'THE AFFAIRS OF OTHERS':
THE DIARIES OF FRANCIS PLACE,
1825–1836

'THE AFFAIRS OF OTHERS':
THE DIARIES OF FRANCIS PLACE,
1825–1836

transcribed, edited, and annotated by
JAMES A. JAFFE

CAMDEN FIFTH SERIES
Volume 30

CAMBRIDGE
UNIVERSITY PRESS

FOR THE ROYAL HISTORICAL SOCIETY
University College London, Gower Street, London WC1 6BT
2007

Published by the Press Syndicate of the University of Cambridge
The Edinburgh Building, Cambridge CB2 8RU, United Kingdom
32 Avenue of the Americas, New York, NY 10013-2473, USA
477 Williamstown Road, Port Melbourne, VIC 3207, Australia
Ruiz de Alarcón 13, 28014 Madrid, Spain
Dock House, The Waterfront, Cape Town 8001, South Africa

First published 2007

A catalogue record for this book is available from the British Library

ISBN 978 0521 883412

SUBSCRIPTIONS. The serial publications of the Royal Historical Society, *Royal Historical Society Transactions* (ISSN 0080-4401) and Camden Fifth Series (ISSN 0960-1163) volumes, may be purchased together on annual subscription. The 2007 subscription price, which includes print and electronic access (but not VAT), is £91 (US $147 in the USA, Canada, and Mexico) and includes Camden Fifth Series, volumes 30 and 31 (published in July and December) and Transactions Sixth Series, volume 17 (published in December). Japanese prices are available from Kinokuniya Company Ltd, P.O. Box 55, Chitose, Tokyo 156, Japan. EU subscribers (outside the UK) who are not registered for VAT should add VAT at their country's rate. VAT registered subscribers should provide their VAT registration number. Prices include delivery by air.

Subscription orders, which must be accompanied by payment, may be sent to a bookseller, subscription agent or direct to the publisher: Cambridge University Press, The Edinburgh Building, Shaftesbury Road, Cambridge CB2 8RU, UK; or in the USA, Canada, and Mexico: Cambridge University Press, Journals Fulfillment Department, 100 Brook Hill Drive, West Nyack, New York, 10994-2133, USA.

SINGLE VOLUMES AND BACK VOLUMES. A list of Royal Historical Society volumes available from Cambridge University Press may be obtained from the Humanities Marketing Department at the address above.

Printed and bound in the United Kingdom at the University Press, Cambridge

For Olwen and Max

CONTENTS

ACKNOWLEDGEMENTS   ix

ABBREVIATIONS   xi

INTRODUCTION   1

EDITORIAL PRINCIPLES   31

THE DIARIES OF FRANCIS PLACE   33

1825   37

1826   49

1827   219

1828   273

1829   295

1830   307

1831   331

1835   341

1836   347

INDEX   353

ACKNOWLEDGEMENTS

This book has taken much longer to complete and has involved many more travails than I had ever expected. Along the way, I have tested the patience of more than one Literary Editor at the Royal Historical Society. I especially owe Aled Jones a great many thanks for his continued support and encouragement. Thank you, Aled. At the Royal Historical Society, David Eastwood was the first to help move this project forward, while Jon Lawrence has finally seen it through to completion. During the publication process, Hester Higton acted as a friendly and expert guide through the sometimes awkward problems presented by the formatting and copy-editing of Place's diary.

Many people offered helpful advice along the way, answered frantic questions, or shared some of their time and knowledge with me. I offer many, many thanks to these people for their time, aid, and friendship: Gregory Claeys, Ruth Paley, Marc Steinberg, Bob Storch, Mary Thale, Joel Wiener, and, at my home institution, Seth Meisel, Becky Hogan, and Mary Pinkerton. I also could not have completed this project without the yeoman (and yeo-woman) help of Joe Jacquess and Terry Hering of the interlibrary loan staff at the Andersen Library who secured for me innumerable obscure articles from around the world. No project such as this one could have been completed without the indirect help of the many British historians who contributed to the new *Oxford Dictionary of National Biography*. Their immense work is reflected in the footnotes of this book. Malcolm Chase deserves special thanks for giving both of his time and expertise in the field of labor history not only to help me finish this project, but also in trying to keep that field alive. Finally, a special note of thanks to Howard Ross, former Dean of the College of Arts and Science at the University of Wisconsin-Whitewater, who managed to extend absolutely essential financial assistance necessary to complete this project.

Work on this book, unfortunately, coincided with both a personal and domestic crisis. To all of those who stuck by me and helped me weather the storm, as it were, I offer my heartfelt thanks and gratitude. John Lombardo, drummer *extraordinaire*, was there in the coffee shop every Monday morning at 9:00 a.m. to listen to my complaints and lamentations. My parents were simply wonderful and supportive. To those I hurt, I offer my most sincere apologies. I hope you find what you want and need. To my fantastic children, Olwen and Max, I offer my love and this book.

ABBREVIATIONS

BL Add. MS	British Library, Additional Manuscript
JHC	*Journals of the House of Commons*
Miles, *Place*	Dudley Miles, *Francis Place, 1771–1854* (Brighton, 1988)
ODNB	*Oxford Dictionary of National Biography* (Oxford, 2004)
PP	*Parliamentary Papers*
TN	*Trades' Newspaper*
Wallas, *Life*	Graham Wallas, *The Life of Francis Place* (4th edition, London, 1925)

INTRODUCTION

Before the diaries: Francis Place, 1771–1825

Historians already know a great deal about Francis Place's life. A catalogue of the evidence produced, collected, or saved by him is truly impressive. There are multiple volumes of correspondence and notes, an extraordinary array of political and social ephemera, thousands of newspaper clippings pasted into volumes of guard books, numerous articles and pamphlets published during his lifetime, an autobiography, and the fragments of a diary.[1] If we include in this accounting the two full-length biographies and the numerous articles in professional journals that have been produced by later historians, there is probably as much or more information available about this individual than most others of his generation.[2] Surprisingly, however, despite this wealth of evidence and the fact that Place's story has been told many times before, there is still a great deal in dispute about him. A brief review of Place's life and career, therefore, would not be inappropriate here.

Place was born in London on 3 November 1771 in a 'sponging-house' opposite the Drury Lane Theatre. This sponging or lock-up house, operated by Place's father for the Marshalsea Court, imprisoned debtors in somewhat more respectable circumstances than were available to them in the Marshalsea debtors' prison. Naturally, prisoners had to be prepared to pay for this privilege and the prices for food, ale, rent, and the like were by all accounts extortionate. Simon Place, Francis Place's father, supported his family for several years from the profits made in this manner. Place recalled the house as clean, light, and very neat.

---

[1] Statistically, the Place Collection in the British Library comprises 95 volumes in the Department of Manuscripts and 180 volumes in the Department of Printed Books.

[2] The most significant publications on the life of Francis Place include Graham Wallas, *The Life of Francis Place, 1771–1854*, originally published in 1898, but I refer to the fourth edition throughout (London, 1925); Dudley Miles, *Francis Place, 1771–1854: the life of a remarkable radical* (Brighton, 1988), and Mary Thale (ed.), *The Autobiography of Francis Place, 1771–1854* (Cambridge, 1972). The new *Oxford Dictionary of National Biography* entry is written by William Thomas: 'Place, Francis (1771–1854)' (Oxford, 2004, <http://www.oxforddnb.com/view/article/22349>, accessed 18 February 2005). The following brief account of his life is drawn principally from these sources.

Place remembered his mother as 'the best woman who ever existed. Clean, neat, kind, cheerful, good tempered, [and] warm hearted.'[3] There is very little else known about her and perhaps Place should be forgiven for this rather hackneyed and melodramatic account he has left of her. The portrait of Place's father, however, is altogether more insightful and nuanced. Not surprisingly, the qualities he most admired in his father were the very same qualities he later most admired in himself while, conversely, those personal characteristics he most condemned or disapproved of became the subject of Place's lifelong interest, and examination.

Place certainly disdained his father's 'dissoluteness', which seems to have included just about every vice imaginable, including physical abuse, neglect, drinking, whoring, gambling, and fighting.[4] Yet he was also ready to dismiss his father's excesses as the reflection of the manners typical of an earlier generation of men. Throughout his life, Place exhibited a pronounced fascination for these facets of eighteenth-century urban life despite his abhorrence of them. This is quite evident from Place's collection of bawdy songs, rude rhymes, and contemporary descriptions of the manners and morals of the common people. Admittedly, he intended to use this remarkable collection of materials to prove that the behavior of the ordinary people had improved dramatically since the mid-eighteenth century, but it may not be too far-fetched to suggest that he was also trying to understand that 'rude' part of both his father and himself.

There was also a great deal that Place admired about his father and the culture from which he had sprung.[5] Thus historians risk grossly oversimplifying Place's complex and ambivalent attitude toward popular culture if they see his later behavior merely as the result of a personal choice between the 'rough' and the 'respectable'. Indeed, Place's attitude was much more complex and multivalent than many would like to imagine. He extolled, for example, the qualities of this dissolute man who was, at the same time, 'to be depended upon in all emergencies good or bad',[6] who 'possessed much resolution and unextinguishable [sic] confidence in his own powers and resources',[7] and 'generally did his business for himself and left nothing undone in

---

[3] Place, *The Autobiography*, p. 21.

[4] Place also included fishing among his father's vices. As an urban exile in the rural Midwest of the United States, I would tend to agree with this categorization; others may not.

[5] Iain McCalman, *Radical Underworld: prophets, revolutionaries and pornographers in London, 1795–1840* (Oxford, 1988), pp. 26–28.

[6] Place, *The Autobiography*, p. 20.

[7] *Ibid.*, p. 24.

any matter which he once took in hand'.[8] The diaries in this volume indeed suggest that these were the same characteristics that Place fashioned for himself: dependable, confident, independent. Not only would it be misleading to crudely distinguish between the 'rough' and the 'respectable', but it would also be misguided to see these independent qualities as in some way 'bourgeois' or middle-class, for they were essential and important aspects of eighteenth- and nineteenth-century working-class culture. As Place himself noted, 'That such a man should have been able to make his way in the world seems strange, that he should have brought himself to ruin and his family to the most perfect state of Distress and yet have recovered again and again appears to us sober people of the present day almost incredible. But such men as he was, were by no means uncommon in his time.'[9]

Place's father was careful to educate both his two sons and his two daughters. Francis Place was sent to a series of day schools and his father had hopes of apprenticing him to the law as a conveyancer. At age fourteen, however, he was apprenticed instead to a leather breeches maker named Joe France. In part, Place explained this turn of events as a result of his resistance to his father's plans: 'I had an antipathy to Law and Lawyers', he simply explained in *The Autobiography*. Yet it also appears to be the case that the thought of such office work repelled him. Understandably, at his age, Place had developed a healthy dislike and disdain for school and was eager to go out to work. Looking back at this decision, he was as incredulous as we all might have been:

> I had for a long time entertained a notion that it was a much greater state of slavery to be compelled to go to school at nine o clock in the morning and remain till twelve, to go again at two, and remain 'till five, having two half holidays in each week, whole holidays at least a dozen times in the year, besides the four usual vacations; than it would be to be compelled to work for at the least twelve consecutive hours six days in the week, with only three holidays at Easter Whitsuntide and Christmas, and this notion was entertained by me as long as I was an apprentice, Strange as this may seem it is by no means uncommon; I have known many boys who thought as I did on the subject.[10]

Within three years, however, Place's master had become bankrupt and, before the age of eighteen, Place had given up his apprenticeship. Over the next several years, he worked at a variety of jobs, sometimes as a breeches maker and sometimes not. At some point, he joined the Breeches Makers Benefit Society and claims to have paid his

---

[8] *Ibid.*, p. 28.
[9] *Ibid.*, p. 24.
[10] *Ibid.*, p. 72.

subscriptions regularly, despite his irregular employment. Most importantly, however, these years witnessed Place's marriage to Elizabeth Chadd in March 1791. He was nineteen, she only seventeen, and their marriage was later followed by several years of great hardship, poverty, and distress. This was especially the case when, in April 1793, the London journeymen breeches makers undertook a strike to raise their wages. Implicated in helping to organize this action, Place was blacklisted and could not find work for the next eight months. During this time, the despair caused by unemployment and poverty was deepened even further by the death of both his father and his first child. Only in December of that year did Place find employment again.

Remarkably, Place's penchant for organization and support of unionization in the trade was not blunted by this experience. By April 1794, he had helped revive the union, begun collecting subscriptions for a new strike fund, and led a movement to secure higher wages for the journeymen breeches makers by taking advantage of the disruption of trade that had followed the previous strike. Place's *Autobiography* suggests that this second unionization effort was successful, despite the absence of a strike or any other form of industrial action. It is likely, therefore, that some sort of negotiated settlement precluded the necessity of a strike. This experience might help to explain Place's later belief that, if left alone, masters and men could resolve their industrial disputes peacefully. However, there were sound ideological reasons for this belief as well, which will be discussed in further detail below. Place's success with the leather breeches makers also seems to have given him some sort of a reputation for organization among the London trades. He claims to have been asked to undertake the formation of similar societies among the journeymen carpenters, plumbers, and several other London trades.

It was at this time that Place first came into contact with the national political reform movement and, in June 1794, joined the London Corresponding Society. His daring and determination in doing so should not be underestimated. Thomas Hardy, the founder and secretary of the LCS, had just been arrested for treason during the previous month, several other early members of the Society who had also been charged with treason were still at large, and the government had recently suspended habeas corpus. Until he left the Society three years later, Place frequently served both as chair of the weekly meetings of the General Committee, a group comprised of delegates from the London divisions, and on the Executive Committee. His resignation was precipitated by a dispute within the LCS over tactics. Place opposed the continuance of mass demonstrations as a tactic likely to secure parliamentary reform in the oppressive political atmosphere of the mid-1790s. In *The Autobiography*, he claims that, at first, he continued to support the actions of the LCS, despite their differences of opinion. This eventually ceased to be the case, however; yet, although he resigned over the issue in June 1797, he never totally lost contact with the Society.[11] In April 1798, Place organized and arranged for subscriptions to be collected and disbursed to the families of a number of radicals who had been arrested and held without trial by the government, a function he continued to perform into 1799. As will be noted in the diary below, he was in fact still collecting funds to support Thomas Hardy into the 1820s, and had maintained contacts with a great many of its former members, including Paul Lemaitre, John Thelwall, Thomas Evans, William Frend, Alexander Galloway, and others.

During these same years, Place never wholly neglected his business. He was determined to establish himself as a master and not return to employment as a journeyman. Unfortunately, this often entailed even more hardship for his family. After several fits and starts, Place eventually rented shop space at No. 16, Charing Cross Road and, after refurbishing the premises, opened a shop there in April 1801. By his own account, he stayed away from politics for the next five years and assiduously cultivated his business. In 1815, his business earned a profit of £1500; in 1816, in excess of £3000; and in the following year he retired from work altogether, aged forty-five.[12] Although his annual income varied thereafter, he never worked again.

Retirement and leisure evoked from Place considerable ambivalence. There was, without doubt, the enormous and often overweening pride that he took in the results of his own hard work, determination, and resolve. These latter qualities, as we have seen, were ones that he similarly admired in his father and were not unknown to working-class culture. Perhaps more significantly, a life of leisure called to mind not just idleness, which Place abhorred, but the lifestyle of the aristocracy, which he wholly detested.[13] The unceasing and almost compulsive dedication that he exhibited to the reform movement, to collecting, to writing, to improvement, and to organizing was a reflection of this drive to make his leisure time both useful and productive. In this, whether knowingly or not, Place made his father's reputation for hard work, dedication, and helping others into his own.

Given Place's abhorrence of the peerage, it is not at all surprising that it was the blatantly corrupt and demeaning actions of the

---

[11] *Ibid.*, pp. 144, 154.

[12] *Ibid.*, p. 226; Miles, *Place*, p. 53; Thomas, 'Place, Francis'.

[13] A point also made by J.M. Main, 'Radical Westminster, 1807–1820', *Historical Studies: Australia and New Zealand*, 12 (1966), p. 189.

aristocracy that ultimately persuaded him to return to active politics. He was appalled when chunks of bread and cheese were tossed to the crowds during the Westminster elections of 1806 and he remained a fixture of Westminster politics for several decades thereafter.[14] His most notable achievements during this period included the organization of the elections first of Sir Francis Burdett in 1807 and then of J.C. Hobhouse in 1820, both of whom were elected as radicals although they both eventually retreated from radical politics. While some historians have doubted the extent to which Place personally contributed to the plan that secured the return of Burdett in 1807, the uniquely successful program certainly bears all the hallmarks of Place's prior trade-union and political experience. By combining a system of subscriptions from electors with detailed committee organization in each parish, the nation's 'first constituency caucus', as it has been called, bore a striking resemblance to the manner in which benefit societies functioned and the LCS was organized.[15] While E.P. Thompson drew attention to the historical significance of Place's apparent retreat from the LCS's claim 'that the number of our members be unlimited',[16] the debt that the British political system owes to the method of subscriptions and grass-roots organization that supported working-class trade unions and benefit societies has never been fully acknowledged.

Place's most significant personal achievements, however, probably occurred during the next decade. Indeed, the early 1820s has often been marked by historians as a turning point in Place's political and intellectual development. However, the precise nature of this transformation is a matter of some dispute. For the biographer Dudley Miles, these years marked the beginning of a 'decade of achievement'. William Thomas, on the other hand, viewed them as years when Place more fully embraced utilitarianism and finally rejected the 'utopian radicalism' of the 1790s. Both assessments largely rest upon an analysis of the same event: that is, Place's role in the repeal of the Combination Acts in 1824. Neither view is wholly wrong, but neither view is wholly correct, either. It is essential to revisit this debate briefly, not only for the light it may eventually shed on our understanding of Francis Place, but also for the new perspectives it may offer for our understanding of the origins of the British working class.

For some, like Miles and Graham Wallas, Place's first biographer, 'the repeal of the Combination Laws in 1824–25 was the most striking

---

[14] Wallas, *Life*, pp. 42–43.

[15] Thomas, 'Place, Francis'.

[16] E.P. Thompson, *The Making of the English Working Class* (New York, NY, 1963), pp. 17–25.

piece of work that Place ever carried through single-handed'.[17] Yet it is possible to overestimate both Place's role in this endeavor and the overall effect of this repeal on trade unionism. Without doubt, the Combination Acts had great symbolic significance, but much work by historians has gone into the now general consensus that the conflicts and struggles between employers and workers were more likely to find their way into the numerous magistrates' courts, courts of request, or mayor's courts, under the terms of the master-and-servant laws, than they were to be prosecuted under the laws of combination and conspiracy.[18] Moreover, while the repeal of the Acts marked a change in law, it certainly did not herald a comparable sea-change of attitudes toward trade unions among the governing classes. That change was to take at least another four decades and await the reforms introduced under the premierships of Disraeli and Gladstone. Finally, Place's own actions may have been overdramatized for, despite Place's renowned planning, vetting of witnesses, and intense preparation of Joseph Hume, the committee chair, the bill was passed into law principally by stealth.[19] Therefore, as many trade unionists of the time quickly realized, the repeal of the Combination Laws had very little effect upon the nature and practice of industrial relations.

If Place's achievement therefore appears to have been rather modest, it may be worth asking precisely what he had intended to achieve. It has often been argued that Place was motivated to seek the repeal of the Combination Acts because of his belief in the efficacy of the market, a belief imbibed through his contact with James Mill, Jeremy Bentham, and the circle of philosophic radicals. However, it would be quite misleading to read Place's actions in this light. Place's determination to repeal the Combination Acts was in many ways an extension of his 'utopian radicalism', perhaps even its culmination, rather than a utilitarian rejection of it. This will be discussed in greater detail below. For now, it is enough to point out that Place certainly believed that, if left to bargain freely between themselves, masters and men would resolve industrial disputes peacefully. Moreover, he held equally strong convictions that it was ultimately the law's repression that compelled workers to form trade unions. 'Men have been kept together for long periods', he wrote to Burdett in 1825, 'only by the

---

[17] Wallas, *Life*, p. 197.

[18] Mark Curthoys, *Governments, Labour, and the Law in Mid-Victorian Britain: the trade union legislation of the 1870s* (Oxford, 2004); Douglas Hay, 'England, 1562–1875: the law and its uses', in D. Hay and P. Craven (eds), *Masters, Servants, and Magistrates in Britain and the Empire, 1562–1955* (Chapel Hill, 2004), pp. 100–101; Robert J. Steinfeld, *Coercion, Contract, and Free Labor in the Nineteenth Century* (Cambridge, 2001), esp. chapters 2 and 4.

[19] See Miles, *Place*, pp. 164–166 for a brief account and Wallas, *Life*, pp. 197–240 for a much fuller one.

oppression of the Laws.'[20] Yet this opposition to the state's role in industrial relations was not a facet of Place's acceptance of the laws of political economy. Instead, for Place, the Combination Acts were part of the British government's legacy of oppression, of Pitt's Terror, the suspension of habeas corpus, Peterloo, and the Six Acts. The diaries below bear witness to the fact that his fight against this legacy continued well past the repeal of the Combination Acts. In 1827, he can still be found encouraging Joseph Hume to introduce legislation to repeal the surviving portions of the Six Acts. In this, as will be suggested below, the influence of Thomas Paine is far more apparent than that of either Mill or Bentham.

Francis Place and the historians

Probably sometime in 1826, Place wrote a brief résumé of his activities during the previous year, and it is this sketchy account of 1825 that precedes the diary proper. It is unfortunate that the diaries begin in earnest only in 1826, even though the Place Papers in the British Library offer volumes of notes and letters covering the repeal of the Combination Acts. A record of Place's efforts in this regard would obviously have been a very welcome addition to our understanding of those events. And historians may have lost something more, because the period after mid-decade was marked by the onset of both relative material prosperity and relative political quiescence. Thus, the most dramatic events of the first third of the nineteenth century are not covered by the diary. Perhaps it is therefore not accidental that Place chose to begin and end his diary at just these points in his personal and the nation's history. And yet there is still much that can be learned. Most importantly, the diary may make a significant contribution to the ongoing discussion among historians over Place's role in London's radical movements of the early nineteenth century. However, to do so, it must be read both for what it says and for what it does not say.

The debate over Place's role in the history of London radicalism was neatly summarized many years ago by Iorwerth Prothero: 'Pre-Chartist London', he wrote, 'has been called "the London of Francis Place". It should, with much greater accuracy, be known as "the London of John Gast".'[21] This quotation, it might be said, encapsulated the political and ideological goals of a generation of labor historians

---

[20] British Library, Additional Manuscripts (hereafter, BL, Add. MSS) 27802, fos 37–38.
[21] Iorwerth Prothero, *Artisans and Politics in Early Nineteenth-Century London: John Gast and his times*, paperback edition (London, 1981), p. 7; see also Malcolm Chase, 'Francis Place: a remarkable radical?', *Bulletin of the Society for the Study of Labour History*, 54 (1989), pp. 60–61.

who came to prominence in the 1960s, 1970s, and 1980s, and who sought to redefine the terms of their trade: artisans rather than proletarians became the center of study, the workshop replaced the factory as the location of agitation, and the experience of workers rather than the history of their institutions became the focus of analysis. In part, this change reflected the ideological riptides of the Left, but Prothero's quotation, more academically, reflected a reaction against the institutional bias and party-political focus that had characterized previous generations of largely Fabian labor historians.

It has often been asserted that the Fabian historians, and in this particular case we are speaking of Sidney and Beatrice Webb and Graham Wallas, had found Place an especially sympathetic character largely because his political tactics were surprisingly similar to their own.[22] Parenthetically, it should be noted that historians who have made this assertion have rarely taken the time either to define or to distinguish the significant differences between Wallas and the Webbs. Still, this claim is not without a good deal of merit. In the Webbs' estimation of Place,

> No one who has closely studied his life and work will doubt that, within the narrow sphere to which his unswerving practicality confined him, he was the most remarkable politician of his age. His chief merit lay in his thorough understanding of the art of getting things done. In agitation, permeation, wire-pulling, Parliamentary lobbying, the drafting of resolutions, petitions, bills – in short, of all those artifices by which a popular movement is first created and then made effective on the Parliamentary system – he was an inventor and tactician of the first order.[23]

A minor Fabian historian, Julius West, made the same point more succinctly: 'Francis Place, the greatest organizer English democracy has ever known'.[24]

The new labor historians, however, were much more ambivalent in their estimation of Place's achievements, an ambivalence that mirrored the new orientation of labor history. Willing to acknowledge the accomplishments both of Place and the older labor histories, historians such as E.P. Thompson nonetheless critically analyzed their shortcomings:

[22] W.E.S. Thomas, 'Francis Place and working class history', *Historical Journal*, 5 (1962), pp. 69–70; Alice Prochaska, 'Francis Place and working-class radicalism in London', *Modern History Review*, 4 (1992), p. 11.
[23] Sidney and Beatrice Webb, *The History of Trade Unionism*, revised edition (London, 1920), pp. 96–97.
[24] See Julius West, *A History of the Chartist Movement* (London, 1920), p. 29. I owe this quote to Malcolm Chase.

Several of the historians who pioneered the study of this period (the Hammonds, the Webbs, and Graham Wallas) were men and women of Fabian persuasion, who looked upon the 'early history of the Labour Movement' in the light of the subsequent Reform Acts, and the growth of T.U.C. and Labour Party. Since Luddites or food rioters do not appear as satisfactory 'forerunners' of 'the Labour Movement' they merited neither sympathy nor close attention. And this bias was supplemented, from another direction, by the more conservative bias of the orthodox academic tradition. Hence 'history' has dealt fairly with the Tolpuddle Martyrs, and fulsomely with Francis Place; but the hundreds of men and women executed or transported for oath-taking, Jacobin conspiracy, Luddism, the Pentridge and Grange Moor risings, food and enclosure and turnpike riots, the Ely riots and the Labourers' Revolt of 1830, and a score of minor affrays, have been forgotten by all but a few specialists, or, if they are remembered, they are thought to be simpletons or men tainted with criminal folly.[25]

In what is certainly his most oft-quoted statement, Thompson announced that 'I am seeking to rescue the poor stockinger, the Luddite cropper, the "obsolete" hand-loom weaver, the "utopian" artisan, and even the deluded follower of Joanna Southcott, from the enormous condescension of posterity.'[26] He might just as well have said that he wished to rescue them from the enormous condescension of Sidney and Beatrice Webb.

To be fair, Thompson was more than willing to acknowledge Place's 'sober manner, his great capacity for organisation, his intellectual application, and his experience of trade union organisation'.[27] However, his scepticism was communicated to those historians who later produced the now-standard histories of early nineteenth-century London radicalism, including J. Ann Hone, Iain McCalman, and Prothero,[28] all of whom sought in part to diminish the centrality of Place in their analyses of working-class radicalism.

As Place's star waned among labor historians, a parallel debate over his goals and ideology episodically made its way into the pages of the historical journals. At nearly the same time that Thompson was issuing his critique of the Fabian veneration of Place, W.E.S. Thomas was publishing a rather withering attack both upon Place's character and his accomplishments.[29] To Thomas, Place appeared rigid, uncritical, uncongenial, sectarian, unrealistic, overeager, tactless, dry, blinkered, and unimaginative, to list but a few of Thomas's

[25] Thompson, *Making of the English Working Class*, p. 592.
[26] Thompson, *Making of the English Working Class*, p. 12.
[27] *Ibid.*, p. 139.
[28] J. Ann Hone, *For the Cause of Truth: radicalism in London 1796–1821* (Oxford, 1982). For McCalman's and Prothero's books, see notes 5 and 21 respectively.
[29] Thomas, 'Francis Place and working class history', pp. 61–79.

more unflattering adjectives. Like Thompson, Thomas was reacting against the 'distorted' and 'exaggerated reputation' that the Fabians had constructed for Place. Unlike Thompson, however, he was eager to emphasize the social as well as intellectual gulf that separated Place from the Benthamites and other middle-class reformers. Thomas suggested that this was, in part, a failure of Place's imagination. Place, in Thomas's estimation, was simply too pragmatic (and perhaps under-educated) fully to comprehend the subtleties of utilitarian philosophy. Moreover, this was also a failure of character: according to Thomas, Place continually alienated those who sought out his help and assistance. Finally, Place's failure to span this gulf between himself and the philosophic radicals was a failure of class. Place was possessed of working-class interests and a working-class ideology. His philosophy amounted to little more than a mixture of Malthusianism, which he did not fully accept, and self-help; his interests lay essentially in promoting working-class respectability and improvement. In sum, Place's outlook and interests went no further than to try to impose his own working-class experience upon the rest of the working class.

More than a decade later, D.J. Rowe responded to Thomas's work.[30] Rowe took direct issue with Thomas's characterization of Place, but the debate still revolved around Place and social class. For Rowe, Place was only 'a temporary elitist' who was distinctly middle-class by virtue of his wealth, his behavior, his education, and his political prejudices. His position in London politics may have been made somewhat anomalous by the fact that he retained a good measure of his working-class radicalism after ascending into the middle class; however, this should not obscure the full extent of his *embourgeoisement*. Rowe wrote that

> Thomas's comment that 'the working classes were certainly the main subject of Place's social and political thinking' is untrue. Place's immediate concern lay with the middle classes. He was a working-class reformer only in his desire to assimilate working men into the middle classes by teaching them middle-class values and getting them to accept middle-class ideas.[31]

As nature abhors a vacuum, so historians abhor consensus. Therefore, there is usually a great deal of interest taken in disputes such as this, interest that in turn often evokes further contributions, even though these later additions, it must be said, often result in more heat than light. However, this was hardly the case here. Prothero's book on John Gast followed in 1979, Hone's book on London radicalism in 1982, and McCalman's remarkable recovery of London's radical underworld in

---

[30] D.J. Rowe, 'Francis Place and the historian', *Historical Journal*, 16 (1973), pp. 45–63.
[31] *Ibid.*, pp. 52–53.

1988, all of which served to undermine further Place's reliability as a witness to the great events of the period and to diminish his role in the making of London radicalism. By 1990, there was little left of Place's reputation and the rather wooden biography by Dudley Miles that appeared in that year resembles in retrospect a tombstone rather than a monument.

Francis Place and the diary

The subsequent neglect of Francis Place coincided with a more general crisis of confidence throughout the historical profession. The so-called 'linguistic turn' of the 1990s brought into question many of the foundational notions of social and labor history, most particularly the relationship between social experience, class, and identity. It also brought in its train a new set of analytical tools that, when abused, made history appear nonsensical. When used with caution, however, these new tools not only helped to deepen the historian's understanding of past people and events but also helped to broaden the ways in which written evidence could be analyzed and interpreted. In the case of Francis Place, such linguistic and interpretive openings may in the end contribute much to our understanding of who he was and what motivated him.

The postmodern legacy has quite properly reminded historians to approach their sources not only with a healthy new measure of caution and circumspection, but also a new way of looking at the evidence historians already have. Thomas, for one, thought Place's memoirs contained a wealth of historical information but were nonetheless unworthy of editing and, by extension, of publication.[32] They were scarcely readable, he wrote, and were comprised mainly of 'enormous catalogues of meetings held, memoranda drawn up (and quoted *in extenso*) and signed'. Place's 'main difficulty', he continued, 'lay in distinguishing the important from the trivial.' Thus, the 'long chronicles of administrative minutiae [in the memoirs] . . . swamp the main issues and cloud causes and effects, and suggest the complete extinction of the idealist by the dry doctrinaire'.[33]

In one sense, these remarks appear to have been based upon an aesthetic evaluation of the memoirs' literary and stylistic merit that made them uninteresting and confusing. However, this unflattering evaluation of Place's memoirs and diaries is probably based upon more than just an aesthetic judgment. It appears also to reflect a

[32] Thomas, 'Francis Place and working class history', p. 68.
[33] *Ibid.*, p. 69.

certain preconceived and largely unexamined notion of the diary form itself.[34] Historians have come to expect diaries to differ from, say, the autobiographical form, by being more spontaneous, by offering a more candid view of the inner self, by being more confessional in tone and substance, and, if not necessarily wholly accurate, then at least more authentic and more immediate. Many years ago, Roy Pascal intimated this critical difference when he suggested that 'the formal difference between diary and autobiography is obvious. The latter is a review of life from a particular moment in time, while the diary, however reflective it may be, moves through a series of moments in time.'[35]

Upon closer examination, however, many of the historian's romantic criteria of the diary appear to be neither essential nor immediately relevant to the form itself. It is in some sense necessary therefore to re-examine what a diary is and is not in order to under-stand what may or may not be learned from it. As noted, diaries appear to constitute a distinct genre precisely because they are assumed to present a more unmediated, honest, and less censored view of both others and the writer's inner self. As a form of evidence, historians therefore consider them to be one of the most reliable of all primary sources. Yet, if one were to examine the basis of this reliance more closely, then significant difficulties and obstacles would arise.[36]

One important assumption is, as Pascal's quote suggests, that diary entries, again as distinct from the autobiographical form, are more immediate and spontaneous literary artifacts, and thus less mediated by conscious selection, memory, and self-reflection. Such a view is indefensible. Logically, no diarist could hope to capture on paper or in any other medium the incalculable number of events, ideas, impressions, and thoughts that occur in an hour, or two hours, much less a day. Thus we are faced by the complicated but not wholly insurmountable problem of identifying precisely the process by which the relatively few events noted or described in a diary are distinguished

---

[34] For much of what follows on the diary form I am indebted to Lawrence Rosenwald, *Emerson and the Art of the Diary* (New York, 1988), chapter 1. See also Fothergill's plea from a different interpretative perspective to perceive 'the character and quality of a given diary not merely as a manifestation of a writer's personality, but as a function of its place in an evolutionary pattern': Robert A. Fothergill, *Private Chronicles: a study of English diaries* (London, 1974), p. 2. My thanks to Becky Hogan for bringing these works to my attention.

[35] Roy Pascal, *Design and Truth in Autobiography* (Cambridge, MA, 1960), p. 3.

[36] Similar recognitions concerning the use and meaning of the genre of autobiography are expressed in Malcolm Chase's 'Autobiography and the understanding of the self: the case of Allen Davenport' in Martin Hewitt (ed.), *Representing Victorian Lives*, Leeds Working Papers in Victorian Studies, 2 (Leeds, 1999), pp. 18–21.

and chosen from the innumerable events that comprise a single day's activities.[37]

It appears to have been the practice of Francis Place to write his diary entries at day's end, a practice he held in common with other prominent diarists, most notably Byron. In contrast, other diarists, such as Pepys, made entries every few days or so.[38] Yet even this temporal immediacy entailed extensive selectivity based upon a number of varying criteria. Place himself testified to this practice in what appears to be a brief introduction written for the diaries, perhaps as late as 1850: 'These diaries must not be taken to include the names of all the persons I saw or all the matters in which I was concerned.'[39] The full effect of Place's selectivity can only be guessed at, however. But there is at least one particularly telling example. Prior to June 1827, Place's contact with the circle of utilitarians, especially James Mill, is frequently noted in the diaries. However, there is no mention of Place's contact with Jeremy Bentham, the leading utilitarian, except incidentally and then only indirectly.[40] This piece of evidence, counterfactual though it may be, might suggest to some historians that the influence of the utilitarians upon Place may have been less significant than had previously been thought. However, on 19 June 1827, more than a year after the beginning of the diary, the following entry appears: 'From Saturday evening to this morning [Tuesday] at nine, no one for a wonder called upon me excepting my my [sic] old very dear friend Jeremy Bentham'.[41] Even this entry may not have been considered unusual at all save for the following additional note written by Place at the bottom of the same page: 'Visits from and to Mr. Benthams have not been hitherto mentioned as each of our houses were as freely entered by either as was his own.'[42]

Such a revelation is indeed remarkable. Unbeknownst to the reader, has Place actually been in direct and constant contact with Bentham throughout this entire period? If so, how can one judge the effect

[37] Georges Gusdorf, who is rather dismissive of the journal and diary form, nevertheless makes a similar point for the writing of autobiographies: there is no apparent reason why it should not apply equally to the construction of a diary. See Georges Gusdorf, 'Conditions and limits of autobiography', trans. J. Olney, in James Olney (ed.), *Autobiography: essays theoretical and critical* (Princeton, NJ, 1980), p. 42.

[38] Mark S. Dawson, 'Histories and texts: refiguring the diary of Samuel Pepys', *Historical Journal*, 43 (2000), pp. 416–417.

[39] See below, p. 51.

[40] See the entries for 18 April 1826 and 15 July 1826, pp. 62 and 117.

[41] See below, p. 264.

[42] As Thomas notes in his study of philosophic radicalism, Bentham's return to his home at No. 1, Queen Square Place, near Charing Cross Road, in 1818 signaled the end of the unique record of correspondence that issued from Ford Abbey. See William Thomas, *The Philosophic Radicals: nine studies in theory and practice, 1817–1841* (Oxford, 1979), p. 41.

this has had on Place, his decisions, and his activities? Should we infer from this reference that Bentham's influence was so pervasive that Place simply accepted without question or comment the great man's presence? Or, conversely, does it mean that Bentham was such a common figure in Place's home that he could safely accept or reject utilitarian principles at will? In short, to what extent can the diaries be trusted as historical evidence if such an important facet of Place's life has been intentionally or unintentionally hidden from view?

To answer these questions, that is, to find out ultimately who the 'real' Francis Place was, the historian must seek another type of evidence. That evidence, ironically, is to be found largely in Place's published writings. Only there can one attempt to analyze and inter-pret the influence Bentham ultimately had upon Place's thinking and his perception of the world. Thus a rather startling inversion has occurred. The recognition of the ultimate impenetrability of Place's daily life in his diaries has forced the historian to seek Place's inner self in the works he presented to the public.[43] It is only in those works that this conundrum can finally be resolved.

Such a radical inversion, however, does not necessarily vitiate the claims of the diary to authenticity. What it does do, on the contrary, is to emphasize to the historian the extent to which the diaries must be understood as a literary construct and not unmediated truth: that is, the extent to which the diaries have to be 'read' as much as they may be quoted. This imposes upon the historian the uncomfortable task of interrogating the diaries as they might also interrogate other secondary sources. The question that must be posed to Place's diaries, therefore, is not necessarily what do they say about the man's 'real' life and ideas; the questions that must be asked are: by what criteria did Place sift and select information for inclusion in his diary, and what does this selection process tell us about him?

For those who are accustomed to approaching the diary as a genre that reveals an individual's 'true' self, this might be an uncomfortable proposition; it necessitates perceiving the diary as a literary artifact rather than as a body of self-evident truths.[44] Georges Gusdorf's des-cription of the 'secret structure' of autobiographies is equally appro-priate when applied to an understanding of how Place's diary functions: 'It does not show us the individual seen from the outside in his visible actions but the person in his inner privacy, not as he was, not as he is, but as he believes and wishes himself to be and to

[43] See Rosenwald, *Emerson and the Art of the Diary*, p. 5.
[44] Gusdorf, 'Conditions and limits of autobiography', pp. 43–44. Again, Gusdorf's recognition of the literary foundations of the autobiography form applies equally to the diary.

have been.'[45] In an important sense, therefore, the self presented in the diary is constructed rather than revealed and, as such, it mimics the narrative form of the autobiography. That is, the diary becomes an effort to tell a story. However, this mimicry must be understood within the unique context of the diary's form. The diary as narrative functions the way it does in large part because of its peculiar relationship to time.

Unlike the autobiography or the novel, the diary is more strictly bound by the thick structure of time: the length of a day most often, but sometimes the week or month, or, very infrequently, the year. This places more rigid limits upon both the extent and depth to which the diarist can compose a story with a noticeable beginning, middle, and end.[46] Arguably, this could even be said to deny the diary any narrative quality whatsoever. Many stories are started in a diary; many fewer are ended. The entire diary itself often withers away or dies from neglect rather than providing a proper ending to a life's story.[47]

However, Lawrence Rosenwald is certainly correct to assert of the diarist that 'each day they have a new chance at writing the perfect entry, the one exact culmination of all its predecessors'.[48] As such, each day or each entry is a new piece of a larger story and the diary itself an episodic accretion of fragmented narratives.[49] In effect, the diary might be said to be an accumulation of beginnings. Edward Said's wonderful explication of beginnings appears to be perfectly appropriate here: 'A beginning gives us the chance to do work that compensates us for the tumbling disorder of brute reality that will not settle down.'[50] Each new entry, to pursue this analogy to Said's point, is therefore both a declaration of intent and an act of exclusion. That is, each entry declares the intention purposefully to produce meaning while excluding not only other writers from the literary space created, but also excluding alternative themes, ideas, events, and 'facts' that are not relevant to the intent.[51] These are what Said calls the 'rules of pertinence' or the authority that guides both writer and reader through the text or diary.[52]

It is of great importance, therefore, to address the following questions: What were Place's 'rules of pertinence'? What were the implicit and explicit rules that governed the writing of his diary? What was the story that he wished to convey? And to answer these

---

[45] *Ibid.*, p. 45.
[46] Rosenwald, *Emerson and the Art of the Diary*, pp. 23–24.
[47] *Ibid.*, pp. 23–24.
[48] *Ibid.*, p. 25.
[49] I owe this insight to Mary Pinkerton.
[50] Edward Said, *Beginnings: intention and method* (New York, NY, 1975), p. 50.
[51] *Ibid.*, chapter 1.
[52] *Ibid.*, p 16.

questions, we have Place's own testimony from April 1826 when he first began keeping the diary:

> I intend for a week or more to keep a diary, not of every occurrence but of such as shew how my time is occupied, since it sometimes happens that I can hardly tell how it has been consumed. I suspect that so much of every mans time, I mean of every mans time who is not engaged in business, is fooled away, that were he to take an exact account of it, he could scarcely fail to be ashamed of himself, and this is probably the reason so few have done it.[53]

One of Place's goals upon beginning the diary, therefore, was to keep track of time, an obviously appropriate task for a diary. However, his was not the same sort of timekeeping that Max Weber ascribed to that arch-capitalist ethicist, Benjamin Franklin, for whom time was money. Place indicates that people in business must treat time in this way, but these merchants and manufacturers were not his intended audience. Instead, the diaries were meant for people of leisure: people like himself who no longer needed to work, who were 'not engaged in business', or who never had worked.[54] Place suggests that the time of these idle men, and they specifically are men, is unknowingly 'fooled away'. If, he claims, they were made aware of the extent of their idleness, if they were presented with 'an exact account of it', their resulting shame, we may infer, would spur them out of their lethargy.

Certainly, there are a good many possible sources for these ideas, but few of them are uniquely Benthamite in origin or orientation. One source has already been noted. Place exhibited a healthy abhorrence of the aristocracy and their lives of leisure and waste. It is possible that this is an expression of emerging bourgeois values, but these ideas may also be found in the vast penumbra of the civic republican tradition that associated luxury with corruption and vice at the same time that it extolled the virtues of an active, participatory, property-owning elite.[55] In this vein, Place may have come to believe that wealth and leisure entailed civic responsibilities that, unless fulfilled, would, or should, evoke guilt and shame. The diary may therefore have been intended to function as a personal record of the active life as well as an example of how civic-minded men of wealth and leisure remained virtuous. This

---

[53] See p. 52.

[54] Place was able to retire in 1817. Dudley Miles suggests that he maintained an annual income of £1100 until 1832, when it was significantly reduced to £400. See Miles, *Place*, pp. 53–56.

[55] J.G.A. Pocock, *The Machiavellian Moment: Florentine political thought and the Atlantic republican tradition* (Princeton, NJ, 1975), pp. 383–400 and 477–505. In a review of Miles's biography, Gregory Claeys briefly suggests such a connection through Place's contact with the writings of Thomas Paine: see Gregory Claeys, 'Whigs, liberals and radicals', *Historical Journal*, 33 (1990), pp. 741–742.

interpretation, it will be suggested below, may also help historians to understand further some significant anomalies in Place's political career.

However, this is not to argue that locating Place within the ideological traditions of civic republicanism explains everything about the man. To do so would be to suggest in effect that he was consistently uniform in his understanding and interpretation of the world around him, a position that is untenable. There are, indeed, other aspects of eighteenth- and early nineteenth-century culture that also apparently contributed to Place's *Weltanschauung*. For example, Place's intent for the diary may have drawn equally upon what Weber called the 'rational asceticism' of English Puritanism.[56] Place was himself an atheist and therefore it is important to understand that he was not consciously adopting an evangelical mode of behavior in order to examine his inner spiritual life. Yet he had received a Christian education, however much he may have suspected his schoolmaster's lack of faith and conviction, and the sense of Place's introductory passage expresses a distinctly evangelical attitude.[57] The language Place employs is redolent of Weber's Puritan divines, who encouraged their flocks to take account of their actions, to measure their worthiness against God's commands, and to avoid the sins and temptations brought about by the acquisition and enjoyment of wealth. 'Wealth is thus bad ethically', Weber wrote of the work of the Puritan divine Richard Baxter, 'only in so far as it is a temptation to idleness and sinful enjoyment of life, and its acquisition is bad only when it is with the purpose of later living merrily and without care. But as a performance of duty in a calling it is not only morally permissible, but actually enjoined.'[58] The diary therefore might express this evangelical attitude toward work and wealth that, by the nineteenth century, had become separated from its religious foundation and thereby secularized.[59]

Interestingly, as Boyd Hilton has observed, the self-denial expressed in this type of secular evangelicalism is at first glance distinctly at odds with the 'hedonistic egoism' most frequently associated with the utilitarians.[60] Yet Bentham himself was not immune to the role that moral reform, such as that envisioned by Place, might play in the

[56] Max Weber, *The Protestant Ethic and the Spirit of Capitalism*, trans. Talcott Parsons (New York, NY, 1958), p. 167.

[57] Place, *The Autobiography*, pp. 44–46.

[58] Weber, *Protestant Ethic and the Spirit of Capitalism*, p. 163.

[59] The process whereby these ideas became secularized is described in Weber, *Protestant Ethic and the Spirit of Capitalism*, pp. 176–183 as well as in E.P. Thompson, 'Time, work-discipline and industrial capitalism', *Past & Present*, 38 (1967), pp. 56–97.

[60] Boyd Hilton, *The Age of Atonement: the influence of evangelicalism on social and economic thought, 1785–1865* (Oxford, 1988), p. 32.

broader utilitarian political reform movement.[61] Indeed, Elie Halévy also noted the strikingly ascetic element inherent in utilitarianism, noting more generally that nineteenth-century British individualism was 'a compound of Evangelicalism and Utilitarianism'.[62]

The historian should not be deterred by the fact that Place could draw on not one but several strands of rational asceticism to establish his 'rules of pertinence' for the diary. Identities are made in just such a way. However, it seems clear that Place's rational asceticism became the foundation upon which he constructed both the form and content of the diary. In particular, he intentionally omitted musings about the characters around him as well as the intense examination of the inner self, both of which we have come to consider fairly typical of the diary form. Significantly, for Place, this was an achievement and not a weakness. The diary was, after all, intended to serve a didactic (that is, a useful) purpose. To engage in such musings was ungentlemanly, showed a lack of respectability, and was even vain. Looking back upon the first year of writing the diary, there is a sense of accomplishment in Place's acknowledgment that 'I had done enough . . . to shew of whom and what the world was composed from the sample which I was connected with, notwithstanding this, [the diary] was not so fully made out as it might be, since I had avoided drawing characters which I could easily have done had I not thought it invidious.'[63] Interestingly, he convinced himself that he had written enough but, when he tried to stop writing, he found that he could not because he had become gripped by 'the devil of vanity'. And so, as a result of this moral failure, the diary continued into the next year.

Such moral precepts pronounced in the diary may also serve to shed further light on working-class writing more generally. A common complaint among literary critics has been that working-class autobiographies frequently avoid the kind of intense introspection typical of the genre, especially as produced by middle-class writers. Some have ascribed this fact to the manner in which class was a more important aspect of working-class consciousness than the travails of the individual. Others, such as Regenia Gagnier, have noted how working-class autobiographers 'worried about their "egotism"', and suggest that this was because working-class writers questioned whether it was

---

[61] Joanna Innes, 'Politics and morals: the reformation of manners movement in later eighteenth-century England', in E. Hellmuth (ed.), *The Transformation of Political Culture: England and Germany in the late eighteenth century* (Oxford, 1990), pp. 109–110.

[62] Quoted in Hilton, *Age of Atonement*, p. 32.

[63] See p. 198. Similarly, Place wrote to Hobhouse in 1819: 'I hate the collector and retailer of anecdotes of his friends or of those he acts with, and I hold him to be a rascal who keeps any account of his own immediate and private intercourse with other men.' Quoted in Miles, *Place*, p. 110. I owe this quote also to Malcolm Chase.

proper to distinguish themselves as individuals in that way.[64] Place's diary hints at a somewhat different conclusion. If Place's writing is taken as a guide, then the differences between middle-class and working-class 'self-writing', as it is sometimes called, may have been based less upon any profound differences in the perception of the self or the relation of the individual to social class and more upon purpose and intent. Place's diary intentionally excluded lengthy introspective and personal reflections because such writings were considered to be morally suspect. They were vain and self-indulgent, a reflection perhaps of idleness and other vices. Place's diary, on the contrary, was intended to promote a certain set of virtues, foremost among which were hard work and responsibility, both of the civic and of the personal kind. In a sense, therefore, Place's diary bears a stronger resemblance to the 'self-help' book of today than to the typical romantic-style diaries of the nineteenth and twentieth centuries.

Nevertheless, the moral underpinnings of Place's activities and beliefs have garnered much less attention than they perhaps deserve. Throughout the diaries it is extraordinarily difficult, if not impossible, to disentangle the moral from the political or the moral from the social. Obviously, the debate between Thomas and Rowe that situated Place either as harbinger of middle-class values or bearer of working-class ideals has proven itself to be a sterile one, but that certainly does not exhaust the analysis of Place's moral world. As I have suggested above, one potentially fruitful line of analysis links Place to the complex moral world of civic republicanism. Mark Bevir rightly warns against reading civic republicanism into too much of the eighteenth and early nineteenth centuries.[65] However, in Place's case such a reading may be justified in large part because we have some of Place's own testimony to support it. Thus, in 1827, reflecting on the ministerial crisis that brought Canning to power, he wrote in the diary: 'Reform proceeds slowly but surely, intelligence amongst the people increases, and both will be accelerated in somewhat the proportion of the law of falling bodies. This is no prophecy, for the march of intellect must necessarily produce its effects, and ultimately terminate in good, that is in a cheap republican government.'[66]

The sources of Place's republicanism are not at all difficult to find. The problem may indeed be that there are too many possibilities rather than too few. Even a cursory glance through the pages of

[64] Regenia Gagnier, *Subjectivities: a history of self-representation in Britain, 1830–1920* (Oxford, 1991), pp. 139–145.

[65] Mark Bevir, 'Republicanism, socialism, and democracy in Britain: the origins of the radical left', *Journal of Social History*, 34 (2000), pp. 351–368.

[66] 19 April 1827 (see below, p. 238).

his diary reveals Place's intense interest in seventeenth- and early eighteenth-century constitutional history, and his reading of Hume's *History*, Godwin's *Commonwealth*, the House of Commons *Journals*, and other similar materials. Of course, Place also had very strong intellectual connections to Thomas Paine. Place's *Autobiography* recalls how his landlord introduced Place not only to the London Corresponding Society in 1794, but also to the works of Paine. Moreover, in 1796, Place was actively involved in the publication of Paine's *Age of Reason*, an event which eventually issued in the prosecution of the publisher for libel.[67]

Perhaps it is unnecessary to tie Place directly to any one author, but many of Place's apparently extraordinary or anomalous actions and ideas begin to make a bit more sense if placed within the context of what Pocock labeled 'commercial humanism',[68] Claeys described as 'commercial republicanism',[69] or Albert Hirschman called 'the Montesquieu-Steuart perspective'.[70] Although there are important and distinct differences between them, all three authors try to make sense of the way in which eighteenth-century writers sought to bring the perceived values of commerce into accord with either classical or Christian notions of virtue. In particular, these historians share the general perception that, during the eighteenth century, there was a paradigm shift in political thought toward the recognition of commerce as an important civilizing and moral agent in the modern world.[71] These so-called commercial ideologists of the eighteenth century, including Paine, privileged the historical importance of commerce and exchange because of its perceived sociological, psychological, and moral power: *Le doux commerce* restrained the passions, elicited the interests, evoked manners, and promoted sociability. Paine was perhaps unique only in his attempt to harmonize this new faith in the civilizing power of commerce with republican ideals.[72]

Such a perspective allows us to make a great deal more sense of Place's activities and ideology, especially in relation to the repeal of the Combination Acts, but also to the Place portrayed in these diaries. As briefly noted above, it has always seemed rather odd that

[67] Place, *The Autobiography*, pp. 126–127; 159–172.

[68] J.G.A. Pocock, *Virtue, Commerce, and History: essays on political thought chiefly in the eighteenth century* (Cambridge, 1985), pp. 48–50.

[69] Gregory Claeys, *Thomas Paine: social and political thought* (Boston, 1989), pp. 46–51.

[70] Albert O. Hirschman, *The Passions and the Interests: political arguments for capitalism before its triumph* (Princeton, NJ, 1977), pp. 69–87.

[71] I have dealt with these issues in a broader context in 'Commerce, character, and civil society: critiques of capitalism during the early industrial period', *European Legacy*, 6 (2001), pp. 251–264.

[72] Claeys, *Thomas Paine*, pp. 5–6.

historians have attributed to Place a slightly incongruous explanation for the causal effects of repeal. It is often asserted that Place was moved to pursue repeal as part of a broad ideological commitment to the application of *laissez-faire* principles of the freedom of contract to industrial relations.[73] The repeal of the Combination Laws would paradoxically lead to the disappearance of trade unions as well as industrial strife, as individuals bargained freely with one another.

In a certain sense, this interpretation is correct. As we have shown, Place did believe that the individuality of contract would result ultimately in industrial harmony after trade unions disappeared altogether. Thus, in June 1825, Place sought to reassure Sir Francis Burdett that, if the revisions to the first repeal bill of 1824 were comparatively minor, 'combinations will soon cease to exist. Men have been kept together for long periods only by the oppression of the Laws. These being repealed, these combinations will lose their cement and soon fall to pieces, and then all will be as orderly as even a quaker could desire.'[74]

However, political economic theory of the early nineteenth century hardly offered any basis upon which to predict the evolution of industrial harmony from the freedom of contract. Indeed the classical economists exhibited almost no interest in individual bargaining, the freedom of contract, or the impact of the Combination Laws. For a variety of reasons, the only extended discussion of wage-bargaining during this era appeared in *The Wealth of Nations*, but even here, as is well known, Smith argued that the interests of employers were in opposition to and not identical with the interests of their employees. Smith's successors virtually ignored the problem of bargaining, relying instead upon some form of the wage fund theory to explain the movement of wages.[75] In addition, the works of Smith, Mill, Ricardo, and the like were characterized by only the most rudimentary engagement with the theory of contracts. While many theorists, both political and economic, assumed *a priori* that freedom of contract was a social necessity, few of them appear to have been either interested in or familiar with the actual workings of the law. P.S. Atiyah noted that 'so far as ordinary contract law was concerned, Bentham was one of the few utilitarians or classical economists to devote even a very brief attention to the question', but even he hardly had anything new or different to say.[76] Moreover, there were

[73] Prothero, *Artisans and Politics*, p. 173; Miles, *Place*, p. 162.

[74] Place Papers, BL Add. MS 27802, fos 37–38.

[75] James A. Jaffe, *Striking a Bargain: work and industrial relations in England, 1815–1865* (Manchester, 2000), chapter 1.

[76] P.S. Atiyah, *The Rise and Fall of Freedom of Contract* (Oxford, 1979), p. 325.

very significant weaknesses in the contemporary law of contracts, especially concerning enforcement, that Bentham as well as the classical economists entirely ignored.[77] Finally, even if the classical economists had shown some interest in either individual wage-bargaining or the law of contract, they certainly evinced little interest in the Combination Laws or their repeal. As one historian has shown, the names of Smith, Malthus, and Ricardo were often invoked during the repeal campaign, but these people themselves wrote almost nothing on the issue.[78]

Therefore, the role of political economy in the repeal of the Combination Laws deserves to be scrutinized in a great deal more detail than it has been. In the case of Francis Place's motivation, a more reasonable argument may be made instead for the influence of the ideas of 'commercial republicanism' upon his opposition to the Combination Laws, a set of ideas most likely, although not solely, to have been inherited from Thomas Paine. First, as the quotation above indicates, Place fervently maintained that it was the system of unjust laws advanced by an unrepresentative parliament that had both 'degraded and demoralized the working people'.[79] His radical republican antipathy to the monarchy, aristocracy, and the injustices they promoted through the tyranny of the law is a palpable theme running throughout these diaries as well as Place's entire political career.[80] Second, for Place, the removal of unjust and tyrannical laws, such as the Combination Laws, would not only obviate the necessity for trade unions, but, more importantly, it would herald the advent of a new social and economic system of liberty and peace, the paramount benefits of commerce. As Paine had written in the *Rights of Man*, commerce was 'a pacific system, operating to unite mankind by rendering nations, as well as individuals, useful to each other'.[81] In a similar vein, Place had written to Joseph Hume, the radical MP and chair of the Select Committee that engineered the repeal of the Combination Laws, that

> The business is really very simple, and it lies in a small space. Repeal every troublesome and vexatious enactment, and enact very little in their place.

[77] *Ibid.*, pp. 515–523.
[78] William D. Grampp, 'The economists and the Combination Laws', *The Quarterly Journal of Economics*, 93 (1979), pp. 501–522.
[79] Place Papers, BL Add. MS 27801, Place to Peter McDougal and William Smith, 1 September 1824, quoted in Wallas, *Life*, p. 220.
[80] For important qualifying remarks concerning the nature of English republicanism, see Mark Philp, 'English republicanism in the 1790s', *Journal of Political Philosophy*, 6 (1998), pp. 235–262.
[81] Quoted in Claeys, *Paine*, p. 79.

Leave workmen and their employers as much as possible at liberty to make their own bargains in their own way. This is the way to prevent disputes. ...[82]

Place's marginal notes to Hume on his own copy of the 1824 bill to repeal the Combination Laws reveal the same sentiment borne out of personal experience: 'I have two formen [*sic*] hired from week to week, or during good behaviour, both have been with me and my son, upwards of 20 years, and no disputes have occurred or ever will occur while the law lets us alone.'[83]

In retrospect, Place's faith in the civilizing power of commerce was largely misplaced. Indeed, in later years there is evidence that, after the repeal of the Combination Laws, he had come to recognize the inequitable distribution of power in a free-market system based upon the individuality of contract. As a result, he awkwardly sought to distinguish between a 'trades union' across several trades and a 'trade club' within an individual trade, only the latter of which was a valid exercise of labor's right to organize.[84] Still, Place was not alone in idealizing the potential moral and social effects of free exchanges. The civilizing power of commerce, and the moral importance of free and equitable exchanges, constituted an important, although sometimes neglected, element of British social and economic thought in this period. It can be traced, for example, in the work of Thomas Hodgskin, Robert Owen, William Thompson, and many others.[85] That these important ideas were eventually subsumed within or displaced by orthodox political economy should not mislead historians into thinking that they necessarily had little influence in their time.

The diary years, 1825–1831

Although his daily entries only begin in April 1826, Place's diary opens with a brief review of his activities during 1825. That year had witnessed a significant upsurge in trade-union activity as a result of the repeal of the Combination Laws, an upsurge that Place thought was only temporary. His legislative lobbying work had yielded other results as well, including the passage of several pieces of legislation for

---

[82] Quoted in Wallas, *Life*, p. 210.
[83] Place Papers, BL Add. MS 27800, fo. 10.
[84] Miles, *Place*, pp. 169–170.
[85] Jaffe, 'Commerce, character and civil society', *passim*; on equitable exchanges, *idem*, *Striking a Bargain*, pp. 29–35.

special commercial interest groups, but his labors on these accounts have not been investigated by historians.[86]

The years for which the diary was most carefully kept, 1826 and 1827, were ones of relative prosperity and political quiescence, especially when compared to the first half of the decade. Entries were made almost daily between April 1826 and July 1827. However, the illness and eventual death of Place's first wife, Elizabeth, in October 1827 virtually ended his interest in the diary. After Elizabeth's death, Place ceased to make daily entries but he did not give up the project altogether. Throughout most of 1828, he contributed monthly entries, although it is not clear whether these were done on a regular basis or retrospectively at some point or points during the year. In the following year, 1829, the entries became even less regular, amounting to extended essays on his activities over irregular periods of time. From January 1830 to February 1831, Place made further irregular contributions to the diary, after which point he neglected the diary altogether. It appears that he tried to revive the diary once or twice in 1835 and 1836, and these brief entries are included here as well.

Again, it is perhaps unfortunate that the political and social issues of great moment did not arise until the end of the period covered by Place's regular entries to the diary. The issues to which he did direct his attention during this period nevertheless reveal the significant demands made upon him by others as well as the demands he put upon himself. The diaries reveal the constant stream of visitors to Charing Cross Road, some of whom sought Place's parliamentary expertise, others of whom came for his business acumen, while still others desired his pragmatic everyday advice. He read regularly during these years, mostly material concerned with the history of the constitutional problems under the Stuarts and the history of working-class manners and morals. Place is perhaps not given enough credit for the careful and assiduous manner with which he demanded the production of written evidence to support these projects, even though his vast collections of materials in the British Library bear ample testimony to that. In *Hard Times*, Dickens brilliantly skewered the nineteenth-century quest for facts, and there is a bit of this utilitarian obsession about Place. However, Place was no mere Gradgrind, although some think he shared some of Gradgrind's personal characteristics. He was, on the contrary, possessed of an intensely historical mind several generations before the professionalization of the discipline. Unlike Dickens's characters, the utility of facts was not an end in itself for Place. They were intended instead to serve a useful purpose, in

---

[86] Among these reforms were the repeal or review of the laws relating to the wool trade, London butchers, tanners and curriers, and hackney coaches.

particular to provide evidence of what he believed was the enormous progress of the working class and the simultaneous failures of an unreformed political system.

Place's political activities during these years ranged across a wide spectrum of issues, including the repeal of the Corn Laws, repeal of the laws governing the press remaining from the infamous Six Acts passed after Peterloo, reform of the laws requiring imprisonment for debt, the founding of the University of London, and many others. There were perhaps three issues, however, that appear more frequently and in greater detail than the others: the ramifications of the Charing Cross Improvement Bill, the fallout from the Greek Loan Scandal, and the machinations following Lord Liverpool's stroke in 1827. The context of many, if not all, of Place's actions and observations in these matters will become self-evident to the reader, yet a brief indication of their significance might prove valuable.

Place appears to have been drawn into the debate surrounding the Charing Cross Improvement Bill (1826) by William Fenn, a commissioner in one of London's local courts of request. The immediate cause of Fenn's opposition to this bill and Place's subsequent support for him was a clause that required the parishioners to pay the curacy of the vicar of St Martin-in-the-Fields. For both men, this clause brought into question the role of the vestry in parish politics, a question that had recently been broached by the passage of Sturges Bourne's Act of 1819, and hence was also a question of the nature of representation in contemporary society.[87] To protect the participatory role of the vestry, Fenn and Place entered into an extensive search of both the history of the parish and its administration, the extent of which was both remarkable and quite revealing of the historicism that penetrated the political debates of the era. Unfortunately, the documentary evidence relating to the origins of St Martin-in-the-Fields was not decisive, and thus Fenn could not prove his contention concerning the custom of the parish. In the end, the case was decided against him.

The Greek Loan Scandal tainted the reputation of Place's closest contact in Parliament, Joseph Hume, the radical MP for the Aberdeen burghs, who had chaired the Select Committee on Artizans and Machinery that investigated the Combination Laws in 1824. The scandal did not erupt until late in 1826, although its roots reached back to 1823.[88] At that time, two deputies from the Greek government

---

[87] For a general history of the parish vestry, see Sidney and Beatrice Webb, 'What happened to the English parish, I & II', *Political Science Quarterly*, 17 (1902), pp. 223–246 and 438–459.

[88] The following is based on the discussion of the scandal in Ronald K. Huch and Paul R. Ziegler, *Joseph Hume: the people's M. P.* (Philadelphia, PA, 1985), pp. 47–54.

had visited London in an attempt to raise money in support of the War of Independence. The money was raised through the issuance of bonds, the scrip of which quickly began to depreciate. Fearing a loss, Hume asked the Greek representatives not only to buy back his shares at the lower price, which they did, but also to repay his losses, which they did as well. In October 1826, these dealings came to the attention of *The Times*, which published a scathing account of the way in which the radicals, especially Hume, had mishandled the affair. Hume, whose reputation had been built in large part upon his dogged attacks upon government spending and mismanagement, was severely shaken by the revelations, and it was chiefly with the aid of Place and James Mill that he saw his way out of this personal and political crisis.

The last of the subjects that occupied a good deal of Place's attention during the diary years was the apparent collapse and reorientation of party politics that took place briefly after 1827, especially the activities of the Whigs in opposition. The diary entries for 1826 contain very few references to national political events, save as they affected Place's particular lobbying efforts. However, Lord Liverpool's stroke in February 1827, unremarked in the diary, and the creation of Canning's coalition ministry with the Whigs in April, evoked from Place an expression of the possibility of further reform.[89] Canning's subsequent death in August and the eventual creation of Wellington's ministry in 1828 certainly put a stop to such wishful thinking. Place's pronounced antipathy toward Wellington is expressed several times in the diary, at one point evoking a comment inserted many years later by Place's son, registering Wellington's much improved reputation. The later events of 1828–1829 are only sparsely covered. The repeal of the Test and Corporation Acts in 1828 is not mentioned at all, while the passage of Catholic Emancipation appears briefly, but only within the format of the monthly surveys of events that Place adopted in the last months of the diary. This seems to attest to Place's relative lack of interest in these matters for, even though his interest in the diary had obviously waned significantly, his notes and entries on Peel's Metropolitan Police Bill, introduced in 1828, are much fuller and more impassioned.

Despite the fact that the frequency of diary entries continues to fall off dramatically into 1830 and 1831, there is little doubt that Place maintained an extremely active role in both London and reform politics. Despite a brief hiatus from politics after his second marriage

---

[89] On the coalition ministries of 1827, see A. Aspinall, 'The coalition ministries of 1827', 2 parts, *English Historical Review*, 42 (1927), pp. 201–226 and 533–559; E.A. Wasson, 'The coalitions of 1827 and the crisis of Whig leadership', *Historical Journal*, 20 (1977), pp. 587–606; Peter Mandler, *Aristocratic Government in the Age of Reform: Whigs and Liberals, 1830–1852* (Oxford, 1990), pp. 23–33.

in February 1830, he soon found himself once again drawing up petitions, being sought out for advice, working for parliamentary reform,
and drafting new legislation. It is perhaps a significant reflection of
the nature of early nineteenth-century radicalism that Place did not
see either the repeal of the Test and Corporation Acts or Catholic
Emancipation as the beginning of 'a transformative moment in British
public life', as it may retrospectively appear to many historians.[90]
Neither augured any fundamental transformation of the British
monarchy or aristocracy, the ostensible object of Place's political
sympathies. For Place, the possibility for substantive political change
only reappeared during the nearly simultaneous illness and death of
George IV and the outbreak of the second French revolution in 1830.
The excitement generated by these events, especially the latter, and
compounded by the general anxiety produced by the Swing rising in
the countryside were the crucial elements contributing to the unique
mobilization for reform that coalesced in 1830–1832. For Place, the
one group that was certainly outside the pale of this reform movement
was the London mob and his advice to the London police on how to
control the mob, whether or not his account is wholly trustworthy on
this point, certainly reveals his antipathy to riot as a form of protest.
Unfortunately, the diaries do not extend into 1832, the year of reform,
and they are only taken up again fitfully in 1835 and 1836.

It is perhaps appropriate to conclude this Introduction with a brief
note on Place's personality, especially since this is often remarked
upon by historians. This editor has great sympathy for the author of
Place's last full-length biography, who described his subject at various
times as arrogant, hectoring, dictatorial, hard-headed, overcritical,
contemptuous, and humorless, a list to which might be added boastful,
self-important, aggravating, and vain. But, much like Place's father,
there must have been some attributes of Place's character and
personality that compensated for these traits. Unfortunately, the form
adopted by Place for his diaries does not readily evoke them, but one
can nevertheless get a sense of what they may have been. First, Place
was intensely loyal to both his friends and family: the first months
of the diary catalogue the extensive amount of time and effort Place
exerted in editing and publishing his son-in-law, John Miers's, account
of life in South America. The diaries also reveal a conscientious 'family
man', at least of the early nineteenth-century variety, who took part in
the education of his children and was out almost daily with Elizabeth,
his first wife. The cæsura in the diary caused by her death and his

[90] See Philip Harling, 'Equipoise regained?: recent trends in British political history,
1790–1867', *Journal of Modern History*, 75 (2003), p. 897.

obvious mourning for her are evidence of just how much he appeared to care for and depend upon her. Place showed a similar caring attitude toward his friends. His efforts to continue to support Thomas Hardy decades after his famous trial are especially noteworthy in this respect.

In addition, Place was a conscientious, dependable, and energetic support to those who came to him for help. His loyalty to Thomas Hardy has already been noted, but the diary is also replete with all manner of assistance that Place provided: legal help, medical care, political advice, business advice, publishing advice, and even engineering advice. The range of people who sought out his help was equally astonishing: politicians, authors, editors, businessmen, trade unionists, and even ladies in distress. Most days of this diary are occupied, to use Place's term, with 'the affairs of others'.[91]

There is no need to choose the 'real' Francis Place from the two personalities presented here. The human character is complex enough to comprehend both. The combination of these qualities suggests, however, something of the turmoil of an outsider, of someone ill at ease in his social surroundings. Seeking influence in the world of politics, he nonetheless disdained its corruption and sordidness; endeavoring to escape the daily toil of the working classes, still he sought to lead them; combative and critical, he was also kind and caring; selfless and generous in the aid of others, he was at the same time proud, egotistical, and vain. Desperate and deprived as a poor, young journeyman, he was uneasy and insecure as a wealthy, middle-aged man of independent means. While Place was of but not in the working class, he was in but not of the middle and upper classes. An atheist and a republican, he was caught in the tide of a society that was increasingly religious and conservative. These were the dilemmas and inner conflicts of an outsider that found expression in this unusual person and in his diary.

---

[91] See, for instance, p. 55, below; there are numerous other instances of the phrase.

EDITORIAL PRINCIPLES

Many of the difficulties one encounters when editing Place's manuscripts have already been thoroughly discussed and described in Mary Thale's introduction to *The Autobiography of Francis Place*.[92] While relatively few sections of the diaries have literally been cut out of the manuscript, several sections have been crossed out or overwritten. In those cases where I have been able to read through the overmarkings, I have presented them in this text as stricken out or, in a very few instances, noted the section as such in a footnote. As Thale noted, perhaps the most confounding aspect of the manuscripts is Place's awkward and sometimes confusing use of punctuation. Commas are often omitted entirely or replace full stops at the end of sentences. Thus, one sometimes finds commas preceding the capitalization of the first word in what appears to be the next sentence.

In this edition, I have sought to alter the original text as little as possible. Therefore, I have added full stops or commas only where they are essential to the comprehension of the text. In all other cases, I have left the text to stand as it reads in the manuscript. In order to avoid disrupting the flow of the text unnecessarily, I have kept the insertion of square brackets indicating these changes in punctuation to an absolute minimum. Brackets have, however, been used throughout the text to indicate sections that are illegible, missing, or contain spelling errors.

I have tried to identify many of the persons to whom Place refers, as well as to describe the context of the events discussed in the diary. In all cases, these references occur in numbered footnotes. Occasionally, Place included footnotes in the diary, but these were often marked with symbols such as an asterisk or a cross; however, in the final year or so of the diary, he included many footnotes and marginal notes without any system of reference whatsoever. All of Place's original notes are given as lettered footnotes, placed above the numbered editorial footnotes at the bottom of the page.

As I have noted in the acknowledgments and in the footnotes, many people kindly offered their knowledge and expertise in tracking down obscure or little-known references in the manuscript. Despite their gracious help, they are, of course, in no way responsible for what appears here. Any errors of transcription or annotation are mine alone.

---

[92] Place, *The Autobiography*, pp. xxix–xxxvii.

THE DIARIES OF FRANCIS PLACE

V. 5.

Memorandums. Diaries Journals.[93]

N°. 1. Memorandums commencing in September   1825.
2. Diary commencing April 9 ending Decr 31.   1826.
3. Diary _ 19 March to 31 Decr. Irregular. ___   1827.
4. Some Memorandums Jany 1828 continually
   irregularly to Decr 31st _____   1828.
5. Some D° in _____   1829.
6. Mr Hume and the New Times Newspaper.   1828
7. Memorandums of some of my occupations
   written at intervals from July 30 to February   1831.
8. D° in January   1831.
9. D° in___1835 and   1836.

These Memorandums &c would have been put into the the [*sic*]
fire, but after consideration I thought they might be useful to any one
who should Edit the Memoir, as they contain parts of political matters
alluded to in other places, and shew the views which I and others took
of them. They are preserved only for this purpose. When they have
been used in this way they should be destroyed.

Brompton 29 Decr 1838

These papers were necessarily written at the moment of the time
mentioned not intended for the eye of any but generally as memoranda
to be revised but as this cannot now be done allowances must be made
for some of the expressions and also for some of the descriptions[.]
22 Feb. 1850.[94]

---

[93] The diaries are to be found in the Place Papers of the British Library, Additional
Manuscript 35146.

[94] A blue-pencil note reading '1874¶' appears across the page here, suggesting that
the diary was reviewed at that time, most probably by Place's grandson, Francis Miers.
According to Graham Wallas, Place's private papers and letters were retained by the Miers
family. They were donated to the British Museum by Francis Miers only after the publication
of Wallas's biography in 1898. See Wallas, *Life*, pp. vii-viii.

1825

1825

No. 1.

Sep. 1825

Memorandums. 1825.[a]

Expectations[95]

   This year, was I expected, to have been a quiet year with me. ~~and~~ I hoped ~~and expected~~ that I should be able to employ much of my time on my projected history of North America. But I soon found myself differently occupied. I had the affairs of several persons in my hands at the commencement of the year but as I was, as I thought, resolved not to enter into any more private concerns of other people which were likely to occupy much of my time, I took what pains I could to finish with those I had already undertaken and ~~then~~ intended to proceed steadily ~~with~~ to the conclusion of my own memoirs, and then with the History of North America. I did neither the one nor the other.

Gaming Funds

   The passion for gaming transactions in the funds and in Joint stock companies which had become almost general and was pursued with an ardour little short of insanity, brought numbers of people to me and in January led me to take up the matter in the Morning Chronicle an account of which may be seen in the papers relating thereto, occupied all my spare time, until after the meeting of parliament early in Feb[y] – and then till the middle of March.

   I do not however consider that my time was unprofitably consumed, the course I pursued and the efforts I made principally in conjunction with M[r] Hobhouse checked some of these fraudulent gambling speculations, and saved the property of thousands of persons from

---

[a] This Paper N°. 1. Volume 5 differs from N°. 2. inasmuch as it is not so mere a Diary but it is pertinent to the Memoir. [Marginal note, written perpendicular to the text.]

[95] This italicized heading and those that follow in this first section of the diary are actually in the margin of the manuscript.

destruction.[96] The number of persons who got introduced to me was considerable and the time thus spent, as well as in corresponding and collating information was great. But before this occupation was ended, commenced another, which consumed all my time, and allowed of no intermission whatever till the end of the month of June, and filled up all intervals to the end of August, and indeed, to the present time has prevented me attending to any thing else except now and then, yet I cannot say that various matters which had gone into arrears have as yet been dispatched. I must make no more promises to myself but must do the best I can to accomplish my purposes.[a]

Combinations

The matter which thus consumed my time was the proceedings of the committee of the house of Commons on the Laws relating to the combinations of workmen, the particulars of which will be found in the Folio book relating thereto and in the Guard book, which contains the documents made use of.[97]

I see by some few memorandums I made at the times mentioned, that on the 30th of Jan[y] M[r] Hobhouse was half way disposed to take up the subject of the Wool Laws to which I had previously paid much attention. My intention was to make out such a case as would induce Ministers to consent to the repeal of the whole of them. I did not expect they would be repealed in the forthcoming session, but I was in hopes that they might be consolidated and brought into one act, and that in the next session a committee might be appointed to enquire respecting them with a view to their repeal. M[r] Hume[98] also seemed well

---

[a] NB They never were accomplished. 1850 [Marginal note.]

[96] John Cam Hobhouse, Baron Broughton (1786–1869). With the assistance of Place, Hobhouse was elected MP for Westminster in 1820. His radical *bona fides* were somewhat suspect, but he was active during this era in attacking government corruption and promoting certain elements of legislative reform, especially the regulation of factory labor and prison reform. The events mentioned here refer to the speculative mania of 1824–1825 and, in particular, to Hobhouse's opposition to the Pasco-Peruvian Mining Company bill. See Ron Harris, 'Political economy, interest groups, legal institutions, and the repeal of the Bubble Act in 1825', *Economic History Review*, 50 (1997), pp. 675–696.

[97] BL Add. MSS 27798–27799.

[98] Joseph Hume (1777–1855), Scottish radical MP. Introduced in 1813, Hume became Place's principal ally in the House of Commons. The nature of their relationship was quite complicated, as these diaries will indicate. Typically, Place claimed responsibility for 'nursing' Hume in the fight for radical reforms and Wallas, following upon this, described Place as Hume's 'schoolmaster'. Based upon evidence throughout the Place Papers, there is no doubt that Place contributed mightily to Hume's parliamentary efforts, especially by

disposed to take part in this affair but the circumstances which soon afterwards occurred totally set all chance of success in this matter aside for the session.[99]

Cutting and Flaying Stat.   *Tax on Leather*

In consequence of my exertions for the Butchers, and the result of those exertions having in the previous session caused the repeal of the "Cutting and Flaying Act," some of the Principal Tanners near London came to me to concert the means of procuring the repeal of the duty on Leather, this was a measure not likely to be entertained, and I declined giving up my time in making the attempt. I had reason to believe that the Law which prohibited Tanners being Curriers and Curriers Tanners, might be repealed. I had spoken with several ministerial members on the subject and had been assured by M[r] William Holmes the Treasury Whipper in, that he was authorized to say that Ministers were disposed to take off the restriction provided they could be satisfied, the duty on leather could be collected with not more trouble and expense than it was at present collected and that the amount should not be diminished. The Tanners were very desirous the restriction should be taken off, but they were unable to devise means by which the duty could be secured. This business therefore was not proceeded with.

6 Acts   *Grey Bennett*   *Case for Mr. Bennett*

On the first of February, The Honb[l] Henry Grey Bennet[100] came to me for the purpose of concerting the means to procure the repeal of the obnoxious acts generally known under the title of – "Six Acts." These are the acts which regulate newspapers and other publications, restrain publications, and punish libel with banishment. At M[r] Bennetts request I made a case for him, which he however returned again

collecting and digesting large amounts of information. However, Place also had a marked tendency to exaggerate his own role in public affairs and thus these claims should be treated with caution. See Wallas, *Life*, pp. 183–184; Ronald K. Huch and Paul R. Ziegler, *Joseph Hume: the people's M.P.* (Philadelphia, PA, 1985); and V.E. Chancellor, 'Hume, Joseph (1777–1855)', *ODNB*, <http://www.oxforddnb.com/view/article/14148>, accessed 18 February 2005.

[99] This paragraph is indented in the manuscript.

[100] Henry Grey Bennet (1777–1836), radical MP for Shrewsbury and early ally of Joseph Hume. In 1824, two of his children died. While recovering from this trauma in Europe, he became ensnared in a sexual peccadillo that ended his political career. See Roland Thorne, 'Bennet, Henry Grey (1777–1836)', *ODNB*, <http://www.oxforddnb.com/view/article/37179>, accessed 27 December 2005.

in a few days, on account of his own ill health and the ill health of his family which would he said compel him to go to Italy, and prevent his attendance in parliament during the session. He did not attend.

A project was named to me by Mr Martineau the Engineer.[101] It was to be a joint stock company for inventions and Patents. Mr Martineau shewed that a society which should act honestly and with judgment might be essentially serviceable to persons who made discoveries and improvements in machinery, chemistry and some of the arts, shipping &c &c. The plan was to raise about 100.000£, or 150.000£, to take a place and build workshops, a laboratory &c – and to encourage persons to come and complete their inventions, which were to be communicated confidentially in the first instance to the acting manager, who was to communicate the information he received and his opinion thereon to four other managers, and they were to permit if they thought proper, the inventor to use their ships, tools, &c &c to perfect his invention, but if the inventor objected to explain his invention to the manager or objected to his explaining it to the other four, then nothing was to be done. The manager was however to be at liberty in some particular cases to have the power to proceed with the inventor without communicating the particulars to any other person. The same rules were to be observed as to Patents. For which money was to be advanced.

In the beginning of March I attended a meeting at a house on Cornhill, present, on our part Mr Martineau Mr Moses Ricardo a brother of the late David Ricardo, and Dr Arnott.[102] We met about a dozen City people very plausible very stupid, yet very cunning people, they had been projecting a somewhat similar society, and their attorney who was present informed us that they had some days before made application to Mr Huskisson[103] to assist them in obtaining a charter, but no answer had been returned. What they had done was

[101]John Martineau, prominent London engineer and partner in the firm Taylor & Martineau, founded in 1820.

[102]The latter name probably refers to Neil Arnott (1788–1874), scientist, inventor, and educator. For a brief survey of his eclectic career, see R.A. Bayliss and C. William Ellis, 'Neil Arnott, F.R.S., reformer, innovator and popularizer of science, 1788–1874', *Notes and Records of the Royal Society of London*, 36 (1981), pp. 103–123 and Bill Luckin, 'Arnott, Neil (1788–1874)', *ODNB*, <http://www.oxforddnb.com/view/article/694>, accessed 27 December 2005.

[103]William Huskisson (1770–1830), one of the principal architects of free trade and 'liberal toryism'. Under Lord Liverpool, he served as president of the Board of Trade between 1823 and 1827, but was ousted from office shortly after Wellington's accession to the premiership in 1828. In A.C. Howe's estimation, Huskisson 'entered office with the needs of a rapidly industrializing state uppermost in his mind. Those needs dictated the removal of impediments to the growth of domestic industries and the export economy.' See A.C. Howe, 'Huskisson, William (1770–1830)', *ODNB*, <http://www.oxforddnb.com/view/article/14264>, accessed 27 December 2005.

proper enough but their notions were very narrow, and it appeared to me their principal object was money making. We laid before them our project and M[r] Ricardo read to them an admirably drawn up paper declaring the object and pointing out the means of conducting the society, it proposed that not more than 10 per cent should ever be paid to any share holder and this only on his real advances and not on his number of shares. It was agreed that our view of the matter was the right one and our resolutions were assented to. Thus the whole seemed to merge into one project. Soon after the meeting it became manifest that the parties we met contemplated a job in the usual stile of Joint stock robberies, and I ~~ceased to~~ attended no more meetings. M[r] Ricardo M[r] Martineau and D[r] Arnott also withdrew and thus the matter ended.

7 Feb a project from Col[n] Torrens[104] to cut a canal across the Isthmus near Vera Cruz to join the Rivers Huasacadio [*sic*] and Chimalapa,[105] See Notes.

Undertook to collect a subscription set on foot for the purpose of raising money for the support of my very old and esteemed friend Thomas Hardy.[106] 100£ a year for the last 3 years.

Consultations and canvassings with Thomas Campbell[107] respecting his project for a College in London, M[r] Hume promised to procure 100.000£ provided I and Campbell would put down the leading points, on paper. This was done by Campbell and several meetings held, but, Brougham[108] tricked Campbell, ousted him from the credit

[104]Robert Torrens (1780?–1864), a prominent political economist and active imperialist. The late 1820s and early 1830s witnessed Torrens's most extensive efforts to promote imperial economic development, especially through the sale of colonial lands to emigrants. See Peter Moore, 'Torrens, Robert (1780?–1864)', *ODNB*, <http://www.oxforddnb.com/view/article/27565>, accessed 10 March 2005.

[105]John Womack has suggested indirectly to me that Place is probably referring here to Coatzacoalcos River and the village of Santa Maria Chimalapa, situated at the headwaters of a tributary to the Coatzacoalcos in Oaxaca. Thanks to my colleague Seth Meisel for posting my query on the Latin American list of H-Net and to Professor Womack for his response.

[106]Thomas Hardy (1752–1832), one of the founders of the London Corresponding Society, whose trial for treason in 1794 became a cause célèbre among radicals. He had become all but bankrupt in 1823. While Clive Emsley is correct in saying that Sir Francis Burdett contributed to Hardy's financial support thereafter, Burdett was not the only one to do so. These diaries indicate that Place actively solicited and collected funds from a variety of persons to help support Hardy. See Clive Emsley, 'Hardy, Thomas (1752–1832)', *ODNB*, <http://www.oxforddnb.com/view/article/12291>, accessed 10 March 2005.

[107]Thomas Campbell (1777–1844), a poet and editor of the *New Monthly Magazine*, first promoted the idea of London University in 1824. See Geoffrey Carnall, 'Campbell, Thomas (1777–1844)', *ODNB*, <http://www.oxforddnb.com/view/article/4534>, accessed 17 March 2005.

[108]Henry Brougham (1778–1868), first Baron Brougham and Vaux. Brougham's long and industrious life spanned a wide range of activities, including contributions to legal reform,

of being the originator, and as Campbell is a simple sensitive creature made him very unhappy. Brougham played so many tricks and acted in such an unprincipled manner as no one can well imagine, but it is probable the money will be raised and I hope the college will be established. All I can do I will do to promote it and Campbell shall if I can obtain it for him or in any way assist to obtain it for him have the credit of being the original professor. See Campbells letter to Brougham and my observations therein.[109]

Undertook for Mr Hume to give him heads for a speech to enable him to move to revive the committee of last session, with a view to the repeal of the laws which forbid the exportation of machinery. Appointed Mess^r Maudslay, Donkin — Bramah, Galloway and Martineau[110] to meet me at Mr Humes on the 23 feb. At this meeting a plan of proceeding was settled and I undertook to put the substance of the conversation into the form of a brief for Mr Hume. See it in the Fol Volume relating to Machinery. Mr Huskisson made some objection to the repeal of these laws, but when on the 24th Mr Hume made his motion Mr Huskisson supported him and a committee was appointed.

I afterwards wrote the Report for Mr Hume for the committee of the Commons on Machinery, it was somewhat altered in the committee. Words were taken out in some places and words were inserted in other places, and as it never came back to me for revision, it contains, bad english and nonsense. None but the London Engineers came before the committee to give evidence notwithstanding Mr Hume gave extensive notice that the committee was sitting and ready to receive evidence. Yet even Ministers were afraid of the clamour which they said would be raised if a bill was brought in to repeal the laws. It was in vain an attempt was made to shew it would not be even a "nine days wonder." Instead therefore of recommending the repeal of the laws Mr Hume was obliged to recommend, a repeal at a future time.

journalism, and the promotion of education. His rather testy relationship with Place, as these diaries reveal, sprang principally from what Michael Lobban diplomatically calls Brougham's political 'inconsistency'. Regardless of his opposition to the politics of 'old corruption', Brougham did not support the expansion of the franchise and thus was not widely trusted by the radicals. See Michael Lobban, 'Brougham, Henry Peter, first Baron Brougham and Vaux (1778–1868)', *ODNB*, <http://www.oxforddnb.com/view/article/3581>, accessed 12 December 2005.

[109]'Letter to Mr. Brougham on the Subject of a London University, together with Suggestions respecting the Plan', *Quarterly Review*, 33 (1826), pp. 257–276.

[110]These were among the most prominent engineers of the first industrial era: Henry Maudslay, Bryan Donkin, Timothy Bramah, son of the famous lock inventor Joseph Bramah, Alexander Galloway, and John Martineau, all of whom Place had arranged to testify before the Select Committee on Artizans and Machinery in 1824, the hearings of which led to the repeal of the Combination Laws.

Another attempt must be made next session. This it is hoped may be effected, without much opposition from any one. See the Report.

March 10 consulted by M[r] Gibson[111] as to the establishment of a Mechanics Institution in Spital Fields, encouraged him to proceed and advised with him as to best methods. M[r] Gibson persevered and an Institution was commenced, it bids fair to prosper. One circumstance is remarkable in my intercourse with the Spital Fields weavers I urged them to become members, but I invariably get for answer that it was likely to be injurious to them, for the first thing done at it was, "hiring D[r] Birkbeck[112] to preach to them in favour of machinery," which they were sure would be their ruin. All argument was useless, the whole body were equally ignorant and scarcely a silk weaver has joined it. These weavers are by far the most ignorant dirty narrow minded ill paid miserable set of journeymen tradesmen in the metropolis, and what is still lamentable, they are very numerous, they will improve very slowly, for their self sufficiency & conceit is equalled only by their ignorance. and filthyness [?]

See notes.

In the month of August applied to by a member of linen drapers shopmen, to organize them into a society for the purpose of lessening their hours of employment by compelling their employers to close their shops at 8 o clock in the winter and nine in the summer. These men are employed from 6 in the morning till 11 or 12 o clock at night. Drew up their address – and rule and orders and took the chair for them at the Crown and Anchor Tavern in the Strand.

See Guard Book for the papers.

Early in the year consulted as to the practicality of an Institution in the City of London somewhat similar to the London Mechanics Institution intended for Clerks and others who could afford to pay 40/a year subscription. Pointed out the means, and set the parties at work, ultimately it was established, many of my friends taking a very decided interest in it.

---

[111] Thomas Gibson was a major London silk manufacturer and an opponent of the Spitalfields Act. According to Marc Steinberg, he was part of a new breed of manufacturer, known as a 'warehouser', who had not progressed through the ranks of the journeymen silk weavers. See Marc Steinberg, *Fighting Words: working-class formation, collective action, and discourse in early nineteenth-century England* (Ithaca, NY, 1999), p. 80. My thanks to Marc Steinberg for this information.

[112] George Birkbeck (1776–1841), an early proponent of popular education and supporter of the efforts to establish both the London Mechanics' Institution in 1823 and the University of London. The reference here obliquely refers to the division that appeared within the movement over the goals and contents of workers' education.

In July in consequence of a recommendation of mine I was waited upon by Mr Bittlestone and Mr Jackson concerted with them the means of a similar establishment at the west end of town.

See Papers Relating thereto.

My son in Law John Miers[113] returned from South America in June having contracted with the Government for Buenos Ayres to set up a mint in that City. Having seen the necessary machinery constructed and obtained an order in Council to ship it he left England ~~about~~ at the End of December for Buenos Ayres.

From his letters journals and notes Mr Miers composed a book on Chile and La Plata, he had not time to revise it but he read it to me correcting it at my suggestions as he went on[.] But as he could not revise it I was obliged to undertake that long and tedious job and to see it through the press – Printing by Messrs Baldwins.[114]

Received as a present a silver cup and cover from the Sailors of Durham – value 50£[.]

Received as a present a beautiful set of knives and forks from the mechanics of Sheffield. Value not known.

I had often been solicited to permit some one to paint a portrait of me but I had steadily refused, there was probably as much conceit in the refusal as there would have been vanity in sitting. In the Autumn however in consequence of a portrait which I praised as a remarkably characteristic likeness of a person I knew, Mr William Tijou[115] persuaded me to sit to the painter for him, and a portrait in water colours was painted. It was said to be a great likeness but I was not quite satisfied with it. I know my own want of firmness on some occasions. I am pretty conscious of my own misgivings but I do not feel that when compared with others, I mean such others as I have known, and have opportunities of observing sufficiently to appreciate their characters, that I am a man infirm of purpose. I have at times shrunk from proceedings or ~~a~~ convictions, and even on a strong suspicion that I could not honestly persevere, but I am not aware that I ever in my life shirked a responsibility or ~~ever~~ when the time for acting came ever held back, on the contrary when it became necessary to do

---

[113] John Miers married Place's daughter, Annie, and subsequently ensnared the family in a great many legal and economic troubles. See the several letters to both son-in-law and daughter reproduced in *The Autobiography*, pp. 252–266.

[114] John Miers, *Travels in Chile and La Plata*, 2 vols (London, 1826). One historian of Chilean mining has called Miers 'a keen contemporary observer': see Claudio Veliz, 'Egaña, Lambert, and the Chilean Mining Associations of 1825', *Hispanic American Historical Review*, 55 (1975), fn. 25.

[115] William Tijou, artist, friend and fellow-collector of songs as well as other material on manners and morals. See, Mary Thale (ed.), *The Autobiography of Francis Place, 1771–1854* (Cambridge, 1972), p. 58.

things, I generally took a lead however disagreeable and unpromising affairs appeared, and have not on any occasion that I know of been reproached with want of courage or energy by my coadjutors. In cases which I have thought of moment, when others have been daunted, or have deserted I have never felt dismay but on the contrary, these have been the occasions on which I have always had the strongest desire to act, and in which I have acted with most confidence in myself and with most energy. But the portrait appeared to me to be that of a man who was infirm of purpose, which upon the whole I do not think I am, so far I was disappointed in the portrait, and as a man who writes of himself should not conceal his opinions of himself I having thus felt put down my opinion. But several persons who know me very well say the portrait is an exact and a capital likeness. Others say it is not sufficiently intellectual. My wife was not well pleased with it she said it was a strong likeness but it was "milk and water," deficient in character and calculated to convey to a stranger a notion of mildness and amiableness which did not belong to me, and so to please her I consented to sit again. The 1st portrait was taken in the dress I always wore at home, except on some very few occasions when there [*sic*] is my wife has company, for I have none except in my own room. It consists of a loose double breasted mint baise coat and waistcoat, and when I have it on as the waistcoat buttons close round the neck I am able to dispense with the, to me, great inconvenience of a neck-cloth. It has been frequently remarked that the difference in my appearance in this dress and in the dress namely black which I wear in the street is rem very remarkable, so it was settled that I should be painted in my black clothes – and this was done. The painter has now I think made a sour likeness, but those who have known me long say that it is much more characteristic than the other, and is perfectly correct as to expression when acting with others on serious occasions and indeed on all occasions when I am not more than usually cheerful. Here is the remarkable matter that every body admits both are strong likenesses, some prefer one some the other, both are intended to be portraits of a serious person, and yet of these portraits both of which are strong likenesses, the one scarcely resembles the other in any particular not even in the general form of the face. This portrait painting job would not have been noticed but for a notion I entertain of myself and the opportunity it may give others who are allied to me a cause for an examination which I know will not when I am dead be unpleasant to them, for if I do not greatly deceive myself they will remember me with pleasure however much they may regret I am no more, and I am sure they have hitherto had and I have no doubt will continue to have reason to respect me as long as they live. I am certain I have done my duty to them, to the utmost of my power in every possible way.

1826

1826

V.5

N° 2. Diary. commencing April. 9. 1826
ending——————————— D[ec] 31.1826

These diaries must not be taken to include the names of all the persons I saw or all the matters in which I was concerned.

I have just now concluded looking over this Diary and request my Executors to burn it with their own hands as soon as it has been examined and such few particulars as some competent person or one of themselves may think are necessary for the elucidation of my memoir, have been used.

11. p.m. 22 Feby 1850 Francis Place

Towards the end of this paper some reference has been made to the Duty on Printed Calico. A paper in relation to the repeal of the Duty is appended to this Diary.[116]

---

[116] This paper has not been included in this edition.

I intend for a week or more to keep a diary, not of every occurrence but of such as shew how my time is occupied, since it sometimes happens that I can hardly tell how it has been consumed. I suspect that so much of every mans time, I mean of every mans time who is not engaged in business, is fooled away, that were he to take an exact account of it, he could scarcely fail to be ashamed of himself, and this is probably the reason so few have done it.

Sunday   April 9 – 1826

Several hours altering the shelves and putting up a number of books which have been accumulating on the floor from want of room.

Mr Charles Blake arrived from Chile – occupied my attention for more than two hours, with relations respecting persons and things in that country – mining projects &c &c and of my daughters departure for Mendoza.

Wrote a short essay on the Pope's Bull for the Trades newspaper.[117]

Read a portion of McCulloch's essay on wages[118] – made a calculation for printing it in a cheap way for circulation. It may be sold for – 2

NB to procure subscriptions to print it.

Made a diagram of the compound motions of the earth and moon and of the sun in respect of the Solar System for the children.

M^r. John Evans the Attorney having at the desire of William Hone[119] requested me to go round to his creditors and endeavour to procure their signatures to a letter of licence. I agreed to do so. Examined his list of creditors, thought it imperfect – wrote to Mr Evans to have it made perfect and for several particulars.

Look at the Mirror and Literary Gazette.

Staid at home all day.

[117] 'The Pope's Bull and the Jubilee', *TN*, 16 April 1826.

[118] J.R. McCulloch, *An Essay on the Circumstances which Determine the Rate of Wages, and the Condition of the Labouring Classes* (Edinburgh, 1826).

[119] William Hone (1780–1842), radical publisher and author, whose parodies of the catechism and the creed brought about his prosecution for blasphemy in 1817. The trials were another cause célèbre among radicals who supported freedom of the press. By the middle of the 1820s, he was in severe financial straits and was imprisoned for debt in 1827. See J. Ann Hone, 'William Hone (1780–1842), publisher and bookseller: an approach to early 19th century London radicalism', *Historical Studies*, 16 (1974), pp. 55–70 and Philip W. Martin, 'Hone, William (1780–1842)', *ODNB*, <http://www.oxforddnb.com/view/article/13659>, accessed 10 March 2005.

Read a portion of Sir F. M. Eden's first volume on the state of the poor prior to the statute of Labourers – Ed. III.[120]

Monday   April 10. 1826

Wrote a long letter to Sir Francis Burdett[121] on the expenses and arrears of the last West[minster] Elections in 1820. The election cost 1600£ and 96£ still remained unpaid – I have paid 130£ and M[r] Henry Brooks[122] who is liable for the 96£ cannot afford to pay it – so I asked Sir F B – to pay that sum on Henry Brooks's account.

Heard at the Royal Institution M[c]Culloch's 3rd Lecture on Political Economy.

Called on M[r] Hobhouse had a long conversation, on the case of D[r] Thorpe, and got a promise of an appointment for D[r] Thorpe to see him and Burdett together.[123]

Walked with my wife, out from $\frac{1}{2}$ 10 to $\frac{1}{2}$ 2.

Read at M[r] Hume's request and for the satisfaction of the seamen of the Tyne and Wear who had written to me on the subject, "a Bill to enable commissioners for trying offences upon the sea" &c &c[,] noted it and wrote to the seamen. The bill if passed into a law as it is at present worded would be an act of injustice towards the seamen.

Read – 6 letters sent to me by M[r] Hume, correspondence respecting the absurd Potteries bill which I noted in the 6 – and about which I conferred with M[r] Mayse the potter.

NB. The bill is bad in every respect and will not be passed.

Read proof of sheet B. vol. II. Travels in Chile and La Plata.

---

[120] Frederick Morton Eden, *The State of the Poor; or, an history of the labouring classes in England, from the conquest to the present period . . . with a large appendix containing a . . . table of the prices of labour; . . . an account of the poor in Scotland, etc.*, 3 vols, (London, 1797).

[121] Sir Francis Burdett (1770–1844) was perhaps the most prominent figure in the political reform movement during the first quarter of the nineteenth century. He represented Westminster in parliament nearly continuously between 1802 and 1837. After a series of very expensive election campaigns, Place played a major role in the formation of the Westminster Committee in 1807, subscriptions to which subsequently paid Burdett's expenses. He was, as Marc Baer has eloquently written, 'a genteel democrat in an age of oligarchy' whose radical politics were anchored in an eighteenth-century defense of the 'ancient constitution'. As Place's diaries testify, these politics were eventually condemned by many radicals as too mild and equivocal. See Marc Baer, 'Burdett, Sir Francis, fifth baronet (1770–1844)', *ODNB*, <http://www.oxforddnb.com/view/article/3962>, accessed 10 March 2005.

[122] Secretary of the Westminster Committee and son of Samuel Brooks, a member of the London Corresponding Society and active in City politics thereafter. See J. Ann Hone, *For the Cause of Truth: radicalism in London, 1796–1821* (Oxford, 1982), pp. 25, 394.

[123] Robert Thorpe claimed in his petition to the House of Commons to have been active on the colonial bench for many years. After returning to England for a year's stay, however, he claimed to have been unfairly dismissed by the Secretary of State for the Colonies and deprived of several other offices. See *JHC*, 81 (1826), p. 323.

Interrupted in the evening by Wm Tijou and Charles Blake – and afterwards by George White[124] a clerk in the house of commons who came to me to tell me "the good news" that ministers had been beaten from their project.

Read the articles in the Bolton Chronicle respecting the miserable state of the weavers and others and containing absurd proposals to fix a minimum of wages and to stop the use of machinery.

Wrote a short paper composed of questions for the Bolton Chronicle.

Mr Fenn[125] respecting D[r] Richards the Vicar who wants a clause in the Charing X improvement bill to compel the parishioners to pay his curate. Refused to see the D^r but took care to defeat his purpose through Mr Hobhouse.[126]

Tuesday   April 11 – 1826

Read as usual – The Morning Chron[icle,] the Morning Herald – the votes of the House of Commons, and looked at the other daily delivered papers from the House of Commons —

Three hours sorting cuttings from newspapers, and sticking, some which relate to, the working people – the conduct of Justices – and South American mining into guard or scrap books.

Charles Blake came with some information respecting S. America.

Long letter from my daughter Annie at Mendoza, she having just crossed the Andes from Chile.

Colonel Bradley, came again with his case, put into the form of a petition to the House of Commons, he is a very ill used man, but has no chance of redress – read his petition to him[,] advised him and sent him to Mr Hume.[127]

Walked with my wife – ½ 1 – to 3.

[124] Clerk of Committees in the House of Commons. Especially active in the campaign to repeal the Combination Laws and editor of several digests of parliamentary activities concerning radical causes.

[125] Mr Fenn, who will appear repeatedly in the diaries, was a commissioner in one of the London courts of request. He is also identified in Place's *Autobiography* as a bookseller in Charing Cross Road (p. 89).

[126] The Charing Cross Improvement Bill was introduced in March 1826 by Charles Arbuthnot to improve east–west transportation through the 'narrow gut' at Charing Cross Road and Bedford Street. See *Hansard*, new series, 15, 21 March 1826, cols 62–69.

[127] Lieutenant Colonel Thomas Bradley, Second West India Regiment. While stationed in Honduras in 1814, Bradley had become involved in a dispute with his superior officer over the command of the military forces there. In the course of that dispute and subsequent military trial, Bradley was arrested, jailed, and dismissed from the service. See *Hansard*, new series, 16, 8 December 1826, cols 321–330; *ibid.*, 14 February 1827, cols 460–471; *JHC*, 81 (1826), pp. 345, 385.

A person respecting Hone's affairs.

Dr Maclean respecting the conduct of the College of Physicians about which he has a book in the press – brought home to me a parliamentary book on Mad houses – which I had lent to him.[128]

Sir Francis Burdett in consequence of my letter of yesterday, will do as requested.

Looked through two sale catalogues of books – marked some for purchase.

Mr Barry to gossip – sent him to Charles Blake.

Mr Carlile[129] – d^o.

Read proof C. vol. 2 Travels in Chile —

Read some papers in the controversy, respecting Irish Absentees.

Mr Russell – the engraver with the plan of Santiago, to consult, respecting the mode of engraving it.

Finished reading McCulloch's essay on wages &c.

Having now no affairs of others which consume much time in doors on my hands I intend tomorrow morning to proceed with my own memoirs, which have not been attended to for many months past.

May. 25. NB. From what follows it will be seen how my intentions were frustrated.

---

[128] Likely *An exposition of the state of the medical profession in the British dominions; and of the injurious effects of the monopoly, by usurpation, of the Royal College of Physicians in London* (London, 1826). The British Library's catalogue entry lists no author; however, the title and author are confirmed in the entry for 26 April below, p. 70.

[129] Richard Carlile (1790–1843), the formidable radical publisher and essayist, was in frequent contact with Place throughout the period of these diaries. Carlile's notoriety was first secured when he republished the works of Thomas Paine, an action that, along with his eyewitness account of the Peterloo Massacre, eventually led to his conviction on charges of seditious libel in 1819. Carlile was released from prison in 1825. He returned to London in January 1826 and founded a joint-stock book company to publish cheap radical texts. At the same time, he became an advocate of birth control and a friend of Robert Taylor, the 'renegade Anglican clergyman', according to Iain McCalman, who advocated a species of mystical deism. It should be noted that, in their admiration of Paine, their advocacy of birth control, and their opposition to the Church and organized religion, Place and Carlile had a great deal in common. See Philip W. Martin, 'Carlile, Richard (1790–1843)', *ODNB*, <http://www.oxforddnb.com/view/article/4685>, accessed 10 March 2005; Iain McCalman, *Radical Underworld: prophets, revolutionaries, and pornographers in London, 1795–1840*, paperback edition (Oxford, 2002), p. 188.

Wednesday   April 12.

Mr Adams[130] respecting the expected arrival of his son from Buenos Ayres.

A long conversation with him respecting certain proceedings – at the Middlesex elections at which Sir Francis Burdett was a candidate, from which I obtained much information – also as to the West^r elections in 1806.

Instructing a farmer sent to me by Mr Henry Drummond,[131] respecting his emigrating to North America.

M^r McCulloch[132] for a gossip – he told me, that on an average of the last three years – the Edinburgh Review had sold 11,000.— Longmans in Consequence of Constables failure have become the sole proprietors – but Jeffrey[133] is to continue as usual to edit it, and it is of course to be printed at Edinburgh.

Occupied all day in the political history of Westminster, made but little progress.

Letters to Douglass Kinnaird[134] and John Smith M. P.[135] requesting them to borrow, Volumes of the Morning Chronicle and some other morning newspaper for the years 1790 and 1796 for my use.

Letter from Sir F. Burdett inclosing his check for 226£. and a note requesting information respecting the Cooperative society.

Wrote him an account of the said society [portion of paragraph excised in original] ... paltry person, a smooth plausible man constantly making pretensions of a desire to devote some portion of his income to good purposes, if any one will point them out to him, and

[130] Apparently a reference to William Adams, a currier in Dean Street, Soho, who had been a member of the London Corresponding Society and remained active in Westminster politics. See Hone, *For the Cause of Truth*, p. 154 *et seq.*

[131] Henry Drummond (1786–1860) was perhaps most well-known as a leading member of the ecstatic Catholic Apostolic church, but he was also, according to his biographer, 'a conscientious and caring landlord and a pioneer of the allotment system'. See Columba Graham Flegg, 'Drummond, Henry (1786–1860)', *ODNB*, <http://www.oxforddnb.com/view/article/8067>, accessed 13 March 2005.

[132] John Ramsay McCulloch (1789–1864), the political economist, was the principal economic writer for the *Edinburgh Review* during this period and the popularizer of David Ricardo. After Ricardo's death, James Mill and others endowed the Ricardo Memorial Lectures and McCulloch was selected as the first lecturer. His lectures in London, and those repeated elsewhere, between 1824 and 1826, were enormously popular and influential. See Phyllis Deane, 'McCulloch, John Ramsay (1789–1864)', *ODNB*, <http://www.oxforddnb.com/view/article/17413>, accessed 10 March 2005.

[133] Francis Jeffrey, one of the founding editors of the *Edinburgh Review*.

[134] Douglas Kinnaird (1788–1830) was a banker, manager of the Drury Lane Theatre, and political radical. He was selected by the Westminster Committee to run in the 1818 election; however, he withdrew during the canvassing in order to give his backing to Burdett. He later served as MP for Bishop's Castle, 1819–1820. See Hone, *For the Cause of Truth*, pp. 280–287.

[135] Most likely this refers to John Smith (1767–1842) who had been, at various times, MP for Wendover, Nottingham, and, between 1818 and 1830, Midhurst.

as constantly discovering when they are pointed out that they are not good purposes, and thus keeping his money in his pocket. He called to cheat me if he could into a belief that it was not wise in him to advance some money to two men shipwrights for the purpose of establishing them in business – which I have no doubt at all it would do, having at his request carefully examined their premises, their books &c &c – This mean fellow having led the men to hope that he would assist them if I upon examination of their affairs thought he ought to do so, now to save the risk of money which can be of no use to him lets these men fall through. They should have the 200 £ of me could I advance it from income, but I cannot, and I must not decrease the amount of my capital which does but just with all sorts of economical cares, support my [section excised] ... his request.[136]

Thursday.   April 13

M[r] Sidney the Printer.[137] This is a shrewd clever man who comes in occasionally, to unburthen himself of his information. He has been relating many curious facts, respecting the bookselling trade, and to many of the present booksellers. he [sic] is a man who discriminates pretty accurately and does not exaggerate, he is therefore a useful communicant —

Letter to John Tester,[138] Robertson[139] has gone to the Kings Bench.

Recommended M[r] Tho[s] Hodgskin for the office of Editor to the Mechanics Magazine.[140]

[136] This paragraph has obviously been heavily edited either by Place himself or one of his executors. As indicated in the text, large portions have been excised from the manuscript, making it impossible to identify the object of Place's disdain. In addition, the portion of the paragraph that remains in the manuscript has been crossed out by several large, heavy lines.

[137] Sidney's was a prominent printing house of this period.

[138] Secretary of the Bradford woolcombers' and stuff-weavers' union. Their bitter and lengthy strike had ended in failure in November 1825. See R.G. Kirby and A.E. Musson, *The Voice of the People: John Doherty, 1798–1854: trade unionist, radical and factory reformer* (Manchester, 1975), p. 40; Iorwerth Prothero, *Artisans and Politics in Early Nineteenth-Century London: John Gast and his times*, paperback edition (London, 1981), p. 160.

[139] Likely a reference to J.C. Robertson who was part-owner of the *Mechanics' Magazine*. The following reference to Thomas Hodgskin appears to substantiate this connection. See Prothero, *Artisans and Politics*, pp. 190–192.

[140] Thomas Hodgskin (1787–1869), the prominent radical political economist. His unique advocacy of the labor theory of value, elaborated in *Labour Defended against the Claims of Capital* (1825), had just appeared. Despite the fact that Place disagreed mightily with Hodgskin, it is plain from these diaries that Place remained on friendly terms with both him and his wife. It is difficult, therefore, fully to accept David Stack's claim that 'Place, who had once promised to act like a father in promoting Hodgskin's career, was by the mid 1820s a positive impediment to his advancement.' See David Stack, *Nature and Artifice: the life and thought of Thomas Hodgskin (1787–1869)* (Woodbridge, 1998), pp. 137–138.

Mr Charles Blake – read with him several papers relating to the people of Chile and La Plata, and on the mining projects in that country.

Mr John Wright,[141] conversation respecting occurrences consequent on the duel between Mr Paull and Sir Francis Burdett, on the conduct of Mr Cobbett on that occasion and on some subsequent proceedings relative to the political history of ~~Chile~~ Westminster.[142] He is to procure some particulars for me.

Walked with my Wife. $\frac{1}{2}$ 1 – to 3.

Mr Barry with notes relative to mining concerns in South America

Mr Blake ——— d^o.

Mr Fenn with a book of items copied from the vestry books of the parish, read them and made notes in the margins for the use of Mr Joshua Evans one of the Counsel in the cause, now going on against our select vestry, the members of which have no legal or customary right whatever to hold the office of vestry men.

> See Papers relating to the Parish of St Martin.

Dr Thorpe, explained to this poor old and much injured gentleman the arrangement I had made with Sir Francis Burdett and Mr Hobhouse respecting his case.

Mr Geo White relative to the laws respecting trade, gave him a book containing references to all the laws respecting wool, and abstracts from many statutes to enable him to furnish Mr Hume with matter for a speech on his intended motion. Mr White informed me that about 40 bobbin net machines had lately gone from Nottingham to Calais, and that they were smuggling out of England and into France lace machines, in parts. The exportation from this country and the

---

[141] John Wright (1770/1771–1844), publisher and one-time confidant of William Cobbett. He was a long-time editor of T.C. Hansard's *Parliamentary Debates*. In 1827, he would become a leading figure in the drive to clean up Westminster's water supply. See Page Life, 'Wright, John (1770/1771–1844)', *ODNB*, <http://www.oxforddnb.com/view/article/30038>, accessed 10 January 2006.

[142] James Paull and Burdett had fought a bitter campaign during the 1807 Westminster elections. Even before polling had taken place, they had fought a duel in which Burdett had been wounded. Paull eventually lost the election and committed suicide a year later. See Hone, *For the Cause of Truth*, pp. 151–161. Mr Cobbett, of course, refers to one of the leading radicals of the day, William Cobbett (1763–1835). During the first decade of the nineteenth century. Place and Cobbett had been political allies. Place, however, later rejected him after Cobbett's 'ludicrous' performance at the latter's trial for libel in 1810. Their enmity became based as much upon political tactics as upon personality. Place, it is commonly noted, rejected what he considered to be Cobbett's inflammatory and reckless actions. Moreover, he was, in E.P. Thompson's words, 'deeply hostile to any open strategy of popular agitation and organisation', a strategy that Cobbett advocated. See E.P. Thompson, *The Making of the English Working Class* (New York, NY, 1963), pp. 612–613 and Wallas, *Life*, pp. 116–117.

importation into that country being prohibited. Mr White explained how this was effected, and proved most completely that no laws could prevent the practice.

Political History of West^r.

Read proof D. Vol. II Travels in Chile – Mr Baldwin the publisher sadly afraid lest it should contain something libellous.

Friday —   April 14.

Compiled from letters a paper for the morning Chronicle on Mining in Chile – took. 3 hours.

At 11. a m. Mc Culloch's lecture on political economy —

Walked with my wife and Caroline to Chelsea over Battersea Bridge and through the market gardeners grounds to the Red House – crossed the water in a boat and home by way of mill bank.

Mr Barry with a translation of the report of Portales to O Higgins in Chile on the then proposed Chile Loan,[143] went through it and corrected it.

A Dr Forster a friend of Mr Lawrence[144] the surgeon called, he lives [remainder of paragraph excised.]

Mr Carlile with Cobbetts Register in which he has attacked Carlile for his "Every womans book."[145]

Mr Blake to examine a translation of Mr Portales's report to the Supreme Director of Chile on Mr Irisarri's proposal for a Loan.

Read in Parliamentary Review on Exportation of Machinery.

[143] In 1822, Antonio José de Irisarri had arranged a controversial loan to the newly independent Chilean government of General Bernardo O'Higgins. José Santiago Portales y Larrain, a prominent aristocrat then in charge of the Chilean mint, was ordered by O'Higgins to submit a report on the advisability of accepting the loan's terms. Portales's report was unequivocal in its rejection of the loan arranged by Irissari. In the meantime, Irissari had signed the contract for the loan. A translation of the Portales Report was included in Miers's book as Appendix C of the second volume. On the context and significance of the loan in Chilean history, see Claudio Veliz, 'The Irisarri loan', *Boletín de Estudios Latinoamericanos y del Caribe*, 23 (1977), pp. 3–20.

[144] Sir William Lawrence, frequently spelled 'Laurence' later in the diaries, was professor of anatomy and surgery at the Royal College of Surgeons. His series of lectures in 1816 and thereafter offered an essentially materialist view of physiology, a view that was attacked by many at the time. See L.S. Jacyna, 'Lawrence, Sir William, first baronet (1783–1867)', *ODNB*, <http://www.oxforddnb.com/view/article/16191>, accessed 19 January 2006.

[145] Richard Carlile, *The Philosophy of the Sexes: or, every woman's book; a treatise on love, etc.* (London, 1826), first published under the pseudonym of 'Dr. Waters'.

Saturday.   [April 15]

Mʳ P. Bingham Editor for Mʳ Marshall of Leeds the proprietor of the Parliamentary history and review,[146] he related some curious facts respecting the tricks which had been played by the booksellers with these volumes, I undertook to get Mʳ Rey to translate the long advertisement into elegant French.

Cutting from newspapers, matters relating – to the people, justices, &c &c

Mʳˢ Wood [?] with Mʳ Blake to consult on the best mode of proceeding to procure the property of her son who had died in Peru. He was in partnership with Price & Co. at Valparaiso & is supposed to have left property to the value of more than 20.000 £, heard her repeat her case and directed her to cause the particulars to be stated in legal form and sent to Mʳ Nugent [Place's insertion: the Brit consul] at Valparaiso, with a request that he would interfere, &c. [remainder of paragraph excised] ... Value.

Coln Bradley, in a sad state poor fellow he cannot get members to support him.

Mʳ Barry with some intelligence relating to Chile Mining gathered from one of the disappointed persons sent out in the Amiga by the Chilean and Peruvian Company.[147]

Sunday   April. 16. 1826

Read in West. Rev.
    United States.[148]
    Madame du Hausset.[149]
    Periodical Literature.[150]
Looked at the Volume of Parliamentary Abstracts sent to me by the projector. Mʳ Marshall. This is a valuable book but it has a defect

[146] The *Parliamentary History and Review* published three volumes between 1825 and 1827. Intended as a political voice for the philosophic radicals, James Marshall was its proprietor and Peregrine Bingham its editor. See William Thomas, 'James Mill's politics: the "Essay on government" and the movement for reform', *Historical Journal*, 12 (1969), pp. 249–284.

[147] The *Amiga* was a ship carrying Cornish miners to work in the Chilean mining enterprises that had recently been begun with British capital. Upon their arrival in Chile, their employers complained that the miners' skills were ill-suited to both the mining conditions and the mineral deposits there. See Claudio Veliz, 'Egaña, Lambert, and the Chilean Mining Associations of 1825', *Hispanic American Historical Review*, 55 (1975), pp. 649–650.

[148] John Neal, 'United States', *Westminster Review*, 5, no. 9 (1826), pp. 173–201.

[149] Henry Southern, 'The private memoirs of Madame du Hausset, lady's maid to Madame de Pompadour', *Westminster Review*, 5, no. 9 (1826), pp. 249–262.

[150] 'Periodical literature: *Parliament History and Review*, &c. for the session of 1825', *Westminster Review*, 5, no. 9 (1826), pp. 263–268.

which is not to be remedied. It contains Reports of committees of the house of commons, but not the minutes of evidence, and these reports are not generally drawn by the most intelligent or most impartial persons[,] e.g. the report of the Committee on Combination Laws is a striking example. Ministers – some of them had lent themselves most absurdly to a few practical men, and provided in a mean, passionate contemptible way to obtain the committee, as they did afterwards in the manner of conducting it. Beaten at all points as they were and afraid of being still worse defeated they heard as little of the evidence in favour of the workmen as they could and refused to hear many others on even the most important point altho these others had been shamefully calumniated, and then to save appearances made a report at variance with the facts, and falsly [sic] reasoned. Thus those who read the report and not the minutes of evidence cannot fail to be misled.

Still the book contains a large mass of useful information, no where else to be obtained but in the parliamentary papers themselves and these are accessible to a few only.

Westminster Review:

Benthams swear not at all[151]

Read to Mr Blake a portion of John Miers book on the Political circumstances of Chile and Peru, for the purpose of hearing his observations, he had come home with the intention of putting the materials he had collected into a book, but having read the volume worked off and heard me read some parts of the second volume he says he has wholly anticipated, and the Mr Miers is a remarkably clear and true account of the countries of which it treats.

Political History of Westminster. 1790–1791.

Was out to day with my wife and Caroline from 1 to 3. in the Regents Park.

Entries made in Political Common Place Book.

---

[151] Peregrine Bingham, 'Swear not at all', Westminster Review, 5, no. 9 (1826), pp. 23–58. A review of Jeremy Bentham's "Swear not at all": containing an exposure of the needlessness and mischievousness, as well as antichristianity, of the ceremony of an oath ... (London, 1817). Jeremy Bentham (1748–1832), the famous utilitarian philosopher and political radical, was a close friend of Place. While Place lived at Charing Cross Road, Bentham lived only a few minutes' walk away, and they regularly visited each other's homes. Initially, Bentham intended that Place should organize and posthumously publish his writings; however, that task eventually fell to John Bowring. Wallas's Life, pp. 79–85, provides a satisfactory account of their personal relationship.

Monday.   April 17.

Several letters to various persons[.]
Wrote a letter to John Miers at Buenos Ayres – containing – accounts – advice of machinery shipped per the John for him.
Also – to my daughter his wife.
Received proofs of his maps and plans from the Engraver, sent with sheets of his book to the Foreign Office, for Lord Ponsonby – our ambassador at Buenos Ayres.
McCulloch's lecture at 11—
Walked with my wife from 12 to 3.
Mr Barry and Mr Blake on South American Affairs.
Read a portion of Mr Miers book to Mr Blake for his observations.
Read proof sheet G. Vol. II.
Employed on Political history of Westminster.
Mr Wood [?], respecting his brothers affairs in Chile, repeated the advice I gave his mother on saturday.

Tuesday   Ap. 18.

Finished Political History of West[minster] so far as relates to the election of 1790 except the details of the proceedings at the election to be taken from newspapers when I can borrow them. NB. by finished I mean, a rough draft has been written.
Walked alone to Clapham and back from – 1 to 3 rather more than 8 miles. Fruit trees very glorious.
Wrote an essay on the utility to the working classes of Mechanics Institutions, urging them to become members – it occupied upwards of three hours.
Piddling among newspapers. 1795–1796. 1797. Westminster politics.
Mr Barry, with information from South America.
Mr Bingham with sundry information – has heard that the Attorney General is about to commence proceedings against Mr Bentham for his pamphlet "Indications of Lord Eldon.["]^{152}

---

[152] Jeremy Bentham, *Indications respecting Lord Eldon, including history of the pending judges' salary-raising measure* (London, 1825). The publishers of this work, Henry Leigh Hunt (1784–1859) and his brother John, were both active in the radical reform movement. Early in their careers, they published *The Examiner*, which at one point included the publication of a 'devastating portrait of the prince regent'. Prosecuted for libel, they were subsequently convicted and imprisoned between 1813 and 1815. Henry's own literary efforts also led to his introduction to and friendship with Mary and Percy Bysshe Shelley, Keats, and Byron, among others. After spending several years on the continent, Henry returned to England in 1825 and tried to resurrect his carreer in publishing. As Place's diary indicates below, he also revived his contacts with London's leading radicals, including Bentham, Hone,

Mr Pickering and Mr Worthington with a small brass bust of Mr Bentham. Lent them a ~~characteristic~~ sketch which is a powerful characteristic portrait to correct the bust by, it is intended to make plaister casts for sale.

Read Proof sheet H. Vol II

~~Packet containing sheets~~

Dr Thorpe, promised to send his note of yesterday to Sir Francis Burdett.

Wednesday   Ap. 19.

Mr Bingham —

McCulloch's Lecture at. 11.

Walked with Caroline ½ 12. To. 3.

Mr Brunel Junr. Promised to go to Rotherhithe to look at the progress he is making with the Tunnel, under the Thames.[153]

Letter from Mr Drew a machinist at Manchester respecting a petition to the House of commons for a repeal of the Laws which prohibit the exportation of Machinery – in reply advised him to proceed – and sent his letter to Mr Hume.

Mr Blake with translation of Mr Portales report to the Supreme Director of Chile respecting the proposal of Mr Irisarri to raise a loan in London for Chile. Wrote a comment on the transaction to be inserted in Mr Miers book on Chile.

Political history of West^r. ~~1805.6.~~ 1795–6.

Mr Carlile to shew me a paper he had composed in reply to Cobbett's attack on him in his register of last saturday.

Mr Robinson the painter.[154]

Mr Barry with information respecting Chile and La Plata mining, given him by Mr Ever [?] Who has just come home overland from Chile to Buenos Ayres —

and Place himself. See Nicholas Roe, 'Hunt, (James Henry) Leigh (1784–1859)', *ODNB*, <http://www.oxforddnb.com/view/article/14195>, accessed 21 March 2007.

[153] Sir Marc Isambard Brunel was engineer for the Thames Tunnel Company, which gained parliamentary and royal approval to construct the tunnel in 1824. Sir Marc's son, the famous Isambard Kingdom Brunel, was appointed resident engineer for the project in 1826, when the previous engineer apparently suffered a nervous breakdown. The first shaft was sunk at Rotherhithe between March and November 1825. See R. Angus Buchanan, *Brunel: the life and times of Isambard Kingdom Brunel* (London, 2002), pp. 22–26.

[154] Perhaps William Robinson, the Leeds portrait painter. See L.H. Cust, 'Robinson, William (1799–1838)', rev. L.R. Houliston, *ODNB*, <http://www.oxforddnb.com/view/article/23887>, accessed 13 March 2005.

Colonel Jones,[155] with four powers of attorney signed – H. Grey
Bennett at Rome 4 April 1826 – witnessed by two persons and attested
by Robert Smith the British Vice Consul at Rome Appointing [*sic*]
Thomas Dean his Atty for the sale of stock belonging to the Mutual
Improv Insurance Benefit Society – Powers sent by the Post to Thomas
Dean Barnsbury Park Islington.

Thursday   Apr. 20. 1826

Up early – composing an essay on the Corn Laws for the Trades
Newsp[r].[156]

D[r] Thorpe. With a note Sir Francis Burdett had written to him
declining to see him or to proceed with his case[.] This is too bad
yet not a bit worse than these members of parliament are constantly
doing. I told the old gentleman not to confide in Burdett or any other
member and not to be disappointed if nothing was done for him.
Sir Francis Burdett last session when the case of Judge Kenrick[157] was
before the house said in reply to M[r] Peel who had said it was a serious
matter to displace a Judge and should not be done but upon such
evidence of his unfitness as should make any other mode useless, Sir
F. B said he would apply the rule to another Judge who had been
dismissed and ruined without there existing any necessity he meant
Judge Thorpe and he then pledged himself to the House to bring the
case before it in the next session and yet notwithstanding this pledge
and notwithstanding he promised me to name a day to see M[r] Thorpe
he now refuses to proceed any further. The poor old gentleman was
greatly distressed – so I dictated a note which he wrote to Burdett
telling [?] him that his pledge to the house had cut him off from every
other member and that in justice he must see him.

Captain Romeo, this singular little man, great beyond imagination
in his opinion, and actually good for nothing – who was so it seemed
to me some years ago – from an examination of himself and his papers
a spy in Italy, came with a petition for money to remove himself[,] his
wife and three children to France. I do not think he has any claim on
me or on any body now, for money and I will give none to him.

Persons like D[r] Thorpe and M[r] Romeo who are wholly occupied
in their own pressing affairs have no mercy on the time of others, and
mine was sadly consumed by them.

---

[155] Colonel Leslie Grove Jones (1779–1839), who would later provide an important link
between Place and Lord Durham during the Reform Bill crisis. See Miles, *Place*, pp. 178–207.
[156] 'Corn Laws – bread tax: to the working people', *TN*, 23 April 1826.
[157] Judge Kenrick was accused of misappropriating money and then charging and con-
victing his accusers of perjury. See *Hansard*, new series, 12, 14 April 1825, cols 1336–1338.

At half past 11. set off to walk to Rotherhithe to see Mr Brunels Tunnal [*sic*]. Found Lord Darnley[,] Lady Darnley and three other women, there with Sir George Cunningham, they were joined by Lord Paget and another well dressed animal whose name I did not hear, who made a singular discovery. On the steam engine being named simply as the engine he observed, that "it must be very hard work for the engine.["] Got away not much liking my company ~~all of whom except Sir George appeared to be as foolish as I know Lord Darnley~~ is. Home at 3 – to dinner.

Mr Barry with a paper on South America.

Mr Hanney [?] to tea.

Mr Anderson editor of the Trades newspaper[158] – says he thinks a dirty trick has been played with the paper I sent on Mechanics Institutions, by some members of the committee who not liking it have destroyed it. NB. Paper sent to me by the post found in Blackfriars Row.[159]

Mr Lang Secretary to the Trades paper[160] respecting the condition of the Journeymen Hatters, the wages have been much reduced in the country and attempts are making here to reduce the wages in all the branches of hatting.

Composing essay on the Corn Laws.

Friday   April 21.

Read proofs Hist. Chile J. K. vol. II.

McCulloch's Lecture.

Mr Fenn came on behalf of some of the persons whose houses are to be pulled down in the Charing Cross improvement, that Sir Francis Burdett and Mr Hobhouse had not done their duty by them, the whole of them being tenants at will and they Sir F. B. & J. C. H. having assented to a clause in the Bill, to permit the commissioners to admit such claims only for compensation as they pleased. I shewed Mr Fenn that this was the proper mode of proceeding – told him I had explained this fully to Mr Hobhouse as the means of procuring

[158] John Anderson, editor of the *Trades' Newspaper*. Both Anderson and the paper's first editor, J. C. Robertson, were often at odds with Place, especially over the issues of the purpose of the London Mechanics' Institution and Place's well-known acceptance of Malthusian principles. John Gast, the London radical, was largely responsible for the management of the paper, which sought to mobilise artisanal opinion and promote their interests. See Prothero, *Artisans and Politics*, chapter 10 and E.P. Thompson, *Making of the English Working Class*, pp. 775–779.

[159] This sentence was inserted between lines.

[160] Jonathan Lang, union leader of the London hatters and early proponent of mechanics' institutions and newspapers. See Place Papers, BL Add. MS 27799, fo. 77.

compensation to lodgers as well as to housekeepers, as had been done when the Great and Little Sanctuaries in West^r were taken down, and that leaving the power in the hands of the commissioners to make compensation to <u>tenants at will</u> included every body who could have a claim.

Mr Fenn is a commissioner of the Court of Requests, and he related several abuses – one of which is, that upon a summons being issued, both parties should attend the court, but in many cases it seems neither attend, and then the court at the instance of the officer grants an execution against the person summoned altho' the case has not been heard and no proof given that any debt is due, the person against whom the execution is issued has no appeal and must either pay the money or go to prison. The officers keep whatever money they get by this practice which Mr Fenn says amounts to several hundreds of pounds now in their hands.

M^r McCulloch – much displeased at the thinness of his audience, as well in the City as in Westminster. Yet his lectures are excellent.

Mr Bingham.

Mr Hobhouse says Mr Arbuthnot agrees that my suggestions respecting further improvements are desirable but that it will be advisable to get the present bill through and make arrangements for extending the plan as the business goes on.

M^r Ed. Wakefield, absurdly pleased with his own marriage which the old fellow represents as a romantic love affair. Indignant at the conduct of his son Ed. G. for the abduction of Miss Turner which he truly says is equally infamous and absurd.[161]

Corrected a paper on Chile mining for Mr Barry.

Wrote to Mr Galloway urging him to get a petition to the house of Commons to repeal the law forbidding the exportation of machinery. The petition to be signed by the London Engineers.

Letter to Mr Hobhouse Charing X improvements, Court of Requests.

Read proof Chile Vol. 2. sheet L.

Collecting matters for history of the common people, and Political History of Westminster.

Walked this day from 1 to 3. with my wife and Caroline.

[161] In the notorious scandal of 1826, Edward Gibbon Wakefield abducted Ellen Turner, the daughter of a wealthy Cheshire manufacturer, and persuaded her that it was necessary for her to marry William Wakefield, Edward's brother. The plot was intended to secure Miss Turner's fortune for the brothers. They were caught at Calais and brought back to England for trial. There the brothers were tried, convicted, and each sentenced to three years in prison. See David J. Moss, 'Wakefield, Edward Gibbon (1796–1862)', *ODNB*, <http://www.oxforddnb.com/view/article/28415>, accessed 10 March 2005.

Note to Dr Thorpe. Burdett will be at home to him any morning he may name.

Saturday   [April] 22.

Rumaging [*sic*] among old newspapers for materials, for Political history of Westminster and history of the common people. It is quite remarkable how very little notice was taken of the people, in any way by the newspapers until within the last few years, in 1796 for example a year of dearth they are seldom mentioned, and never except as objects of charity, as animals to be fed to prevent them becoming furious. It is only within the last 10 or 12 years that they have become any part of the community deserving of any attention whatever.

Mr Adams respecting his son now probably on his way to England and respecting the Court of Requests of which he is a commissioner.

Captn. Romeo. M^r. Wright. D^r. Thorpe. M^r. Blake. M^r. Barry.

Walked from 4 to 6 with my wife.

Mr Combes the accountant respect Miers's estate.

Read proofs. Miers's Chile sheets M. and N.

Read Dr Forster's "Somatopsychonoologia. Shewing the proofs that, Body, Life and Mind considered as distinct essences cannot be deduced from Physiology."[162] It is like the Docter [*sic*] himself a strange performance. He appears to be Idealist and spiritualist, Materialist, and Catholic. It is however a good justification of Mr Laurance.

Read in Dupuis Origine de tous les cultes.[163]

Mrs Hodgskin requesting me to procure the editorship of the Mechanics Magazine for her husband.

Sunday   [April] 23.

Rumaging [*sic*] among newspapers same as yesterday. Read in Stephen's Life of Horne Tooke.[164] Looked at the several weekly publications viz. Republican Cobbetts Register – The Mirror, Literary Gazette, Every day Book – Mechanics Register and Trades Newspaper. NB this is always done, in the course of the week. generally [*sic*] on Saturdays and Sundays.

---

[162] Thomas Forster (pseud. Philostratus), *Somatopsychonoologia: showing that the proofs of body, life and mind, considered as distinct essences, cannot be deduced from physiology, but depend on a distinct sort of evidence. Being an examination of the controversy concerning life carried on by MM. Laurence, Abernethy, Rennell, and others* (London, 1823).

[163] Charles François Dupuis, *Origine de tous les cultes, ou religion universelle* (Paris, an III de la République (1795)).

[164] Alexander Stephens, *Memoirs of John Horne Tooke, interspersed with original documents* (London, 1813).

Looked at Dr Forsters pamphlet on the evil consequences of drinking spiritous liquors, which he sent to me with his other book yesterday.[165]

Collating Titles and contents of Chapters, arranging plates and maps for the printer, Vol. I. Miers's Chile.

Cobbett offended at a paper I wrote respecting his ignorance of the principles of trade threatens to attack me. He does not see that in wasting his time on Carlile he is damaging himself in respect to his contemplated return to parliament. But this is of little consequence since he can only sit for a purchased Borough. No place where any shew of election exists will return him, and even if he had a chance any body might destroy it by a single appeal, exposing his recommendation to sow [?] Bank Notes while 100 great fires were blazing in London.

Walked from half past 4. with my wife, Frank – and Jenny round the Regents Park.

Mrs Mill before going into the country.

Wrote to Mr Smith of ~~Bolton~~ Manchester.

—— to Mr Hobhouse on Court of requests, and repeal of Laws which prohibit the exportation of Machinery.

Monday   [April] 24.

Rummaging among newspapers same as yesterday.

McCulloch's lecture. This and the pr[e]ceeding lecture on Economy and Banking are very clever and should be printed separately.

Mr Marshall of Leeds for a gossip conversation, on political economy, and politics, also respecting his book the Parliamentary Review and Debates, as to the probability of those who hold Hansards Debates joining him, promised to talk with Mr Wright the editor on the subject.

Walked. $\frac{1}{2}$ 1 to 3 – my wife, Jane and Caroline. Hyde Park.

Mr Wright, in consequence of Cobbett having been announced in some of the papers as likely to become a candidate for Westminster, shewed him that Cobbett stood no chance, ~~and~~ but that if he did, nothing would be more easy than to destroy that chance by a single hand bill, which I assured him I would write if it became necessary.

Mrs Harwood, to consult me respecting the property of her late husband Col^n Harwood, agreed to go with her to some Barrister a friend of hers whenever he should name a time.

Mr Geo White. with some curious anecdotes respecting house of commons matters. All the clerks have been ordered to conclude the matters in their hands by the 5 may.

[165] Thomas Forster, *Physiological Reflections on the Destructive Operation of Spirituous and Fermented Liquors on the Animal System* (London, 1812).

Mr Anderson.

Mr Barry.

Captn Romeo, for money, gave him none, he has no fair claim on me or any body.

Read. Dupuis. Origine &c.

Edinburgh Review. N° 86.

1. Banking Systems of England. By McCulloch[166]

2. Watertons wanderings.[167]

Looked at the other articles.

Tuesday.   [April] 25.

Rummaging – newspapers.

Pasting into guard books.

Dr Gilchrist[168] – respecting the Mechanics Institution. The Committee last night appointed a deputation to me and Brougham – object to raise money to discharge debt.

Talked of Cobbett and his absurd intention of standing for Westminster[.] [T]he D^r says he has seen him on the subject, and that he is obstinate. He is acting in direct opposition to the advice of his friends. This might have been expected. A man so conceited, so utterly worthless, and reckless, a man so very ignorant of almost every thing worth knowing, and who has all his life long conducted himself with a total disregard of the feelings, and without any desire to do justice to any one must necessarily misconduct himself. He will ultimate blackguard every one who is now assisting him.

Dr Thorpe. Mr Aimé.

Met Mrs Harwood at Mr Tyndale's chambers, went into the particulars of her claim to dower, which Mr Tyndale says Mr Brown the Attorney witholds [sic] improperly – Learnt the law of the case, and agreed to see Mrs Harwood at Mr Browns tomorrow morning at 10.

Mr Blake. Mrs Chatterley – respecting papers in the hands of Mr Nettlefield [?] the attorney promised to get them from him, if possible.

Mr Hobhouse. Apprehensive that if Cobbett stands for Westminster, it may provoke a ministerial candidate to stand also. This is probable.

[166] 'Thoughts on banking', *Edinburgh Review*, 43, no. 86 (February 1826), pp. 263–298.

[167] Sydney Smith's review of Charles Waterton, *Wanderings in South America, the North-West of the United States, and the Antilles, in the Years 1812, 1816, 1820, and 1824* (London, 1825), *Edinburgh Review*, 43, no. 86 (February 1826), pp. 299–315.

[168] A likely reference to John Borthwick Gilchrist, a philologist of South Asian languages, who helped found the London Mechanics' Institution. See Katherine Prior, 'Gilchrist, John Borthwick (1759–1841)', *ODNB*, <http://www.oxforddnb.com/view/article/10716>, accessed 29 March 2005.

Mr Toplis[169] from the Mechanics Institution to concert means of obtaining money to pay debts, promised to write to Mr Brougham on the subject in hope that I shall be able to induce him to persuade Lord Grosvenor to subscribe a thousand pounds which he all but promised me last year he would do.

Mr Carlile – respecting Cobbett.

Writing – memoirs respecting the working people in London.

Wednesday.   [April] 26.

With Mrs Harwood at Mr Brown's the attorney in Welbeck S^t. Mr Brown explained the whole matter very clearly. Mrs Harwood has a life interest in a sum of money from the sale of an estate of her late husband[.] Mr Brown administered to his will as a creditor, he received the money, and bought 3 per cents. with it to the amount of £1100 – he pays Mrs Harwood the interest.

M^r McCulloch's Lecture.

Rummaging Newspapers.

Mr Hobhouse – to complain of Dr Thorpe, whose pertinacity has offended him.

Mr Barry.

Walked with wife. 1 to 3.

Dr Maclean with sheets B. to Q of "An Exposition of the state of the Medical Profession" – which at his earnest request I promised to read, and to make such remarks on as occurred to me as useful.

Letter Mr Ashby at Erith, respecting his mill &c and desiring to borrow 350£. Answered. No.

Mr Evans respecting Mr Hone's affairs. Hone owes £6000. and has nothing to offer worth any mans acceptance, nothing can be done for him. Mr Evans is to tell him so, but he is to tell him also that if he thinks it likely, that his creditors will accede to his proposal I will for his satisfaction make it to some of the most important by way of ascertaining what can be done.

Read proofs. Chile. Sheets. O and P. Wrote to Mr Baldwin to accelerate the printing.

Made up the appendixes and the preface ~~and~~ for the printer.

Two applications for employment at the expected election for Westminster.

Told Mr Hobhouse what indeed I had told him three years ago that I would on no account whatsoever go out of the house to assist in the election but that I would do any thing I could at home, and would see

---

[169] Toplis was a member of the organizing committee of the London Mechanics' Institution.

him, and half a dozen others at any time, but that I would not be seen
by any body and every body who might chance to call upon me.

Conversation on the same subject with Mr Bickersteth.[170]

Thursday.   [April] 27.

Mrs Chatterley respecting some papers in the hands of M^r
Nettlefield the attorney. Promised to procure them for her. Wrote
to Mr Nettlefield.

Rummaging Newspapers.

John Mill,[171] sundry, matters.

Thomas Wilkinson, Journeyman Silver Plater and secretary to the
trade at Birmingham deputed to London, in consequence of the
masters having struck against the men. A remarkably genteel sensible
young man. Gave him letters to introduce him to the trades in London.
See the Address of the Silver platers in Guard Book.

Ed Review. Timber trade an article containing much ~~good~~
information well reasoned, by McCulloch.[172]

Proofs – sheets. Chile. Q. and R.

Wrote a paper for insertion in the Trades Newspaper, recommending "An Essay on the circumstances which determine the rate of wages
and the condition of the labouring classes, by J. R. McCulloch Esqr."[173]

Colonel Bradley with a printed copy of his petition which Mr Hume
is to present to the house of commons on monday next, requesting
me to inclose one in a letter to Sir Francis Burdett. Did so.

At home all day.

Friday.   [April] 28.

Thomas Wilkinson from Birmingham gave him instructions how
to proceed.

Benj^m Lomax from the Shipwrights.[174]

McCulloch's lecture.

Walked from 1 to 3 with my wife.

[170] Henry Bickersteth, radical barrister and original member of the Rota Club, a dining
club formed in 1818, whose reform-minded members included John Cam Hobhouse, Sir
Francis Burdett, and Lord Byron.

[171] John Stuart Mill (1806–1873). As this diary reveals, Place was in frequent contact with
the Mills and often met with John Stuart separately from his father.

[172] 'Considerations on the timber trade', *Edinburgh Review*, 43, no. 86 (February 1826),
pp. 341–356, arguing for the benefits of reduction or elimination of all timber duties.

[173] McCulloch's essay was published in 1826. Place's article, 'Wages: to the working people
and their employers', appeared in the 14 May 1826 issue of the *Trades' Newspaper*.

[174] Benjamin Lomax was one of the leaders of the Thames Shipwrights' Provident Union
along with John Gast. The Union was established in 1824. See Prothero, *Artisans and Politics*,
p. 165.

Letters and papers respecting the breaking of steam looms at Blackburn.[175]

M[r] Barry with a letter from Arequipa in Peru describing the country, and its diseases, both, miserable.

Political Hist[y] of West[r].

Saturday   [April 29].

Rummaging among Newspapers.

M[r] Hubbard the inventor of the walking cane gun[,] pocket blunderbuss and folding chair, all curious inventions. His lock being by far the most simple, recommend him to apply it to all the percussion guns and grant licenses under his patent to others to use it. Wished for sometime past to see him to tell him this. His lock cannot be cocked by pulling the gun through a hedge, or by striking it against a stile nor in any way, unless intended and done by the fingers.

Bradford Secretary to the Seamen of the port of London for advice, the South Shields Seamen have misbehaved &c &c

Walked with my wife and Jane, $\frac{1}{2}$ 12 to 3.

D[r] Thorpe has had a satisfactory meeting at Burdetts pleased with this on the old mans account, but it will terminate in nothing useful to him, except consolation.

Political history of Westminster.

Sunday   [April] 30.

Arranging papers and pamphlets.

Looked – at Cobbett, the Republican, The Mirror, Every day Book, Lit Gazette.

Read – The Metimpsycosis – the Smugglers – Weddings – &c in Blackwoods Magazine.[176]

Deputation of two sensible men from the Coopers, to state the depressed situation of their trade and to ask advice. They gave me a history of the present and former conduct and manners of the men in their trade – promised to put down the information on paper.

D[r] Maclean with the remainder of the sheets of his book An Exposition of the state of the Medical Profession &c —

Parl. Hist[y]. West[r]. Newspapers.

---

[175] The 1826 depression sparked the widespread destruction of power looms by the Blackburn handloom weavers. The machine-breaking quickly spread to other parts of East Lancashire and eventually to Manchester. See Kirby and Musson, *The Voice of the People*, pp. 41–42.

[176] Articles appearing in *Blackwood's Magazine*, 19 (May 1826).

Monday.   1. [May]

My good old friend Mʳ George Ensor[177] just arrived from Ireland, full of all sorts of information.

MᶜCulloch's lecture 11 to 12.

Walked with Mʳ Ensor – ½ 12 to 2.

D° – my Wife – 4 to 6.

Corrected Proofs Chile sheets S. and T.

John Beveridge seaman from N Shields to request me to endeavour to procure him employment under Government at Plymouth. Promised to make a case for him. He is a good honest man and sometime secretary to the Seamens Association.

Letter from Bolton respecting the rioting and steam loom breaking in Lancashire. Bolton Chronicle giving an account of the proceedings of the Rioters, and both letter and paper saying that the people have been set on by the Government spies.

In the evening Mʳ Geo White from the House of Commons, in a state of high exultation. Canning had proposed to the house to let out the foreign bonded wheat on a duty of 12/ the quarter and to permit the importation during the recess of corn at the same rate of duty. An act to be brought in and to be passed through all its stages tomorrow.[178]

This is a masterly stoke. The whole matter has probably been got up by ministers. A disposition to break the steam Looms has existed for some time and of this disposition ministers were well informed, yet no precautions were taken, and no troops were kept near enough to the places where the steam looms were in work to prevent their being broken while the spies of Government were urging the people to break the looms. It was not seen [?] in what way the corn laws could be got rid of, it was my opinion as well as that of my friends that the power of the Landowners in the two houses would be too great for us to hope that we should be able to procure a repeal of the Corn Laws, and here it is done by Ministers by a coup de main. The whole country is alarmed at the state of the manufacturing population, and willing to do almost any thing to appease the starving people, a meeting is to be held in the City tomorrow, troops are sending [sic] off by canal boats with orders to proceed by day and by night, every body

---

[177] George Ensor (1769–1843) was an Irish-born radical and long-time acquaintance of Place. Ensor's numerous publications included books attacking established religion, on parliamentary reform, workers' education, and legal reform, all issues close to Place's heart. See Hone, *For the Cause of Truth*, pp. 223, 250, 288; Francis Watt, 'Ensor, George (1769–1843)', rev. Marie-Louise Legg, *ODNB*, <http://www.oxforddnb.com/view/article/8822>, accessed 10 January 2006.

[178] *Hansard*, new series, 15, 1 May 1826, cols 764–774; 2 May 1826, cols 784–831; 5 May 1826, cols 914–956; 8 May, cols 971–1007.

is in a state of doubt and anxiety, when down came the ministers and proposed to repeal the Corn Laws. The proposal must be entertained, the aristocracy are struck dumb, and are powerless – perhaps the most important step ever taken by the government has been taken. It will be the peoples [*sic*] own fault if the act which is to be for a year, be not made perpetual, and free trade in all its branches will assuredly follow.[179]

This will be a memorable session.

Mr Wright with particulars respecting Cobbett.

I omitted to observe that at the commencement of the session Ministers proposed to the leading advocates for the Corn Monopoly to accede to a repeal of the Corn Laws on a duty of 15/ the quarter on wheat, and on other grain in proportion. This was rejected, and now they must put up with the sum which Mr Jacob has in his report recommended.

Tuesday.   2. [May]

Looking back at the contents of this diary it seems that my time is idled away, and yet most certainly it is not so. I am satisfied that I am doing something useful, almost every day. It seems also that my time is not occupied, for how it may fairly be asked can the whole time have been consumed in such matters as have been noticed. To this I reply that I am intensely and continually occupied and cannot find time to go on with those things I desire to go on with, namely my own memoirs, and the projected history of the United States of North America; neither can I see how I shall ever obtain time unless I quit London, and consequently remove myself from all chance of being useful in the way I am at present useful.

It is now 12. o clock at noon and nothing seems to have been done. At 8, I began to read the Chronicle containing a lame account of the highly important debate of last night in both houses of parliament. Then I looked at the Herald, then at the parliamentary papers delivered this morning. Then I wrote a letter to Mr Smith of the Bolton Chronicle on the state of the workmen, their mistakes in respect to machinery and the relative bearings of machinery[,] population and wages, for insertion in the Bolton Chronicle [. . .] the [. . .][180] the stock exchange as a Stock Broker he remained an hour giving me an account of transactions among our Merchants and dealers in the City, as of atrocious a character that persons not conversant with these people would think could be deserving of the least credit, and yet I have no doubt they are all true . . . did not relate these as matters are

---

[179] 'It was the peoples fault', added later, over this entry, in Place's hand.
[180] Sections excised in original.

usually related which are mere calumnies but as things in which he "unfortunately" had had no shame; clever things done by people who when compared with himself were silly people, and this produced no feelings beyond envy of their good fortune and regret that he so much more of a clever fellow than they should not have participated in. "Damned clever things, as you as well as I know, and all fair, for a man in dealing must get money."

Before [...] was gone in came [...] the Attorney to whom I had recommended [...] to raise some money for him on leasehold property in his profession, and while I was getting rid of them in came Mr Ensor, who was followed by Dr Thorpe whose absence was waited for by Mr Charles Blake, who came in with a pamphlet printed in Chile, from which I am to have an extract for Mr Miers book on Chile. It is now, a quarter to 2. and my wife has been waiting to walk with me for an hour but as yet I have had no time to shave myself.

This is pretty much the way in which a large portion of my mornings are consumed. But inasmuch as I thus obtain information of almost everything worth knowing of public matters, as well complying with the wishes of those whom I can really be useful to I do not discourage people from coming to me. I however admit but few people after 3 o'clock, yet my time is occasionally consumed by intruders in the evening and this, I frequently regret without being able to prevent it, but by shutting information [...] to obtain.

Thus it [...] how fully my time is occupied and that it is all but impossible that any day can be long enough for me.

Captain Romeo with his pitiful case. I have distributed his letters which is all I can do for him.

It is now half past 2. and I am as usual to dine at 3.

Abstracts of the Annual Expenditures copies to the Morning Herald and Trades Newspapers.

Paper on Chilean mining and loaming to the Herald.

Walked [...] my [...] and Caroline.

Read Proof sheet V. vol. 2 Miers's Chile.

Mrs Harwood respecting her affairs promised to go to Mr Gilbee in Sloane S^t on Thursday morning.

Not being able to induce William Tijou to produce the accounts between himself and his father, wrote to Mr Tijou, informing him of that fact.

Mr Barry respecting Chilean mining.

Looked through Sir Fernando Gorges, America painted to the life[181] till half past 11. p.m. and then went to bed.

---

[181] Ferdinando Gorges (1629–1718), *America Painted to the Life: the true history of the Spaniards proceedings in the conquests of the Indians, and of their civil wars among themselves, from Columbus his first discovery to these later times*... (London, 1658–1659).

Wednesday.   3 [May].

Arranging papers respecting the state of the people in the Cotton Manufacturing Districts.

McCullochs Lectures.

Mr Geo. Ensor. Went with him to Meyer the engraver, saw his portraits &c &c –.

Sticking papers on Poor and population into guard book.

Dr Thorpe with 17 Testimonies of respect from inhabitants of Canada and Sierra Leone, Grand Juries &c —

Mr Thomas Hodgskin and his Wife.

Sir Richard Phillips and his son. Sir R told a curious tale of his troubles and solicited advice which he is sure not to follow.

Mr Fearon[182] from Alderman Waithman[183] to procure my assistance towards returning him for the City of London.

Looked over Thelwalls Panoramic Miscellany for April.[184]

Reading the debate in the house of commons last night and taking down heads for an essay for the Trades Newspaper.[185]

Mr Carlile with a long letter to him on his every woman book,[186] and an essay on the present riots in Lancashire for my opinion on the latter. [C]ame in at nine p.m. and staid till ten, gave me a copy of his newly printed book. Good Sense – corrected [?] a book for his use.

Write to Mr Anderson Editor of the [. . . .]

---

[182] Henry Bradshaw Fearon, a London wine and spirits merchant, or perhaps a brewer, who had been active as a deacon in the Freethinking Christians church and in radical City politics generally. See Hone, *For the Cause of Truth*, pp. 224, 302; McCalman, *Radical Underworld*, p. 73.

[183] Robert Waithman (1764–1833), a prominent City politician, who served several terms as its MP, was elected an alderman (hence Alderman Waithman) in 1818, was sheriff of London and Middlesex, 1820–1821, and Lord Mayor, 1823–1824. His radicalism was deemed too moderate by some who decried his support of rate-payer rather than universal suffrage, and triennial rather than annual parliaments. Nevertheless, he was an important figure in the parliamentary reform movement, in defense of freedom of the press, and the anti-corn law movement. See J.R. Dinwiddy, '"The patriotic linen-draper": Robert Waithman and the revival of radicalism in the City of London', *Bulletin of the Institute of Historical Research*, 46 (1973), pp. 72–94; Michael T. Davis, 'Waithman, Robert (1764–1833)', *ODNB*, <http://www.oxforddnb.com/view/article/28406>, accessed 10 March 2005.

[184] *The Panoramic Miscellany: or, monthly magazine and review of literature, science, arts, inventions and occurrences* (London, 1826). It appears that only one volume of this magazine was ever issued. The renaissance of interest in Thelwall, whose activities in the early 1790s made him 'the most prominent and articulate member of the reform movement', according to the *ODNB*, has sparked several important contributions, especially, E.P. Thompson, 'Hunting the Jacobin fox', *Past & Present*, 142 (1994), pp. 94–140 and Gregory Claeys (ed.), *The Politics of English Jacobinism: writings of John Thelwall* (University Park, PA, 1995). My thanks to Greg Claeys for identifying this publication.

[185] The debates concerned the Corn Laws: *Hansard*, new series, 15, 2 May 1826, cols 784–831. Place's article appeared as 'Breaking of machinery and breaking of the Corn Laws', *TN*, 7 May 1826.

[186] Richard Carlile, *The Philosophy of the Sexes* (see p. 59, note 145).

Thursday   4 [May].

Looked at a pamphlet 'Eunomia" [*sic*] at Mr Thelwalls request, for
his Magazine, but the work is too puerile and ridiculous for me to
write a line on it.[187]

Went to Hans Place Sloane Street to a Mr Gilbee, who informed
me that Col^n Harwood had the third of an estate in Granada which
was however mortgaged. That the Estate was sold for 16.300 £ and
that unless Mrs Harwood did something to set aside her dower, she
was intitled to one third of the sum the estate was sold for. Promised
Mr Gilbee that I would see Mr Brown and request him to explain to
me how the one third had been disposed of.

Went to Smithfield and Queen Hithe [*sic*], to see Mr Hones
principal creditors in the hope of making some arrangement in his
affairs – none likely, wrote the particulars to Mr Henry L. Hunt.

Mr Henry Drummond with a proof of his new edition ~~letter
to Home [*sic*] Summer~~[188] Essay on the currency,[189] Mc Culloch had
been objecting to some of his statements, Mc Culloch is wrong and
Drummond is right.

Read proof sheet X. Chile.

D^o ———— —— Y. – D^o.

Writing an essay for the Trades newspaper till half past 12. p. m.

Friday.   5 [May].

Continuation of the essay. S. iii

Mc Culloch's Lecture

Went with Mr Ensor to my old friend Galloway's factory to shew it
to Mr Ensor.

Completion of the essay.

Mr Tijou and his son, with their partnership accounts, which is
nearly at an end, and they are about to separate. Mr Tijou acts
generously, his son meanly, went through the accounts, and suggested
the mode of settling the whole affair[.] Mr Tijou quite willing to

[187] *Eunomia. With brief hints to country gentlemen and others of tender capacity: on the principles of
the new sect of political economical philosophers termed Eunomians: which principles are applied to the
grand question, "'What is money, its office and effects in society?" The question again "Set at rest forever."
With some strictures upon banks and the banking system, in answer to the Right Hon. Sir John Sinclair,
Bart., Malachi Malagrowther, Sir Robert Peel, Bart., and all the rest of the philosophers, advocating "cheap
currency", which "gives your districts the impetus". Under Sir John Sinclair's grand plan, hereunto appended.*
(London, 1826).

[188] Henry Drummond, *Cheap Corn Best for Farmers Proved in a Letter to George Holme Sumner,
Esq., M.P., . . . by one of his constituents* (London, 1825).

[189] Both a third and a fourth edition appeared in 1826 under the title, *Elementary Propositions
on the Currency* (London). The first edition appeared as *Elementary Propositions Illustrative of the
Principles of Currency* (London, 1819).

consent thereto. Wm Tijou not so willing – they are to come again on monday afternoon.

Read proof – sections i & ii of the article for the Trades newspaper.
Read sheet Z. Chile —
Made copies, abstract of the accounts for Mr Tijou and his son.
Looked through a sale and a booksellers catalogue.
Read proof at 11. p. m. of the article for the Trades newspaper.

Saturday.   6 [May]

Letter to Mr Hume on his speech last night, in which he did what I told him he would be sure to do, regret him being persuaded not to propose a bill to repeal so much of the act 6 G. IV. c. 107 as related to tools and utensils.[190] Urged him to bring in a bill, and sent him a sketch of the bill.

Mr Wilkinson from Birmingham gave him instructions respecting apprentices and some other points respecting the journeymen platers of Birmingham.

Mr Hansard and the printer one of Hones' creditors on Hones affairs, which he thinks are hopeless. A long conversation on books and booksellers by which I obtained some curious information.

Mr Ensor with a number of anecdotes.

Captn Sheriff R.N.[,] Lord Cochranes[191] friend, to tell me of various matters respecting Lord Cochrane and also respecting Greece, State of the steam vessels, their enormous ordnance Long [?] 68 pounders to throw red hot shot. Some suspicion that Galloway had and still continued to delay the construction of the steam engines in consequence of the injury it might do to his interests in Egypt where his son now is, assured Captain S that from my long and intimate acquaintance with Galloway I would undertake to say that no possible amount of money nor any other consideration would induce him to delay the completion of the engines, a single hour.

---

[190] Hume had presented two petitions to the House, one from the machine-makers of Manchester and the other from their workmen, requesting the repeal of the laws prohibiting the exportation of machinery. See *Hansard*, new series, 15, 5 May 1826, cols 908–914.

[191] Thomas Cochrane (1775–1860), naval hero and 'enlightened mercenary'. After establishing his reputation for cunning and success in the Revolutionary and Napoleonic Wars, he went on to sell his services to several national independence movements, including those of Chile, Peru, Brazil, and, in this case, Greece. Cochrane's participation in the Greek War of Independence was premised upon his command of specially built British and American war steamers. See Andrew Lambert, 'Cochrane, Thomas, tenth earl of Dundonald (1775–1860)', *ODNB*, <http://www.oxforddnb.com/view/article/5757>, accessed 10 March 2005.

Much conversation on the compensation [?] effects of high pressure and condensing engines for the naval service, and the advantages to be expected from Brunels gas engine should it be found to answer.

Looked at Cobbetts Register and the Republican.

Looking back to tuesday April 11. I see myself disencumbered of the concerns of others and prepared to go on with my own memoirs, yet it will be seen that I have not as yet touched them since that time.

Mr Aimé with N. American maps and some books.

Mr Thomas Tooke, a long conversation respecting the measures proposed by Mr Canning as to bonded corn &c – Mr Tooke had collected the opinions of many City people on the subject and these upon the whole were favourable to Mr Cannings project.

Mr Barry. Hullotts have compromised their actions against the Morning Chronicle.

M^r ~~John~~ Henry L Hunt on Hones affairs he is a young man not sufficiently accustomed to the ways of the world to understand why Hones creditors should refuse to accept his proposition.

Proof. Sheet. 2A. Chile

Looked at the Mirror[,] the Literary Gazette, and two catalogues of Book sales.

At home all day.

Sunday.   7 [May].

Assisted Mr Hunt to make some extracts from Cobbetts Register.

Corrected a sheet for Richard Carlile.

Wrote the title page and an exordium to form an advertisement for John Miers's book on Chile &c.

Sticking cuttings from newspaper respecting the working people, the riots in the manufacturing districts, &c into guard books.

Read a portion of McCullochs book on political economy.[192]

Walked with my wife from half past 4 to 7.

Annoyed by Mrs Harwood, on her affairs, most uselessly for a full hour.

Translating with Mr Blake some matters relating to the finances of Chile, from a report of certain commissioners, for appendix C. of John Miers's book.

Instructing Blake in the process of copper refining, and gave him some M. S. S. on the subject, as he expects employment in the Copper works in Persia.

---

[192] Perhaps J.R. McCulloch, *A Discourse on the Rise, Progress, Peculiar Objects, and Importance, of Political Economy*... (1st edition, Edinburgh, 1824; 2nd corrected and enlarged edition, London, 1825).

Monday.   8 [May].

Mᶜ Culloch's Lecture.

Note from Galloway wished to see me on something of great
moment to him. Went to him when it turned out that he had heard the
surmises respecting his keeping the machinery in hand lest it might
affect his interest with the Pacha of Egypt. He was exceedingly hurt
and called upon me to justify him to the members of the Greek,
war committee. I told him what had passed with Captⁿ Sheriff, and
promised to see Mʳ Hobhouse the chairman of the Greek committee
on the subject.[193] Read several letters which had passed between the
committee and Galloway. The committee have not made sufficient
allowance for the magnitude of orders they to [sic] have given, and
Galloway did wrong in undertaking to complete such an order in so
short a time. Went over the factory and saw the number of men more
than 100 at work on the machinery – the work is ponderous, and
particularly well executed as to workmanship, and being fully satisfied
that he has done all that he could do and more by far than any other
engineer either would or could have done, I have undertaken to say
so to several members of the Greek war committee.

Saw Mʳ Tindall on Mʳˢ Harwoods affair this counsellor who seemed
to very positive a week ago did not I now found understand the matter
and I agreed to see Mʳ Gilbee and get certain particulars to enable
him to understand it.

Mʳˢ Chatterley on her affairs, told her what she was to do.

Mʳˢ Harwood on hers —

Walked from half past 4 to 6 with my wife

Mʳ Tijou on his affairs, I had seen his son who at length admitted
that his father had acted liberally towards him, he consented to the
proposal I had made, as did also Mʳ Tijou. Promised to put the matter
into form [?], for Mʳ Tijous attorney to draw the necessary papers.

Captⁿ Romeo with his begging letters, gave him several names.

It is now 8. p. m. and my day so far has been almost wholly consumed
in the affairs of others.

Gossip with Sir R. Fergusson [sic] M. P.[194] and another gentleman a
stranger respecting, Cobbetts threat to stand for Westminster.

Read paper left by Richard Doane, case of Mʳ Buckingham.[195]

---

[193] The Greek Committee was composed of radicals and free traders sympathetic to the
War of Independence. Formed in 1823, its leading members included Sir Francis Burdett,
John Cam Hobhouse, Joseph Hume, John Bowring, and Jeremy Bentham.

[194] Sir Ronald Craufurd Ferguson, MP, Dysart burghs 1806–1830; Nottingham borough
1830–1841.

[195] Mr Buckingham, editor of the *Calcutta Journal*, was banished from India for publishing
anti-government remarks. See *Hansard*, new series, 18, 9 May 1826, cols 1004–1014.

Tuesday.   9 [May].

Sticking cuttings from newspapers respecting the state of the trade and the riots in Lancashire &c.

Went with Mr Ensor to see the Tunnell [*sic*], from eleven to two.

A long gossip with Messrs. Ensor Torrens, and McCulloch respecting the conduct of ministers respecting Corn and currency, and also respecting a dispute at the Political Economy Club on Monday last, on value.

Mrs Chatterley on her affairs

M^r McCarthy on his Biangular Stone pavement, has an order to lay down a sample opposite Coutt's Banking House in the Strand but wants money to pay wages gave him a note to Mr Evans as the most likely person to procure him the money.

Mr Tijou and his son, after a long debate, settled the matter, and Mr Tijou set off to his attorney to have the papers drawn up.

Mr Russell from Sydenham with the three maps for John Miers's book went over them.

Proof sheet. 2. B. corrected.

Mr Thelwall begging of me to write him an article on currency for his Magazine, promised to do so.

Mr Parkes of Birmingham[196] and Mr Carlile of Fleet S^t the first with various information, the second with a printed sheet for me to correct, did correct it.

Mr George White to tell me of a conversation he had had with Mr Charles Grant M. P.[197] respecting the article in the Trades paper yesterday.

Apropos of this paper it seems that an additional number was printed in the expectation of an increased sale, but that not one remained on sunday afternoon, that many persons wanted it who could not get it and that the demand was considerable on monday morning. None were however re-printed instead of which notice should have been given by posting bills that on account of the demand a second edition would have been ready for delivery this morning. But a committee will never manage any thing of this sort as it should be managed.

---

[196] Joseph Parkes gained prominence as a successful Whig election agent, active dissenter, and reformer. See Philip J. Salmon, 'Parkes, Joseph (1796–1865)', *ODNB*, <http://www.oxforddnb.com/view/article/21356>, accessed 19 January 2006.

[197] Charles Grant (1778–1866), first Baron Glenelg, MP for Inverness burghs (1811–1814; 1814–1818) and Inverness-shire (1818–1835).

Wednesday.   10 [May]

Wrote a letter to Mr H. Drummond in answer to his question "Why do you not call a public meeting in Westminster on the Corn Laws?"

Read or rather looked at the Chronicle the Herald, and the parliamentary papers delivered this morning.

At 10. Mr Wright and Mr Carlile with a proof sheet of Life of Wm Cobbett for my advice, detained me till nearly 11. And having to shave &c. was too late to attend McCulloch's Lecture.

In comes that very worthy old man Thomas Hardy, with two M. S. Respecting Corresponding Society and United Irishmen. curious information.

Called away to Mr Wm Lee the High Constable of Westminster to hear his case respecting a claim on Parliament for remuneration, and to request my interference in his behalf. Think he has a just claim and will do what I can. Authorized him to use my name to Mr Hume and if necessary, he is to request Mr Hume to call upon me.

His departure was waited for by Dr Maclean who had seen Mr J.C. Hobhouse and had past by [?] made an appointment for me to see him on the subject of his book.

Detained by Mr Cruden[198] late Mayor of Gravesend with an account of the removal of the Custom House from that place, and the proceedings thereon. My opinion is that the 400 watermen who are said to be put out of employment by the removal of the Custom House, are 400 smugglers whose avocation has been spoiled.

Went to Mr Hobhouse. a long conversation on Greek affairs, and Lord Cochrane who has sailed from Flushing in a small unarmed vessel for Greece. Found Hobhouse exceedingly displeased with Galloway, and disposed to believe that he had purposely delayed the machinery, on account of his business with the Pacha of Egypt. Cochrane had written to the committee, insisting upon it that Galloway had sold himself to the Pacha. Satisfied him I believe that Galloway was incapable of such conduct, and endeavoured to convince him of what I have no doubt is the fact that, no Engineer would have done more than he has done. The folly was two-fold – 1– in giving so large an order to any one man, 2. in Galloway undertaking to do what neither he nor any other engineer could have accomplished. Maudslay refused to take it because he was overpowered [?] with business and this was in fact the case with all the London Engineers. Much conversation on other subjects.

Went to Hans Place to Mr Gilbee who was not at home —

[198] Likely a reference to Robert Pierce Cruden, mayor of Gravesend in 1817 and 1818. He would later be re-elected in 1831. My thanks to Deborah Saunders of the Centre for Kentish Studies for this information.

Mr Thelwall with a plan for the improvement of Ireland, desirous to interest me therein. Like all such projects it is delusive and the paper which I have read is in some particulars, greatly exaggerated.

Bell rings for dinner

Dinner hardly over when Mr Blake came with a draft of an agreement respecting mining in Persia. It was a project set up by the [resident?] from Persia and a young man a sculptor for a joint stock company to search for and to work mines in Persia. An absurd if not a fraudulent scheme. Told Blake to have nothing to do with the project of a company but, if there was any intention to mine and they were willing to send him and another or two out to enquire and report, and would give him the security of some respectable persons here for payment of salary &c – I saw no reason why he might not undertake the enquiry and report faithfully.

Blake was turned out by Mr Hume who had various things to consult upon – Greek Committee – Exportation of Machinery Corn Laws. His resolution of the 4th May which we went through seriatim. He has shewn some very material defects in the money concerns of the Treasury and Exchequer. Talked over the matter of Mr Lee the High Constable, he will do whatever as an honest man he might do. Mr Peel has promised to procure for me the information I require as to the number of houses at different periods in the Metropolis from the parish books.

Went away soon after 6. Tea and then came Mr Rintoul,[199] who has become the editor of the Atlas Weekly paper, a paper twice the size of any now printed as a weekly paper, went over all the matters connected therewith. Rintoul is probably the best man that could have been found to conduct the new paper. Prospectus – inserted.

This occupied me till half past 8. p. m. And so go my days pleasantly enough to me, but how far useful with what in some other way they might be I cannot say.

Sheet. 2. C. Chile – read proof.

Mr Barry, had been at a meeting of the Directors of the Chile and Peruvian mining company, where some very curious scenes passed. They have only £14.000 left in Exchequer bills and owe some considerable sums while their expenditure in Chile and Peru amounts to 600£ a week. Mischief will soon come of this swindling concern.

Mr Carlile with another proof of his Memoir of Cobbett.

$^{1}/_{2}$ past. 10.

Letter to Mr Hume with the motion for Mr Peel.

---

[199] Robert Stephen Rintoul, editor of the Benthamite paper *The Atlas* and, after 1828, founder and editor of *The Spectator*.

Thursday.   11 [May].

Sticking papers in Guard book respecting the cotton weavers.

Wrote letter to Mr Smith of Bolton. Mr George White respecting the bill to be drawn for Mr Hume, looked at the act. 6. G. 4. c.107. S.99 – and settled the wording of the ~~act~~ bill.

Mr Carlile with some more of the memoir of Wm Cobbett, corrected it.

Went to Hulmandles respecting the lithographed plates for the book on Chile. Hulmandle lives in Great Marlborough S^t.

Thence to Galloway in West St Smithfield and related the substance of my conversation with Mr Hobhouse[.] One of the steam vessels the perseverance 400 tons, answers admirably she will leave the river on Monday – and probably join Lord Cochrane off Weymouth.

Went to the Lord Mayor at the Mansion House on Hones affairs.

~~After~~ Home at 3 – to dinner.

Read Mr Hales pamphlet on the state of the weavers &c.[200] – read his letter to Mr Hume and Mr Humes' [*sic*] replying in M. S. Wrote a few words as a head for Mr Humes letter to the Trades Newspapers next sunday.

Wrote a short article on the Corn bills now in the house of Commons, for the Trades newspaper.[201]

Mr Anderson editor of the Trades newspaper, he had been ordered by the committee of trades to insert the whole of Mr Hales, absurd pamphlet in the paper, which he had refused to do.

Mrs Harwood on her affairs.

Read proof sheet. 2. D. Chile.

Mr Blake to consult me, as to what salary he should demand from the Persian mining projectors, they appearing willing to send him out, to make enquiries. He is to request 800£ for the first year and to have all his expenses paid.

Sat from ½ 10 to 12 at night looking at a parcel of girls dancing quadrilles, in the dining room.

Friday.   12 [May].

Arranging sundry papers.

Letter from Galloway, inclosing copy of another he had sent to the Greek War Com^t

Mr Wright respecting memoir of Cobbett.

[200] William Hale, *An Address to the Manufacturers of the United Kingdom stating the causes which have led to the unparalleled calamities of our manufacturing poor; and the proposal of a remedy* ... (London, 1826).
[201] 'Corn Laws', *TN*, 14 May 1826.

Mc Culloch's lecture 11– to 12.

Went to Mr Gilbee on Mrs Harwoods affairs, – home at 2.

Abraham Samida from two to 3. – he has been summoned to the Court of Common Pleas as a special juror, q. will they let him sit, he being a jew. Annoyed by his pertinacity and nonsense, respecting phrenology.

Reading sundry matters relating to the working people. Distress is terrible indeed.

Mrs Harwood, with a letter to Mr Tooke

Dr Gilchrist from the mechanics Institution urging me to procure money for them.

Mr Toplis on the same subject, advised with him respecting different modes of inducing persons to give money

Letter from Mr Lomax Junr requesting me to procure employment for him as secretary to some gentleman.

Mr Barry.

Mr Banvise [?] respecting the state of the Western Literary Institution.[202] Undertook to induce some persons to take shares.

Rummaging among newspapers till 12. p. m.

Saturday.   13 [May].

Wrote a letter to Sir F. Burdett to request him to inclose Mrs Harwoods letter to Mr Tooke and to recommend him to pay the money he is to give M^{rs} H – to me, for her.

Looking at Catalogues – for 3 book sales

Honb^l Douglass Kinnaird on the subject of the forthcoming West^r Election, the Anniversary dinner on 23 May – and case of Mr Buckingham.

Mr Geo White from the House of Commons he has been appointed clerk of the committee on Mr Buckingham's case, and being desirous to serve him, had made some extracts from his petition, went through them, advised with him and sent him to Douglass Kinnaird who is Buckinghams right hand.

Dr Maclean respecting his book, he wishes me to persuade Mr Hobhouse to name the subject in the house. Will speak to M^r H – respecting it.

<hr />

[202] Founded in London in 1825 'for persons engaged in commercial and professional pursuits': see *Laws of the Western Literary Institution . . .* (London, 1834). Reports of its lectures were carried regularly in the *Trades' Newspaper*, although there it was frequently referred to as the Western Literary and Scientific Institution.

At the Appolonian from 2. to 3. Walked with my wife and Caroline, from 4 to 6.

Read draft deed dissolution of partnership between Mr Tijou and his son made observations, theron, and wrote to Mr Sheriff the Atty – requesting an interview.

Rummaging among old newspapers till 12.

Sunday.   14 [May].

Looking at newspapers and weekly publications.

At 10, set out for a walk with Frank, went by St Johns Wood to West End over one tree hill and round the Hampstead heath to Frogmore, thence across the fields and over Primrose Hill home at two o clock.

Rummaging among old newspapers till dinner time at 3.

D° after dinner. Finished examination of newspapers – 1797 – 8 – 9 – and 1800 – principally Times Chronicle, and Cobbetts Porcupine, and cut from them all that related to the state of the people West^r and Political Societies.

Mr Barry late in the evening with a paper respecting Chile Mining companies, corrected it and gave him a note to the editor of the Morning Herald.

Monday.   15 [May].

Arranging books, lately purchase and entering them in catalogue.

John Beveridge Seaman, with his case, read it with him, told him he had no particular claims but that I would consult with Mr White about him.

Mr Bingham respecting, a history he was going to have compiled of the last session of Parliament.

Mr King and my son Fred. Mr King has been some time at Taylor and Martineaus and says Fred^a may acquire a great mass of information if he takes pains to arrange [?] it.

Mr Henry Leigh Hunt, on Hone's affairs and other matters.

Long letters from Bolton le Moor and 4 country papers, took two hours to look them through.

Read and corrected proofs sheet 2.E. 2.F. 2.G. Chile.

Read, part of the trial Hanniford master v. Hume captain of the Tweed.

Mr Anderson, promised to write an article for the Trades Newspapers on Mr Hales's pamphlet.

---

^a One of my sons who was at this time a clerk in Martineau and Taylor Factory. [Footnote.]

Mr Carlile – on various subjects particularly as to his taking a large house in Fleet Street, he left me at $\frac{1}{2}$ past 10 p. m.

In the day, walked from 4 to 6 with my wife.

Read both yesterday and to day part of M^r McCullochs, book on Political Economy.

Made part of a Glossary of the Spanish and Indian words in Miers's Chile.

Tuesday.   16 [May]

Wrote part of an article for the Trades Newspaper on Mr Hales's Pamphlet.[203]

At 11 – attended Mr Sheriff on the business of Mr Tijou and his son, agreed that Wm Tijou was behaving meanly towards his sister and not very honestly towards his father. Resolved to have an account of all the money transactions during the partnerhip.

Went to Mr Tijou at his house near the Vauxhall Bridge, and thence to Wm Tijous in Greek St Soho, W^m very ill behaved and ill disposed to furnish an account, told him I would employ an accountant.

To Hulmandles respecting the plates to Miers's Chile.

Packed up, and directed to Lord Ponsonby at Buenos Ayres for John Miers, Copies of the Maps, Plates and letter proofs to sheet V inclusive Vol. II.

The Jew Samida on his case —

The poor crazy woman Miss Hammertons on her case.

Charles Blake and Mr Barry read to them sundry extracts from Mr Miers book on Chile.

Making a Glossary to Miers's book

At 11 p. m. wrote a letter to John Miers at Buenos Ayres.

To bed at 12.

Wednesday.   17 [May]

Sorting Parliamentary Papers.

At nine the Jew Samida read his memorial to the Treasury and was obliged to write a new one for him. This occupied me till 11. o'clock.

Mr Wright, respecting Cobbett.

M^r Ed Baines Junr, who has just returned from his nine months travels in France.

[203] 'Mr. Hale's Address on a Minimum of Wages', *TN*, 21 May 1826.

Met old Mr Tijou at Mr Sheriffs his attorney at 12. Much conversation respecting his dissolution of partnership with his son, who has both cheated and bullied the old man. Settled the matter at the end of two hours.

To Mr Foster at Calverts Brewhouse in Thames Street on Miss Hammertons affairs.

~~At dinner time Mrs Chatterly~~[204]

Mrs Hodgskin with some papers from her husband.

Miss Hammerton, much more insane than many of the people she left behind when she quitted St Luke's – promised to go home to her friends.

Mr Barry, he had been at a meeting of the Chile and Peruvian Company, Directors related some curious particulars of these swindlers.[205]

Looking at sundry Parliamentary Papers and Journals of the house of Commons, and writing the remainder of the article on Mr Hale's pamphlet proposing a minimum of wages – went to be[d] at 1 o clock.

Thursday.   18[May].

Arranging Parliamentary Papers.

Walked with James Mill to Cheapside home again at 11. a. m. As I am here a recorder of time more than of opinions I shall not say why it has happened that such friends as Mill and I are, his name has not before appeared in this diary.[206]

John Colls.[207]

Mark Wilkes – the Rev^d.

Long letter from Longson at Stockport[208]

[204] Remainder of paragraph is heavily blacked out. To his children's great chagrin, Place married Mrs Louisa Simeon Chatterley in 1830, about two and a half years after the death of Elizabeth. The two later separated, in 1851.

[205] The last two words of this sentence appear to have been pencilled out and overwritten with the words 'these matters'.

[206] James Mill (1773–1836), political philosopher and 'Bentham's chief disciple'. Place was introduced to Mill in 1808 through their mutual acquaintance, Edward Wakefield. In turn, Mill introduced Place to Bentham in 1812. According to Graham Wallas, Place began to replace Mill as Bentham's principal companion after the former's appointment to India House in 1819. Especially in the early 1820s, Place and Bentham worked very closely together. They lived within minutes' walking distance of each other and, according to Place's diary, they frequented each other's homes regularly. See Wallas, *Life*, pp. 65–86; Terence Ball, 'Mill, James (1773–1836)', *ODNB*, <http://www.oxforddnb.com/view/article/18709>, accessed 10 January 2006.

[207] Perhaps Bentham's amanuensis.

[208] William Longson, a delegate from the Manchester weavers to the select committee on the Combination Laws, later fell out with Place over the issue of a minimum wage.

Letter from Wilkinson Birmingham

Walked from 12 to 3 with Caroline over Primrose hill – country looked gloriously.

Making Glossary for Miers Chile

Occupied for nearly two hours with Mr Smith the Laceman respecting the intended election for Ald^n Waithman arranged some matters relating thereto.

Charles Blake.

Sticking cuttings from newspapers respecting the working people.

bed – at $\frac{1}{2}$ 11.

Friday.　19 [May].

Glossary Miers's book.

McCulloch lectures at 11 —

Looked over a booksellers catalogue half an hour.

Walked with my wife from half past 12 till 3.

Glossary completed.

Mr Thelwall respecting his magazine and the improvement of Ireland scheme

Young Mr Waithman and a Mr Harrison, gave them letters to some persons in Westminster who are likely to assist them.

M^r McCulloch for a gossip.

Read, the two letters, from Longson and Wilkinson, wrote answers to them.

Mr Carlile from $\frac{1}{2}$ 9 to $\frac{1}{2}$ 10 p. m.

Looked at Cobbett's Register, the Republican and the account in the morning herald of Cobbett's proceedings at Preston with a view to his being elected to Parliament for that place.

Saturday.　20 [May]

Arranging parliamentary papers.

At eleven, went to the India House

At twelve, set off with John Mill to his fathers at Dorking – rode to Streatham, walked to Mitcham, thence to Carshalton, thence of over the downs to the N. of Banstead, across the race course at Epsom and through the fields and lanes to Burford Bridge and arrived at Mr Mills at, $\frac{1}{2}$ past 5.

Mr Mill and M^r McCulloch arrived by the coach at 6 – spent the evening as such evenings are usually spent in dining crawling about the Garden and talking, not nonsense I hope.

Sunday.   21 [May]

Mill, McCulloch, I and John, out before 9 – walked to Norbury Park, and through it – crossed the London road and climed [*sic*] Mickleham down, thence through Sir Lucas Pepys's grounds, – and up the valley to the top of Box Hill along the hill descended at Burford Bridge – and home at one, where we found Mr George Ensor, walked about and gossipped [*sic*] till dinner time. Spent the evening as usual.

McCulloch went away by the coach at 5 o clock. I have said I am not going to draw characters or portraits but it is with difficulty I refrain from doing this with the odd creature McCulloch. But it would not be fair to do this with one who is so much the cause of mirth in others.

Monday.   22 [May]

Rose early breakfasted before 7 – saw Mr Mill and John off at 7 – took leave of Mrs Mill and the children at half past 7 – and walked off with Mr Ensor up the ravine we[,] John Mill and I[,] came down on saturday and away to Headley thence to the Epsom race course, past Banstead, and away across the downs and dropped into the turnpike road at Sutton was overtaken by Newmans Brighton Coach, and got a cart to the Elephant and Castle at Newington and walked home, which I reached at ½ 1. found an accumulation of Newspapers pamphlets and letters.

Corrected 2. H. 2. I. Miers's Chile. Wrote letter to Mr Coombs respecting the accounts in Miers's estate.

Mr Hobhouse respecting Westminster anniversary dinner to-morrow, and the forth coming Westminster Election.

All the evening looking over the Newspapers, weekly publications and Henry Drummonds pamphlet on the Currency.[209]

Tuesday.   23 [May]

Read Mr Drummonds pamphlet

Wrote part of an essay for the Trades Newspaper in reply to Mr Ensor[210]

Mr Anderson – with sundries.

Mr Geo White – d^o

Il Chevalier Bozzelli & a french woman with a recommendation from D^r and Mrs Gilchrist to procure him employment, promised to

---

[209] Henry Drummond, *Elementary Propositions Illustrative of the Principles of Currency* (London, 1819), a third edition of which appeared in 1826.

[210] 'Observations on Mr. Ensor's attack on the political economists', *T.N*, 18 June 1826.

send copies of Mr Gilchrists letter to, Thomas Campbell Mr H. L. Hunt, and Mr Miller, for their magazines.

Walked $\frac{1}{2}$ 12 to $\frac{1}{2}$ two with my wife

Corrected sheet 2 K Miers Chile.

Mr Samida the Jew who had served on two special juries, read and again corrected his memorial to the Treasury.

Mr B. Tooke on Mrs Harwoods affairs.

Mr Tijou and Mr Blake

Mr Carlile, looked over many plates to obtain a figure for his engraver to copy.

Extracts, manners of the people.

Wednesday.   24 [May]

Finished the essay in reply to Mr Ensor.

Dr Maclean on the subject of the College of Physicians.

Captn Romeo on his begging business

M^r McCarthy on his new pavement, he cannot induce any one to assist him with money, this I regret.

Mr B. Lomax on his affairs, helped him to compose a letter to that rich and ~~shabby fellow~~ man Morrison to advance him money to pay his workmen which he can do without risk.

Mr Thelwall.

Corrected, the last sheet of Vol. 2 Miers's Chile. Title page and table of Contents

Read Edward Gibbon Wakefields narrative of his abduction of Miss Turner.

Reading in Dr Macleans new book An Exposition of the state of the medical profession.

Thursday.   25 [May]

Sticking papers respecting the Cotton and Silk manufacturers.

Dr Thorpe – nearly an hour

Col^n Bradley not much less

M^r McCulloch —

Mr Ensor —

Mr Fenn on Parish affairs. about an hour and an half

Reading in Dr Macleans Book.

Mr Anderson – from the Trades paper

Mrs Harwood on her affairs.

Putting up papers of my own writing in a volume
    to bed at 12.

Friday.   26 [May]

Revising and extending the paper in reply to Mr Ensor at the request of the Editor of the Trades Newspaper.

Corrected the last sheet of Vol. 1. Miers Chile, containing the Preface and Glossary this completes the work.

Went to Mr Barry in Great Ormond Street and thence with his aid and that of his spanish clerk, corrected the Gossary [sic] to Mr Miers book. Took the proof to the publisher in Paternoster Row.

Mr Saml Miller. ⎫
                                  ⎬ idle gossip.
Mr Kennedy –   ⎭

Mr Geo Ensor —

M^r M J^a Evans —

Read a long examination of Edward G Wakefield in the Herald.

Looked over two catalogues, Book sales

Mr Lomax – on his affairs.

Rummaging among newspapers for matters relating to West^r and the manners of the people.

A long letter from Paul Lemaitre[211] on several subjects – replied to it seriatim.

Reading in Dr Macleans Exposition

Looking at the girls and boys my wife had collected to dance quadrilles, from ten to twelve p. m.

Saturday.   27 [May]

Sorting parliamentary papers.

Mr Lomax, Morrison is shuffling with him.

M^r McCulloch. 2 hours on various subjects.

Mr Barry with a paper on South America, gave him a note to the editor of the Morning Herald

Mr Blake.

Reading sundry papers relating to the manners of the common people making extracts therefrom.

Made a list of the public meetings of the London Corresponding Society.

Looking up the books of the last Westminster Election as they will soon be wanted.

Reading in Dr Macleans book.

211 Paul Lemaitre, gold-watchcase-maker, former member of the London Corresponding Society, and active in City politics thereafter.

Looked at the Republican, Cobbett[,] the Mirror, and Literary Gazette.

Sunday.   28 [May]

Arranging books and papers which had accumulated during the week.

Walked with Frank my son over Camberwell hill, to Norwood, above Sydenham and home at three to dinner.

Sorting cuttings from Newspapers in 1796 and 7 – respecting Westminster politics and – London Corresponding Society, and sticking them to sheets of paper, for future use.

Reading some curious matter relating to the manners of the french in a french book lent me by Mr Aimé.

D^o the life of Devil Dick, a book which contains some curious matters of English Manners – from Mr Aimé.[212]

   to bed $\frac{1}{2}$ 12.

Monday.   29 [May]

Looking at a quarto volume of tracts relating to Bridewell and Bethlem Hospitals, for manners &c.

Read Life and character of Mr Alderman Barber late Lord Mayor of London, and made some extracts relating to manners and the liberty of the press General warrants &c. – [213]

Omitted to say I was with my wife from 12 to $\frac{1}{2}$ past two at the Opera house to see the Society of arts distribute their annual prizes [?], the house was lighted as usual on opera nights before the curtain, a raised platform was put over the orchestra and part of the stage, at the back of which were raised benches to the proscenium, the house was crowded with spectators.

Mr Carlile, on sundry matters.

Mr John Fordham, Banker and farmer from herts, in the course of two hours he gave me much useful information, respecting the state of the country in his neighbourhood, banking[,] farming, labourers, crops, roads, and waggons. Reading life of Devil Dick.

[212] Perhaps Daniel Defoe's *Anecdotes of a Scoundrel; or, Memoirs of Devil Dick: a well-known character. By an invisible spy, etc.* (London, 1726?), or Billy Bradshaw, *The Droll Life, Singular Adventures, Pranks, and Rogueries, of the Notorious Billy Bradshaw, Esq; better known by the name Devil Dick, a jack of all trades* ... (London, 1808).

[213] John Barber, Alderman of London, *An Impartial History of the Life, Character, Amours, Travels, and Transactions of Mr. John Barber, City-Printer, Common-Councilman, Alderman, and Lord Mayor of London. Written by several hands* (London, 1741).

Tuesday.   30 [May].

Mr Smith of Piccadilly to induce me to join him and others,
in making arrangements for the forthcoming Westminster Election,
heard all he had to say, but refused most positively to attend any
meeting or to quit my house in any business relative to the election,
on any account whatever. Consented to see him and any two others,
on the business and to assist them by doing any thing I could do at
home.

Mr Ensor who leaves London to-day.

Reading and noting Life of Devil Dick, notes occupy 8 pages, the
book exceedingly characteristic of the manners of the people 70 or
80 years ago.

Made memorandum of my conversation with Mr Smith.

Col^n Diggins on his affairs – shewed me a friendly note to him
from the Duke of York inclosing one from Mr Huskisson to the Duke,
excusing Canning from not giving Diggins a consulship. Canning says
he has 500 Candidates some of whom he must serve.

Wrote an address to the electors of Westminster who are to meet
this evening, on election business.

A son of Mr Alderman Wood[214] to interest me for his father,
promised to do all I could in the way he requested, namely to procure
some westminster men to assist him in canvassing in their respective
parishes.

Mr Jackson on West^r Election, gave him the sketch of an address –
the Local Register – some printed papers and some instructions.

Mr Blake and Mr Tijou on d^o —

Messr. Clark, De Vere[215] – Jackson & Smith from the meeting of
Electors, With a request that I would draw up resolutions to be
proposed at a meeting at the Crown and Anchor on Thursday next.

Mr Douglas Kinnaird and Mr Joshua Evans appointed to a sub
committee, to wait upon me at 4 p. m. tomorrow when I am to have
the resolutions ready for them.

Wrote a declaration and resolutions, but being interrupted by M^r
Barry did not finish them till after 12 at midnight.

---

[214] Matthew Wood (1768–1843), prominent London politician, alderman from
Cripplegate, sheriff of London and Middlesex, Lord Mayor, and MP for the City. He
was a key supporter of Queen Caroline, scourge of the Durham and Northumberland coal
trade to London, and chairman of the House committee on metropolitan improvements.
See Anita McConnell, 'Wood, Sir Matthew, first baronet (1768–1843)', *ODNB*, <http://www.
oxforddnb.com/view/article/29889>, accessed 10 March 2005.

[215] This name is variously spelled 'De Vere' and 'De Vear'. I have maintained Place's erratic
spelling throughout.

Wednesday   31 [May].

Occupied all day long in sorting, arranging and selecting books for the Westminster Election.

Mr Rintoul to procure a copy of Mr Miers book, to make extracts for the Atlas Newspaper.

Mr John Wright.

Mr Douglas Kinnaird and Mr Joshua Evans, for the business of the election, went over the resolutions I had prepared, and made a few verbal alterations.

Made copies and sent them to Sir Francis Burdett and Mr Jackson.

Mrs Harwood on her affairs.

June. 1826.

Thursday —   1 [June].

Occupied the whole day in sorting[,] arranging and sticking papers in the guard books, respecting the Westminster Elections in 1818 – and 1819.

Letter from Mr Morrison who had refused to discount either of the two bills for the Lomax's [*sic*] – Gave Lomax my acceptance for the 100 £ and a letter to Morrison telling him I could not refrain from an effort to establish these men in business, and requesting the mean mercenary creature to discount the bill, which he had written to me not to accept.

Thomas Hardy on sundry matters. Colonel Jones, on Henry Grey Bennets affairs,

Charles Blake ~~on d^o~~

Mr Adams on Westminster Election matters.

[Friday]   June. 2.

All day sorting, arranging and sticking papers relating to Westminster Elections 1807 – to 1820.

Wrote to Mr Hobhouse on the same subject.

Mr Hobhouse at Noon

Mr Hobhouse – at – 4 – p. m.

For particulars see minutes Westminster election same date.

Mr H. Drummond at – 5 to 6. Walked with my wife from $^1/_2$ 6 to $^1/_2$ 8.

Mr Carlile and Mr Hassel,[216] the latter this day released from Newgate where he had been confined two years for selling Paine's Age of Reason in Carlile's shop. He is a sedate, moral, excellent and very extraordinary young man and will probably rise to some eminence.

M^r De Vear & Mr Jackson at 10 p. m on West^r Election business.

Saturday   June 3.

Arranging papers elections 1820

Instructing a clerk in the business of the forthcoming election.

Mr Wright on sundry matters.

Mr Blake ——————— d^o.

To Wimpole Street on Mrs Harwoods affairs.

[216] Richard Hassell was 'Carlile's brilliant young volunteer shopman', according to McCalman, *Radical Underworld*, p. 184.

To Red Lion Wharf Thames S^t respecting the exportation of an Hydraulics Press to Constantinople for Messrs Martineaus.

Sir Francis Burdett on Election business – and respecting the Western Literary Institution. Walked with my wife from 5 to ½ 6.

Arranging papers writing minutes and remarks election 1820.

Mr Barry.

Mr Geo White.

Looking at sundry periodical publications, till 11. p. m.

Sunday.   June. 4.

Sorting arranging & sticking papers relating – to Westminster[,] the Correspondg Society, and parliamentary reform, 1763 – to 1811. nearly all day.

Mr Tijou in the morning. ⎱
Mr Jackson ───────── ⎰ elections

Messrs. Clark. de Vear. Jackson, in the evening – with a placard.

M^{rs} ~~Chatterley~~ [illegible]

Monday.   June. 5.

Wrote, letters on election business to Mr Kinnaird and Mr Shelton[.]

Mr Fenn with something very like evidence to shew that, the parish of St Martin was a parish only in name until the time of Elizabeth, and that in her time, there were not as many housekeepers in the parish as 49, the number set up by the present vestry as sanctioned by prescription [?].

M^r McCulloch, on leaving London. Well pleased with Miers's book which he says he will endeavour to get reviewed in the Edinburgh.

Wrote letter to John Miers at Buenos Ayres to go in the Ship John with sundry Iron work —

Walked from 12 to 3 with my wife

M^r De Vear on Election business

Mr Wright – d^o – respecting Cobbett at Preston.

Mr Charles Blake who has a prospect so he says of being sent to Chile by Mr Jacob.

Called on Mr Brown in Mrs Harwoods affair – he says Mrs Harwoods dower was a third of Mr Harwoods property in the estate, that her life interest was valued at 33£ a year and that he laid out money to produce her that sum.

Mr Barry.

At the General Meeting of the Western Literary society from ½ 7 to ½ 10.

Arranging papers on Parliamentary reform – and Westminster.

Tuesday.   [June] 6.

Arranging papers. &c.

Mr Jackson on Election business

Mr Smith on D^o – promised the one and then the other to prepare the business for the General committee which is to meet tomorrow evening.

Wrote a resolution for the committee – wrote a letter also to be sent by them to Sir Francis Burdett. D^o – to be sent to Mr Hobhouse.

Gave Mr Smith a letter to Mr Hobhouse informing him what I was doing.

Mr Hobhouse, with the draft of an address to the electors, for my opinion.

Mr Toplis – with an account of the two french silk looms – and some information respecting the mechanics Institution.

Mr Hackett, the clever builder, who assisted in planning and putting up the Lecture room of the Mechanics Institution to request me to promote his interests as a carpenter in the London College.

Mr Lemaitre Junr. on sundry matter relating to his fathers affairs.

Messrs Jackson De Vere & Smith on election business – read sundry papers to them, and other various proceedings.

Wednesday   [June] 7.

Thomas Hardy with a bundle of papers relating to Middlesex, Westminster and Parliamentary Reform.

George White sundry matters.

Wrote letter to William Adams at Portsmouth.

Mr Adams on the business of the election and respecting his son.

Went with Mr Toplis into the City to see a newly invented patent [?] power loom weaving silk, saw two, placed side by side, the power was on by turning a wheel, both looms making good work, one out of very bad materials. These looms differ from the french loom about which much has been said and are very superior to it. They are the property and partly the invention of Mr Kendall of Pater-noster Row. They must come into use generally they are very simple and the work is as flexible as that made by hand. Saw the work made in the french loom it is not saleable.

Walked with my wife from 4 to 6.

Mr Jackson and Mr Adams on the business of the election, drew up resolutions for the meeting and an order of business.

At half past 8 Mr Jackson again on business of the election.

Mr Fenn, on matter relating to the parish, some very curious and singular discoveries made in the books at the Vestry relative to the history of the parish – particularly respecting an ~~large~~ endowment of a large quantity of land which does not at present belong to the parish. Enquiry to be made respecting the time and manner of the parish being dispossessed of this land.

Arranging papers

Writing an essay for the Trades Newspaper, on Machinery.[217]

Thursday.   [June] 8

Writing the essay for the Trades

Walked from 12 to 3 with my wife.

~~Mrs Chatterley on her affairs~~.

Mr Jackson, M^r De Vere on election business.

At night Mr Jackson —

M^r De Vear.

In the afternoon Mrs Harwood on her affairs.

Sundry persons on the election occupied me from 5 till $\frac{1}{2}$ 11 p. m.

Friday.   9. June

Writing the essay for the Trades[.] At 11 went to Covent Garden and there from the top of a shed saw the election of Sir Francis Burdett and Mr Hobhouse.

Home at 1.

Mr Samida with his case for the Treasury.

Walked from $\frac{1}{2}$ 2 to 2. to 3 with my wife[,] Jane and Caroline.

Mr Tijou. Mr Blake. M^r De Vear Mr Jackson on the Election – Mr Smith[.] Promised to draw up an address to conclude the business of the committee on tuesday next.

William Adams arrived with his child from Buenos Ayres, spent the evening with him, his father and sister. he and the child remain here.

Saturday.   [June] 10.

Examining and sorting the papers given me by Mr Hardy.

Mr Wright on Preston election

Walked with my wife.

Reading Mr Adams's narrative

[217] This does not appear to have been published.

Spent the evening with Mr Adams
Mr Hume on City Elections

Sunday   [June] 11

Sorting and sticking the papers given me by Mr Hardy.
Walked with my wife 1 – to 3.
Sticking papers.
William Adams's journal.
Spent the evening with Mr Adams.

Monday.   [June] 12

Arranging election papers.
Mr Fenn with a book of extracts from the Parish book for me to
revise, to be laid before counsel.
Mr Carlile on matters relating to a house he is taking in Fleet Street,
advised him to go to Dr Gilchrist &c &c
Mr Blake – Robinson – Barry —
Read Mr Fenns book very carefully and made notes thereon.
Examining Newspapers – 1806 for matters relating to Westminster
William Adams in the evening.
Mrs Harwood on her concerns.

Tuesday.   [June] 13.

Newspapers. 1806
Thaddeus Connellan the extraordinary Irish teacher, with his
several books, in Irish and English, gave him a note to Sir Francis
Burdett, and one to Mr Hobhouse.[218]
Mr Fenn, went through his book on parish matters.
Mr Thelwall respecting his magazine.
Saw Mr Tindall in the Temple on Mrs Harwoods affairs, but do not
as yet clearly comprehend the law of the case[.] Must see the deeds in
Mr Gilby's possession.

---

[218] Author of *An Irish English Primer, intended for the use of Schools; containing about four thousand Irish monosyllables, with their corresponding explanation in English: together with a few of Æsop's fables, in Irish and in English* (Dublin, 1815), the third edition of which had recently appeared as *An Primér Gaóidheilge lé na bhrígh a Saicsbhearla. The Irish-English Primer to the Irish Language: intended to assist the native Irish in learning English through the medium of the Irish Language . . .* (London, 1825), as well as Irish dictionaries and Irish translations of extracts of the Bible. According to Dudley Miles, Place had known Connellan since the late 1810s and had for many years promoted his efforts both to train teachers and to extend Irish literacy. See Miles, *Place*, pp 104–105.

Walked from 1– to 3. with my wife.

Mr Adams on his own and his son's affairs.

Mr Adams and Mr Joshua Evans on Westminster Election business. William Adams.

Mrs Harwood – on her affairs, received from her a large parcel of papers from Mr Tooke,[219] they relate, to his estate at Tompoen [?].

M^r De Vere and Mr Green, a meeting called this evening at the Crown and Anchor, gave them the papers I had drawn up for the meeting[.] All my spare time occupied in examining and cutting from newspaper accounts of West^r and Midd^x Elections in 1806.

Wednesday   [June] 14.

Sorting newspapers. West^r 1806.

Mr John Evans on legal business.

Walked over Primrose Hill &c. 12 to 3.

Mr Anderson on business of the Trades newspaper

Mr Carlile respecting the means of getting into his new house.

In the evening, with Mr Wm Adams Mr Barry and Mr Blake, much talk and comparison of sundry matters and opinions respecting South America.

Thursday.   [June] 15.

Sorting and sticking papers West^r 1806

Mr Connellan respecting his interview with Sir Benjamin Hobhouse, with whom he had breakfasted, settled the matter of a letter he is to write to Sir B.

A Gentleman respecting some property I hold of one Ashby, consumed 2 hour

Mr Lang secretary to the Trades newspaper on business

Walked with Caroline $^1\!/_2$ 12 to 3.

Mr Connellan with his letter, made some corrections.

Mr Lang again —

Looking at Newcourts Repertorium[220] for evidence respecting the plea set up by the vestry for prescription, 1 as to their being a vestry at all 2 as to the number 49 vestrymen. They can prove neither, we can prove 1. the commencement of the Parish 2. that it did not contain 49 houses for ages.

---

[219] Perhaps William Tooke, a prominent London attorney.

[220] Richard Newcourt, *Repertorium Ecclesiasticum Parochiale Londinense; an Ecclesiastical Parochial History of the diocese of London; containing an account of the Bishops of that sea [sic] . . . the Deans, Archdeacons, and Prebendaries, and of the several parish churches within . . . the diocese, etc.*, 2 vols (London, 1708–1710) commonly referred to as Newcourt's *Repertorium*.

Sticking, cutting respecting West^r elections in 1806.

Friday.   [June] 16.

Sorting and sticking Election papers 1806–7
Mr Fenn, on the parish dispute, went through several particulars,
examined Newcourts Repertorium, promised to write a statement for
the purpose of shewing that St Martin is not an antient parish and
can have no claim to a prescriptive right.
Occupied till 5. p. m.
Mrs Harwood —
Went out at 6 to St Johns Wood to see the place whence the Balloon
is to go tomorrow, home at 9.
The rest of the evening with Mr Adams.

Saturday.   [June] 17

Till one o clock arranging sorting and selecting books and papers,
West^r Elections in 1818. 1819. 1820
Mr Jackson and M^r D Vear, with resolution &c passed on tuesday
at the Crown and Anchor, put them in form as I did also a sheet of
paper to be issued to those who are willing to collect money to pay
the expenses of the election.
Westminster election papers.
Went with Mr Barry at 4. p. m. to see Messr Cornillot and another
ascend with a balloon. home at 9.
Evening with Mr Adams.

Sunday.   [June] 18.

Letter to Mr Wallis Spital Fields weaver respecting his trade, offering
to assist them in organising themselves.
Went [?] walked with my wife to Wallis's house at ~~Hackney~~ Elizabeth
St Hackney road – home at 3 to dinner.
Westminster Election papers – till 9 – William Adams till 11.

Monday —   [June] 19.

Writing an essay on currency for Mr Thelwall – for his magazine.
Sundry matters Westminster elections.
My own memoir till 12. p. m.
In the afternoon Major Turnbull
After him Dr Gilchrist on the affairs of Richard Carlile.
Walked with Caroline from, 4 to 6.

Tuesday   [June] 20

From 7 to 11 – on my own memoir
John Mill on sundry matters.
Walked from 12 to 3 with my wife.
Mr Henry Drummond to tell me of the proceedings at the Surrey
Election and to ask me what he as Sheriff of the County was to do
respecting the changes of the constables &c —
Charles Blake on Chile affairs
Reading Mr Woods book on rail roads.[221]

Wednesday   [June] 21.

Writing to John Miers at Buenos Ayres.
My own memoirs.
Two Miss Spencers on poor mad Miss Hammertons concerns,
promised to assist them in procuring some money for her support.
Walked from $^1\!/_2$ 12 to 3 with my wife
Looking over and cutting from a volume of the Times newspaper
for 1790 Westminster Election, &c in that year
Dr Gilchrist on Carlile's affairs, the Gymnasium and Mechanics
Institution.
Mr Barber Beaumont, he gave me an account of his and the La
Plata Agricultural Company's proceedings and of the total failure of
the project, a certain loss of 11,000£ and the chance for a much greater
loss, but he added that the forfeited shares amount to about the same
sum, 200 persons [?] have been sent out, and great difficulty exists as
to disposing of them in any way.
Went with Charles Blake in the afternoon to see a Balloon go up
with Mrs Graham and Miss Hooks. Ascent put off on account of the
weather it being gloomy and boisterous.
Till 12 p. m. at the Times newspaper.

Thursday —   [June] 22.

My own memoir for the year 1806 this includes the West^r Election
of that year, worked hard at it for 6 hours.
Walked 1 to 3 with my wife.
Finished memoir year, 1806. The reference to so many books is
necessary in this work that the progress is very slow.
Thomas Hardy for a gossip.

[221] Perhaps Nicholas Wood, *A Practical Treatise on Rail-Roads, and Interior Communication in General; with original experiments, and tables of the comparative value of canals and rail-roads* (London, 1825).

Richard Carlile on his affairs.

George White with letters from G[r]avener Henson the ingenious mechanic and lace maker at Nottingham. He has made an improvement in the lace machine which enables him to work figures on the net which have hitherto been worked only by hand, he has sent up specimens and says his machine will do more work and do it much better in 10 minutes than a woman can do in a day. This is a very important improvement.

Reading the 68 N° of the quarterly Review – just published.

Mrs Harwood on her affairs at 10 p. m. left a tin box containing sundry pieces of plate.

Friday.   [June] 23.

Finishing my memoir. 1806.
Walking alone 1. to 3.
Mr Aimé
Mr John Wright
Reading Quarterly Review and extracting certain particulars as items of the improvement of society since 1740.
Mr Henry Drummond on Sundry matters – again invited me to spend some days next month at Albury. But I shall not go.
Walked with my wife and Caroline from 6 to 8.
Sticking cuttings from newspapers Westminster Election. 1790.

Saturday.   [June] 24.

Examining papers West^r Election 1790 —
D° London Corresponding Society 1797, sent to me by Thomas Hardy.
Col^n Torrens quite elated with his return to parliament for Ipswich. He says he cannot be unseated, by any petition. But Mr Drummond says his opponent is equally certain that the return is false and will be revised, he has resolved to petition the house and has retained the attorney General Mr Denman and Mr Gurney.
Mr Hobhouse with a letter from his father for Thady Connellan, much talk on political matters.
Westminster papers.
Walked with my wife and Caroline 7 to 9.
Reading Quarterly Review.

Sunday.   [June] 25.

Nearly all day arranging papers materials, for history of west^r elections, Corresponding and other political societies. Reading Parliamentary debates relating to Mr Paul[l] and Westr. 1806. 1807.

Mr Wm Tijou }
Mr Blake   } William Adams

Monday.   [June] 26.

From 7 to $^1\!/_4$ past 8 writing my own memoir, for 1807. Breakfast, and looking at Morning Chronicle and Herald till 9. Memmoir [*sic*] from 9 till nearly eleven – From half past 11 to two out principally on Mr Carliles business.

Dinner – from 3 to 5 memoir – Tea and gossip with my wife and Mrs Hodgskin till 6 —

Walking with my wife from $^1\!/_2$ 6 to 9

From 9 to 12– my memoir.

Two or three persons looked in but I lost very little time with them.

Tuesday.   [June] 27.

Seven to eight memoir.

Breakfast – newspapers.

Nine to twelve memoir. finished it for 1807 to 2nd May. Chapter V.

Mr John Wright about Preston election. 1 to $^1\!/_2$ walking.

Dinner at 3. till then looking at some papers sent to me by Mr Thwaites of the Morning Heral[d] a dispute in the west of England between the Revd Matthew W Place and a Roman Catholic Priest

Mr Henry Drummond on the affairs of his Shrievalty and payment of constables, and with a letter and plan for a safe and secure currency from a Mr Palmer a Bank Director. The director has a confused notion of the subject

Reading. "Abernethy on the origin of and treatment of Local diseases and on Aneurisms."[222]

Charles Blake who wants to write a review of Miers book for the Quarterly Review. Told him to write to Murray the bookseller and to tell him so.

Walked from 7 to 9 with my wife.

Reading Abernethy.

---

[222] John Abernethy, *Surgical Observations on the Constitutional Origin and Treatment of Local Diseases; and on Aneurisms* (London, 1809), which went through a number of subsequent editions.

Wednesday   [June] 28.

Writing several letters.

1. To Sir Richard Phillips who sent me a copy of his "Illustrations of the Interrogative System of useful and liberal Education"[223] with a letter requesting me to give him the names of persons in various parts of the country with whom he might correspond. Did so.

To John Richter.

To Henry Richter.

To M[r] Smith at Bolton with a copy of Torrens's book on the Corn Laws,[224] requesting him to use the Bolton Chronicle as much as possible for the purpose of inducing a multitude of people to petition for a revision of the corn laws in the next session of parliament.

Thaddeus Conellan with a letter to the Duke of Northumberland for assistance, dictated a postscript and the proper address in hopes of obtaining him an interview.

M[r] Blake on Chile matters.

My own memoir. Election for Westminster in 1807.

Went at [?] 5 p. m. with my wife and Caroline to White Conduit House to see M[rs] Graham and Miss Stokes go up with a balloon. home at 9.

M[r] Carlile on his own affairs.

Thursday.   [June] 29

My own memoir.

D[r] Gilchrist on sundry matters.

M[r] Fenn on parish affairs, he is now completely master of his subject has laid his abstract before M[r] Scarlet who has given a very decided opinion in his favour, but M[r] Fenn fears he will not put the case to the court in its plain simple form and disposed to do it himself – advised him not to attempt it as he does not understand the practice of the court nor how much he can call upon his adversaries to prove.

M[r] Wright —

My own memoir.

Walked with my wife from 7– to 9.

Finished my memoir for 1807.

[223] Richard Phillips, *Illustrations of the Interrogative System of Education* (London, 1820?).
[224] Robert Torrens, *An Essay on the External Corn Trade*, 3rd edition (London, 1826; first published 1815).

N. B. the memoir from the number of books and documents necessary to be examined occupies a great quantity of time and goes on but slowly.

Friday.   [June] 30.

Nearly the whole day at my memoir excepting 1 to 3 when I walked alone and ½ 8 to 10 when I walked with Charles Blake.

Saturday   July. 1.

Read with William Adams the commencement of his diary. Route from Mendoza to S Juan, and on the road to Famatima, needs great amendment and extension before it can be fit for part of a book.

Mr Lambert and Mr Smith Gold Lacemen for me to draw up a memorial to the Privy council for trade, to obtain a drawback on Gold and Silver wire.

Mr Blake with an essay on Chile mining intended for insertion in the M[orning] Chronicle, corrected it for him.

My own memoir —

Mr Carlile on his affairs, [illegible]

Reading in Mr Buckinghams Oriental Herald. Vols 6 and 7.

Walked with Mr Robinson the painter and Caroline from 7 to $\frac{1}{2}$ 9.

Sunday.   [July] 2.

Sorting papers —

Writing memorial for the Gold Lacemen

Finished my memoir to 9 feb 1810 and chapter X.

Walked from 7 to 10 with my wife.

Monday.   [July] 3

Sorting papers – cutting from Newspapers

O. P. riot in 1809–10 – Westminster meeting in feb^y – Committal of John Gale Jones to Newgate and Sir Francis Burdett to the Tower in 1810.

Walked in the evening – 7 to 9 with my wife.

Mr Fenn in the morning two hours on Parish matters.

Tuesday.   [July] 4.

Sorting papers &c. – 1806 to 1811

Dr Gilchrist respecting a motion he wished to make at the India House respecting the education of Writers and respecting Carliles affairs.

William Adams.

Charles Blake.

Mr Anderson. Trades newspaper and Spital Fields Weavers, accounts respecting

Read preface to the 5th Volume of the Mechanics Magazine in which Messrs Knight and Lacey condemn Mr Robertson for his conduct towards Dr Birkbeck and others and towards the Mechanics

Institution, but they have omitted to say that they encouraged him in his vile conduct and made common cause with him in the act he did to that Institution at its commencement, of which I have given an account in my observations on the establishment of that most excellent institution.[225]

The elections have now closed and the degraded people have as usual returned a set of miscreants to the house of Commons, but this is to no very great extent their fault. they have no choice. Very few indeed are the places for which any man can hope to be returned without spending a large sum of money, and those who are willing to spend large sums of money simply to enable them to serve the country are still fewer, and it is really of little importance except in some few cases which of the pretenders is chosen. Thus it happens that a large majority of those who compose the house of commons are as little qualified and as little worthy to sit in a house which should really represent the people as it is perhaps possible to collect together in any way. When some years ago a member said that if the first 688 men that crossed Westminster Bridge were brought into the house these would be as wise and as honest a set as then composed the house, he did not exaggerate the matter. He who really knows how the members are chosen or rather how they get there, and who they are will not if he act honestly ~~that it is~~ deny the truth of the assertion. Many persons whom I see tell me of the infamous conduct carried on at this general election, and infamous enough the conduct of both candidates and voters is, but it is none more so than in former times, and in the present instance it has not been as extensive as usual. But the moral as well as the intellectual improvement of society is partaken of by the Press and matters are related and commented upon which a very few years ago would have passed as matters of course without notice, but now the Daily and Weekly and country newspapers one and all so far as I have seen have exposed the nefarious practices at many places and have reprobated them in a becoming manner, thus the villainies of the candidates as well as those of the electors are laid before the public, and those who have never taken the trouble to enquire what was the practice formerly think the atrocities they read of are either now committed for the first time or are much increased. Thus bad observers of events are deceived on both points, but the matter appearing new the sensation is the stronger. Even in Westminster in 1806 open bribery or all but open bribery was practised with impunity. In 1818 a good deal of similar sort of work was done

---

[225] According to Place, John Knight and Henry Lacey claimed that Robertson preferred 'a literary miscellany' to more useful knowledge. See Place Papers, BL Add. MS 27823, fos 375–378.

by both Whigs and Tories and the newspapers were not only silent
on the occasion but they countenanced the villainy by applauding the
conduct of those who perpetrated it. This will however do no longer
and the Reporters as well as the Editors and Proprietors begin to see
that their interest is most likely to be promoted by the course they have
taken. Of these infamies I have preserved [?] a few specimens ~~from~~
cut from newspapers. The example set by Westminster has certainly,
not been lost, either in this or in any other respect.

The number as well as length of the advertisements inserted in
newspapers have ~~both~~ been small and short when compared with the
general elections prceeding [*sic*] this which has just closed.

Up to this day I have done scarcely any thing beyond giving a dry
detail of events which have occupied my time, if I continue this diary
as I probably shall for some time longer I shall make observations and
comments occasionally

Walked from 7. to ½ 9 ~~alone~~ with Wm Adams in the evening.

Wednesday.   [July] 5.

Sorting and cutting newspapers Westminster matters, for 1810.

Mr Wright. he had been employed by the Hanleys to compile
a mountebank Gazette to be published daily during the election
at Preston at which Cobbett was a candidate, he did so, and elven
[*sic*] Nos were printed and distributed, but as he made no particular
bargains as to money he now fears he may not be paid.

Mr Fenn with a very clever paper and a very conclusive paper
against our parish vestry, ~~totally~~ completely disproving ~~any~~ every claim
to custom, which they have set up or can set up.

Mr Thomas Campbell and Dr Strachan from Canada – the D^r has
a project of a College or University for Canada in which he says he
shall succeed.

Much conversation about the London University – when I
suggested a plan for inducing persons to take shares.

Mr Chas Blake. Gave him a letter of introduction to Mr Campbell
for the purpose of getting him employed on his New Monthly
Magazine.

Walked 7– to ½ 9. my wife & Caroline.

Sorting papers 1810.

Thursday.   [July] 6

Sticking papers into guard book 1810

Mr Barry —

Mr Blake, had seen Mr Campbell and had undertaken to write a series of letters relating to S. America if Mr Colburn the proprietor should approve thereof.

Mr Blake again he had seen Thwaites the editor and proprietor of the Morning Herald to whom I gave him a letter of introduction, and had engaged to write 6 letters for his paper.

Mr Evans respecting Buenos Ayres he wishes to be employed as refiner and assayer to the mint there, told him to write a letter to John Miers and that I would also write recommending him. He ~~had~~ left a note before he came away from Buenos Ayres which Mr Miers had noticed in his correspondence with me.

J. W. Brooks respecting his fathers estate, which is likely to be wholly wasted by the stupidity of the executors the cupidity of the Lawyers and the malicious [blank]^{226} of Spratly his son in law who could have caused [?] the affair to be settled two years ago and could do so now if he would. This man by refusing to sign papers which would enable the executors to sell the property will probably ruin as many as a dozen persons.

Waited on Mr Wm Tooke on the business of the University told him that if squads of three persons would go round in coaches to those who have taken shares and induce them to take more, get from them the names of others likely to become share-holders and then wait upon these persons a large number of shares could be disposed of. Offered to make one with two others, and to go day by day until as large a number as possible were disposed of. Promised to see him again on Monday.

Walked 7– to ¹/₂ 9 with my wife.

Friday   [July] 7.

Sticking papers relating to West^r 1810.

Wrote an essay for the trades Newspaper at the conclusion of the year since its establishment.^{227}

Went to Henry Brooks on his affair

To Miss Spencer on poor Miss Hammertons – agreed to have her placed in the insane ward at Guys Hospital, and to assist in procuring her some 10 or 12 £ a year for clothes and comforts [...] a larger sum. Miss Spencer says Miss Hammertons is desirous of going there. Guys is the best place in England, see it described in the commons committee on Mad Houses where there is a plan of the insane ward.

---

^{226} The blank space appears to have been intentional.
^{227} 'The *Trades' Newspaper*: to the working people', *TN*, 9 July 1826.

Made a drawing for a glass fountain inkstand.
Walked from 7 to $\frac{1}{2}$ 9 with my wife.

Saturday   [July] 8.

Sticking papers relating to West^r 1810
Burdetts committmen [*sic*] to and escape from the Tower.
Mr Campbell he had been at the council of the intended London
University where the plan suggested by me to induce persons to
become shareholders had been discussed. It seems that some time
ago Brougham had spoken of me as of a person who could if he chose
be very useful in promoting the object of the council and particularly
in the sale of shares, Mr Wm Tooke having cogitated on the matter
and knowing that I had taken a very decided part promoting other
societies, and that my efforts had on these occasions been useful,
requested me to see him in the hope of our being able to form
a plan to dispose of shares. My plan having been mentioned, was
immediately admitted to be useful, and fit to be proceeded upon,
Brougham concurred in this but objected that my name if mixed up
with the College might be injurious on account of the Infidel opinion
I was, (he said) known to entertain. It is more than probable that my
opinions on these matters were unknown to all the members of the
council excepting those with whom I am rather intimately acquainted.
Dr Gregory on hearing this from Brougham became alarmed and
shewed himself, so Campbell says, a narrow bigot. Campbell objected
to Brougham and Gregory, and some others that my opinion had
any thing to do with it, that it was well known that the council itself
contained men of various religious opinions, and some notorious free
thinkers, and that if exceptions were taken they would go round.
Campbell said he would go with me and endeavour to dispose of
shares.
    The conduct of Brougham is as usual that of a shuffling lawyer, his
is much better known as an Infidel than I am and he is known too as
I am not known and cannot be known to be a shuffler in Politics. I
will challenge him to go round with me to sell shares and I dare say
he will do it.
    Nobody else called upon me and I was closely occupied till 12 at
midnight in Westminster affairs. How much reading and thinking it
requires to enable me to write a single line.

Sunday.   [July] 9.

    Occupied as yesterday – without any interruption till 7 p. m. when
I went out with my Wife and Jane, came home at $\frac{1}{2}$ 9 —

Monday.   [July] 10.

Occupied as yesterday till $\frac{1}{2}$ 11 and then went to Mr Tookes, chambers in Grays Inn.

Went with Mr Tooke to the office of the University – arranged a plan for making lists of persons to be waited on – and a list of those likely to consent to go round[,] came home at 2. Found 7 country newspapers containging [*sic*] accounts of the state of the poor manufacturers in Lancashire Yorkshire – and Cheshire and a Montrose Paper containing an account of the Election of Joseph Hume, with which as I had some fears I am well pleased.

Col^n Torrens on several matters relating to what he is to do in Honb^l House, arranged some matters respecting petitions against the Corn Laws.

Wrote an essay for the Trades newspaper, on Mechanics Institutions and Machinery.[228]

Walked from 7– to $\frac{1}{2}$ 9 with my wife. Read over the essay for the Trades newspaper.

Tuesday   [July] 11.

Looking over parliamentary papers. Examining accounts respecting Greenwich Hospital.

	£
Income ——————————————	187.345
Pensioners ————————— 2710	
	£
Cost of Pensioners – not more than	90.000
So that the charges are —————	97.345

that is more than the whole expense occasioned by the pensioners – Mr Hume must look to this. The Paper. is N° 377. 17 May. 1826.

Read in the morning Herald some account of the Parish of St Martin in the Fields, Mr Fenn came and we read the acts 23 and 28 Henry VIII respecting the exchange of lands with the abbott of Westminster, and also the act of the same king, settling the bounds of his Palace at Westminster. Agreed that Mr Fenn should push his enquiry as far as possible. Wrote to Mr Thwaites of the Herald for the address of the person who supplied this information.

[228] 'Defence of the London Mechanics' Institution', *TN*, 23 July 1826.

Went with my wife to St Lukes Hospital to learn what steps must be taken to insure [*sic*] admission of poor Miss Hammerton into the incurable ward of Guys Hospital for insane persons.

Writing part of a long letter to John Miers at Buenos Ayres.

Mr Robinson – Mr Blake.

Mr Barry on sundry matters.

Looking at Mrs Mercy Warrens history of the American Revolution in 3 vols sets, it appears to me to be a useful book.[229]

Wednesday.   [July] 12.

Removing books to make way for the carpenter to put up some shelves in the library.

Writing letter to Mr Miers.

Copying act. 28 Hen. 8 c. 12 respecting the limits of his palace at Westminster. Examining and writing some observations on Aggis's maps of Charing Cross and the Strand &c – 1578. Norden. 1593 —

Correcting and adding to a papers written by Mr Barry on South American Loans.

Walked alone from 6 to half 9 – went to Highgate and across to Hampstead Heath thence by Pond or Pound Street across the fields to the Regents Canal on the Hampstead Road, and home, weather very delightful.

Finished letter to Mr Miers.

Wife gone to the Lyceum Play House with Jane, Miss Waterfield and Mrs Miers.

Thursday.   [July] 13

Reading in Mrs Mercy Warrens history of the American Revolution.

Wrote to Henry L. Hunt, and to Thomas Campbell recommending an unfortunate gentleman the Chevalier Bozzelli for literary employment.

Read and corrected for Mr Blake the first of an intended series of letters on Chile, intended to be inserted in the Morning Herald.

Working hard, replacing and arranging books in the new shelves, which occupied me from noon till night.

Had a conversation a day or two ago with a person who had been master of a vessel, on the subject of homeward freight on vessels shut out by the blockad[e] of Buenos Ayres. It seems that the English masters instead of landing their cargoes at Monte Video as they might

[229] Mercy Warren, *History of the Rise, Progress, and Termination of the American Revolution* (Boston, MA, 1805).

do on account of their consignees, refused to break bulk and return home under the persuasion that they shall receive homeward freight, this he assured me they could not receive, and this afternoon Mr Edward Ellis[230] told me he believed that under the circumstances of the case, he thought they would not be permitted to receive even the outward bound freight. He is to enquire for me.

At home all day.

Comparing some statements of the number of persons committed for crimes in London and the country. In the Manufacturing and Agricultural counties, wrote about a page on this subject.

Friday.   [July] 14.

Reading in the Leeds Mercury and in the Leeds Intelligencer, Letters written by Mr Ed. Baines Junr.[231] the first from Rouen and the last on the question respecting machinery.

Cutting and sticking sundry essays and accounts of meetings in the manufacturing countries, respecting the state of the people and of trade.

Went at 12 to the London University chambers, to see what had been done with respect to going about to collect shares – appointment made for tuesday.

Mr John Smith M.P.	Mr G. Grote Junr[232]
Lord Auckland ————	Mr Warburton[233]
Thos Campbell ————	Jas Mill

have consented to go round, Mr Coates is making out [a] list for the purpose.

Went to Miss Spencer on Miss Hammertons affairs. Home at 2.

Wrote to Mr Shelton and Mr Banvise urging each of them to take a share.

[230] Edward Ellice (1783–1863), wealthy merchant and MP for Coventry, although he briefly lost his seat in 1826. Place variously spells his name 'Ellice' and 'Ellis'.

[231] The son of Edward Baines, Sr, proprietor of the Leeds Mercury.

[232] George Grote (1794–1871). One of the group of utilitarian radicals around Bentham and Mill, later elected to the first reformed Parliament as MP for the City of London. See Joseph Hamburger, 'Grote, George (1794–1871)', ODNB, <http://www.oxforddnb.com/view/article/11677>, accessed 19 January 2006.

[233] Henry Warburton (1784–1858), political economist, friend of David Ricardo, leading exponent of the founding of a London University, and radical member for Bridport, Dorset. See H.C.G. Matthew, 'Warburton, Henry (1784–1858)', ODNB, <http://www.oxforddnb.com/view/article/28672>, accessed 10 March 2005.

Out from 4 to 6 on John Miers's business. Looking at Sir Egerton Brydges's book on the "Population and Riches of Nations[.]"[234]

M[r] Meabry my Co Executor and Trustee under the late M[r] Miers's will talked much on the matter of our trust. Everyone of the legatees in England have shewn themselves particularly dishonest people. I have spent a vast quantity of time, and taken great pains to make the most of the property, have incurred scarcly [sic] any law expenses in the administration of a most complex estate, and have in every way saved every shilling of expense that could in any way be saved, yet these people who but for me would have had the whole property wasted in law and Chancery suits, now concur with Abbott the man whose character and conduct they used to describe as infamous and with whom some of them would hold no converse, all now or nearly all are supporting or backing on to file a bill in Chancery against me, on a pretence that money I received from their brother John and expended again on his account, belonged to them and not to him. I will do them strict justice notwithstanding, but I will have as little intercourse as possible with them. These people are great fools, for I had offered to give John Miers a receipt in full for the whole sum between £3000 and £4000 he owes me to enable them to receive as much as he may have left when he returns to England, but I shall not now withdraw any part of my claim, but shall take from him all he can pay me.

W[m] Adams just returned from the N of France whither he has been on business.

Read an excellent paper in the Scotsman on Sir James Graham's pamphlet on Corn and Currency.[235]

As usual, read Cobbett's Register for tomorrow, certainly a most singular production, knowing as I do the extreme egotism of Cobbett his propensities and weakness. I take this register to be a proof of his insanity whence I infer that the time is not very distant when he will either die or be confined.

Saturday.   [July] 15.

Write Miss Hammerstons case, and made a copy of it. Took it to Miss Spencer in Great Russell Street and having read it to her took it

---

[234] Sir Samuel Egerton Brydges, *The Population and Riches of Nations, considered together, not only with regard to their positive and relative increase, but with regard to their tendency to morals, prosperity, and happiness* (Paris, 1819).

[235] James Graham, *Corn and Currency; in an address to the land owners* (London, 1826).

to M^rs and Miss Rankin^a who are to give it to the Treasurer of Guy's Hospital.

Went to Drury Lane and thence to Clifford Inn, to bail Mr Joseph Webb^236 who has been arrested by his bookseller.

Thence to Carlile's in Fleet Street, home at 2.

Mr Mill on sundry matters one of which was to induce me to review the Life of Major Cartwright for the Westminster Review, which I consented to do – much conversation on various subjects, he is writing a review of the last session of Parliament [–] talked over some of the most material points – settled others respecting the London University, he will go with me on thursdays to dispose of shares.

Mr Felix Wakefield for some information on one or two subjects of small consequence.

A young gentleman named Urquhart sent to me by Mr Bentham, to learn something of the public character of Lord Cochrane, as he U—— is going to Greece. Gave him the information he required as far as I could.

Mr Barry on S[outh] A[merican] matters. Black^237 will put the letter I corrected for Barry into the Chronicle on monday.

Dr Gilchrist on London University matters, he will go with me on 4 mornings each week.

Hunting out dates, when Parliamentary reform was discussed &c

Sunday.   [July 16.]

Reading Sir E. Brydges on Political economy, the book abounds with faults and errors, but there are some shrewd and useful observations in it, some of which I copied into a common place book, for the purpose of quoting them hereafter, to the working people.

Hunting up papers on Parl[iamentary] Ref[orm].

Walked from 7 to ½ 9 with my wife.

Monday.   [July] 17.

Wrote several letters to persons to request them to take shares in the London University.

---

^a Regents Park [Footnote.]

^236 Bill-broker and member of the so-called Peckham Lodge circle of infidels and freethinkers that circulated around Timothy Brown. He later became a follower of Carlile. See McCalman, *Radical Underworld*, pp. 75 and 255, n. 17.

^237 John Black, editor of the *Morning Chronicle*.

Went out at ¹/₂ 11 to the University Chambers. Mʳ Coates had not been able to settle for going around tomorrow.

Went at one, with Frank[238] to the Bricklayer Arms, thence by coach to Blackheath, thence through Morden College – to Bexley and Hall Place on Foot. From Hall Place where we had business to transact, to Bexley Heath over shooters [*sic*] Hill and through Greenwich Park to Greenwich, thence in a Coach home at nine.

Mʳ Coates from the University, he had made an arrangement for Wednesday morning.

Tuesday.   [July] 18.

Finished a letter for John Miers and sent it to the foreign office to go in Lord Ponsonby's bag to Buenos Ayres.

Read a long letter of Wᵐ Longson's in the Bolton Chronicle on a minimum of wages.

To Mʳ Hume 9 Bryanstone Sqʳ he was in the Country.

Mʳ Aimé on sundry matters.

Making and arranging lists for the London University.

¹/₂ 6 to Mʳ Mill's. —

Wrote to Mʳ Galloway respecting the London University.

Read a portion of the M.S. Life and sufferings of James Blincoe.[239]

At Mʳ Mills' [*sic*] – from ¹/₂ 6 to 10 p. m

Read Life and Correspondence of Major Cartwright till ¹/₂ 12.[240]

Wednesday[.]   [July] 19.

Reading Life of Cartwright.

Out from ¹/2 9 to 2. with Dʳ Gilchrist and Mʳ Geo Grote on University business – waited on 19 persons, were favourably received, some promised to give the names of their friends and some also to increase the number of their shares.

Making a report of the days work. Sent report and a letter to the Office of the University.

Mʳ Barry —

Mʳ Thelwall much conversation on the state of society at the present time. Thelwall like every one else except Mill, croaks sadly – Trade is ruined, the manufacturing people are starving, and a crisis approaches. It is all nonsense – notwithstanding there are some thousands of

---

[238] Francis Place, Jr, born 22 June 1798.

[239] A reference to *A Memoir of Robert Blincoe, an orphan boy; sent . . . to endure the horrors of a cotton-mill*, published in 1832 by John Doherty. This had obviously been circulating in manuscript several years before it came into print.

[240] F.D. Cartwright (ed.), *The Life and Correspondence of Major Cartwright*, 2 vols (London, 1826).

working people in a dreadful state of want still, the quantity of profitable business now doing is much greater than it was in the average of 7 years to the year 1822. and there are more people who are not in want but are well off than there ever was before except perhaps in the years 1824–5. I have no doubt at all that there are more people proportionally well provided for than there were at any time for three years together since 1794.

A race has been run between the improvement of machinery and the increase of population and population has beaten machinery.

Read Life of Major Cartwright till 12. at night.

Thursday.   [July] 20.

Examining Smith. 62 additional plates to the antiquities of Westminster making remarks on Nordens survey[241] and Smiths plates of the Sanctuary,[242] &c &c.

Mr Geo White, a person has applied to him to sell a borough which returns two members for £28,000 –. promised him to mention it to Mr Drummond who some time since talked of buying such a borough.

Mr Meabry my Co-executor and Trustee in Miers's estate. Keighley had been with him, and seemed resolved to commence a suit against me for the 600£ before mentioned —

Looking at Smith's Antiquities of Westminster but could get nothing from it.

Walked ½ past 12 to ½ past 2 with my wife – went on business to Mr Wm Miers – Mr Coombes – and Mr Nettlefield.

Went at half past 3 to the council of London University. met there. Messrs. T. L. Goldschmidt – J. Hume – Mill – Tooke – Macaulay, John Smith, G. Grote and some others – made arrangements for Monday Tuesday – and Thursday. home at 6.

Col^n Torrens.

Looked at some books purchased today.

D^o — at a book sale catalogue —

Life of Major Cartwright.

Friday.   [July] 21.

Cutting and sticking – papers relating to the working people.

[241] Any of the various editions of John Norden, *Speculum Britanniæ: an historical and chorographical description of Middlesex and Hartfordshire. Wherein are alphabetically set down the names of the cities, towns, parishes, hamlets, houses of note &c. in those counties* (first published London, 1593).

[242] John Thomas Smith, *Antiquities of Westminster; the old Palace; St. Stephen's Chapel (now the House of Commons), &c. containing two hundred and forty-six engravings of topographical objects, etc. (Sixty two additional plates, etc.)* (London, 1807–1809).

Read a long account in the M[orning] Chronicle of Dr Paris's
book on diet and regimen.[243] I have never yet seen a book on this
subject, which shewed that the writer had clear ideas, and certainly
Dr Paris from the account of his book has a very confused notion of his
subject. Dr Kitcheners book, furnishes excuses for every one to do as
he pleases. Mr Abernethy's is confused and embarrassing – the whole
that is certainly known on the subject might be comprised in a few
pages. Moderation is recommended by all, but ~~every one~~ generally a
man judges of his own moderation, not from his reason, not from his
knowledge, but from his desires. I attribute the sound health, strength
and cheerfulness I enjoy to my moderation, but my moderation would
be excess of indulgence to some, probably starvation to others. I judge
as well as I can from effects and endeavour to subdue my propensities
to evil, thus I avoid every thing which produces flatulency, or acidity,
of which, when I do not take sufficient care, I get an early notice of
my impropriety, but the generality cannot accurately observe these
matters nor easily ascertain the causes of what they do observe, some
knowledge of anatomy, and physiology is necessary to enable a man
to approximate to right conduct in these matters and this kind of
knowledge is confined to comparatively but few.

Reading life of Major Cartwright

Walked with my wife from 7 to ½ 9 p m

Read and corrected, a letter for Charles Blake on S. America to be
inserted in the Times —

Read for four hours in the course of the day – Life and sufferings
of Robert Blincoe.

Saturday[.]   [July] 22.

Sorting a number of pamphlets to be sent to the binder's.

M^r. Anderson with a proof of my essay on Mechanics Institutions
&c &c urged me to permit my name to appear as the writer in an
advertisement to the Essay saying it contained some account of the
life of M^r. Place, as it would sell 1000 additional copies of the paper,
this I refused.

Read life of Blincoe till 2 o clock. Intend to have its contents verified
and then to print it.

Went to Hoxton to look for a man who has made an ingenious
pump.

Went at ½ five to the Cobourgh Theatre as it is called – never was
in this house before, – it was saturday night yet the company was

---

[243] John A. Paris, *A Treatise on Diet, with a view to establish . . . a system of rules for the prevention
and cure of the diseases incident to a disordered state of the digestive functions* (London, 1826).

very superior in dress and manners to what it used to be at the Royal Circus and at Astley's when I was young – the house was crowded at half price, and much blaguardism [*sic*] in the gallery, yet not nearly so much as formerly.

My Wife took me to this place with Jane and John. It rained heavily when we left the house, no coach could be procured and we walked through the heavy rain all the way home, which we reached, before 12. o clock.

Looked at some french books left by M^r. Aimé and got to be[d] at 1. p. m. [*sic*].

Sunday.   [July] 23.

Sorting, cutting and sticking papers from the John Bull in 1821 relating to the Queen.
Reading – Life of Major Cartwright
Reading – Voltaire —
Making a list of persons and arranging the names for the London University.

Monday.   [July] 24.

From ½ past 9– to ½ past 3 with M^r. Warburton, G. Grote, D^r. Gilchrist in hunting up shares for the London University.
Wrote a report of our proceedings for the council, of the University.
Walked from 7 to 9 with my wife.
M^r. Barry with his book – on South America —
Looking at some french books till 12.

Tuesday.   [July] 25

Making a list of persons to be waited upon, by M^r. John Smith M. P., Joseph Hume M. P. – and myself to induce them to take shares in the London University.
Out from ¼ past ten till ¼ to 4 with M^r. Hume and M^r. Smith.
Wrote a report of our proceedings for the council of the university.
M^r. Wright.
M^r. Charles Blake with a letter on Chile, which I corrected.
Sticking papers relating to the Queen.

Wrote a letter to Sir Richard Phillips on the West Review and his absurd desire to have his foolish book of social philosophy puffed in it.[244]

Wrote a letter on sundry matters to M[r]. Smith of Bolton in reply to one from him received this day.

M[r]. Geo White who has undertaken to have a fair copy of the Life and sufferings of Robert Blincoe made and has promised to bring me some more cases of the same kind.

M[r]. Barry.

M[r]. Carlile.

Wednesday.   [July] 26.

Cutting and sticking – from the John Bull in 1821 – matters relating to the Queen.

Out from 11 to 2. on University of London Business.

Cutting and sticking —

Out with my wife from $\frac{1}{2}$ 6 to $\frac{1}{2}$ 8.

Wrote out names and arranged them in order for tomorrow morning – for London University —

Thursday.   [July] 27.

M[rs] Harwood on her affairs.

M[r]. Jn[o]Wright.

From half past nine to $\frac{1}{2}$ 1 with M[r]. Mill and M[r]. Z. Macauley beating up for person to take shares in the London University.

Making out a report of proceedings. Reading on sundry political and other matters which had been laid by from want of time.

M[r]. Thomas Campbell on matters relating to the University.

M[r]. Coates – on d[o] —

M[r]. Carlile.

Sticking papers relating to the queen. Read two very long letters from Manchester on the state of the people, and an essay of Richard Hassells on the same subject in the Republican.

[244] Perhaps a reference to *The Hundred Wonders of the World, and of the Three Kingdoms of Nature, described according to the best and latest authorities, and illustrated by engravings,* first published in 1818. A subsequent edition appeared in 1826. Phillips was a popular author of catechisms and grammars who wrote under many pseudonyms, this book having appeared under the name Rev C.C. Clarke.

Friday.   [July] 28.

Writing an essay for the Bolton Chronicle on a minimum of wages[245]
[–] this took me six hours.
Out from 1 – to 3.
Sticking paper. Distressed Manufacture
Out from 7 – to ½ 9 with my wife
Reading Life &c Major Cartwright

Saturday ~   [July] 29

Making out a list of persons likely to take shares in the London
University.
Thomas Campbell on similar business.
Richard Hassell for instruction respecting the poor Laws.
Out from 12 to 3 at M^r. Humes on sundry matters.
M^r. Fenn with Whartons Historia de Episcopatis [*sic*] and
~~Denanis~~ Decanis Londinensibus[246] – translated with him part of
the Instrumentorum Quodam [*sic*] and Historiam sides Londinenius
spectantia I – so much as related to the boundaries of St Margarets
parish – a. d. 1222 – from which it appears that the parish of St Martin
in the fields had then no existence.
Examined also with M^r. Fenn so much of Newcourts Repertorium
as relates to these matters, and so much also of Partons History of the
Parish of St Giles as relates to the same subject.[247]
Reading Life of Major Cartwright.

Sunday   [July] 30.

Examining further into the origin of the Parish of St Martin.
Writing till 6 p. m. – an essay for the Bolton Chronicle, on
machinery, wages and population.
Out with my wife from 7 to ½ 9.

Monday   [July] 31 —

Revised the essay for the Bolton Chronicle
Read it to Major Torrens.

[245] 'Minimum of wages, population, &c.'. See copy in Place Papers, BL Add. MS 35154,
fo. 121.
[246] Henry Wharton, *Historia de Episcopis et Decanis Londinensibus: neonon de episcopis et Decanis
Assavensibus a primâ sedi utriusque Fundatione ad annum 1540* (London, 1695).
[247] John Parton, *Some Account of the Hospital and Parish of St. Giles in the Fields, Middlesex*
(London, 1822).

Geo White with an essay on the same subject for the Trades newspaper – read it

M^r. Wright.

M^r. John Maclaren from the Bough [?] Mechanics Institution. wishing me to become a patron. consented.

Out from 1 to 3. looking for a pump invented by a M^r. Aust.

Examining further respecting the Parish of St Martin in the fields and am quite satisfied there was no such parish until Henry 8, made one.

Wrote letter to M^r. Hume.

Wrote letter to M^r. Campbell.

D^o ——————— M^r. Bowring[248] – all in the business of the University. Entered some books in my catalogue.

---

[248] John Bowring, confidant of Jeremy Bentham and first editor of his collected works. Bowring was active in many radical causes, including the founding of London University, acting as secretary of the Greek Committee, and editing the *Westminster Review*. See Gerald Stone, 'Bowring, Sir John (1792–1872), *ODNB*, <http://www.oxforddnb.com/view/article/3087>, accessed 29 March 2005.

August

Tuesday.   [August] 1.

Making a list of persons to be called on – and at 10 a m went with M^r. Hume and M^r. Campbell to the persons on the list to induce them to take shares in the London University.

Out from 10 to 3.

Making a list – as above for M^r. Warburton, Bowring and self for tomorrow.

Corrected the remainder of Mr Blakes letter on Chile.

Read in Vol 37 Transactions of the Soc Arts – an account of M^r. Austs pump.

Read in the Scotsman an excellent essay on profits.

Looked at Blackwoods Magazine a double number for Augst. 1826.

Wednesday.   [August] 2.

Reading for manners of the people Ordinary of Newgates account of convicts &c – 1706–1745. two vols 12 mo.

At $\frac{1}{2}$ 9 – went with M^r. Thomas Campbell to M^r. Bowring (M^r. Warburton did not keep his appointment) and then to various persons respecting the London University – out till half past three.)

Made a report of the business & sent it to M^r. Campbell.

Made a report of yesterdays proceedings and sent it to M^r. Hume.

These reports to be laid before the council of the university tomorrow.

M^r. Barry with City news – ~~Anglo~~ meeting of the Chile and Peruvian company at which he had been present.

M^r. Anderson Editor of the Trades newspaper.

M^r. Js^a Evans and his brother on sundry matters.

In our route [?] to day on University business we called on M^r. Thomas Kinder jun^r – the celebrated manager of the first Peruvian Loan swindle with Paroissien and Garcia del Rio.[249]

---

[249] Thomas Kinder floated the first Peruvian loan in Britain in 1822. James (or Diego) Paroissien and Juan García del Río were the ministers to London sent to secure recognition of Peru's independence. Paroissien, English by birth, was surgeon general in the trans-Andean expedition of José de San Martín that liberated Peru. See John Lynch, *San Martín: Argentine patriot, American liberator*, Occasional Papers no. 25 (University of London, Institute of Latin American Studies, 2001); W.M. Mathew, 'The first Anglo-Peruvian debt and its settlement, 1822–49', *Journal of Latin American Studies*, 2 (1970), pp. 82–83; Ron L. Seckinger, 'South American power politics during the 1820s', *Hispanic American Historical Review*, 56 (1976), pp. 243–244.

Kinder is an ignorant yet very smooth plausible, cunning fellow, one of the most ill looking miscreants I ever saw. He has a countenance and manner and form which says plainly – beware of me.

Looking at Blackwoods magazine.

Thursday.   [August] 3.

Examining on a large map the bounds of the ancient parish of St Magaret [sic] Westminster.

Concerting matters with M^r. Fenn relating to the Parish of St Martin.

Reading Ordinary of Newgates reports &c.

Reading and noting Partons History of Giles – for matters relating to the parishes of St Margaret and St Martin.

Read an attested copy of a grant of Land by King James for a Burial ground for St Martins Parish – which declares that King Henry 8 built the church and constituted St Martins a parish, and the reasons for his having done so.

Reading – Le Compere Mathieu.[250]

Went at 7 – p. m to see a pump made by M^r. Aust at a place in Old Street – The pump is an excellent contrivance but too little known. home at 9

Reading Le Compere Mathieu.

Friday   [August] 4.

Occupied for 6 hours drawing the boundaries of St Margarets Parish as antiently settled by an ecclesiastical award – the boundaries of St Martins parish when taken from it and of St Paul St Ann St James and St George when taken from that of St Martin. They are all outlined, on a large map for the use of the council [sic] the Judge and the Jury when the trial shall come on.

Reading sundry matters relating to the Westminster parishes.

Walked from 7 to 9 with my wife.

Writing an essay on Machinery &c for the republican.[251]

Saturday.   [August] 5.

Correcting and finishing the essay for the Republican.

M^r. Fenn on parish matters.

[250] Henri Joseph Du Laurens, *Le Compère Mathieu* (London, 1829).
[251] 'Machinery – Mechanics' Institutions'. See copy in BL Add. MS 35154, fos 116–117.

M^r. Blake with his 6th and last letter for the Morning Herald – corrected it.

M^r. Hume, a satisfactory report of proceedings at the council of the London University.

Reading on parish matters.

D^o. Compere Mathieu

Out from ½ 6 to 9 with my wife

Sunday   [August] 6

Almost all day ~~correctin~~ collating newspapers – 1797 – to 1812 matters relating to trade, condition of the people, and seditious meetings proceedings and prosecutions.

Reading sundry weekly publications.

Wm Adams on the state of his fathers affairs in reference to his coach [?] making partners – neither of them are honest men – all rogues to one another.

Reading – or rather as Bentham says squiring – "the last man"[252] —

D^o – Compere Mathieu.

Out walking with my wife 7 to 9 —

Monday —   [August] 7.

Occupied same as yesterday – Out at the Mechanics Institution in the morning.

M^r. Anderson – reprobated his conduct as misleading the people in what he said in yesterdays paper, respecting repeal of taxes as likely to amend their situation.

Out with my wife — 7– to ½ 9 went up Mill Bank to see how Lord Grosvenors plans for destroying the Garden grounds and landing the earth excavated from the London and St Katherine's docks were proceeding.

Wm Adams.

Tuesday.   [August] 8.

Reading a curious pamphlet 1716 Letter to a Country Gentleman shewing the inconveniences which attended the last part of the Act for triennial parliaments.[253]

[252] Mary Shelley's 1826 novel.
[253] *A Letter to a Country Gentleman, shewing the inconveniences, which attend the last part of the Act for Triennial Parliaments* (London, 1716). Attributed to Daniel Defoe.

NB. This is a whig pamphlet and contains their reasons for septennial parliaments.

Out from $\frac{1}{2}$ 10 till $\frac{1}{4}$ past 2 hunting all over Hoxton for a M^r. Aust the inventor of a pump.

Out at 4 – to a turner to get a model made for a fountain Inkstand.
Sorting newspapers &c &c
Mill promised to go to his house at Dorking on Monday next.

Wednesday.   [August] 9.

Sorting papers till 11 —
Out from 11 to 3 at the London Dock to see a ship fitting for Van Diemens Land. Thence to the St Katherines Dock to see the excavations there.

Out at 4 to a turner to get a model made for an Ink stand.

M^r. Bowring – a long conversation respecting M^r. Bentham's will. M^r. B made his will in 1817 when I was with him at Ford Abbey making me his executor and leaving me 1000 £ for the purpose of arranging and printing from his M. S. S subsequently Mill and I supposed he had made Bowring his executor. This does not appear to be the case, but Bowring has reason to fear that he has altered and complicated his will, and that his ~~will~~ M. S may not be properly attended to.

Promised Bowring to write an article for the Westminster Review – a sketch of the history of Parliamentary Reform.

M^r. Carlile on sundry matters.

M^r. George White, this poor devil seems unlikely to be able to raise the money necessary to pay his first instalment on the money he owes at the time. I prevailed upon his creditors to wait for it.

Sorting. Newspapers.

Thursday.   [August] 10.

Sorting newspapers —
M^r. Wright – with a small pamphlet the poor mans Friend – &c exemplified by William Cobbett.[254]

M^r. Barry – respecting his spanish book now in the hands of Murray the Bookseller. M^r. B— came to consult on the best mode of dealing with Murray for the publication of his book, and for a translation to be elucidated by plates and descriptions copied from a large and very curious Indian picture painted on both sides.

---

[254] Anon, *The Poor Man's Friend, or, companion for the working classes: giving them useful information and advice: being the system of moral and political philosophy laid down and exemplified by William Cobbett* (London, 1826).

Went at 4 to the new London Dock to see how the excavation was going on. home at 7 – went into several of the narrow lanes near May Fair and through May Fair to look at the poor people and their children – They are generally much cleaner and much more healthy than they formerly were.

Sorting newspapers —

Reading Compere Mathieu

Looking at the ridiculous and still more ridiculously written novel the last man.

Read with much satisfaction an article on the Hamiltonian system of education the 87 N° for June 1826 of the Edinburgh Review.[255] It is a system I have long recommended and very nearly the system I adopted in teaching myself, and long since practised in teaching arithmetic to others.

Friday.   [August] 11.

Reading Edinburgh Review.

Sorting newspapers, nearly all day.

Out from – 12 to 3.

Several persons called but as I have neglected to insert any thing in this diary until the present monday Augst the 14th I cannot recollect particulars.

Arranging with M^r. Aust and M^r. Money[256] respecting the putting up a pump in the kitchen and the course of the pipe thence to the well in the cellar under the print [?] house – Oh. my walk was to the new London Docks.

Saturday —   [August] 12.

Pulling down the stone in the tailors shop, with the bricklayer, and building it up again. It was necessary that I should be present all the time as the hot air flue to my room is connected with the stone, and I know that unless I directed the laying of the bricks that it would either be made useless or would let in the soot and smoke from the common flue, thus time goes.

Went to Thames Street and bought a new bottom part to the stove. In the evening read in the Edin^g Review.

[255] Sidney Smith, 'Hamilton's method of teaching languages', *Edinburgh Review*, 44, no. 87 (1826), pp. 47–69.

[256] Place's carpenter.

Sunday.   [August] 13.

Reading Dying speeches and Ordinary of Newgates account of malefactors – for manners and morals of the people.

Read and corrected a paper written by Charles Blake for the New Monthly Magazine.

M^r. Toplis – on the new silk loom. On Hagues, paddle for steam boats – explained to him its peculiar action. Sundry other matters relating to Machinery and Austs pumps —

Consented to have my name put on the list as a candidate for the committee of the London Mechanics Institution.

Monday.   [August] 14.

Arranging papers – cut from newspapers – relating to the condition of the working people – distress in 1811 [–] 1812 – machine breaking in 1812–16 – Distress in 1822.

Ts. [?] Set off at 3. p. m on a visit to M^r. Mill at Dorking.

M^r. Hackett an ingenious carpenter a man of a comprehensive understanding as to buildings, he came to communicate with me as to some particulars relating to the intended buildings of the London University – Gave him a letter of introduction to M^r. Coates at the University Chamber.

Had some conversation with my daughter Mary respecting advances made by William Adams to my daughter Jane and also with Frank on the same subject with a view to stopping such advances. Cautioned Jane also. Adams is half crazy, and by no means explicit as to his own affairs and yet he complains that he has not a friend in the world, not being able to appreciate himself he does not see that it depends upon a mans own self whether he have friends or not. He is absurd, will not conform to the customs of the world, but expects the world shall conform to his notions, and administer to his absurdities while he is to make no returns, nor any acknowledgement, and this is insanity. His conduct makes my wife very unhappy, she persuades herself that his conduct towards his wife must have been bad, and as she was her favorite [sic] child she is frequently very unhappy in consequence of her surmises.

Walked with Mill to Denisons.

Tuesday.   [August] 15.

Reading and extracting from Partons History of St Giles.

D^o Encyclopedia [sic] Progressive till 1 o clock.

Walked over Box Hill, to Headley round to Mickleam [sic] —

In the evening to Denisons.

Wednesday.   [August] 16.

Parton.

Encyclopedia [*sic*] – till 1—

Walked through Norbury Park to Fetcham, and home by the side of the river Mole.

There was a considerable run of water at Leatherhead Bridge and for some little distance above it, and at a small distance above this again there was not a drop of water in the river the bed of which was a dry lane of loose gravel. Above this near Burford Bridge there was a run of water about half as much as at Leatherhead Bridge. Mills House is called the Grove and the garden runs down to the river under Box Hill. Hence there was a run of water in a larger volume than at Burford Bridge. On the South Bank of the river at the bottom of Mill's garden is a small swallow as they are here called, that is a place, where the water is absorbed, I saw it running in and heard the noise it made in descending, the sound was just such as water would make on falling among large pebbles and discursing [?] through or amongst them.

On the opposite side of the river a little higher up is another swallow and there must be others of greater capacity lower down, or the whole of the water could not be absorbed. Made a section of the river to shew how it water might be absorbed and again regurgitated.

Thursday.   [August] 17.

Out but little to day.

Reading and extracting from Parton[,] Encyclopedia – Progressive.

Letter written to Bowring.

Reading a portion of a curious M. S on the political moral and commercial state of Egypt, written by a Capt[n] Pringle of the Royal Engineers, who has been for some time in Egypt, and is now employed on the Government survey of Ireland.

Friday —   [August] 18.

Concluded reading in Parton, arranged the extracts, and wrote notes by way of elucidation and comment. Many Proofs that S[t] Martins was not a parish until made one by Henry 8.

Encyclopedia – &c

Walked to Ranmer [Ranmore] Common and to White Down[s], home as usual to dinner at 5. p. m.

In the evening – climed [*sic*] box hill on the steep side, with Mill's 3 eldest daughters, got up by means of the box bushes —

At 8. p. m. went up Denisons hill home at ten.

The moon at the full, not a cloud above the horizon, no vapour, bright and clear beyond anything I ever saw before. The outline of the hills, and the trees on Dorkins Glory sharply defined.

{This beautiful spot has was [*sic*] I am told been destroyed and the path across the Glory shut up by the proud young M^r. Hope – the Beast of the cut picture: 1850[257]

The days as clear and beautiful as any one can conceive, hot, of the roasting kind, not close or stewing. Glorious fine weather.

Saturday   [August] 19

A long letter from John Miers at Buenos Ayres, filled with disappointments and misfortunes, nothing was going right with this painstaking persevering excellent and clever man.

Finished reading Captn. Pringles M. S. It is a very curious, and no doubt faithful narrative. Undertook to arrange the matter, to elucidate some parts and to adapt it for the Westminster Review.

Walked to Dorking – Butler Hill along the Wathing Road and round Peter's Park, at Betchworth – and thence along the banks of the Mole home at 5 to dinner.

Joined by John Mill and M^r. Graham – afterwards by M^r. John Austin. Walked up Denison's Hill and round by the fields to Dorking thence home by 10 p. m.

Sunday.   [August] 20.

Made a plan of the house; ground floor and bed room floor.
Playing about with the children till 11. a m.
Walked to White Down, thence to Wotton Park – thence to Lanes inn [?] to see a bath, and by Bury Hill to Dorking – thence home at half past 3. — Dined at – 4 — Off in the coach towards home at 5 – home at half past 8.

Monday.   [August] 21.

Many letters and papers, to see to,
Wrote a long letter to M^r. Miers.
Wrote several other letters —
Read a number of small papers and saw half a dozen persons
Walked from 4 to half past 6 with my wife to the cutt at the top of Mill, or Thames Bank.

[257] This sentence was inserted at a later date.

Arranging and sticking cuttings from Newspapers respecting the present state of the people in the Cotton and Silk manufactures.

Tuesday.   [August] 22.

Writing letters to
M^r. Frend[258] – Carlile – Coombs – Bowring – Anderson —
M^r. Fenn a long consultation respecting evidence, from sundry documents as to St Martin Parish.
Out from 11– to 3– on sundry matters of business.
Saw in the course of the day —
M^r. Sydney on Geo White affairs
Mrs Kenney – on hers —
M^r. Service [?] on his.
M^r. Barry ——— d^o.
M^r. Jno Evans sundries.
M^r. Auban respecting a review of John Miers's book for the Westminster
M^r. Charles Blake.
M^r. John Mill who introduced his friend M^r. Horace Grant.
Walked – 7– to 9 with my wife.
Wrote letter to M^r. Smith at Bolton in reply to one from him.

Wednesday.   [August] 23.

Sorting and arranging the Sessional papers sess – 1826
M^r. Anderson with sundry matters of information.
Reading Parliamentary report on Emigration.[259]
Walking with my wife from 4 to 5
Reading Edinburgh Review
M^r. Aimé respecting some books
Giving directions to Money the carpenter at M^r. Mills respecting the shelves in his library.

Thursday.   [August] 24.

Reading – Report and minutes of evidence on Emigration.
Out from 11– to $^1\!/_2$ 12 – on various matters of business.

[258] William Frend (1757–1841), member of the London Corresponding Society, close friend of Place and freethinker. He initially managed the relief fund established for Thomas Hardy and was active in London radical politics. See Place, *The Autobiography*, p. 182, n. 2; Hone, *For the Cause of Truth*, p. 17.
[259] *PP*, 4 (1826), *Report from the Select Committee on Emigration from the United Kingdom*.

Reading Report on Emigration —

A long conversation with a sensible man a M^r. Taylor just returned from Valparaiso. He gives some reason for hope that some amendment is about to take place in the opinion and in the government of the people of Chile – He brought me a long letter from Dr Leighton.

M^r. Henry Drummond, a long conversation on Languages and Language learning.

M^r. John Evans – sundry law matters.

M^r. Robinson who gossiped away an hour and a half of my time.

Reading – in N° 10 Westminster Rev.

Friday.   [August] 25.

Reading and noting Report on Emigration.

Out with my wife and Caroline from twelve to 3.

M^r. Fenn on Parish matters.

Reading – &c Emigration —

D^o – Millers Retrospect of the 18th century – Surgery Phisiology[260] [sic]

M^r. Carlile and M^r. Hassell – sundries.

Saturday.   [August] 26.

M^r. Eyton Took [sic],[261] with some account of his experience in his journeyings to the north &c &c

M^r. Roebuck[262] – d^o —

M^r. Barry – d^o – he had been since yesterday with some stock exchange people, and came to tell me what passed and of the frauds contemplated respecting, the pretensions of the Pasco Mining company.

Paroissien and a Sir Wm Temple acting as his secretary were at Potosi and the accounts they have written of the climate of that place are in direct contradiction to the experience of William Adams, who took minutes during his residence there. They say that the climate is fine, bracing, and the country salubrious. But they do not say that the heat is very great in the middle of the day and that it freezes

[260] Samuel Miller, *A Brief Retrospect of the Eighteenth Century. Part first . . . containing a sketch of the revolutions and improvements in science, arts, and literature, during that period*, 3 vols (London, 1805).

[261] William Eyton Tooke, son of the political economist Thomas Tooke and close friend of John Stuart Mill. He committed suicide in 1830.

[262] J.A. Roebuck, close friend of John Stuart Mill, who would later work with Place on the National Political Union and the Parliamentary Candidates Society. See S.A. Beaver, 'Roebuck, John Arthur (1802–1879)', *ODNB*, <http://www.oxforddnb.com/view/article/23945>, accessed 19 January 2006.

every night, and is consequently a climate to kill every european who attempts to remain there. Wm Adams says the air is so attenuated that a stranger cannot walk a hundred yards at a sharp pace without being winded, and that Captn Andrews has been obliged to sit down and recover his wind when walking at a moderate pace from his own to Adams lodgings a distance of some two hundred yards and yet Andrews is a healthy well travelled man.

M^r. Blake for an extract from Dr Leightons letter from Valparaiso.

M^r. Fenn with copies of letters from Henry 8 – to the abbot of Westminster and sundry other papers relating to the parish of St Martin.

M^r. Russell of Exeter respecting sending his son to Hannover to Mrs Hodgskins father.[263]

Out from 4 to 7 with my wife. Reading or rather examining Caulfields Anecdotes &c of Remarkable characters for notices of manners.[264]

M^r. Graham, to make enquiries respecting the mode of assessing the poor rate, and the relative amount charged on land and houses.

Sunday.   [August] 27.

Read in N° 1of the sixpenny tract the Bull-dog in which I among others am blackguarded.

Reading and noting Emigration Rep^t.

Examining for evidence of manners Caulfields – account of extraordinary characters – in 4 volumes.

Reading and noting progress of literature in U.S. North America in Millers retrospect.

Extracting from letters from Chile for Charles Blake.

Monday.   [August] 28.

M^r. Fenn, with digest of evidence respecting the parish of St Martin. And also respecting the conduct of the parish paving committee respecting people selling fruit in the street.

Examining the papers left by M^r. Fenn several hours.

Out walking three hours – Revising M. S. Respecting Egypt.

---

[263] Thomas Hodgskin's wife, née Hagerwich, was born in Hanover. They met after Hodgskin had been encouraged to visit and report on the German state by James Mill.

[264] James Caulfield, *Portraits, Memoirs, and Characters, of Remarkable Persons, from the Revolution in 1688 to the End of the Reign of George II*, 4 vols (London, 1819).

Tuesday.   [August] 29.

Reading and noting Parliamentary Report on Emigration.
Out walking 3 hours —
Writing an essay for the Bolton Chronicle
Reading. Westminster Review.
D° – Millers retrospect for manners.
Sundry persons called today and yesterday.
Evening from 7 to 10 at Tijous.

Wednesday.   [August] 30

Fourteenth Report of Commissioners of Revenue – Stamps.[265]
Out at 11 – to Rotherhithe – thence to London Docks – to hunt
up a Captain Hatch who has dishonoured his acceptance for 100 £.
This bill was given by Hatch to two Shipwrights in part payment for
the repair of a ship, and as I wished to serve these men I procured the
money for the bill, which I now fear I shall lose. Home at 3 —
Emigration Report.
Long letters from John Tester, Bradford
Wrote an answer to them.
Looked at and made extracts from several books relating to Egypt.

Thursday.   [August] 31.

Emigration Report —
Wrote several letters.
Walked from 1 to 3 with my wife
Emigration report —
Egypt —
M^r. Black who is going out to Greece with the deputy Orlando –
promised him letters.
Wm Tijou on his family affairs.

[265] PP, 10 (1826), *Fourteenth Report of the Commissioners for Inquiring into the Collection and Management of the Revenue Arising in Ireland, and into Certain Departments of Revenue Arising in Great Britain.*

September

Friday.   [September] 1.

Emigration Report to folio. 170.
Jaˢ Mill – sundry matters.
Walked with my wife. 12 to 3 —
Mʳ. Fenn on Parish matters
Reading and noting. Histoire de L'Egypte sous le gouvernment de
Mahommed Ali – par M. Felix Mengin.[266]

Saturday.   [September] 2.

Sundry weekly publication – among them Nº 2 – of the Bull Dog.
Hunting particulars from several books relating to Egyp [sic] —
Mengin – noting – and writing a paper on – for the Westr Review.[267]
Life of Dʳ Clarke
Recent Discoveries in Africa.
French Official life.[268]
At home all day.
Saw nobody.

Sunday.   [September] 3.

Reading M Mengin's work – comparing his account with itself and
other information and writing a portion for the Westminster Review.
At 5. p. m. with my wife to Mʳ. Galloway – at his earnest entreaty to
converse respecting the steam engines he had made for the expedition
in favour of the Greeks to be commanded by Lord Cochrane. On
Lord Cochranes return from S. America he came to me several times,
he was very desirous to accept offers which had been made to him
to take command as Admiral of the Greek Navy. I heard what he
had to say and offered such doubts and made such objections as
appeared to me likely to be useful to him and I particularly cautioned
him not to accede to any proposal which might be made to him
unless he saw that a sufficient force was provided for him and also
a years pay for his officers and was secured in the hands of some
principal house in the City of London. I observed that he had twice
committed, first in Chile and second in Brazil, and had been ill

[266] Félix Mengin, *Histoire de l'Egypte sous le gouvernement de Mohammed-Aly, ou récit des
événements . . . qui ont eu lieu depuis le départ des Français jusqu'en 1823*, 2 vols (Paris, 1823).
[267] The review article would eventually appear in vol. 6, no. 11 (July 1826) of the *Westminster
Review*, pp. 158–201.
[268] Three articles that appeared in the June 1826 edition of the *Edinburgh Review*.

used in both services, and I endeavoured to impress upon him as much as possible the necessity of acting with great circumspection. He promised accordingly and as on former occasions omitted to do any one material thing. Circumstances not connected with Greek affairs made it necessary for him to leave England and reside on the continent but before he set out an arrangement was made for the purchase of vessels, the building and fitting up of five steam vessels, and the supplying them with guns of 62 to carry 62 lbs red hot shot. I was originally and without my consent put upon the Greek committee, which I attended on one occasion at the particular desire of several of the members but as I saw there were no men of business in the committee and that some of the most active among them were mere tricksters I did not again attend, and did not consider myself a member of the committee. No sooner was it settled that Cochrane should go to Greece and he had accepted the offer than all communication with me ceased, I was no longer consulted neither was I informed of any steps which were taken. I afterwards learned that Sir Francis Burdett M^r. Hobhouse and M^r. Ellice had been appointed a committee to see to the arrangements respecting the vessels &c destined for Lord Cochrane, I saw Hobhouse frequently but he neither hinted to me the existence of any such committee, nor ever gave me the least hint of what was going forward, he spoke to me occasionally of Greek affairs and of Lord Cochrane probably for the purpose of ascertaining from time to time what I might happen to have learned on the subject but as I knew nothing beyond what I had seen at Hagues the Engineers who were making some boilers for Galloway, and what I saw at Galloways, who was making the boat engines, whence I drew my own inferences I was ignorant of what was going on. On Saturday May 6 Captⁿ Sheriff Cochranes friend called – (see the memorandum under that date ante) – see also under date Monday 8 May conference with Galloway and – also – Wednesday 10 May my visit to Hobhouse – and Galloway Thursday 11 May. At this time I did not know of the appointment of Burdett Hobhouse and Ellice as a war committee. Three more useless inefficient men could not have been found in London, and the consequences have been such as I should have predicted had I been informed at the time, of their appointment. It now comes out, that the vessels which have been built draw a great deal more water than they were to draw, and that not one of the boilers has capacity to produce a sufficient quantity of steam. They were made according to the orders of Lord Cochrane a foot narrower and several feet shorter than Galloway recommended. All the boats are useless, but still no great blame is imputable to Galloway beyond that of his permitting himself to be induced to take an order which he ought to have known he did not possess the means of completing within months of the time he undertook to complete it. Here too both Lord Cochrane and his brother Major Cochrane were to blame, that it was not possible for Galloway to make the engines in time. All three of them knew well enough as well from what they had heard as from their own experience that every new plan for fitting up steam vessels had been more or less defective and in most cases unequal to the expectations of the parties who made the experiments, and they should have made one of the smaller engines and tried it on board a hulk. So far all three are highly censureable. But as for the three war committee men, they knew as much about steam vessels as steam vessels know of them. As it is the vessels are useless and notwithstanding the failure has led to an ingenious and probably more efficient mode of setting boilers than any hitherto adopted. Greece and its independence has been at least for the present sacrificed to the ignorance and absurd conduct of these six persons.

Had they or any one of the 6 applied to me as they ... [indecipherable] in the first instance, none of this mischief would have happened. We should have discussed the merits of the new arrangement of the boilers, and should have certainly had a trial. We should have found five engineers, to have made each of them one double-engine, and we should have managed to have had such an inspection of the vessels while building as would have either prevented them drawing more water than they ought to have drawn, or if that could not have been wholly prevented, we should have found the means of adapting the engines to the vessels – [several words crossed out]. We should have gone into the matter, and my habits would not have permitted me to have done less than I have mentioned. I should have given all the time necessary to such an important business should constantly have attended to it, and seen with my own eyes every thing as it went on. It is now said both in the Greek committee and out of it, that Hobhouse contrived the whole matter to get Cochrane out of the way, lest somebody should set him up at the General Election in opposition to him at Westminster.

Monday.   [September] 4.

Diligently at work on the article on Mengin's book for the Westminster Review. Found it necessary to consult many other books.

M^r. Sidney respecting M^r. Whites affairs and also respecting his project of a cyclopedia for the working people. Dr Birkbeck will be the editor.

Walked from ½ past 6 till ½ past nine with my Wife round the Regents Park.

Tuesday   [September] 5.

Diligently at work on the article for the West Review.
~~Read in~~
Walked as yesterday from $\frac{1}{4}$ 4 to 7 —
Read in the evening. West Review and Quarterly Review.

Wednesday   [September] 6

As yesterday – at home all day.

Thursday.   [September] 7.

As yesterday.
Omitted to notice that on monday last Colonel Marbot, came to
me with the first volume of M Comte's book on legislation, and a letter
to introduce him to my acquaintance.[269] A long conversation with this
well experienced and intelligent man on the affairs of France, highly
instructive to me.
Several persons have called in but as I have refused to see any one
after 2. p. m. I am now much more at ease than usual.

Sunday.   [September] 17.

The last ten days have been occupied almost wholly on the article
for the Westminster Review which I have just completed. Read the
whole of the two Volumes, more than 1000 pages, corresponded with
M^r. Galloway on the subject and read some long letters from his son
Thomas who has been two years in Egypt putting up machinery. This
is the first article written by me for the Westminster Review. I know
that some persons write in Reviews for money and that a few like
myself write with a view to benefit others much more than for the
money. This article has cost me a fortnights hard labour upon an
average nine hours a day, and it will be seen or it may be seen by those
who read this and then look at the article whether such an article does
credit to me or is any thing but an example of how much time a man
may occupy to very little purpose.
NB. I never received a shilling for any thing written for the
Westminster Review.
Several persons have called and I have bestowed a small portion of
time on their affairs out of doors.
Walked generally about $2\frac{1}{2}$ hours with my wife daily.

[269] Charles Comte, *Traité de législation ou exposition des lois générales suivant lesquelles les peuples
prospèrent, dépérissent ou restent stationnaires*, 4 vols (Paris, 1826–1827).

Out to day from $\frac{1}{2}$ 11 to 3 – went to look at two houses near the Bricklayers Arms Kent Road and on the way home went on the works at the new London Bridge – the abutment on the surrey side is above high water mark, and so are the two piers on the same side, the centerings up on the second and partly so on the first arch at both of which some courses of stones turning [?] arches are laid, the centerings are enormous frames of woodwork.

In the afternoon. Mrs Kenney [?] to request me to interfere in their concerns with M^r. Reece the bookseller of whom they were purchasing his business in Percy Street. Reece having agreed for the sale and ~~agreed~~ to the draft of a legal deed for this purpose sold the business without M^r. Kenneys knowledge to another person and sent him back 140£ he had rece[iv]ed from Kenney. It is a most serious affair for Kenney. Promised to go about this business tomorrow morning.

M^r. John Galloway with the M. S respecting Egypt which had been sent to his father for perusal and correction, told me some curious particulars respecting the country.

M^r. John Fordham, who also told me some curious particulars respecting the harvest, the situation of the farmers and the consequences to them of the order in council to permit the importation of certain sorts of grain.

Read some of Sir Astley Coopers lectures – in the Lancet.

Read about 50 pages of Captn Heads rough notes on the Pampas. They do not so far contain any thing new, but they are very lively and entertaining. Capt Head was not long enough in the country to understand the people and he mistakes them much. He talks too of the Pampas as of a paradise of which they are as nearly as possible the reverse.[270]

Read the rascally publication the "Bull Dog" N° 4.

Monday   [September] 18.

Rectified the M. S for the West^r Review from the information received last night from M^r. John Galloway and sent it with a note to M^r. Bowring.

To M^r. Kenney found upon going into his case that it was not to be remedied, but that he had good grounds for an action against Reece if he chose to proceed against him. He has been most shamefully used.

Sorting and sticking papers relating to the working people. Wrote a letter of recommendation for Charles Blake to the Hammersmith Bridge Company, he is soliciting the office of Clerk —

---

[270] Francis Bond Head, *Rough Notes Taken during Some Rapid Journeys across the Pampas and among the Andes* (London, 1826).

D^o – for M^r. Service [?] D^o – to the Commissioners of turnpikes trust north of the Thames.

M^r. Carlile with a curious essay sent to him for insertion, in the form of [a] letter to M^r. Peel pointing out the evil consequences of the law as it now stands as to the offence of Pederasty and recommending its revision. Advised Carlile not to send it but to forward it to M^r. Peel.

Read 70 pages Captn Heads notes.

Read some M. S – respecting Egypt sent by Captn Pringle.

Tuesday.   [September] 19

Sorting &c. Papers

M^r. Barry with some curious particulars respecting the Rio de la Plata Mining company.

M^r. Blake.

Reading to p. 140 Capt Heads book.

Out with my wife two hours.

M^r. Burnet of Devonport having made me a present of his book, "A Word to the Members of Mechanics Institutes"[271] – read it rapidly – a curious collection of facts and opinions some of the latter silly enough; some shrewd and useful. Upon the whole the book will do good.

Writing to John Miers at Buenos Ayres.

Wednesday.   [September] 20.

Examining some papers and conversing with M^r. Fenn on parish matters.

11. to 3. out alone – a long conversation with M^r. Mill at the India House – respecting Westminster Review, the conduct of the editors and particularly of M^r. Southern. Matters relating to the London University principally in respect to a defect, in the specification of the contract as pointed out to me some days ago by M^r. McWilliam the surveyor.

Read the remainder of Captn Heads book, the captain's like another Captain, Hall, makes a very amusing book – principally by means of his imagination, and enthusiasm, some of his tales are pure inventions.

Enticed by my wife and persuaded by my son Frank to go with her to the English Opera House in the Strand to see – "the last Guerilla" – a piece enough to make a dog sick – and then Miss Clara Fisher, who when quite a child played several characters as a prodigy and fools paid large sums of money, to be <u>amused</u> by her, she is now rather a pitiful looking young woman, with a bad voice no figure and an impediment

---

[271] Richard Burnet, *A Word to the Members of the Mechanics' Institutes* (Devonport, 1826).

in her speech, she personated several characters as successfully as such an insignificant person could do. This short interlude was followed by "Presumption" (Frankenstein) a most tiresome absurd ill written and worse performed mass of sad nonsense. Have promised to go with my wife to the Haymarket Theatre on Friday.

NB. have never seen the new Haymarket Play house, and never but once before, the English Opera House.

Thursday.   [September] 21.

Wrote letters – to M^r. Hume in reply to his request to send him information respecting corporations and the way in which they impede trade commerce &c.

To M^{rs}. Harwood, and to M^r. Tooke and her affairs.

M^r. Barry. Corrected and arranged for him, a prospectus of the book he has printed. "Noticias Secretas de America." Secret Report on South America &c – by Ulloa and Juan. The object is to obtain subscribers at 2-12-6 a copy. The book is beautifully printed in royal quarto.[272]

Out two hours with my wife.

M^{rs}. Kenney on her husbands affairs.

In the evening M^r. and M^{rs}. Kenney to tea, staid gossiping 'till nearly midnight.

Friday   [September] 22.

M^r. Barry early with his paper.

M^r. Fenn. Went to the Vestry room to examine some of the parish books with M^r. Joshua Evans my friend the barrister. Met there M^r. Fenn and his attorney M^r. Burke. I think & so does M^r. Evans that we shall oust the vestry.

Walked round Holland House Kensington with my wife.

Col^n Torrens, respecting the corn laws and other matters he is to moot in Parliament.

M^r. Fenn to report progress as to the parish books.

Undertook to make a tabular digest of the matter for the use of counsel.

Went to please my wife to the Haymarket Playhouse for the first time since it has been rebuilt. Saw an Interlude or Comedy in one

---

[272] Jorge Juan y Santacilla and Admiral Antonio de Ulloa, *Noticias Secretas de America*, ... *escritas* ... *segun las instrucciones del* ... *Secretario de Estado* (London, 1826).

act called A day after the Wedding or a wifes first lesson,[273] a good lesson if people could take it on governing their tempers. It was well played all the characters being properly sustained. This was followed by the Clandestine Marriage especially well played, but not equally well dressed, half the performers being dressed in the fashion of 70 years ago and the other half in the fashions of the day.[274]

Then came the Burletta of Midas.[275] This vulgar low lived piece was got up to shew Madame Vestris's legs.[276] This Madame Vestris is a notorious [blank] who has noodled several foolish fellows to spend large sums of money on her, and it is said has annuities to the amount of 800 £ a year. She like most such women has wit and humour and modes of making herself excessively agreeable for a time, without having any passion whatever for the fellow she fools, but she also has her [crossed out] likings and therefore keeps a young man the son of a bookseller in Pall Mall as her cherie Amie. This I learned a year or more since from the bosom friend of the young man and from others. This Madame Vestris whom every play going person has run to see is in height about the middle stature or rather beneath it, but she is exquisitely formed, her arms naked from the shoulders seem equal to her legs which are both alike an uncommon thing in a woman and both set equally well in at the knees. She is just so nearly upright in her person and carries her head so well as to be straight without losing grace and ease. She is probably one of the best figures of a woman in existence, not a very handsome but lively and engaging face, defective from the lower lip to the throat. She seems to have given an impulse to the liking in the audience of the old debauchery which was very much out of fashion on the stage. It will not be revived now. Fawcett some time ago talking with me on these subjects said, Oh I thought we were going to be really respectable, but now all the whores have got carriages. This account of the matter was a fine piece of acting and would make an admirable scene in a comedy.

Saturday.   [September] 23.

M[r]. Barrys prospectus – arranged a portion of it to be inserted in the list of M[r]. Murrays books in the next quarterly review to appear on the 29th.

---

[273] Marie Thérèse De Camp, *The Day after the Wedding; or, a wife's first lesson. An interlude* (London, 1808).

[274] George Colman and David Garrick, *The Clandestine Marriage: a comedy* (London, 1766).

[275] Kane O'Hara, *Midas: an English Burletta* (London, 1764).

[276] Eliza Vestris, the first actress-theatre manager on the London stage, was well-known for her shapely and attractive legs.

M^r. Hodgskin, some conversation respecting his lectures at the London Mechanics Institution, when I told him he was deluding the audience and confirming their prejudices to their injury.[277] Hodgskin has behaved ill. He boasted to the audience that he was one of the most active persons in establishing the Institution, and claimed credit on that account, but he did not tell them, that he and Robertson had when they found they could not govern the Institution as they pleased, done it all the disservice they could, that they were the means of preventing others of us procuring money by donations which we could have easily done to have paid all the expenses of an outfit, and consequently the Institution would have owed nothing instead of owing as it does now full 5000 £. He did not tell them that he and Robertson and McWilliam alarmed the working men in the first committee and induced them to accept a much worse set of regulations than those which Hodgskin and Robertson had themselves in a sub committee agreed to. Neither did he tell them that he and Robertson clandestinely withdrew the subscription books from the booksellers, stopped the subscription and the accession of members as far as this could effect these two purposes and that they never either gave a correct account of the money which had been received or ever gave up the original minutes of the first committee, and that the consequence was the minute book does not contain any account of the proceedings of that committee. The minutes were in existence for I drew them myself and read them to the committee for approval and they were approved. Now I would expose this trickery as well as some other dirty tricks in which M^r. Brougham was concerned were it not that by so doing I should injure the society, and thus as is usual people are deceived and imposed upon by rogues and shufflers an[d] silly people who know they will not be exposed by honest men because honest men will not through them do injuries to others.

Out ½ 12 to 3– with my wife
Out from – 4 to 6– on sundry matters of business.
Reading Darwins Zoonomia.[278]
Sorting papers   Riots – among [?] the miners in 1816.

Sunday.   [September] 24.

Sorting and sticking papers.
Distress in 1811 – 1812 – 1813 —
D° ——— Luddites — d ——

---

[277] Eventually published as Thomas Hodgskin, *Popular Political Economy: four lectures delivered at the London Mechanics' Institution* (London, 1827). These lectures elaborated and extended Hodgskin's analysis of the labour theory of value.

[278] Erasmus Darwin, *Zoonomia: or the laws of organic life*, first appeared in 1794–1796.

Reading Darwins Zoonomia —

Reading in Bibliotheque Populaire[279]

L'Evangile – being history of Jesus Christ from the Evangelists but without any account of his miracles or other supernatural matters – the book contains 128 pages 4 inches long and three inches wide, it has been prosecuted at Paris and thousands have since been sold privately.[280]

Reading Darwins Zoonomia.

Monday.   [September] 25.

M^r. Fenn with the first part of the brief for counsel respecting our [?] select vestry for revisal – Read it carefully and commented on it. It is very ably drawn.

Papers – Luddites, Distress – in 1811 – 1812 – 1813.

Out from ½ 4 to ½ 6 with my wife.

Reading – Bibliotheque Populaire art. Diccionnaire [*sic*] Feodal.[281]

Wrote to M^r. Peel inclosing to him an article from the Republican on Church Yards and burial places in London. (The shutting them up)

Read for correction a small portion of Wm Adams Journal of a journey from Mendoza to Potosi by a route never before travelled by an Englishman – and from Potosi to Buenos Ayres, by the common road.

Tuesday.   [September] 26

M^r. Mill a long conversation on the conduct of the editors of the Westminster Review, and on the means necessary to establish it.

Reading M^r. Wm Adams's Journal.

Sir Richard Phillips with a crude notion of Legislation – "founded on benevolent motives." And another equally crude notion of finding out modes, "to discover the truth."[282]

Out from 4. to 6 with my wife

Went to a man to make enquiries respecting a person who has long been plundering Sir John Swinburne and found her to be a drunken

---

[279] *Bibliothèque populaire* (Paris, 1826) was a collection of historical, literary, and scientific texts for popular edification.

[280] *L'Evangile* was the fourth volume of *Bibliothèque populaire*.

[281] *Dictionnaire Féodal* was the third volume of the collection *Bibliothèque populaire*.

[282] Likely Richard Phillips, *Golden Rules for Social Philosophy: or a new system of practical ethics* (London, 1826).

woman of bad character. The man and his family in a horrid state of poverty and misery.

Reading respecting Silk Business in 1822–24.

Wednesday   [September] 27.

Finished reading Wm Adams's Journal
Out from ½ 11 to 2.
Write a letter to Jn° Swinburne including information collected this morning.
Making up my catalogue of books.
M^r. Barry with a spanis[h] book respecting Columbus, Behaim [?], and M. Otto.
Thomas Hardy with some particulars respecting the late M^r. Horne Tooke
Read Mrs Centlivre's comedy of the "Bold Stroke for a wife" – Mrs Inchbalds "Remarks" – her account of Mrs Centlivre preceding "The Busy Body" – and the biographical sketch of M^rs C – in the "Biographica Dramatica."[283]
Went to see the play with my wife.
The piece was upon the whole well got up – some of the coarser expressions retained in the play as printed by Mrs Inchbald in 1806 from the Prompt book were omitted, and some words in several places were judiciously inserted. The parts of the quakers were greatly overacted, but this very circumstance drew forth the applause of the audience. We were in a front row of the dress box near the centre of the house, and had of course the command of the pit. It is sixteen years since I was in this house and since that time the appearance of the pit has changed a good deal. Comparing the appearance, dress and behaviour of the company in the pit with ~~they~~ what it was 30 years ago, ~~they~~ it may be called a dress assembly, and the conduct of the audience corresponded to their very respectable appearance. The company in the boxes was thin and inelegant the pit was crowded.
A foolish piece called the Scape Goat followed[284] – and then the "Magpie or the Maid"[285] – a piece loosely put together, but containing some good sentiments which notwithstanding they were meant for clap traps, are useful.

[283] It is likely that Place refers here, and later in the diaries, to Elizabeth Inchbald's multi-volume *The British Theatre: or, a collection of plays, which are acted at the Theatres Royal, Drury Lane, Covent Garden, and Haymarket . . . with biographical and critical remarks, by Mrs. Inchbald . . .* (London, 1808.)

[284] John Poole, *The Scape-Goat: a farce in one act* (1824).

[285] Most likely any one of the several adaptations of L.C. Caigniez and J.M.T. Baudouin d'Aubigny, *La Pie voleuse* (1815) presented on the English stage as *The Maid and the Magpie.*

Thursday.   [September] 28.

Writing some pages. "Manners and Morals."
Out from ½ 11 'till 3 – at the London Dock on business.
Reading and noting M^r. Mill's article on Church Establishments
in N°. 10 West^r Review[286] – the notes are to aid me, hereafter as to
the mode of persecution sure to be adopted by any church when
it becomes dominant. Making references from the Index of the
Reprinted Reports of the House of Commons, Respecting Trade and
Manufacturers.

Friday.   [September] 29.

Writing – several letters on the Corn Laws – to induce those written
to – to get petitions for their repeal ready for the meeting of parliament.
Out from – ½ 12 to 3 —
Out from ————— 4 to ½ 6
Collecting materials for the article on parliamentary reform for the
West Rev[287]
Saw several persons

Saturday.   [September] 30.

M^r. Fenn on parish business
M^r. Barry with an affidavit he made in the cause Irissari v Clement
developing some curious circumstances respecting the Chile loan –
The cause being compromised the affidavit was not read.
Out with my wife and Caroline from 4. to ½ 6.
Copying a chart of the Atlantic Ocean, containing the voyages of
Columbus, from a spanish book published last year at Madrid and
containing a copy of Columbus's log book —
M^r. Tijou and M^r. Carlile in the evening.
Looked as usual at Cobbetts Register, Carliles Republican and the
Trades Newspaper.
M^r. Hume on several subjects but especially the Corn Laws.
M^r. Lang from the Hatters, with a man from the Carpenters to
consult respecting petitioning against the Corn Laws.

[286] James Mill, 'Ecclesiastical establishments', *Westminster Review*, vol. 5, no. 10 (April 1826),
pp. 504–548 – a review of Charles Butler's *Vindication of the Book of the Roman Catholic Church*
and R. Southey's *Vindiciæ Ecclesiæ Anglicanæ*.
[287] This article eventually appeared as a review of *The Life and Correspondence of Major
Cartwright*, entitled 'History of Parliament', *Westminster Review*, vol. 8, no. 16 (October 1827),
pp. 253–303.

Sunday.   [October] 1.

Copying the Chart of Columbus's 4 voyages.

M^r. Blake with a spanish paper respecting the Chile Loan.

Looked as usual at the Mirror, Hones Every day book[288] – and the London Literary Gazette.

Writing part of an article on the Chile Loan for the Morning Herald Newspaper.

M^r. Carlile at 9. p. m.

Monday.   [October] 2

Finished the article for the Herald

Read it to M^r. Barry.

M^r. Anderson Editor of the Trades Newspaper on sundry matters. Out with my wife from 1. to 3.

Read a large portion of the brief for council on parish matters, it is very ably drawn.

A long conversation with M^r. Fenn respecting M^r. Peel's new Jury act and the conduct of the Magistrates under the act – will endeavour to get it amended. {Succeeded in several particulars.[289]

Note from M^r. Hume he will take up the subject of burying persons within London &c &c – to obtain particulars.

M^r. Wallace and another Spital Fields weaver, they gave me a long account of the state of their trade, and made arrangements to procure petitions against the Corn Laws.

M^r. Meabry my co executor and trustee in Miers's estate on the business of that estate, and the evil disposition of most of the Legatees, and also the dishonest conduct of William Miers.

Tuesday.   [October] 3.

Wrote to M^r. Drummond giving him an account of the efforts making in London and in various other places to petition against the Corn Laws.

M^r. Fenn on parish business

[288] William Hone, *The Every-Day Book: or, everlasting calendar of popular amusement, etc.*, 2 vols (London, 1826–1827).

[289] This bracketed note was apparently added later. According to Douglas Hay, Peel's 1825 Jury Act transferred responsibility for returning lists of qualified jurors from petty constables to more respectable churchwardens and overseers of the poor. See Douglas Hay, 'The class composition of the palladium of liberty: trial jurors in the eighteenth century', in J.S. Cockburn and Thomas A. Green (eds), *Twelve Good Men and True: the criminal trial jury in England, 1200–1800* (Princeton, NJ, 1988), pp. 322–323.

M^r. Northouse editor of the Glasgow free press, he gave me much information respecting the cotton manufacturers. Encouraged him to request an interview with M^r. Robinson the Chancellor of the Exchequer[290] to state to him the facts he had related to me and to request him to take of[f] the tax of 2^1/$_2$ on the printing of every square yard of cotton as one means of increasing the employment of the starving people by lowering the price and increasing the demand for printed cottons, and also on the ground that, the gross revenue was about 1.250.000 £ of which 50.000 £ only reached the Exchequer.

D^r. Thorpe to canvas me in favour of one of his sons who wishes to be preacher at St Georges Hospital.

Out ^{1}/$_2$ 12. to 3 with my wife

With M^r. Henry Drummond from 4 to 5 on Corn Law and Negro slavery, devised means to procure petitions against the Corn Laws

Read very carefully in the Morning Chronicle of the 30 Sep a long account of the meeting of the County of Lanark respecting the condition of the starving weavers.

Reading Emigration Report.

Wednesday   [October] 4.

Reading emigration report.

M^r. Northouse, had followed my directions and obtained an audience of M^r. F. Robinson – explained his case fully and suggested to M^r. Robinson the injurious nature of a tax which took 1.200.000 from the purchases of printed calicoes while the exchequer received only 40.000. The figures are M^r. Robinsons. M^r. Northouse is satisfied M^r. R——— will if supported repeal the tax. Undertook to recommend to my correspondents in the cotton districts – to memorialize M^r. R the Treasury and petition ~~the~~ parliament – for the repeal.

Much conversation with M^r. Northouse respecting the state of the people near Glasgow.

Captn Henderson – on Chile matters

M^r. Blake – sundries.

M^r. Barry — d^o.

Out with my wife – 1– to 3 —

Reading the Quarterly Review No. 68. The character of the work much changed. Praises Burke for advocating, Liberty.[291] Says the French have not only benefited by their revolution but all the world

[290] Frederick John Robinson, Viscount Goderich, Chancellor of the Exchequer, 1823–1827.

[291] Richard Wellesley, 'Prior's life of Burke', *Quarterly Review*, 34, no. 68 (September 1826), pp. 457–487.

has also benefited, and will continue to do so. Condemns our Law system in toto, and calls for Codes.

Squiring Blackwood.

Thursday.   [October] 5.

Reading and making notes from the Quarterly.
John Mill —
M^r. Mill.
Out from ½ 11 to 3 – at the London Docks.
Out with M^r. Mill 4. to 5 —
Reading Emigration Report.

Friday.   [October] 6

Extract making sundry matters related to manners.
Out from ½ 11 to 3 with my wife and Caroline.
Reading in Quarterly Review. Articles – Life of Mad[ame] Genlis,[292] which contains a good account of French and English morals and Manners.

Humphreys, on Real Property – an able review recommending, M^r. Humphrey's proposal to divest the laws relating to real property of ambiguity, fraud and roguery – by a Code.[293] But both M^r. Humphreys and the reviewer admit a great deal too much as necessary for the management of real estates. Exact definitions of the law of succession are necessary not because the land has any peculiar property in itself distinct from other kinds of property but to prevent litigation and expense. The true – and the only truly useful thing that can be done is to put an end to all feudal rights and claims, to extinguish the property as real property and henceforth to let its administration be precisely the same as that of personal property. Justice can be done in no other way. It will come to this some day when people grow wiser. No registration would be necessary – or conveyancing might be done by schedules.

Reading the Republican and Cobbetts Register.

M^r. Northouse highly delighted with an interview he had at my persuasion procured with M^r. Wilmot Horton[294] who kept him to dinner much talk of emigration, of the starving scotch weavers which

[292] Richard Chenevix, 'Memoirs of Madame de Genlis', *Quarterly Review*, 34, no. 68 (September 1826), pp. 421–456.
[293] Charles Edward Dodd, 'Humphreys on the laws of real property', *Quarterly Review*, 34, no. 68 (September 1826), pp. 540–579.
[294] Robert John Wilmot-Horton (1784–1841), under-secretary of state for war and the colonies, 1821–1828, and an 'obsessive' advocate of state-aided emigration. See

will come to nothing. M^r. N. read a paper on the subject which he had drawn up for M^r. H.

Saturday.   [October] 7.

Writing an essay on Political economy for the Republican – took much pain with it, to prevent cavillers doing mischief.

M^r. Barry with a project to emigrate the poor Irish to Spain. He proposes to give up a year of his time provided his expenses are paid to go to Madrid and procure leave from the King to set down in Estramadura a large number, say 200,000 Irish catholics. He says the country is suitable[,] is depopulated and now wholly uninclosed [sic], that he has no doubt he can obtain the land for this purpose for nothing, to be held of the Crown – and of certain Grandees at an easy quit rent, to commence in two years after location, that all the emigrants would require on the voyage and Journey would be oatmeal and potatoes, and as much more of the same kind of food as would last for 6 months when they would be able to provide for themselves, and thus if about 1000 persons were thus established in several parts of Estramadura, they would soon invite others, vast numbers of whom would go at no more expense to Government than the use of transports and the expense of oatmeal, potatoes and salt herrings for the voyage and the journey, that including a family of 5 persons he supposes the whole expense would not exceed a pound a head, instead of 22£ or 25£ to Canada. Recommended him to M^r. Northouse and M^r. Northouse to him. Nothing will come of this project.

M^r. Blake – sundries.

M^r. Drummond, to tell me that he had good reasons for concluding and he named them that Lord Liverpool alarmed by the Landowners, had made up his mind to treat the subject of the Corn Laws as an open question, that is, not as a minister to interfere, that is, not to call upon his supporters to do any thing, that is, to abandon the measure altogether, as one sanctioned by the Government.

Sunday.   [October] 8.

Looked at the Trades Newspaper which in the hands of M^r. Anderson is becoming any thing like a teaching paper to the people and will shortly be extinct.

Hones every day book.

Literary Gazette.

Eric Richards, 'Horton, Sir Robert John Wilmot-, third baronet (1784–1841)', ODNB, <http://www.oxforddnb.com/view/article/13827>, accessed 10 March 2005.

Writing a number of Letters to persons in the Manufacturing Counties, to induce them to get petitions sent up for the repeal of the Corn Laws.

Monday.   [October] 9.

Writing letters as yesterday.

M^r. Barry, on his emigration project, he is to call upon M^r. Wilmot Horton and lay his plan before him, write a note – for him to M^r. Horton – and instructed him what to say at his interview for the purpose of proving to M^r. H – that he – M^r. Barry was not an adventurer. It will come to nothing.

M^r. Hume on sundry subjects – a long conversation.

1. Repeal of the duty on calico printing – promised to speak to every body likely to assist, it seems from enquiries made before a committee of the house that the duty, including all expenses amounted to no less than 30 per cent on the wholesale piece of cotton goods – and yet that Government did not receive so much as 10 per cent. This tax is bad in every way that a tax can be bad.

2. M^r. Hume proposes to move an amendment on the address to the King on his speech on opening the new Parliament – he wants me and Mill to assist him in framing it – he is to send, his own views to me – and I am to do what I can, to promote his purpose.

Out from 1. to 3– and from $\frac{1}{2}$ 4 – to 6 with my wife.

Reading. Emigration Report —

D^o Mignet – Histoire de la Revolution Francaise.[295]

Tuesday.   [October] 10.

Reading Emigration report and noting d^o

Out from 12 to 3.

Reading Lords Reports on the dignity of a peer[296] – origin and constitution of the house of commons, for the purpose of ascertaining facts, for an article for the Westminster Review, History of Parliamentary Reform —

M^r. Carlile in the evening.

Several persons called.

[295] François-Auguste-Alexis Mignet, *Histoire de la Révolution française depuis 1789 jusqu'en 1814* (Paris, 1824).

[296] The House of Lords published several reports and papers on the dignity of peers in 1826; however, volume 9 included a specific historical section. See *PP*, 9 (1826), *Second, Third and Fourth Reports from the Lords' Committees on the Dignity of a Peer of the Realm etc., etc.*

Wednesday —   [October] 11

Reading and sorting as yesterday

Report Lords – Dr Allens able remarks on d° in Edinburgh Review, Brady's Introduction to Old English History.[297] All day till 7 o clock at night except from 1 to 3. when I was out for one hour walking with my wife – and at the Chapter Coffee House with M^r. Northouse, on the project of a sunday newspaper to be called the London Free Press, which he has concerted with M^r. Hume who is to come to me on saturday on that and other subjects. Suggested to him that as the money was to be raised (2000) by shares of 20 £ each, it would be advisable to appoint two or three trustees who should receive the money and pay all outgoings – that these trustees should of course appoint him editor and another person as manager, he the editor having nothing to do with either the management account or money concerns, and know [?] nobody but the trustees, that as M^r. Ridgway the bookseller had taken a warm interest in the matter, he should be requested to be one of the trustees.

At 7 – p.m. – received N° 11 Westminster Review, in which is inserted my article on Egypt,[298] of which I am ashamed. M^r. Bowring who is no man of business could not manage to send me the proofs and the consequence is, that the article has nearly 100 errors in it, ~~nearly all~~ many of the names of places and persons are wrong spelt in many cases so absurdly lettered as to shew, an ignorance quite disgraceful to the editor, and by inference to the writer.

Read the article on Chile and La Plata – written by someone who is utterly ignorant of the country, written too in a "hop step and jump" manner, poor and miserable scarcely fit for the lowest magazine. {written by Southern. I suppose when half drunk.[299]

Thursday.   [October] 12.

M^r. Northouse had another interview with M^r. Wilmot Horton when he learned that, Horton and his master Lord Bathurst, who is as stupid as a post, intended to give the Corn Law question the go by. Horton urged as a reason, in which the sapient M^r. Northouse concurred that for a time the introduction of foreign corn would injure

[297] John Allen, 'Lingard's *History of England*', *Edinburgh Review*, 42, no. 83 (April 1825), pp. 1–31. Place mis-states the name of the author of the book under review. A second part of this review, not covering 'Old England', was published in the forty-fourth volume, in June 1826.

[298] 'The state of Egypt', *Westminster Review*, 6, no. 11 (July 1826), pp. 158–201.

[299] Henry Southern, 'Travels in Chile and La Plata', *Westminster Review*, 6, no. 11 (July 1826), pp. 202–230 was, in part, a review of John Miers's book.

our manufactures, because the Poles and Germans would not want manufactured articles but Gold & silver!!!

A long conversation with M^r. Mill on M^r. Hume's intention to move an amendment on the address, at the opening of parliament. Agreed to dine with Hume and discuss the matter with him, but if necessary to consult previously on the several subjects, the heads of which he is to give me on saturday,

Some talk on the sad way in which the Westminster Review is conducted, and the means of putting it on a better footing – Major Cartwright and reform, and the way in which Biography should be written. Parliamentary Review &c &c

Yesterday, Mary engaged herself as daily governess to Jno Talbot Esqr for three weeks – and to day comes with a proposal that Jane should take the situation of Governess in the family, to which Jane consents and is to see Mrs Talbot tomorrow morning to settle terms. Of the attainments of these girls, any one might be proud, they are to an uncommon extent acquainted with the grammars of the English – French, and Italian Languages, conversant with that of the Latin, the German and Spanish, know a good deal of Algebra and something of Mathematics, play pretty well on the Piano especially Jane, who also to a considerable extent understands the principles of perspective and draws, not badly. They are both extremely industrious in the acquisition of book learning – good geographers and well read in history.

A long conversation with Colonel Torrens on the most prominent matters likely to be brought before parliament in the ensuing session – what part he should take – how he should conduct himself – who were likely to work with him – what certain members would do – and the means of keeping himself independent of cabals, which never fail to compromise a mans usefulness.

Out alone half past 4. to 6.

Reading and correcting a proof of a petition for the repeal of the corn Laws, drawn by Col^n Torrens.

M^r. John Fordham – much information on the state of the agricultural labourers and their probable condition supposing the Corn Laws were repealed. M^r. F. does not understand the principle of wages and therefore draws erroneous conclusions, he for instance supposes that if the taxes on beer, malt &c were taken off, the labourers would be able to buy beer, he does not see that the real wages of the labourer in a redundant population are no more than according to the habits of the country will enable him to subsist and propagate his race and that he must have the same real wages, and will have no more while the population is redundant, whether the taxes remain or are all repealed.

Reading Mills – Logical article in the West Review[300] – on the formation of opinion which, notwithstanding the heterogeneous way in which he used the word <u>mind</u> is a very clever essay.

Friday.   [October] 13.

Reading – in West^r Review M^r. Bowrings article on the Greek Committee and Count Palma's pamphlet.[301]

Squiring Mrs Grote's article on Mad Genlis,[302] compared it with that on the same subject in the quarterly.

M^r. Grahams article on pleading well done[303] – and likely to be useful —

Coln. Torrens went over the draft of the petition for repeal of Corn Laws – and sundry other matters.

M^r. Fenn on M^r. Peels Jury bills. M^r. Dawson had again addressed a circular note to the Sheriffs &c of caution respecting the defects and inconveniences occasion[ed] by some clauses in the bill which he on the part of M^r. Peel disclaimed as his, and gave notice that the bill would be amended in the next session. Agreed with M^r. Fenn that there was only one way to make the bill efficient in respect to special juries and that was to define the qualification.

M^r. Geo White – talked the matter over again – agreed that the best way would be to propose that instead of a bill to explain and amend the Jury bill, it was advisable to make an effort to procure the Jury bill to be repealed and to reenact it ~~with~~ in an improved form so as to have only one act of Parl relating to Juries. That as there ~~was~~ is as much in the act which is useless – and as useless words and enactments are generally mischievous, we agreed that each of us should recast the act then meet and discuss the matter, and when complete, that M^r. White should take it to M^r. Dawson, and that in the meantime M^r. White should apprise M^r. Dawson of what we were doing.

M^r. Oliver.

M^r. Barry.. [sic]

Out – from ½ 1 to 3.

[300] James Mill, 'Formation of opinions', *Westminster Review*, 6, no. 11 (July 1826), pp. 1–23.

[301] John Bowring, 'The Greek Committee', *Westminster Review*, 6, no. 11 (July 1826), pp. 113–133: a review of Count Palma's account of the steam-boats used for Lord Cochrane's expedition.

[302] Harriet Grote, '*Memoirs of the Countess of Genlis*', *Westminster Review*, 6, no. 11 (July 1826), pp. 134–157.

[303] George G. Graham, 'Law abuses: pleading – practice', *Westminster Review*, 6, no. 11 (July 1826), pp. 39–62.

M^r. Wm Tijou's from ¹/₂ 4 to 6. – with his three sisters respecting an arrangement with their father to settle a further sum of 1500£ on them, which he has partly promised me he will do.

Carried by my wife to the Haymarket playhouse – saw The Purse[304] – and the Jealous wife,[305] both well performed.

Read the Republican.

Saturday.   [October] 14.

Carefully correcting the revise of Col^n Torrens's petition against the Corn Laws.

Drawing up a motion for M^r. Hume for a return of the number of Houses in all the Parishes – extra parochial places, Precincts and liberties within 5 miles of St Pauls cathedral, a plan for making the return, and the form for digesting the information into a table.

Drawing up for d^o a motion for a return of all burial places within the same limits – the size, situation and other description of each such place, and the number of bodies buried or deposited in each during the last 3 years ending at michaelmas 1826.

M^r. Blake.   M^r. Barry.

M^r. Northouse on the subject of his intended weekly newspaper, has made an arrangement with M^r. Merle respecting the management. He and M^r. Merle have adopted all my suggestions and will act on them – this is a great deal more than I expect will be done – and if they so far deviate as to commence the paper hastily and before at the least the 2000£ have been paid into the hands of the trustees, the paper will not succeed. The prospectus is to be sent to me to day for correction.

Out from ¹/₂ 12 to 3 – with my wife.

[Paragraph scratched out and unreadable.]

M^r. Robinson the painter, who told me of the state of the fine old banquetting hall of K[ing] John at Eltham, which I will take a walk to see.[306]

Sunday.   [October] 15.

Finished reading Report on Emigration.

---

[304] William Reeve, *The Purse, or Benevolent Tar* (London, 1794).

[305] George Colman, *The Jealous Wife: a comedy* (London, 1761).

[306] Likely a reference to Eltham Palace, Greenwich, which in 1827 would become the subject of a popular campaign to save the Great Hall from demolition. J.M.W. Turner was one of a number of contemporary artists who popularized the ruins. The site became a Royal Palace in 1305, thus long after the reign of King John.

M^r. Blake, a long lesson to him on his own conduct and manners, and advice to him how to conduct himself, in future with a view to his own advantage in the world.

Out from ½ 1– to 3 with Frank.

Reading – noting and extracting from the Lords report 1820 on the dignity of a peer.

M^r. Carlile, ½ 9 – to ½ 10.

Monday.   [October] 16

Reading some of Mrs Inchbalds remarks on the Inconstant – the Beau's Stratagem – the Provok'd Wife – and the Provok'd husband – D^o in the Biography Dramatica D^o Chalmers's Biographical Dict. with a view to the elucidation of manners – read also the Provok'd Wife, and squired the other plays and wrote three pages of observations this occupied me from 11 – to ½ 12 last night, and from ½ 7 to ½ 8 and from 9 to ½ 11 this morning. Thus goes much time to little purpose, and yet what can one do better, that is what that is better can be done by me just now.

Piddling among books even in this way is however trifling a real source of great enjoyment, which never fails, never surfeits, and never makes a man worse while it seldom fails to make him better or at least prevents him getting worse as he grows older, for I am decidedly of the King of Prussias opinion that if man could live for ever they would be too depraved to be endured by one another, that is, the whole race with few exceptions do become more wicked as they advance in years, at least until their desires become somewhat languid, and the consequent lives of quiet induces [*sic*] them gradually to withdraw from active exertions in the affairs of the world, for it is quite certain that those who are unable from any cause to do this until absolutely incapacitated do become worse and worse to the end of the chapter.

Went with – my son Frank – M^r. Wm Tijou – and M^r. Watkins to Woolwich to see the dock yard, but principally the Smith Shop which has been completed since my last visit. This is the grandest thing of the kind in the world – the Blowing machines – and hammers are worked by two steam engines – the weight of ~~the~~ each of the two large tilt hammers is ~~4 ton,~~ 4 ¼ tons, and each fall through the distance of about a foot. Went on board the Kings new Yatch [*sic*] which M^r. Tijou is guilding.

Dined at M^r. Tijous at 6 – and remained there till 11.

Tuesday.   [October] 17.

Found some copies of the prospectus of the London Free Press, left by M^r. Northouse last night, – on each of which was written that the subscription was to be paid to me. Wrote to M^r. Merle M^r. Northouse's coadjutor to say I had not authorized him to say this and that I should decline receiving the money.

Out from 11. to 3 – on sundry business respecting – two shipwrights – at Rotherhithe thence through the Surry [sic] Docks – home.

Looking at Mrs Inchbalds Remarks on some plays in her edition – and at Biographica Dramatica – for matters relating to manners.

M^r. Thelwall respecting some lectures on English Literature, which it is wished he should deliver at the Western Literary Institution.

Wednesday   [October] 18

Last day of the State Lotteries. thus has at length – this demoralizing nuisance but [sic] put an end to. let us hope that no plea of necessity will be again admitted as valid for again permitting a state lottery.

Examining the Indexes to the Volumes of the Commons Journals for matters relating to

1. Parliamentary – Reform
2. Westminster
3. St Martins. Parish

Found a petition from the Vicar and Church Wardens of St Martin, 8 W. III. in which they claim to be a select vestry in consequence of a faculty obtained from the Bishop of London in 1662 and confirmed in 1637 [sic; recte 1673][307] This will put them out of Court.

Made a copy, from the entry in the Journals – of petitions from St Margaret, St James, and St Martins, wrote a short comment and left it with M^r. Fenn. Think it is quite conclusive against the Vestry.

Out ¹/2 11 to 3 – at M^r. Barings on account of Chas Blake. At the London Dock as yesterday. Obtained him employment as a clerk in the Country house of Messrs Barings.

Examining Indexes of Journals – and Journals – as before.

Thursday.   [October] 19.

M^r. Mill a long conversation on various subjects Political Economy Jurisprudence – &c &c.

[307] See *JHC*, 11, 2 March 1696, p. 481 in *Journal of the House of Commons: volume 11: 1693–1697* (1803), pp. 480–486, viewable at <http://www.british-history.ac.uk/report.asp?compid=39257&strquery=select%20vestry>, accessed 16 August 2006.

M^r. Eyton Tooke, to return some parliamentary reports respecting Ireland on which he has written an article for the Westminster Review which he requested me to read in M. S.[308]

Out from 12. to 3 – on the business of M^r. Tijou and his daughters – Gave M^r. Sheriff the Attorney – instructions to convey the sum of 1500£ part of the money to be paid by Wm Tijou to the use of his sisters. – $^1/_2$ 1– to 3 with my wife.

M^r. Barry on sundries ——

M^r. Blake, gave him the best advice in my power as to his duty and his conduct at Messrs. Barings.

Wrote out the form of a petition against the Corn Laws for the Sailors of the Tyne and Wear, to serve as a model for the working classes in that neighbourhood.

M^r. Fenn on Parish business

Write to M^r. Parkinson of Sunderland Steward to the Loyal Standard Association of Seamen declining to accept a bill to complete the payment for a ship the seamen have had built.

Searching the Journals Dom Com[309] for matter relating to Parliament and Parliamentary Reform, Westminster and the Act 1. E. 1. c. 7. and making extracts.

At 10. p. m interrupted by Dr Forster who staid till nearly $^1/_2$ 11[.] He had some metaphysical notions which he wished to expound. Locke he said made a mistake respecting personal Identity, it did not L— supposed consist in memory. I am not the person I was at one year of age because I do not remember the sensations I then had. This said Dr Forster follows from the doctrine of Locke altho he means to prove the contrary. I had sensations when I was a year old of which I am not now conscious, ergo. I am not the same person, thus Locke mistakes. Dr Forster was delighted with his discovery but could not persuade me that it was worth any thing. Of what use can it be to ascertain, if that be possible whether I am or am not the same identity I was – a year, a day or an hour ago. That I am – I – at this instant is in fact all I can know, and all that I need be concerned to know for any useful purpose, all the rest may be taken for granted either way, as far as reasoning is concerned, for it can never make any difference in the result, be the inference either the one or the other.

Friday.   [October] 20.

Hunting the Journals – &c as yesterday.

[308] W. Eyton Tooke, 'State of Ireland', *Westminster Review*, 7, no. 13 (January 1827), pp. 1–50.
[309] I.e., *JHC*.

M^r. Calder respecting the payment of an annuity granted to me by a M^r. Smith for whom he is a trustee. M^r. C— explained the nature of his trust and promised payment in future.

Out from $\frac{1}{2}$ 11 to three with my wife – to Paddington to collect some rents – and to Brompton Square to see . . . [crossed out] Mrs Chatterley respecting the payment of 300£ or 400£, to a M^r. Oliver on account of Goods to be shipped to his son in law M^r. Savery. [This sentence crossed out.]

Colonel Jones – has recovered a book of mine which I lent to the Hon^{bl} H. G. Bennett some years ago, but will not let me have it unless I go and breakfast with him, which I am to do tomorrow morning.

Hunting – the Journals – principally for particulars respecting the Triennial Act – 16 Charles. 1.

M^r. Hodgskin respecting his translation Baron Du Pins work, Mathematics Practically applied,[310] and respecting the intended popular encyclopedia —

At night looked at the Comedy "Made a wife and have a wife"[311] which my wife, Frank and Jane have gone to see – induced thereto by their desire to see my friend Kenneys new piece – "The [illegible]."[312] It is remarkable that Mrs Inchbald in her remarks on this comedy, merely says that the women are detestable, when the truth is that the whole of the characters without one exception are detestable.

Saturday   [October] 21.

Breakfast with Colonel Jones and his lady at N$^{\underline{o}}$ 7 Upper Gloucester St Dorset Square, and got my book. A very curious scene occurred after Mrs Jones retired with a creditor of Henry Grey Bennets – with whom Jones quarrelled but as it is neither fair nor useful to expose ones friends private weaknesses I shall on this as on other occasions mention no particulars.

Home at 11 – made some notes on Manners in reference to the Comedy "Made a wife and have a wife"

Out with my wife at 1 – went over the extensive Coach Manufactory of Hobson Adams and Co – Late Hatchetts in Long Acre – then walked till 3.

---

[310] Baron François Pierre Charles Dupin, *Mathematics Practically Applied to the Useful and Fine Arts by Baron C. D.: adapted to the state of the arts in England by G. Birkbeck* (London, 1827).

[311] Perhaps a garbled reference to Elizabeth Inchbald's own *Wives as They Were and Maids as They Are* (1797).

[312] Playwright James Kenney (1780–1849). Unfortunately, the handwriting at this point is illegible. It appears that only one new work of Kenney's appeared in 1826: *Benyowsky; or, The exiles of Kamschatka*. However, one of his most popular comedies, *Love, Law, and Physic*, appears to have been re-staged in 1826 as well.

M^r. Blake with a petition he had copied for repeal of the Corn Laws.

[Paragraph crossed out.]

M^r. Aimé, some conversation respecting books, and prices of Books.

M^r. Fenn went through the first 7 volumes of Commons Journals looking for matters relating to the Parishes of St Margaret, and St Martin.

A long letter from M^r. Farrar at Bradford Yorkshire.

In our conversation this morning Col^n Jones shewed pretty clearly that in some parts of the country much more evil was produced by the Courts of Request than would be exist were the law to declare that no one should have any remedy for any sum under five pounds.

Hunting the Journals – Dom Com.

NB. This has been one of the finest days ever seen at any time of the year. A Glorious day.

Sunday.   [October] 22.

Sorting and arranging parliamentary papers —

D$\underline{o}$ d$\underline{o}$ letters from William Adams and his wife in South America. To be bound in volumes.

Reading in the Parliamentary History portions of the reign of Charles I – This portion of our history always makes me uncomfortable and I never look at it with out pain. That a miscreant king should have the power to inflict so much misery on a people as this sad rascal did is lamentable indeed had he 50 heads he ought to have lost them all, long before his miscreant head, fell from the block, if it would have prevented mischief. It is hardly less painful to contemplate the condition of even the mass of the better sort of people as they are called, ignorant, superstitious, wilful and childish, the very few who could and would have done them service were unable and thus, the nation reverted to kings again, to a base a domineering aristocracy, to proscriptions and murders and excessive taxes and many miseries and misfortunes which might have been avoided.

Reading and correcting part 3 of M^r. Fenns Brief – 15 folios.

Looking at a french copy of "Le Decameron de Jean Boccace." {Bought yesterday for M^r. Best – an illustrated copy.

Nobody called to day but M^r. Blake with some papers —

|| NB This day just the reverse of yesterday. it has been a continually raining since day break, with a very thick and gloomy atmosphere.

Monday.   [October] 23.

Sorting and arranging the letters from South America, written by
Wm Adams and his wife – to be bound on one quarto volume.

M^r. Holland Wine Merchant of Coopers Row, with a letter from
M^r. Prowse the accountant &c introducing him and a spanish
refugee named Argelick – who has some wine which he says in [sic]
100 years old, and M^r. Prowse supposes that I can introduce him
to some gentlemen like [sic] to become purchasers. They left two
samples, which with their card, I promised to give to M^r. Hume and
M^r. Hobhouse.

M^r. Geo White on sundry matters

Hunting the Journals Dom Com. and making extracts.

M^r. Blake late in the evening to report on his situation at Barings.

Long letter from Squire Farrar at Bradford respecting the working
people and petitioning for repeal of the Corn Laws

Tuesday —   [October] 24.

Pulling the gas stove in my room to pieces, stopping the brickwork
with cement and putting the stove together again.

M^r. Hume, with heads of matters for his intended motion of an
address to the King on his speech at the opening of Parliament. Went
through them all with him, suggesting alterations as to matter and
form, adding some particulars, and taking away others, occupied full
two hours in this way – If what he will say could be fairly reported in
the newspapers it would produce a great sensation. This matter is not
to be talked about since no one can be relied on to assist as every one
ought to do, and because the whigs if they knew what he meant to
do would supersede him by some miserable nonsense of their own, as
it is they will do next to nothing and M^r. Hume will be able to shew
many very important matters to the people through the house.

Out from 1 to 3 – [crossed out]

Reading and noting from Hansards Parliamentary debates for
M^r. Hume

M^r. Carlile respecting reprinting the article Ecclesiastical
Establishments from the Westminster Review

Copies from Journals Dom Com – an article for M^r. Fenn.
St Martins Parish.

Wednesday.   [October] 25.

Writing an essay for the Bolton Chronicle on the Equalization of
Wages and Minimum D^o.

M^r. Barry – says the wines left by M^r. Holland are very fine. M^r. Hume who says he is a judge of such wines is to have a sample of each, and will endeavour to serve the Spaniard.

Making out a statement of the Estate of the late John Miers – to this day.

Reading and noting Parliamentary Debates for M^r. Hume.

M^r. Fenn with some curious papers relating to the parishes of St Giles – St Margaret – and St Martin copied from papers in the British Museum.

M^r. Frederick Birkennorin [?] on his return from the East Indies after an absence of 13 years, very little altered. Much conversation on the country about Calcutta – manners of the natives and residents – war with the Burmese &c &c – many curious particulars gleaned from him.

Looking over some accounts in the matter of Miers estate.

Out from 4 to 6.

Hunting and Noting from Journals Dom Com – matters relating to Parliament.

Thursday.   [October] 26.

Cleaning the sashes taken from the ceiling of my room this morning – to be put up again tomorrow morning. This occupied me and John till $^1/_2$ 11.

[Crossed out.]

Mrs Chatterly respecting [Crossed out] wrote to his father – to request him to sell stock and and him p pay me from 300£ and 400£, and in a letter to [crossed out] he wrote a note to me to receive it and to pay it on his account [crossed out].

Reading some curious M S. respecting Church Yards, Burial Places, and the customs of ancient and modern nations respecting the dead. These papers were sent to me by Hume, for the purpose of being noted for his use in parliament. On my sending him a letter which appeared some time since in the Republican on the nuisance occasioned by burials in London and other towns, he with his usual industry, and desire for information wrote to several learned persons, travellers, &c for information, as well natives as foreigners, and thus obtained the papers, I have been reading.

Hunting Journals Dom. Com.

M^r. Blake.   M^r. Carlile.

Friday.   [October] 27.

Reading the very clever article on the age of Chivalry, by John Mill in the 11th N<u>o</u> Westminster Review.[313]

Reading – long letter from John Miers at Buenos Ayres.

Wrote 12 pages observations thereon advice, news, and accounts relating to his family.

Extracts – relating to improvement in London – connected with – its Salubrity. In respect to the St Katherines Docks now excavating – about 7000 persons will be expelled from perhaps the worst rookery in all London, certainly the worst when its extent is considered —

John Mill – respecting some Parliamentary Books —

W<u>m</u> and Edward Ellis. some conversation respecting the ship W^m and Henry sent by the Blockading Squadron at Buenos Ayres to Rio, with the machinery for the mint in her. Wm Ellis supposes the underwriters will pay me the insurance.

Hunting Journals Dom Com Vol. 7. matters relating to parliament.

Saturday.   [October] 28.

Reading – several small periodical pamphlets – as usual.

Marking on portion of Harwoods Large Map the spaces occupied by the London Dock, and intended to be occupied by the St Katherines Docks.

Out from – 11 – to 3 – on sundry matters of Business. viz. M^r. Oliver – the attorney – respecting M^r. Evans my attorney – respecting – some houses at Paddington – and in the New Kent Road – met Mr. Mc Creevy who told me some particulars respecting the state of Printing. M^r. Calder who told me a long story about a trusteeship from which he has to pay me 40£ a year. M^r. Cullen the barrister a long conversation respecting the Greeks, Burdett – Hobhouse – Ellice – Cochrane – Galloway and Hume. To Leadenhall Street to inquire the character of a M^r. Maynard who wishes a lease of the two houses in the Kent Road – he will not do.

Went to M^r. Henry Drummond at 4 – he shewed me a very good paper on currency he had written for the Literary Gazette in reply to an article in that publication. Much conversation on the Corn Laws – Currency – and Jury Laws.

M^r. Evans the Bookseller and Auctioneer of Pall Mall, he told me some news respecting the present state of the bookselling business – and the comparative value of books.

[313] J.S. Mill, 'Modern French historical works – age of chivalry', *Westminster Review*, 6, no. 11 (July 1826), pp. 62–103.

Col^n Torrens – is willing to do all he can to get a meeting of such Titled and other landowners as may be willing to publish a declaration against the Corn Laws – M^r. Drummond says he must cooperate with M^r. Whitmore.

Looking over two, Booksellers catalogues.

Hunting Journals Vol. 7.

Sunday —   [October] 29.

Bell klanging [*sic*] all the morning.

Reading "a Philosophical Dialogue concerning decency" &c – g [?] to 1751.[314]

Writing an article for the Trades Newspaper.

Hunting Journals and making extracts. Vol. 7.

Reading – Parliamentary History same period.

Monday.   [October] 30.

Arranging papers, and making some extracts.

M^r. Geo White and M^r. Sidney one of his principal creditors – full two hours investigating M^r. Whites affairs which terminated in a resolution to call a meeting of his creditors and propose to them to take an assignment of all his property now and hereafter until his debts are paid.

M^r. Ireland an old acquaintance whom I had not seen for many years he is going out to New Holland and wished me to assist him if I could to procure him a grant of Land. He is to state his case in writing, and I am to get some one, to make interest for him at the colonial office – this must be through M^r. Hume.

M^r. Barry respecting some Plates of Chilian costume, much talk of what passes in the City respecting Burdett Hobhouse Ellice and Hume in respect to the Greek Committee Greek Loans &c &c

Reading some parts of a translation from the Spanish of a quarto volume, "Historical Investigations upon the principal discoveries of the Spaniards in the Ocean in the 15 cent^y and beginning of the 16 cent^y in answer to the memoire of M. Otto respecting the true discoverer of America &c &c Madrid – 1794."[315]

---

[314] Samuel Rolleston, *A Philosophical Dialogue Concerning Decency: to which is added a critical and historical dissertation on places of retirement for necessary occasions, together with an account of the vessels and utensils in use amongst the ancients* . . . (London, 1751).

[315] Cristóbal Cladera, *Investigaciones históricas sobre los principales descubrimientos de los españoles en el Mar Océano en el siglo XV. y principios del XVI: en respuesta á la Memoria de Mr. Otto sobre el verdadero Descubridor de América* (Madrid, 1794). Otto's memoir, referred to in the title, appears to be lost.

Notes respecting manner[s] in 1751 and 1756. from books published at these periods.

Hunting Journals. Vol. 7 and making notes.

Tuesday   [October] 31.

Long letter from M^r. Longson of Stockport in vindication of his conduct in which he shows plainly that he is a great rogue. I shall take no notice of him.

Letter from M^r. Northouse regretting that I should refuse to have my name inserted in his prospectus for the London Free Press – as the receiver of money for shares, he is like many others who never take the trouble to make themselves acquainted with the whole of a case but content themselves with as much as suits their immediate purpose. If I had received the money as he proposed I should have made myself personally responsible for its application, and might have been compelled to return it to the parties that paid it to me, notwithstanding I had paid it for the establishment of the paper – shall write to him tomorrow. People busy he tells me in getting up petitions as I requested for repeal of the Corn Laws.

Letter from M^r. Baines of the Leeds Mercury requesting inform-ation as to the expected conduct of ministers in relation to the Corn Laws.

M^r. Samida with a bundle of papers relating to his case with the Treasury respecting the sale of some cotton under peculiar circum-stances. I am to draw up a petition to the House of Commons for him. &c &c.

A long conversation with M^r. Bruce respecting Greek affairs – Hume, Burdett Hobhouse Ellice and Bowring.

M^r. Barry same subject he had been conversing with some City men on Change [?] and other places and he says there is but one opinion of the conduct of these gentlemen and that is detrimental to their character.

Copying from Journals Dom Com Vol. 7 – time of the Common-wealth. There was too little knowledge in the land at this time to turn the propitious circumstances to account in the right way. And then as now too little honesty in many public men, or a good and popular government would have been established.

A long conversation with M^r. Mill on Greek affairs and the parties concerned. Both of us regret exceedingly that M^r. Hume should have been induced to have taken Greek Scrip, or to have had anything to do personally with the money. And more so that his love of money should have induced him to take the difference to make up the loss he had incurred.

~~That~~ May [?] M{r}. Hume's connection with the Greeks Loan which has now brought obloquy on him he is much to be blamed, he should not have taken the scrip at all nor in any way have touched their money or stock. I told him this and supposed he would not do either. When however he was afterwards accused by the Greek deputies of impeding the cause of Greece in consequence of the scrip he held, he came to me and said he would sell and put up with the loss. This was the first time I heard that he had taken scrip, I was very sorry, but having heard what he had to say advised him not to sell at so considerable a loss as he must at that moment sustain but as there could be no doubt that the price would rise to hold the scrip until it came to par and then to offer it to any one in the Greek committee, saying I never intended to deal in Greek scrip or bonds or to make money in any such way, take these Bonds who will, now that the market is still rising, and I shall be done with them. I gave this advice seeing that the obloquy of holding scrip at all was upon him, and that to hold it could do him no further harm, and that thus openly dispossessing himself of them would free him from all further imputation. He however persisted and told me afterwards that he had sold at a loss of about 1200£ which he said he did not mind. But he never told me that the loss had been made up to him. If he had hinted at any such transaction [it is] probable I should have advised him on no account to take the money. It was however his love of money which in this case overcame his prudence. So far as an ex parte case can go he seems to have acted very reprehensibly and can scarcely fail to have his usefulness greatly impaired by the transaction.

Wednesday.   1. November

Reading in Blackwoods Magazine
Writing letters to
   M^r. Baines – Leeds
   M^r. Northouse – Glasgow
   M^r. Bingham
Looking at accounts in Miers's estate and making out forms for W^m
Miers to fill up respecting certain sums of money received by him.
   Out with my wife 1– to 3.
A couple of hours in the dining room with a parcel of young folk
collected for dance.
Reading Noctes Ambrosianae in Blackwoods Magazine for
November.[316]
Reading – carefully, a long article by McCulloch on the Corn Laws
in the Edinburgh Review. Vo. 44 – p. 319.[317] This is by far the best
essay which has appeared on the subject, notwithstanding his account
of tithes is not correct. He says tithes are not a tax on farm produce
in this country but a charge on rent, and he endeavours to prove
it by shewing that a large portion of the land is tithe free, but he
has erroneously persuaded himself that the price of raw produce is
governed by the untithed land, and not by the tithed land, he has
failed to shew this. Raw produce is raised in price by the tax of tithe.
   Reading a letter from M^r. McDougal cotton spinner Glasgow,
promising to procure petitions against the Corn Laws, and giving
me a terrible picture of the state of the people, in the western part of
Scotland.
   M^r. John Evans on sundry law matters.
   Looking at my wife's company from 11– till 1– a m.

Thursday —   [November] 2.

Looking at the 5th Report of the Commission of Woods and Forests
improvements near Charing Cross the Strand &c &c[318]
   Out from 12 to 3 with my wife
   Reading in Edinburgh Review articles.

[316] John Wilson, 'Noctes Ambrosianæ, No. XXIX', *Blackwood's Magazine*, 20, no. 119 (November 1826), pp. 737–756.
[317] J.R. McCulloch, 'Abolition of the Corn Laws', *Edinburgh Review*, 44, no. 88 (September 1826), pp. 319–359, a review of 'Mr. Jacob's *Report on the Trade in Corn, and on the Agriculture of the North of Europe. Presented by Order of the House of Commons, 14th March 1826*'.
[318] *PP*, 14 (1826), *Fifth triennial report of the Commissioners of His Majesty's Woods, Forests and Land Revenues*.

I. Independence of the Judges, hung upon a pamphlet of Lord Kinnaird respecting the election of Scotch Peers.[319] So long as there are Peers, it is perhaps advisable that those who sit for Scotland should be appointed in the best possible way, instead of the present which is one of the worst possible ways. But both Lord Kinnaird and the Reviewer talk sad nonsense of the loss and inconvenience the public sustain, from the sons of scotch peers being prohibited from sitting in the house of Commons for Scotch Burghs. Of what real use these sons of Scotch Peers, could be to the people in any way cannot be shewn. It is very probable that not one of them unless better qualified than they at present are would be elected by the people did the choice of representation really and truly belong to them.

The Reviewer has spun out his article to great length, for "the seller [?]" for certainly he might have said all he has said about the judges good as it is in about $\frac{1}{3}$ of the space he has occupied.

II. Letter of Madame Maintenon and the Prince Montbary [sic] written I suppose by Sir James Mackintosh it has all the air of his Holland House toad eating about it.[320] It is just such a paper as a man would scribble down off hand as he read or looked over the books, for the purpose of picking up small talk. The books seem however to be characteristic and useful, and so is the concluding page of the Review of the them [sic], in its warnings of the consequences to nations, of having Kings and Courts. The page has I apprehend been written by Jeffrey as a summing up of the subject. It is a remarkable circumstance that contrary to the usual course of events Jeffrey as he grows older grows less whigish [sic], and more of a republican.

iii. Licensing system.[321] A lively well written satire on the system – proposing the only true remedy – doing away with Licensing altogether, or rather permitting every one who chuses to take a license and open a public house. Had Grey Bennett not disgraced and exiled himself as he had done the Licensing system would have been destroyed. His conduct is the more lamentable as we have no man in the House of Commons to fill his place.

Commons Journals. Vols. 6 and 7

---

[319] Henry Brougham, 'Independence of judges', *Edinburgh Review*, 44, no. 88 (September 1826), pp. 397–413, review of Charles Lord Kinnaird, *A Letter addressed to the Peers of Scotland* (London, 1826).

[320] Place was correct: James Mackintosh, 'Court of France', *Edinburgh Review*, 44, no. 88 (September 1826), pp. 413–441, review of *Lettres inedites de Madame de Maintenon à la Princesse de Ursins and Memoires de M. Le Prince de Montbarey*.

[321] Sydney Smith, 'Licensing of alehouses', *Edinburgh Review*, 44, no. 88 (September 1826), pp. 441–457, review of Thomas Edwards, *A Letter to the Lord Lieutenant of the County of Surrey, on the Misconduct of Licensing Magistrates, and the Consequent Degradation of the Magistracy* (London, 1825).

Godwin's History of the Commonwealth[322]
Humes – England – Salmons Chronology till past 11. p. m

Friday.   [November] 3 —

55. years of age.

M[r]. Fenn with some curious documentary evidence extracts from records respecting the Parish of S[t] Martin in the fields. Examined them and made arrangements for a judicious use of them in the forthcoming trial.

M[r]. Black with a project which some man has to set fire to the sails of vessels. Told me some curious matters relating to Greek affairs, and of some persons in respect to transactions in the Greek Loans. He sails for Greece in a few days. The ship he is to go in has been detained some weeks because no one would advance money to pay her freight. She is loaded with Guns & balls for the Greek service, and the Balls are now to be sold to pay the freight – so she will carry Guns but no balls for them.

M[r]. Mitchell respecting the affairs of M[r]. Geo White.

Received 12 petitions from Bradford Yorkshire to be presented to M[r]. Marshall[323] against the corn laws —

Colonel Torrens who had also received 12 petitions from Bradford. Much talk respecting the new parliament & the course which will probably be taken by ministers, by the paltry whigs and by the no party men. There is some chance that a nucleus will be formed in the new House of Commons of a few men who are too discreet to join the worn out palsied Whigs, and are better informed on the true mode of Legislating than men have hitherto been. Cautioned Torrens against joining the Club at the Clarendon in which the miserable whigs stultify every fresh catched member.

Out this day from 1 to 3 with my wife

Looking at "the London Spy complete in 17 parts" – 4th. Ed – 1753 – for manners

Edinburgh Review. Art. Phrenology a priding [?] unreadable article.[324]

Journals Dom Com – till 11. p. m

---

[322] William Godwin, *History of the Commonwealth of England from its Commencement to the Restoration of Charles the Second*, 4 vols (London, 1824–1828).

[323] John Marshall (1765–1845), MP for Yorkshire, 1826–1830.

[324] Francis Jeffrey, 'Phrenology', *Edinburgh Review*, 44, no. 88 (September 1826), pp. 253–318, review of George Combe, *A System of Phrenology*, 2nd edition (Edinburgh, 1825).

Saturday.   [November] 4.

M[r]. Hume has a letter in the Morning Herald addressed to the Editor in reply to some remarks of his, on his M[r]. H— s conduct with respect to the Greek Loans. And in the same paper and in the M. Chronicle, is an address or appeal to the public and a set of documents explaining the transaction, from these it appears that M[r]. Hume having become a commissioner for the first Greek Loan after he had taken the bonds was called upon to consent to the sending of some part of that loan to Greece, but that owing to the civil war then waging in Greece and the uncertainty into whose hands the money might get he refused to consent, and was in consequence accused of refusing his consent on account of his own interest in respect to the stock he held, this induced him to sell, the Greek deputies became the purchasers and held the stock until it rose above par, and then they who had gained the difference offered to pay it to him and he accepted the offer having sold at a loss after refusing to wait, and as his love he should not have accepted the offer, his love of money however got the better of his understanding, or he would have forseen [sic] the probability of what has now happened, and the mischief the imputation could do to his reputation, and the mischief to others through him. It is much to be lamented that he took the money.

All the morning sorting and sticking cuttings from newspapers – relating to Trade – Corn – Manners [–] Law &c &c

Reading London Spy for Manners.

Note from M[r]. Hume evidently written under strong feelings, requesting me to come to him tomorrow morning at 11 – and to persuade M[r]. Mill to accompany me. Inclosed [sic] was a note to Mill which I sent to him with my note M[r]. Humes note to me and received for answer. "We must by all means see him. If you call here at half past 10 we will walk through the Parks together.["]

Reading in Edinburgh Review an excellent article on the "Parliamentary Reports and Review.["][325] Only a little too whiggish here and there, a good and pretty fair castigation of the self importance of some of my friends.

A dull article on the Established Church.[326]

M[r]. Barry [–] he says City people are not satisfied with M[r]. Hume's explanation, he they say should not have been a scrip holder in the first instance and should not in the second have taken the money from the Greek deputies, and in this I am compelled to concur with them.

London Spy for manners.

[325] Henry Brougham, 'Parliamentary history', Edinburgh Review, 44, no. 88 (September 1826), pp. 458–490, review of Parliamentary History and Review (London, 1826).
[326] Thomas Arnold, 'The Church of England', Edinburgh Review, 44, no. 88 (September 1826), pp. 490–513, review of An Episcopalian, Letters on the Church (London, 1826).

Sunday.   [November] 5.

Arranging books and paper.

Out from ten to two, with M^r. Mill at M^r. Hume's. Found him somewhat agitated, but satisfied that he had done no wrong to any one. He had he said resolved to return the money.^{a} To this he was evidently induced as well by his own feelings as by those of his wife, ~~and~~ by the Times Newspaper which called upon him to do so and by the John Bull which had to the surprise of us all, justified him in the transaction, regretting however his taking the money, and suggesting that he should return it. Mill was of opinion at first that he had better return the money. I saw no reason why he should do so. The money would not go to the Greek Government and he would not be thought one bit better of for throwing it away. Mill thought there were a considerable number of well meaning weak minded persons who would be satisfied with Humes conduct if he returned the money, and so thought Hume. ~~To the~~ I maintained that more people would conclude that he kept the money as long as the matter was unknown and only paid it when he was by fear compelled to do so, and further that they would say, knowing as we do M^r. Hume's attachment to money he would never have paid so large a sum had he not been quite conscious that he had no just right to hold it. ~~Finally Mill~~ Another reason was that if he paid it before tomorrow it would be said that he kept it till the last moment and then only paid it to stop the mouth of Luriottis.^{327} It was at length agreed that, he should not tender payment, until it was seen whether M Luriottis would reply tomorrow to M^r. Humes statement I contending that no good could result from his paying the money at all, and that if M Luriottis did not reply to M^r. Humes statement that he M^r. Hume had no more to say and no more to do. Finally it was settled that M^r. Hume should meet me and M^r. Mill at my house tomorrow afternoon a little before 5 o clock, to determine the matter. The mischief which arises in consequence of men who act in public matters forgetting the strict course they ought to pursue and shutting themselves as to all personal considerations out of the question is dreadfully mischievous. I can say most truly that nothing but this determination on all occasions in the many public and difficult circumstances in which I have acted has alone preserved

^{a} That is the amount of the difference he has received. [Footnote.]

^{327} Andreas Luriottis, one of two deputies (the other being Jean Orlando) sent by the Greek government to arrange foreign loans in order to assist the Greek independence movement. See G.F. Bartle, 'Bowring and the Greek Loans of 1824 and 1825', *Balkan Studies*, 3 (1962), pp. 61–74 and Robert E. Zegger, *John Cam Hobhouse: a political life, 1819–1852* (Columbia, MO, 1973), pp. 120–137.

me from imputations of self interest with which among all the vile accusations against me I have never been charged.

Advised M^r. Hume very strongly to avoid mixing himself up in any way with either Ellice or Bowring, both of whom are jobbers and [deletion] as indeed that letters and papers in M^r. Humes hands prove, altho I wanted no proof beyond my own knowledge of the men and their conduct on particular occasions.

Reading the concluding sheet of M^r. Fenns brief – for correction.

Noting a coloured map for counsel.

London Spy for manners —

Godwins History of the Commonwealth.

Monday   [November] 6.

Writing some pages respecting Manners and Morals.

M^r. Fenn on Parish affairs read with him two statutes in Latin in the Statutes at Large 23 Hen^y 8 relating to exchanges of Land in the Parish of St Margaret Westminster and comparing the same with maps to shew that the parish of St Martin did not then exist.

Wrote a paper for M^r. Hume as an explanation of his connection with the Greek Loan transactions.

A long letter from M^r. H. Drummond on the licensing system, sent it with some alterations to the Morning Chronicle.

M^r. Geo White on his affairs.

M^r. Hume and M^r. Mill. M^r. Mill had seen M^r. Colson, M^r. Hay [?] – M^r. Black M^r. Brougham M^r. Grote and several other persons every one of whom were of the opinion that M^r. Hume should not because he could not return the money to the Greek deputies without doing more harm to himself and to the public by lessining [sic] his utility than he would do by keeping it. The reason were [sic] that it would be said he had bribed Luriottis to silence, he Luriottis [illegible] known [?] to be a man trick – and also that he would not have given back the money, had he not been conscious that it was not his own.

A long talk on a project of Broughams for a tract society which if it could be carried into effect would be of great use.[328] But my opinion is that it will fail. Mill goes into it with Brougham and Denman & Lushington and others[329] – It is to publish two sheets periodically octavo double columns for sixpence each number to contain a treatise, on morals or politics – or political economy – or science – and they calculate that the sales will pay the bookseller, give him profit and pay

[328] The origin, it appears, of the Society for the Diffusion of Useful Knowledge.

[329] Thomas Denman and Stephen Lushington, both MPs, both later judges, both worked with Brougham in the defense of Queen Caroline.

also those who are to compose the essays. My fear of failure arises from the price, ten times as many would be sold for 3^d as will be sold for sixpence. The only way to have even a chance of a large sale is by giving the bookseller about 150£ or 200£, to make the intention thoroughly known, and that it is to be conducted under the auspices of the men who are promoting it, and this must be attended to at once.

M^r. Marshall to give Ellis's lectures on Political economy at Leeds, and a reverend gentleman is to do the same at Hallifax [*sic*].

Occupied thus till 6. p. m

Attending the creditors of Geo White did him all the service I could, agreed that he should assign his property – and consented to be a trustee for the creditors with M^r. Sydney – and M^r. Harrison the Printers.

Home at 9 – Reading Godwins Commonwealth.

Tuesday.   [November] 7.

M^r. Flight the organ builder with an account of an invention by which he was to make his fortune, by a newly invented paddle wheel for steam boats. After much cunning to conceal in what way the wheel was to act I found that the paddles moved perpendicularly in dipping and rising – I then told him that it was an old plan, that his paddles were regulated by an excentric [*sic*] wheel which had been used more than 10 years ago – he admitted that I had described the invention, and there poor fellow his fortune ended.

M^r. Geo White and his brother on his affairs.

M^r. Sydney a conversation with him respecting the publication, talked of by M^r. Mill yesterday. It came out that this was the Popular Cyclopedia about which M^r. Sidney had frequently consulted me, but in a new form. M^r. Sidney says he is willing on reasonable terms to go into Brougham's project, but agrees that for so cheap a work, it is necessary that my views as to making it notorious should be taken by the Brougham-ites & says he will have nothing to do with it unless they do take means to make it sufficiently notorious, but will go on with his own project of a Popular Cyclopedia. Promised him to explain all these matters to Mill. If Brougham's party will subscribe money enough and see that it is judiciously laid out, the work will pay. If not – not.

Letter from Seamen of South Shields on Corn Law Petitions – replied to it.

Letter from Joe [?] Parkes on Parliament and Chancery, with a bundle of my collections on Parliament.

M^r. Toplis, on matters connected to the London Mechanics Institution the expenditures of which exceeds its income, on mechanics as a science and respecting lectures on mechanicks [?] which he is going to read at Plymouth and Exeter.

M^r. Barry with some Spanish books.

M^r. John Mill.

Perusing draft for a deed to convey to me in trust 3285£ due from Wm Tijou to his father. 1500£ to be the property of M^r. Tijous 3 daughters and the difference to be received by me and paid to him.

Reading Godwins Commonwealth.

Wednesday.   [November] 8.

Note from M^r. Bowring mentioning a calumny respecting him at Brooks's propagated on my authority – note in reply – that not one word was true nothing having been said on my authority.

M^r. Geo White on the detail of his affairs, settled the course he is to follow.

Out from 12 to 3.

Mrs Austin on the affairs of her brother M^r. Philip Taylor – after much conversation I promised to see M^r. Philip and M^r. Edward Taylor tomorrow morning at 11.

Note from M^r. Ed Taylor wishing my assistance.

M^r. Neal, to say Mrs Austin having seen her brother M^r. John Taylor wished me to see her again before I saw her brothers – to call upon her at 11 tomorrow.

M^r. Tooke on sundry matters.

M^r. Miller M^r. Humes secretary with several notes from his friends all advising him not to return the money. A letter also from M^r. Hume to M^r. John Black of the Chronicle for my perusal to see if there was any objectionable matter in it, saw nothing but what ought to be said, ~~and~~ told him so in a note, ~~and~~ advised him to shake off the whole matter and go on preparing himself to move an amendment to the address on the opening of parliament, and by no means to permit the circumstances in which he is placed to impair his utility.

Thus occupied till 6. p. m.

M^r. Blake – M^r. Barry with some curious spanish prints relating to Bull Fights.

Wm Adams – conversation on the country about Famatina in S America.[330]

Godwins Commonwealth.

[330] Famatina, in the province of La Rioja, Argentina, was the site of several silver mines that had attracted British capital investments. My thanks to Seth Meisel for this information.

Thursday.   [November] 9.

Out soon after 9 am. With Mrs Austin on her brothers affairs.
Thence to the Manufactory in the City Row – a long conversation on
the embarrassed state of affairs of Taylor and Martineau and the best
mode of settling them. A long debate on the propriety of an address
written by M^r. Edward Taylor respecting the British Iron Company
from which his brother M^r. Philip had been removed as manager
and M^r. David Muskett who appears to be an incompetent person
being put in his place. Convinced them apparently that it would be
injudicious to print M^r. E Taylors address – or to appeal in any way
to the public. Thence to M^r. Richard Taylor who had advised the
publication – he not being at home left a note, to stay him. Thence to
George St Westminster to M^r. Austin to say what had occurred.

A long letter from M^r. Hobhouse at Paris telling me what I was as
well acquainted with as he could be, this is as a ruse to introduce, as he
has done at the end a complaint against Galloway and an imputation
to clear himself. This is brought in merely en passant, ~~he~~ and then
comes a request that I will write to him at Dover on his return home
on the 11– or 12–. He wants to feel his way, and to have a letter from
me which if in his favour he may shew & which if not in his favour he
may not shew, but having thus ascertained my opinion act accordingly.
I shall not write but will examine him when he comes to town and tell
him freely my opinion. There is a note from Cochrane in the papers
to day in which he exculpates, Burdett – Hobhouse – Ellice – and
Ricardo, and insinuates blame on Galloway. That Galloway is greatly
to blame cannot be denied and ought not to be concealed, but he
is not one jot more to be blamed than Cochrane himself and those
whom he has named, and perhaps less to be blamed than most of
them.

Looking through 3 Sale Catalogues of Books.
Reading Godwins Commonwealth.

Friday.   [November] 10.

Finished examining the Parliamentary History: Vol. II – and
commenced Vol. III – for matters relating to Parliaments and Reform
of Parliament.
Making extracts from Vol. 3.
Reading Godwins Commonwealth.
———— several small publications.

Saturday   [November] 11.

M^r. Geo White on his affairs, advised him how to proceed.

Wrote to M^r. Jackson on Parish business.

M^r. Tijou with a draft of his will, badly done, promised to write one out tomorrow. Much conversation on his affairs, particularly respecting his daughters. Went over the draft of a deed to convey 500£ to each of them from the money due to him from his son Wm Tijou in which I am to be Trustee.

Colonel Jones – about Bowring – he was the man who told B— what had been said at Brooks's. Bowring like a fool as he is, took my note to Bentham and almost persuaded him to deny [?] ~~that~~ for Bowring that he did not owe him 3000£ by a public declaration to that purpose in the newspaper.

M^r. James Brooks respecting his Fathers estate and the conduct of some of the parties.

M^r. Chapman – foolish gossip.

M^r. Gilbee, who has promised to see M^r. Brown the Attorney and endeavour to persuade him to continue Mrs Harwoods [inserted] her payments from her Dower which he has lately suspended.

Parliamentary History. Vol. 3.

Godwins Commonwealth.

Sunday.   [November] 12.

Arranging papers and books.

M^r. Jackson the publican with a number of papers and the lease from the Commissions of Woods Forests and Land revenues of a house he has built near the Regents Park for a tavern on the faith of having a licence which the Justices are now endeavouring to prevent him having preference being given to a man who has not laid out a shilling and for a house with a clause in the lease forbidding the house to be a public house, read his papers and advised him what to do.

M^r. Blake —

Out from 1 to 3 —

M^r. Carlile on sundries but more particularly respecting reprinting Ecclesiastical Establishments from the 10th Number West Rev.[331] Wrote to Bowring ~~the~~ on the subject.

M^r. Wm Tijou on his own affairs and to consult on those of the Western Institution.

Index to the Journals of Dom Com Vo. 2. hunting for references respecting parliament.

---

[331] Mill, 'Ecclesiastical establishments', pp. 504–548.

Monday.   [November] 13.

M^r. Geo White and M^r. Sidney on M^r. White's affairs – concerted measures to stay proceedings against him.

Yesterday M^r. Hobhouse on his return from the Continent came to me and we had a conversation on the aspect of affairs and respecting the circumstances relative to Greece. M^r. Hobhouse had seen Lord Cochrane at Marseilles, he was resolute in his purpose and said he would finish the war with the Turks in 3 months if he had the vessels he wanted. M^r. Hobhouse was very anxious as to the course he ought to take, and my advice to him was that he should make no appeal and no explanations in a public manner, he was exceedingly vexed to hear that he was inculpated, and endeavoured to shift the blame on Cochrane, saying he went out of town and when he came back to London he to his surprise found that Lord Cochrane had given the order to Galloway for the Steam Boats, and he had therefore nothing to do with it. This I observed was his fault and that it was an enormous fault, he being one of three into whose hands these matters had been put, he as well as Burdett and Ellice were bound to see the business properly executed, and not to permit either Cochrane or anyone else to act as if he and he alone was the war committee. He is to come to me to day to talk further on the subject.

Out this morning with my wife from 1 to 3.

[Section crossed out.]

Made M^r. Tijous will, he has now done justice to the utmost of his power to all his children of both families. To his legitimate family he has behaved handsomely all his circumstances considered.

Writing to John Miers.

Reading in Hume and Godwin period of the Commonwealth.

Hunting for information in Vol V. Statutes of the Realm.

Tuesday.   [November] 14.

Writing several letters some on my own some on other peoples business.

Out from ½ 10 to 3. At the Western Institution to meet M^r. Papworth the surveyor. Went with him and a committee of the society to view Dibdins Theatre in Leicester Place and a house &c in Leicester Fields formerly occupied by Sir Joshua Reynolds for the purpose of ascertaining, if either, or which of the two would be most eligible for the purposes of the Institution. M^r. Papworth is to report.

[Section crossed out.]

With M^r. Papworth over a house which he had been building for M^r. Ackermann at the Corner of Beaufort Buildings Strand. A singularly well adapted house for the purposes intended.

At 4. M^r. Hume and M^r. Ald^n Wood a long conversation respecting Greek affairs and, parliamentary matters. M^r. Hume is recovering his spirits and will proceed as he intended – on the Kings Speech.

M^r. Hobhouse, a long conversation on Greek affairs, he detailed seriatim the whole of the business respecting Cochrane and the Steam Boats. It seems that Orlando and Luriottis engaged Cochrane to go out as the Admiral of the Greeks, but that when they came to terms Cochrane demanded 57.000£ should be paid to him in advance, this the deputies were unwilling to pay and they referred the matter to Burdett, Hobhouse & Ellis, who all concurred in the impropriety of paying the money to Cochrane. After disputing for four days, Cochrane agreed to take 37.000£ which the deputies were willing to pay him provided he would sign an agreement to take the command, this he refused. The deputies then said they would pay the money if Burdett Hobhouse and Ellice would receive it and guarantee as far as they could that Cochrane would take the command, this they also refused, at length it was agreed that the money should be paid into the hands of Sir Francis Burdett, to be by him paid to Ld Cochrane, how and when he should by circumstances think himself warranted in paying it. The money was accordingly paid to Burdetts account at Coutt's, & laid out in Exchequer bills which are now at Coutts. The interest has been paid to Lady Cochrane. This was the whole of the transactions in which they were concerned they never were a war committee and never undertook to do any thing. The ordering of the steam boats was wholly the affair of the deputies and Cochrane who of course did as they pleased. Thus if what M^r. Hobhouse says is correct neither he nor Burdett nor Ellice are at all to be blamed in this affair. The most remarkable circumstance in this affair relating to Hobhouse is that he did not on Sunday last tell me, he had nothing to do to do with the matter to do with ordering the steam boats and that neither he Burdett nor Ellice had ever undertaken to do any thing in the affair.

M^r. Hobhouse brought some long letters addressed to me from Bolton which had been lying at his chambers more than two months. Reading them and replying to them.

Commons Journal. Vol. I for matter relating to the Bill of Rights.

Godwin from $\frac{1}{2}$ 10 to near 12. p. m.

Wednesday.   [November] 15.

Received a number of copies of the Article Ecclesiastical Establishment reprint from the Westminster Review, sent copies, to several persons. N. B. this and other tracts are paid for by a subscription, of those who take them for distribution.

M^r. Adcock to shew me some plates and drawings for a work on steam engines, by Dr Birkbeck & Henry and James Adcock, they are beautifully got up and all the parts are singularly well expressed.[332]

Letter from South Shields on the Corn Laws – Answered d^o.

Looking over a sale and a booksellers catalogue.

Out at 12. to M^r. Nettleford [remainder of paragraph crossed out]. Home at $\frac{1}{2}$ 3.

Examining Journals – Dom Com Vol. I. Petition of Right.

Vol – 5. Statutes of the Realm D^o.

M^r. Carlile. at 10. p. m.

Godwins Commonwealth —

Thursday.   [November] 16

Geo White he must surrender to the Kings Bench this morning we cannot save him from two of his smaller creditors who are absurd and vindictive. Hope yet to be able to settle his affairs.

M^r. Sidney on Geo Whites affairs and respecting the Tract society. it is agreed to go on ~~with~~ as the society is to furnish the means of making the project known as I suggested to Sidney and if they do this sufficiently and use these means discretly [sic] the thing will go on at least for a considerable time and do much good, but it will not produce profit to the society as they seem to persuade themselves it will.

M^r. Hayne, the engineer, he has some improvements in machinery which he wishes me to see. He is extremely anxious for the return of John Miers to join him in his business.

Colonel Jones says that Hobhouse's explanation as far as it goes is well enough, but that he has not stated the whole of the case, that altho not formally appointed to be a war committee it was already understood that Burdett Hobhouse and Ellice were to manage all matters relating thereto in England, that he and all concerned fully expected it of them.

M^r. Charles Austin[333] a long conversation on sundry matters relating to Political Economy and Jurisprudence

Out with my wife from 1. to. 3 – At M^r. Mill's who has the Gout and cannot stir out.

[332] George Birkbeck . . . and Henry and James Adcock, etc., *The Steam Engine Theoretically and Practically Displayed*, nos 1–2 (London, 1827).

[333] Charles Austin was a prominent London barrister and rather 'unorthodox Benthamite'. See Wilfrid E. Humble, 'Austin, Charles (1799–1874)', *ODNB*, <http://www.oxforddnb.com/view/article/906>, accessed 19 January 2006.

Col[n] Torrens who is somewhat puzzled with the annoyance of his pretended Whig friends, who he says are advising him not to do any thing this session of Parliament, telling him that if he does he will be called a talking busy fellow and that he will lose himself. Were he to follow this advice they would say at the end of the session that he was a poor useless creature. I advised him as I have often done before, not to make speeches, but to say whatever he thought was necessary on subjects which he thoroughly understood, and not to go beyond them, that he would thus if he had any discrimination soon ascertain his own standing when he might act accordingly. The fact as I told him is that the whigs already dislike that the people who are likely to petition as well as those who are petitioning against the Corn Laws, are much should advert to Colonel Torrens in the way they are doing, and still more to hear as I have taken care they should hear that already many petitions have been sent to him.

M[r]. Thelwall to read a letter he had sent to the John Bull Newspaper in consequence of John having said that he was the Kings Lecturer and had changed his principles – a matter not worth notice.

M[r]. Fenn on Parish affairs.

Extracting from Journals. Dom Com matter relating to the Triennial act. 1640.

D[o]– May's history of the Parliament.

Reading Godwins Commonwealth.

Friday.   [November] 17.

A large packet of letters from poor crazy Miss Hammerton – returned these with a note – to say I would not see her, but would attend to her requests as was proper if made to me by some friend of hers.

M[r]. Geo White —

M[r]. Sullivan an absurd Catholic some [illegible] on superstition.

To M[r]. Mill at ½ one home at 3 —

M[r]. Hume, will send me on sunday his draft of the proposed amendment to the Kings speech, on sunday which I have promised to examine, and report to him respecting it.

M[r]. Barry.

Reading and Noting. Hume. Rapin.[334] Rushworth[335] – early part of the reign of the intolerable miscreant Charles. 1. Taking notes

---

[334] Paul de Rapin Thoyras, *The History of England, as well Ecclesiastical as Civil*, trans. Nicolas Tindal (London, 1726).

[335] John Rushworth, *Historical Collections of Private Passages of State, weighty matters in Law, remarkable proceedings in Five Parliaments. Beginning the sixteenth year of King James, anno 1618, and*

&c – How any man who has the least claim to understanding can palliate the conduct of this atrocious man and his advisors seems very strange. And who that reflect on the circumstances which then took place, and the probable result of the proceedings of the court had they not been most manfully opposed by the singularly great and good men in the house of commons can withold [*sic*] the praise preeminently due to them. Not that we have any lack of such men now, but constituted as the house of Commons ~~now~~ is such men will not put themselves to the expense trouble and inconvenience of endeavouring to procure a seat in such a den.

Saturday.   [November] 18

Rapin. Rushworth —
Geo White and a person whom I engaged to make up M^r. Miers's accounts.
Mrs Chatterley. Coln Torrens
Out from 2 to 3—
Rapin Rushworth Journals Dom. Com.

Sunday.   [November] 19.

At work hard all day at Rushworth Rapin – Hume, Nelson and the Journals of the House of Commons in the early part of the Reign of Charles. 1.
One hour sawing wood for exercise. the day miserably wet and foggy.
In the evening M^r. Joseph Parkes much interesting conversation respecting M^r. Bentham his connection with Bowring and the state and preservation of his M. S. M^r. Parkes as well as every one else who is really a friend to M^r. Bentham, regrets that he should be so much as he is under the control and management of Bowring, but this seems at present to be unavoidable. Bowring gives much of his time to him, dines with him, and takes him out with him now and then, and for this Bentham undoubtedly owes something to Bowring. Bowring also panders to him, is his toad eater, and can therefore command him, and as something of the sort is necessary to M^r. Benthams comfort, to deprive him of Bowring without substituting some one in his stead would if it could be done, make him unhappy.

ending the fifth year of King Charles, anno 1629. Digested in order of time and now published by John Rushworth, 7 vols (London, 1659–1701).

Monday.   [November] 20

Met the person who is to make up Miers's estate accounts at 10 o clock went through some of the accounts and set him to work – thence to the City on business home at $\frac{1}{4}$ past two and found waiting for me M^r. Hobhouse. a long conversation on the Greek Steam Boats, the conduct of Lord Cochrane ~~and~~ Galloway and the Greek Deputies Himself Burdett and Ellice. Advised him as well as I could. Advised him also to pay to Ransoms, the balance overdrawn nearly 100£ ~~at Ransoms~~ above the subscription received ~~to~~ toward defraying the expenses of the last Westminster Election.

M^r. Parkes came in the morning and said that he had mentioned what I had told of him of M^r. Humes intention to move an amendment to the address on the Kings Speech to M^r. Marshall of Leeds the Member for Yorkshire who was desirous of seconding M^r. Hume.

At $\frac{1}{2}$ past 3 M^r. Hume came with his address. Went through it paragraph by paragraph and word by word, made it as perfect as we could, omitting several important matters, for the purpose of making it short and quite clear to the commonalty. Agreed to write to M^r. Marshall to say M^r. Hume was willing he should second him and would be at home to him from nine to twelve tomorrow morning – Wrote to M^r. Marshall accordingly.

Writing to John Miers at Buenos Ayres – and to Dr Leighton at Valparaiso, until this minute half pas[t] 9. p. m.

Picking out references for M^r. Hume, respecting some words and the form of expression in his address to shew if necessary to the house that the language is parliamentary, and has been used at various times, by eminent men and also by both Houses in former times.

Tuesday.   [November] 21.

Writing to M^r. Say at Paris,[336] on the state of affairs here, particularly respecting Greece, and also respecting my son Tom who is at Paris. In this letter I have I think fairly and clearly stated the matter respecting Cochrane Galloway, Burdett, Hobhouse, Ellice Bowring and Ricardo's and as M^r. Say will probably shew the letter to some of the members of the Parisian Greek Committee I have had a copy made, that should any thing be hereafter said the parties named, all or any one of them may see what I have said.

Omitted yesterday to say that M^r. Hume and I were interrupted by Colonel Torrens, to whom however some advice which may be useful

---

[336] Jean-Baptiste Say (1767–1832), the French political economist, first met Place in 1814. They remained in contact with one another thereafter.

was given. But Torrens it is evident is playing a game in which he may
not and I hope will not be a gainer. He admitted that he did not mean
to take a manly decided part, as M[r]. Marshall has done but to act
cautiously, that is to feel his way to some place or office for the sake of
the money which he like others who live beyond their incomes, often
endeavour to make a seat in parliament subserve.

In his Register of Saturday last Cobbett says if no one will call
a meeting in Westminster on the Corn Laws he will. The City has
not, Southwark has not, many other places have held meetings and
Westminster ought to meet. But it happens that in Westminster, those
who call meetings are generally left to pay a considerable portion
of the expense which must be incurred. The three last meetings
cost me nearly 24£ and I will not again except indeed upon some
extraordinary emergency put myself forward in any public matters
of this sort. Westminster is a singular place. The Electors will come
to meetings when the preparations have been made but will neither
attend to the matters necessary to prepare for a meeting nor subscribe
towards the expenses. They will vote for a popular candidate even
when by doing so they offend a large number of those who deal with
them but they ~~would~~ wil[l] let any ministerial man walk over the
course unless the whole of the preparatory matter ~~was~~ were done for
them and unless all the expenses [were?] provided for. For after all
there never was so many as 150 out of the 16,000 who on any occasion
contributed any money, not perhaps so many as 100 who gave ~~so much
as~~ each 20/− some few have however given larger sums, and many
have subscribed pretty often.

Wrote letters to M[r]. Doherty[337] at Manchester on Corn Laws and
Reform of Parliament.

[Paragraph crossed out.]

Wrote an essay for the Bolton Chronicle on equalization of wages.
Object to procure a select committee of the House of Commons on
the subject.

Rushworth. the Parliament 18 Car. I 16 Jany. 1621. to 19 Dcr 1621.
making notes till ½ 10 p. m.

Wednesday.   [November] 22.

Omitted yesterday to notice that the King went in State to open
the Parl[iament]. He came along the Street. The day was fine, but the
concourse of people and carriages was much less than usual. There
was no particular cause of complaint either against the King or his

---

[337] John Doherty (1798–1854), well-known trade unionist, political radical, and later
factory reformer, to paraphrase the subtitle of Musson and Kirby, *Voice of the People*.

ministers, but on the contrary more than usual cause to be satisfied with both. The King is quiet and does not interfere[,] he has lately given several sums of money 1000£ at a time to the subscription for the Spital Fields weavers and to the cotton weavers in the north. The Ministers had done much for trade and had on the apprehension of a scanty harvest on their own responsibility opened the ports to admit certain kinds of grain, which was pretty generally acknowledged by the people to be a wise measure. Still the attendance was small and the applause but partial. The fact is and it is of much importance the reverence for Royalty is greatly decayed. The persecution of the late Queen went a considerable way in breaking down this absurd and mischievous reverence.

~~Out from 12 to 3 at M^r. Mills part of the time – and at home to see the King pass and repass to the houses –~~

~~Reading and noting Rushworth Rapin and the Statutes of the Realm till nearly 11. p. m.~~

~~Thursday.~~   ~~23.~~ Reading the debates in the two houses last night Mr Hume made an excellent speech and moved his resolutions[338] – Mr Marshall seconded them. This is well, Mr Marshall has thus at once cut the Whigs and taken a most decided part. Of those paltry, juggling Whigs – those mean pitiful panderers, those false friends to the people not one was found to support Mr Humes motion, useful as it could not fail to be and called for as his propositions are by the country.

Mr Humes propositions were just such as on former occasions Sir Francis Burdett would have been proud to have had put into his hands, excepting perhaps that which alluded to the Corn Laws and he would have made a speech which the country would have responded to. But he too is among the Whigs, and so is Hobhouse. Two such men are really not proper to represent Westminster any longer, and Westminster will do well to change them whenever others can be found who will take a decided part for the people.

Canning's allusion to Portugal is ominous as to the course the Govern^t will continue to take, never to be without an excuse for a war on account of some foreign object of no importance to this country, but which they are resolved to have an excuse for whenever it may

---

[338] Hume's amendments to the King's speech included calls for the reduction in the size of the standing army, abolition of government pensions and sinecures, reduction of taxes and abolition of the Corn Laws, reform of the criminal laws and the House of Commons, Catholic emancipation, and a reversal of English policy in Ireland. The measure was supported by 24 members of the house and defeated by a majority of 146. *Hansard*, new series, 16, cols 50–61.

suit their purposes to divert the attention of the people that way for their own purposes.[339]

M[r] Hobhouse – vexed that M[r] Hume had made his motion and that he had been obliged to vote for it. He admitted the matter was good, but said Hume was not the man to do it, and this too when he knew that Hume was the only man who would do it. M[r] Hume had communicated his intentions to Brougham so that the party knew well enough that it was only because they had not taken the matter up that he did. But M[r] Hobhouse is right, in the way he looks at the matter. M[r] Hume was not the man to produce an impression upon the house, – and the reason is that as the Whigs will support nothing which is not done by themselves, and thus M[r] Hume being supported by neither of the "Battalions of the well paid Regiment," he is not the man to produce much effect upon it. But M[r] Hobhouse mistakes when he persuades himself that M[r] Hume is not the man out of the House. M[r] Hume did not expect even so much support as he received. but The amendment contains matter not only good in itself but congenial with the feelings of the mass of the people and among them it will be properly appreciated.

Colonel Torrens. he confessed that he paired off to avoid voting. He said the discussion was intolerably dull, and this is no doubt correct, for it was repugnant to both battallions [sic]. I told him that was of no consequence, it was not to the House that M[r] Hume and M[r] Marshall and M[r] Dawson[340] spoke but to the people and to them the matter would not be dull.

M[r] Hume. very well satisfied with what he had done and pleased with M[r] Marshall. He said Sir Francis Burdett would if he had spoken have supported him. He should then have spoken. M[r] Hume was in a room up stairs before he made his motion, and here he read it to several of the left hand battallion [sic], one wished him to say nothing of Ireland – another nothing of the army – others – nothing of the revenue, of the Law, – of the taxes – until not one bit would have been left – he had the courage to disappoint them all and to do his duty.

Long letters from Bolton describing or rather noticing the miserable state of the poor people there, and a printed copy of a petition to the house of commons against the Corn Laws. Replied to it.

Mr. Blake —

M[r]. Geo White respecting a M.S in my possession. "Correspondence between M[r] [Spencer?] Percival [sic] and M[r] John Brown." Browns Widow wishes to make money of it. Recommended White to

---

[339] Canning had recently stationed British ships at Tagus to protect Portugal's borders and thus maintain 'an honourable peace'.

[340] Alexander Dawson (c.1771–1831), MP for Louth, 1826–1831.

obtain her consent for him to give the M.S to Mr Canning and take her chance of his making her a present.

William Adams, gave him as note of introduction to Mr Baldwin the bookseller,[341] for the purpose of ascertaining whether he will undertake on his own account to print Adams's Journal of his travels, from ~~Mendoza~~ Buenos Ayres to Chile – thence to Mendoza, San Juan[,] Famatina, Potosi, and back to Buenos Ayres.[342]

Rapin – Reign of James. I.

Godwin – the Commonwealth.

Out to day from ½ 1 to 3—

Thursday.   [November] 23.

Letters from Dr Leighton – on Chile.

D^o. Sunderland on Corn Laws.

Stitching papers in Guard books – Corn, cotton, &c &c —

Out from 12 to three, on Mr Mill's affairs – d^o. – Tijou's

Colonel Torrens, some matters relating to a petition against the Corn Laws which he has to present to night.

Mr Blake with some extracts from Prior relative to manners.[343]

M^r. Mealey on Miers's affairs.

Reading for Extracts. Rapin. Rushworth. Reign of James I. – Commons Journals till ½ 10.

Friday.   [November] 24.

Commons Journals. 1 & 2 James. I.

Arranging – list of Geo Whites creditors

Out at ½ 11 – obtaining the signatures of White's creditors to a Trust deed —

Much interrupted yesterday in the evening – which I regretted, did but little in parliamentary inquiry.

A long conversation with Mr Paskin[344] the Clerk at the vote office at the House of Commons respecting several of the members and on some matters relating to the house.

[341] Baldwin's was a prominent London printing house throughout the first half of the nineteenth century. See Ellic Howe (ed.), *The London Compositor: documents relating to wages, working conditions, and customs of the London printing trade, 1785–1900* (London, 1947), p. 44.

[342] Neither Adams's project nor Brown's correspondence with Perceval appear ever to have been published.

[343] Perhaps a reference to the poet Matthew Prior (1664–1721).

[344] Charles Paskin, deputy to James Mitchell, the deliverer of votes and printed papers. My thanks to Dr Margaret Escott of the History of Parliament project for her help in identifying this individual.

Home at ½. 2.

Reading some long and well written articles in the Scotsman newspapers, on Metaphysics – New Home – society – and a vindication of M[r] M[c]Culloch from the censure of some miscreant in Blackwoods Magazine.[345] NB. it is seldom I notice this sort of reading – or mention the person with whom I have conversation when from home.

At ½ 8 M[r] Hume from the House in considerable agitation in consequence of the truly infamous attack upon him in the Times Newspaper.[346] John Smith[347] and several other members had persuaded him to commence an action against the Editor, every body he had spoken to or rather every one and, they who had spoken to him advised him to take this course, he said his own family and all his immediate family friends were hurt beyond expression and thought he must put a stop to such infamous calumnies and imputations. I advised him on no account whatever to commence any law proceedings. 1. Nothing he would do in this way would tend to clear him of imputations. 2. He had said and, now further said that he had on a former occcasion [sic] of an infamous calumny in the Times, told the editor in a letter that he would neither prosecute for libel, nor bring any action. And were he now to do so his letter would be published with all sorts of insinuations and all sorts of calumnies. 3. That so far from silencing the Rascally editor of the Times he would be giving him a premium to continue his abuse since the way in which he would be able to handle the matter pending the suit, would more than pay him by the increased sale of his paper than all the costs and damage would amount to and this he well knew, and this was a principal reason with him for doing as he did.

4. That if only small damages should be awarded it would be taken as a complete defeat.

5. That he would in a short time have as much character remaining as he desired to have, and that no effort of his could procure him more

6. That as he had cast himself forward as the advocate of the people in favour of free trade, for all acts of retrenchments, as he had been and still was preeminently the friend of the working people he had made himself the Target for all who hated the people, as well as all

---

[345] *The Scotsman*, 11 and 15 November 1826.

[346] *The Times*, 24 November 1826. This was a continuance of *The Times*'s October revelations of the so-called Greek loan scandal, in which Hume and several others, including John Bowring, J.C. Hobhouse and Edward Ellice, were implicated in the manipulation of private bonds floated for the Greek independence movement. See R.K. Huch and P.R. Ziegler, *Joseph Hume: the people's M.P.* (Philadelphia, PA, 1985), pp. 47–51.

[347] John Smith (1767–1842), MP for Wendover, 1802–1806; Nottingham borough, 1806–1818; Midhurst, 1818–1830; Chichester, 1830–1831; and Buckinghamshire, 1831–1834.

who could get money by such conduct to shoot at ~~him~~. But like the
Iron Target in Hyde Park which had been bruised all over he must
stand to be shot at, and like that target if he did stand however he
might be bruised he would never be shot through by even the rifles of
the Times and Cobbett.

7. That he must screw his courage to the sticking place and not
shrink in the least.

8. That he should send his former correspondence with the Times
to the Morning Chronicle accompanied by a short note saying he was
still resolved not to prosecute, but that no man however infamous he
might be would have done as the Editor of the Times has done were
he not assured that he should not be criminally prosecuted.[348]

Mr Hume is exceedingly sore and almost wearied. No one in
the rascally house will stick back and edge to him and present
circumstances make him not only doubt of his own usefulness, but
almost determine him to abandon what he sees is no recompense for
the labour he undergoes for the public. But he has only to persevere
and a short time will set him right again. Preeminently useful; he must
make up his own mind to be more than usually assailed, this to be
sure he knows, and would I have no doubt be at once reconciled to
his circumstances were there only one staunch man to act with.

Journals– Dom Com – from – 4 to 11 – saving the time occupied by
Mr Hume and in Tea drinking.

I endeavour to keep up Hume as I keep up myself, by asking this
question what better can I do. I know the very little value of life. I
know what a contemptible thing it is to live at all, if that living is to be
subject to the control of others in such a way as to make ones comfort
to depend on the opinions or the acts of others, and in this I suspect
I excede [sic] all my acquaintance, that active as I am in the concerns
of others my opinions are all my own, never in my own case asking
or receiving the advice of others, and being wholly independent of
any thing that can be either thought or done by others in respect to
my own happiness. I have limited my desires, so as [to] bring all that
is necessary and more than is necessary within my reach and have I
think brought myself to that state that no possible event can make me
uncomfortable for 24 hours; bodily pains excepted.[349]

---

[348] This correspondence, relating to the publication of an allegedly slanderous letter in
1825, appeared in the *Morning Chronicle* of 28 November 1826.

[349] Place later added: 'I have since had more to prove the supposition correct since the
above was written and most especiall [sic] during the last five years than all that occurred
if all my former long life had been compressed in the same time; even after it [sic] amount
had been doubled – yet thanks to former reasonings I have neither lost my chearfulness [sic]
nor ever been <u>unhappy</u> during 24 consecutive hours. aged — 78 3 Nov 1849'. The date '22
February 1850' was also added here later.

Saturday.   [November] 25.

Reading. Dryden's Amphitryon for manners.[350] Prior Poems – d[o.]
Out at 12. on Mr White's business one of the principal creditors
having refused to sign and having defaced the deed by erasing his sons
name as a trustee with his pen, the matter must I conclude remain as
it is.
With M[r] Mill 1½ hours – home at 3.
M[r] Blake.
Commons Journals. Vol. I Jac. I. notes —
Godwin's Commonwealth.

Sunday.   [November] 26

Deputation from the Coopers respecting their business —
Charles Blake – out with him from ½ 10 to ½ 2 – over Hampstead
and Highgate Hills.
Making out account current – for D[r] Leighton writing to him and
copying the account current
Writing to M[r] King Liverpool
William Tijou on his affairs two hours.
Finished Journals Dom Com first session first Parl Jac. I –.
Reading in the evening. Memoirs of Captain Rock.[351]

Monday.   [November] 27

Write – Letters – 1. To M[rs] Leighton Edinbro
Messr Elliott – Messr Keating
Cap[t] Henderson – all in D[r] Leighton affairs.
At 10 – M[r] Sidney on White's affairs.[352] He told me a curious tale
respecting the intended tract Society.[353] Brougham finding that his
coadjutors would not subscribe any money, and unwilling to relinquish
the honour and glory of being the prime manager, took the matter
from Sidney (who had purchased the plates for a part of the work
and some M.S.S – for 150£) and gave the rights of publication
which did not belong to him to Longmans. Sidney hearing this

---

[350] Amphitryon, or, the two Socia's (London, 1690). A comedy after Molière with music by
Henry Purcell.
[351] Thomas Moore, Memoirs of Captain Rock, the Celebrated Irish Chieftain. With some account of
his ancestors. Written by himself. (Paris, 1824). Thomas Moore (1779–1852), the Irish nationalist,
poet, and confidant of Lord Byron.
[352] Perhaps a reference to George Sidney, a London master printer. See Howe, London
Compositor, pp. 119, 169; Alison Ingram (comp.), Index to the Archives of the House of Longman,
1794–1914 (Cambridge, 1981).
[353] That is, the Society for the Diffusion of Useful Knowledge.

went to Longmans – told them what had occurred, and said if they went on with the work he would bring an action against Brougham for compensation for the damages he had sustained. Upon which Longmans refused to go on with the work until a meeting had been held, and a meeting was therefore to be held yesterday, the result of which Sidney did not know. There is nothing extraordinary in this. It is another only of the pranks Brougham is ever playing.

Mr Goe [*sic*] Morland with a project for a small pamphlet to shew the farmers, that the corn laws were a disadvantage to them. Offered to write it, but then as usual I feared I must also print it at my own expense, so there that ends.

Mr Anderson of the Trade Newspaper he had several subjects to talk of, but of no importance whatsoever, he however remained until turned out by Colonel Torrens with whom a long conversation respecting the House of Commons. He as usual paltering and shuffling. I told him of the meanness of those who like himself not supporting Mr Hume and said if I were Mr Hume I would soon set myself right with the House as well as with the people by at once bringing in a bill for the total repeal of the Corn Laws in just as many words and thus put an end to the hostility of the house to me, by compelling them at once to attend to the subject.

Thomas Campbell[354] – now Lord Rector of the College at Glasgow. He also told me a curious anecdote. [Sentence crossed out.] Brougham advised him not to expect to be elected Rector as he would be opposed by Mr Moncrief of Edinburgh.[355] That he Brougham who was the Lord Rector knew that Moncrief must from the interest he had in the College and the feeling of all toward him be elected on which Campbell wrote to some of his friends not to trouble themselves further in the matter. This however caused them to make inquiry when it turned out that Moncrief had been named only to one of the electors and to him by Brougham himself. Brougham all the time professing to Campbell to be desirous of his appointment.

Mr Hume, in fair good spirits – advised him to lose no time in coming before the house on the Corn question, and telling the Speaker

---

[354] Thomas Campbell succeeded Brougham as rector. According to his biographer, Campbell 'took the duties of his office with unprecedented seriousness, examining the management of the university and protecting the interests of the students. Such was his popularity that he was re-elected for two further years, to the considerable annoyance of the authorities, who considered his third re-election to be illegal.' See Geoffrey Carnall, 'Campbell, Thomas (1777–1844)', *ODNB*, <http://www.oxforddnb.com/view/article/4534>, accessed 17 March 2005.

[355] Perhaps a reference to Sir James Moncrieff, Dean of the Faculty of Advocates in the mid-1820s. See James Coutts, *A History of the University of Glasgow from its Foundation in 1451 to 1909* (Glasgow, 1909), p. 548.

he now should resume his speech at the point which the bad manners of gentlemen had on Friday induced him to leave of[f].[356] To tell them plainly that he was speaking to the people through the house and would lose no opportunity of doing so.

To attack Canning, thus, the Right Honb[l] Gentleman had told them in an almost Regal manner, much indeed in the manner of the Stewarts that the house should not discuss grievances until it was convenient to him. [sic] and had named his time as Feb or March next. Not to be trusted [?] Ministers had fomented tumult on other occasions and might do so on this. But whether they did or not, it was hardly to be expected that the people who had born [sic] almost unequalled privations would remain quiet when they saw that the house had refused to listen to them but starving and forlorn as they would be tumults must be expected, and then these would be made excuses to postpone the matter. See it would be said the exasperated state of the people see the necessity of the standing army see the tumultuous state in which the country is, and then say is this the time to discuss so momentous a question as the Corn Laws, and thus if it so pleased Ministers the matter would have the go by – That he felt a strong inclination which he thought he should indulge of Bringing in a bill to repeal these laws. He will not do all this because he absurdly has some remains of respect for the Den.

Thus without intermission except about half an hour for dinner have I been occupied until now $\frac{1}{2}$ past 5.

Dr. Gilchrist just returned from Spa in Germany.[357] Much alarmed at the state of the Mechanics Institution and much vexed at the conduct of some toward M[r] Hume.

Rapin reign of James. I.   reading
                                                    &
Captain Rock ———   noting.

Tuesday.   [November] 28.

I see by the papers this morning that M[r] Hume did last night in the house, allude to what he was saying on Friday night, – mentioned his expectation of tumults during the winter if the Corn Law question

---

[356] *Hansard*, new series, 16, 24 November 1826, cols 135–136, where Hume's opening remarks on the Corn Laws were allegedly 'coughed down'. See *ibid.*, 28 November 1826, cols 143–144 for Hume's brief speech on the Corn Laws before the House, which was intermingled with a defence of his own actions in the Greek loan affair.

[357] John Gilchrist, a Scots surgeon active in radical causes. Organiser of the 'Shamrock, Thistle and Rose' committee in support of Queen Caroline in 1820–1821. Prothero, *Artisans and Politics in Early Nineteenth-Century London: John Gast and his times*, paperback edition (London, 1981), p. 143.

was not discussed, and also his intention if it were not done to bring in a bill himself to compel discussion. But as M{r} Canning was not in his place he said but little, most likely intending to say more on another occasion.

The Morning Chronicle has inserted the correspondence between M{r} Hume and The Times, with the suggestions I sent the Editor. The Herald has acknowledged the receipt of the letters in a note to me and advises M{r} Hume to treat the matter with contempt. This is indeed all he now has to do.

Out ½ 12 to 3 – most of this Time at M{r} Hobhouses – where I met Colonel Jones who is desirous in the event of a vacancy to stand for Sudbury.[358] A long discussion on the actual position of M{r} Hobhouse. Col{n} Jones who is a straight forward, manly fellow started the conversation by telling Hobhouse that he was not a man of business which is not only affirmed but proved. This gave us both the opportunity of saying what in the event appeared to have been the wish of each of us, we went over the conduct and character of several members and compared them with that of Hobhouse, and with his peculiar situation as member for Westminster – shewed him how he trifled with himself and with his duty – told him what the people said of him and assured him, that unless he did his duty in a very different way than that he had been accustomed to he would never be again elected for Westminster. He understood himself so little and his situation so much less that he was quite confounded. However he had a number of facts stated to him and the means of verifying them given him. But his habits are so averse from business and he is so mistaken in himself and is withall so ~~feeble~~ infirm of purpose that he will never fill his place as the member for Westminster ought to do. Burdett stood for the people when no one else did, and he therefore lives in their remembrance and altho now of little use, the people will not probably abandon him.

M{r} Hume on his way to the house.

Reading and noting till nearly 11 p.m. Parliamentary History. Hume's History, and Petyts Jus Parliamentarium, Jac. I. –[359]

---

[358] Jones's election address was later published as *Begin: to the electors of the Borough of Sudbury* (London, 1826).

[359] William Petyt, *Jus Parliamentarium: or, the ancient power, jurisdiction, rights and liberties of the most High Court of Parliament revived and asserted* (London, 1739).

Wednesday.   [November] 29.

Mr Aust with the model of a very curious and useful garden engine.

Sent, statements and tables, relating to half pay in the army, (intended to be used by Mr Hume tomorrow in the house of Commons) to the Morning Chronicle and the Morning Herald Newspapers.[360]

Out from 1 to 3 at Mr Mills.

At 4 Mr Northouse with a long paper in explanation and defence of Mr Hume read it over – discussed and corrected it. Mr Northouse intends to procure its insertion in the Morning Chronicle. It is a plain honest paper, which Northouse has been induced to write in consequence of the violent abuse daily contained in the Times Newspaper.

At 5 Colⁿ Jones with a sketch of an address to the electors of Sudbury discussed it – much conversation on the Greek affair – Burdett Hobhouse Hume Ricardo &c til ¹/₂ 6.

At Tea Mrs Hodgskin and my daughter Mary, conversing on the Memoirs of Goethe, and the conceit of the man in writing so many particulars of himself.[361] He could do nothing said Mrs Hodgskin that he did not ~~thin~~ believe the world would think of importance because he was the doer. And am I not also doing what will be justly liable to the same imputation – Is it advisable to go on, Is it not advisable to burn this diary. These are questions which will soon be resolved.[362]

Journals Dom Com – Jac. I – til ¹/₂ 10
Godwins Commonwealth till 12.

Thursday.   [November] 30.

Mr Henry L. Hunt with Mr Marriot proprietor of the Taunton Courier, to shew a proof of the Newspaper printed on calico, and to advise with me as to the state of the Law.[363] Mr Marriott supposed that if he paid the duty on the calico he printed, say 2 ¹/₂ the square yard he would not be liable to the Newspaper stamp, and then he could afford to sell the paper or whatever else it might be called for ^d5 instead of ^d7.

[360] *Hansard*, new series, 16, 30 November 1826, cols 183–195. Hume attacked excessive military expenditures and argued that generous allowances created much 'dead weight' in the military.

[361] Goethe's *Memoirs* had been published in London in 1824.

[362] Place later added to the diary at this point: 'My Executors may burn them. Sept 1838.'

[363] Joel Wiener notes that printing on calico was not an uncommon means by which publishers sought to evade the various 'taxes on knowledge'. Richard Carlile, for example, published two almanacs on calico in the early 1830s, one of which was titled the *Untaxed Cotton Almanack*. See Joel H. Wiener, *The War of the Unstamped: the movement to repeal the British newspaper tax, 1830–1836* (Ithaca, NY, 1969), pp. 15, 17–18. My thanks to Professor Wiener for bringing this to my attention.

I have no hesitation in saying that if the law be construed as all penal laws ought to be construed ~~that~~ this mode of printing is not liable to the stamp duty on Newspapers. But a difficulty exists as to the mode of regulating the printing of calicoes as the law may be made to mean that the whole piece of calico shall be printed before the duty can be levied and the piece marked, and this will effectively prevent the printing on Mr Marriotts plan as he must cut up the piece before he prints – As however Mr Brougham is just now on the qui vive as to the press I gave Mr Marriott a letter of introduction to him, in which I recommend him to Broughams special attention.

Out from 1 – to 3 – at Mr Miers's inspecting the accountant who is making up the books belonging to that estate.

Col^n Torrens – who thought as every whig will be sure to think that Mr Hume, did not act prudently last night in presenting to the House the Petition of the Rev Robt Taylor complaining that he being a deist could not be sworn in a court of law or justice[364] – Mr Hume was supported by Mr W. Smith of Norwich.[365] Told Torrens I expected he would say Hume had not acted prudently – that this was said of every man who when every so little out of the beaten track, and that if none were imprudent in their sense of the word there never could be any improvement but on the contrary we must go perpetually worse and worse and worse, that all innovation every attempt at improvement was imprudent, and that every great reformer who had existed was imprudent, and that so far as the individual was concerned most of the great reformers were actually imprudent men notwithstanding the greatest good had resulted from their imprudence. That Mr Hume was in the vulgar acceptations of the word imprudent, inasmuch as he confirmed the prejudices of many against him personally, but that he was doing what was really beneficial to the nation could not be doubted by any one who looked back to only the few last years, ~~and~~ observed what was the state of men's minds then, ~~and~~ who observed what they were now and reasonably calculated in what this state would be a few years hence. That Mr Hume had done no more than advocate as became a member of the legislature the right of every individual to profess his belief or disbelief in matters of opinion,

---

[364] See *JHC*, 82 (1826–1827), 29 November 1826, p. 44 and Hume's presentation of the petition to the Commons in *Hansard*, new series, 16, 29 November 1826, cols 171–172. Robert Taylor was prominent in the 'radical underworld' of the late 1820s and early 1830s. He founded the deistic Christian Evidence Society in London in 1824, was convicted of blasphemy in 1828, and published several infidel tracts throughout the period. See Iain McCalman, *Radical Underworld: prophets, revolutionaries and pornographers in London, 1795–1840* (Cambridge, 1988), pp. 188–191.

[365] William Smith (1756–1835), MP for Sudbury, 1784–1790 and 1796–1802; Camelford, 1791–1796; and Norwich, 1802–1830.

and prayed that no man should on these accounts be stigmatised or rendered incapable of performing any duty or holding any office. That Mr Humes conduct in these matters marked the progress of thinking. 10 years ago no man would have dared to have written the petitions and consequently no man in the house would have presented such a petition had it been written. When only about 3 or 4 years ago Mr Hume presented petitions from Carlile his wife and sister, the house was all but up in arms, altho they only prayed for the mitigation of unjust and uncommonly severe sentences, while now the house very patiently heard a petition read from an avowed Deist who told the house that he publicly preached Deism in a chapel every sunday and had it discussed on one evening in every week, but the house did more than this it sat quiet and suffered a foolish fellow who took the part of the Gospels against the petitioner to be very severely reprehended, and put down as Torrens confesses in such a way as will make him very cautious how he interferes again.

M^r. Barry.

Write a number of letters to those who subscribe annually for the maintenance of that worthy old man. Thomas Hardy.

Journals Dom Com. Vol – I. till 10 – p.m

Godwins Commonwealth.

Friday.   [December] 1.

Had determined last night to close this diary with the month. Half afraid that I was sadly trifling – and half disposed to believe as I suppose others have believed that it really was worth the trouble it had cost. Was decided at last by the reflection that I had done enough to shew, even if it were worth shewing what the course of my life was, a course not very likely so far as I could calculate to undergo much change, as also to shew of whom and what the world was composed from the sample which I was connected with, notwithstanding this, was not so fully made out as it might be, since I had avoided drawing characters which I could easily have done had I not thought it invidious. All then that can be accomplished by this diary has been accomplished, in future it must be a repetition of similar event[s] and circumstances, transacted with the same and different persons. It may then be closed – so said I – and now this morning the devil of vanity having muted all the other spirits here am I continuing the diary.

Well then I request those in to whose hands it may fall hereafter, to take from it only such parts as may be applied to some useful purpose, if any such parts there are, that is to request they will be more discreet than I am,[a] a request in such a case which is most likely an idle request.

M[r] Marriott of Taunton, he had seen M[r] Brougham, who was decidedly of opinion his publication was not a newspaper under any existing law, but was not so certain of its not being a pamphlet under [the] Six Acts – and consequently liable to a stamp unless it contained the quantity of two $\frac{1}{4}$ sheets and was sold for [d] 6 – In this M[r] Brougham is mistaken. It may be liable to the penalties of the act as a pamphlet containing news but not to the stamp duty.

One difficul[ty] occurred to me and that was the excise on printed calico[.] I do not see how under any act the duty can be levied if the piece of goods to be printed be cut up in parcels before it is printed. Sent M[r] M—— to a calico printer in Garrett Lane Wandsworth, with a proposition for printing calico so cut up, for the purpose of ascertaining how he would accomplish it, or why it cannot be accomplished. Sug[g]ested also the weaving in of coloured threads at certain distances, thus paying the duty on the piece and then cutting it up in the presence of the exciseman.

M[r] Henry Burgess with his pamphlet – Letter to Canning – on Bills of Exchange[,] Country Bank notes and Bankers – gave me two copies.[366]

[a] Note – to take from it as soon as possible. [Marginal note.]

[366] Henry Burgess, *A Letter to the Right Hon. George Canning, to explain in what manner the industry of the people, and the productions of the country, are connected with, and influenced by, internal bills of*

Colonel Bradley with a long list of papers relating to his case which he wished Mr Hume to move for.[367] Shewed him that this could not be done unless Mr Hume, was prepared to say he would follow up his demand with a motion which he was not prepared to do. Promised to shew the paper to Mr Hume, to explain it to him and to let Col^n Bradley know the result.

Dr Thorpe for advise in his case – told him nothing would be done for him, altho there was no reason he should not do all he could, as while there's life there's hope, a forlorn hope in his case. He has been very ill used and from mere compassion, ministers should give him a small pension even if his having spent all his life in their service did not intitle [sic] him to some small remuneration in his old age.

Out on Thomas Hardy's business from 1/2 12 to 3.

At 4 Thomas Hodgskin, he said the matter respecting the People's Library, the Longmans and Sidney had been amicably arranged, and that it was to be a bookselling concern and he was to superintend the publication. It may now go on. Longmans have settled the price to contributors at 10£ a sheet, At this rate they will obtain a few good articles from those who do not write for the money but are willing to give their time for the public good, but they will soon be either obliged to double the sum or the matter will be a mere vile, abridgment from other publications. 20£ a sheet, would as to quantity of matter be much below the price paid for either the Edinburgh Quarterly or Westminster Review, and not more than is paid by the New Monthly magazine.

Writing to Mr Hobhouse on the subject of our conversation the other morning – in consequence of what he said to my son in which I have pointed out to him the evidence of his being no man of business and offering him the case of Mr Samida the heads of which I inclosed [sic], in my letter, cautioning him not to undertake to bring the matter before the house of commons unless he could make up his mind to hear Mr Samida at length patiently – read his papers and fully understand the case in all its parts.

Commons Journals – Rapin – time of Jac I. —

Godwin's Commonwealth.

exchange, country bank notes and country bankers, Bank of England notes, and branch banks, etc. (London, 1826).

[367] Lieutenant Colonel Thomas Bradley, Second West India Regiment. While stationed in Honduras in 1814, Bradley had become involved in a dispute with his superior officer over the command of the military forces there. In the course of that dispute and subsequent military trial, Bradley was arrested, jailed, and dismissed from the service. See Hansard, 8 December 1826, cols 321–330; ibid., 14 February 1827, cols 460–471; JHC, 81 (1826), pp. 345, 385.

Saturday.   [December] 2.

Letters to collect subscriptions for Thomas Hardy.
Col^n Bradley with papers in his case which I have promised to read.
M^r. John Marshall M. P. and his son M. P.[368] various topics –
discussed a project for a Reformers Club, somewhat of the kind as
the Atheneum and other such clubs but on a smaller scale, at first –
M^r. Marshall to draw up a plan – as many known reformers as possible
to be induced to make lists of names – a meeting of some 25 to be
selected and these to settle the plan and then summon such others as
they may think proper to commence the club.
M^r. Hobhouse – sundry matters – gave me 20£ 4 years subscription
for Thomas Hardy.
Colonel Jones. he is resolved to go to Sudbury and see how the
people are disposed, and will then publish his address.
These one after another occupied me from 11 to 3 – and from 4
to 6.
Reading some of M^r. Burgess's pamphlet. M^r. Burgess like many
other men sees nothing but just his own project and is too little
informed in political economy to be able to write usefully.
Journals – Rapin – Hume
Reading Godwin.

Sunday.   [December] 3.

I hate to go out of the house when it rains, I hate to go out after
dinner because I have no time to myself until that time, even that
is encroached upon, and thus as may be seen I am able to read but
little and to write still less. Thus it happens that I do not take as
much exercise as I ought to take. Intended a long walk this morning
but turning [?] too, to put up the books, and pamphlets which had
accumulated for a month, I staid at home until it rained and then
made this a shuffling excuse to stay at home, and was occupied all day
long in sorting arranging &c &c —
In the evening reading Godwins Commonwealth.

Monday.   [December] 4

Resolved to go out, when in came M^r. Fenn with some matters of
so much moment to his action which will come in a few days that I
could not refuse to cooperate with him.

---

[368] William Marshall (1796–1872), MP for Petersfield, 1826–1830, and later member for
Leominster, Beverley, Carlisle, and East Cumberland.

Then came Geo White before I could shave myself and he had much to say. 1. as to his own affairs which are unfortunate enough and 2nd respecting Torrens – Marshall – Warburton, and several other members of parliament, the state of the house in respect to them and other matters all conveying information and all interesting to me.

Just as I was done with him and before he went away came M^r. Hobley bringing with him a M^r. Hulme, a Pawnbroker, whose case is one of the most extraordinary I ever heard. Hulme, employed one Tennant an Attorney with whom he at length disagreed, and then he employed another attorney. Tennant then – sent in his bill of costs, but did not sign in as in law he was bound to do to make it a legal demand. Hulme however sent it to his attorney to have it taxed and settled. The new attorney not contemplating any mischief did not proceed with the taxation as fast as he might have done. One evening last week as he was about to close his shop a man offered him some goods for purchase which he refused, and as soon as his shop was shut another man knocked at the door and asked the boy who opened it for M^r. Hulme. Hulme was at this time letting [?] some watches in the parlour for sale the next day ~~and~~ his wife went to the door and told the man who was a stranger that M^r. Hulme was not at home. This was a trick it seems to have an excuse to sue at a commission of Bankruptcy against him, at the suit of Tennant, and on friday evening a messenger seized the whole of his property, under a Commission of Bankruptcy issued that afternoon. The man was almost mad so I gave him a note to Hobhouse in the expectation that he would consent to bring the matter before parliament.[369]

In comes Colonel Bradley with a long pressing story of what he had been doing and desiring assistance to enable him to go on, and before he was gone Hubley and Hulme returned from M^r. Hobhouse saying if I would draw up a petition and get from Hulme the state of his case in writing he would bring it before the House this evening. Instructed Hulme how to draw out his case and to come to me again at four o clock to meet M^r. Hobhouse. Drew up a petition simply stating facts and praying the house to interfere [?] since by the nature of the process Hulme was debarred all remedy both at law and in equity. This brought ~~to~~ me to 3 o clock when just as I was sitting down to dinner in came Colⁿ Torrens to talk to me of a petition he was to present to night from Bolton, and at 4 came M^r. Hobhouse and M^r. Hulme, examined M^r. Hulme, explained the law of the case to M^r. Hobhouse shewed him that no blame attached to the commissioners but that Hulme could do nothing ~~to~~ that would prevent his name

[369] See *JHC*, 82 (1826–1827), 4 December 1826, p. 75.

going into the Gazette as a Bankrupt notwithstanding as he stated in the petition that he had more than seven times as much property as the whole of his debts amounted to, that he would be put to an enormous expense to get the commission superseded, and would then probably find no course in law by which he could either procure compensation or punish Tennant. That the only chance he had to save his reputation was the petition with such a discussion of his case as he M^r. Hobhouse could provoke in the house.

From this time till 6 reading a letter from the mechanics of Sheffield who had called the meeting on the Corn Laws and answering it, till 6 o clock tea time, during which a discussion with M^r. William Tijou and my son Frank respecting the state of the Mechanics Institution and the remedies proposed, until put an end to by M^r. Hume from the House of Commons, who related to me that Hobhouse had presented the petition, had made a good statement, that there had been a pretty fair discussion and that so far the object aimed at had been obtained. Talked of the abuse heaped upon him and of the conduct of the country newspapers in supporting him, said it was now [a] matter of perfect indifference to him what they said. Talked of the petition from Birmingham for the repeal of the laws which prohibit the exportation of Machinery. Had sent it to M^r. Huskisson, who would not consent to repeal the law, but was willing to grant licenses to export such machinery as upon application to him might not appear objectionable. Agreed to draw up for M^r. Hume Reasons for the repeal of the law, and concerted with him a plan to induce our friends to attend on Wednesday and support the petition. M^r. Marshall, M^r. Warburton, to canvas for assistance at the Political Economy Club this evening. M^r. Hume left at ^{1}/2 past 8.

Drawing up reasons &c. as promised.

Thus has all my day since 10 o clock in the morning till now and I may say till nearly 12 at night been consumed in matters no way relating to myself personally and yet such as under the circumstances of the cases I could not avoid.

~~Monday~~
Tuesday.   [December] 5.

Letter from J. Parkes Birmingham respecting parliamentary pamphlets &c.

D$^{\underline{o}}$ M^r. Smith – Bolton giving a sad account of the state of the people there.

Out before 11– to Col^n Torrens on the subject of M^r. Hume's motion or notice for tomorrow night relating to the exportation of

Machinery.[370] Was not a little disappointed at finding Torrens utterly ignorant of the subject, and that notwithstanding his knowledge of Political Economy he talked like a silly old woman of impeding the French manufacture of cotton goods, and affirmed that to impede them even to a small extent, and for the short period of a year was reason sufficient for us to refuse to repeal the law which prohibited the free exportation of Machinery. He most absurdly supposed that France could not manufacture as much machinery as was required. But he is a poor creature and will make no figure as an opponent of ministers in what is bad, and will not be worth their purchasing.

At M^r. Humes, went through the paper I had prepared, he making all the objections which had been urged both within and without the house, found them all and every one of them answered in the paper and I believe refuted and so M^r. Hume thought.

Home at ½ 1.

M^r. Northouse with his project of a weekly newspaper. Went through with him the whole of it, advised him and told him, that I had no doubt of its success, provided he could procure a sufficient sum of money – namely not less than 2000£ to start with.

Wrote an article on the state of the people, and made some comments on the convictions and executions of persons for Horse stealing and sheep stealing given to me by M^r. Hume. The object – to shew that sanguinary laws cannot be executed, and that since they cannot be executed they serve as an encouragement to the commission of crimes. Sent them to the Morning Chronicle.

Journals of the house of Commons time of James I.—

Wrote several letters – to Wooler[371] – M^r. Smith at Bolton. M^r. Papworth to request him to find a carpenter who would take my son John apprentice.

Wednesday.   [December] 6.

This being a most miserable day heavy rain, foggy atmosphere, cold and uncomfortable – resolved to stay at home and do several things which had been laid aside, but I did none of them. First came M^r. Fenn, on parish matters, read with him, several papers relating to his suit and promised to attend the consultation at M^r. Scarlets tomorrow evening – Brougham and [illegible] Evans the consulting counsel.

---

[370] Hume presented a petition from the machine makers of Manchester: see *Hansard*, new series, 16, 6 December 1826, cols 291–298; *JHC*, 82 (1826–1827), p. 99.
[371] T.J. Wooler, radical editor of the *Black Dwarf*, which had ceased publication in 1824.

M^r. Toplis, respecting the Library for the people. Brougham had partly [?] made him promise to write the articles on mechanics, advised him to do so.

M^r. Henry L. Hunt – respecting M^r. Marriotts project of a newspaper on calico. Brougham has seen M^r. Sykes the Solicitor to the Commissioner of Stamps. M^r. Sykes said he had no doubt he could find law in some act of parliament which would reach the case of news – as a newspaper be it printed how or what ever it might be printed on. M^r. Marriott is nevertheless resolved to adventure. M^r. Marriott has ascertained that he can have the calico stamped in the piece and can legally cut it in pieces before he prints it.

M^r. Doanne from M^r. Benthams respecting the people's library. Told him the whole of the circumstances relating to that publication.

M^r. Wm Jones. Burdett. to pay his subscription to Thomas Hardy an hour and a halfs conversation on various matters principally the increase of knowledge among the people since 1793 – A Good right thinking fellow this as usual.

Dr Gilchrist, respecting the Newspaper projected by M^r. Northouse and his being a trustee.

A letter from M^r. Hume sent to him by the committee of Woollen manufacturer journeyme[n] at Frome requesting him to present and to support their petition, to prevent the use of certain machinery – such as Gigs – shearing frames &c – Wrote a letter to the committee.

Wrote to M^r. Samida on his case and to M^r. Hobhouse on M^r. Samidas case, and it is now six p. m.

Mr Elliot respecting the drugs ordered by Dr Leighton at Valparaiso.

M^r. Keating – d^o – d^o —

Journals Dom Com. James. I —

Rapin – d^o —

Thursday.   [December] 7.

Colonel Bradley on his case. He has drawn it out as a narrative and accompanied it with letters to the Duke of York, Earl of Liverpool and Lord Bathurst – promised to read his narrative.

Read his narrative. His is a case of great hardship and singular injustice, but he may as well keep quiet, he has no remedy and will have no redress.

Letter from M^r. Hobhouse he will undertake M^r. Samida's case.

Statement from J. J. Tanner against whom M^r. Hulme petitioned the house. Tanner convicts himself out of his own mouth, and makes his case more than it was – Noted the case for M^r. Hobhouse, to enable him to reply to Horace Twiss[372] – and Bankers from both Commissioners of Bankrupts who have a counter petition to present from Tennant.

M[r]. Hobhouse who wrote the notes to my dictation for his own use. If this man would but learn how to work he would make a figure.

M[r]. Hume. he complained of the way in which the debate was reported this day respecting Machinery Exportation. It was to be sure very badly done – left me two letters to read one from a Pole on Exportation of machinery, well written.

Wrote an article on Peels speech for the Trades newspaper.

M[r]. Barry with some information respecting Buenos Ayres —

M[r]. Blake d[o] and several characteristic anecdotes of some of the leading people there and here. Money has been sent 50.000£ which cost [?] 110.000£ to buy ships for Buenos Ayres, but as this will go into the hands of Hulletts, it is plain to me that Hulletts, John Parish Robertson, and Rivadavia,[373] mean to make a job of it.

Last night on the presentation of a petition in the house of commons from a member of [the] machine makers praying that the law prohibiting the exportation of machinery might be repealed, Coln Torrens commenced pretty openly to do what Nathaniel Brassey Halhed[374] tried as he said for 17 years in vain to accomplish. I have stood said he, "for 17 years at the back of ministers with my soul in my hand, to sell it to ~~ministers~~ them and they would not buy it." Torrens to the surprise of those who did not thoroughly know him, talked in precisely the same strain as Huskisson and Peel, only that he went much further than either of them, in direct contradiction to his own writings. It will not do, he has been too precipitate and will be of little consequence for the administration to think him worth purchasing.

Rapins England. Vol. 2. Jac. 1.

Attended consultation at M[r]. Scarlets[375] chambers present M[r]. Scarlet, M[r]. Brougham, M[r]. J. Evans – Barristers – M[r]. Burke the Attorney M[r]. Fenn the Client, and myself.

---

[372] Horace Twiss (c.1787–1849), MP for Wootton Bassett, 1820–1830; Newport (Hampshire), 1830–1831; Bridport, 1835–1837.

[373] The connections between the banking firm Hulletts and Bros. and Bernadino Rivadavia, later president of Argentina, dated back to 1824 when their relationship regarding the Rio de la Plata Mining Company came under scrutiny. See Jonathan Harris, 'Bernardino Rivadavia and Benthamite "Discipleship"', *Latin American Research Review*, 33 (1998), pp. 144–145.

[374] Nathaniel Brassey Halhed (1751–1830), MP for Lymington, 1791–1796.

[375] James Scarlett (1769–1844), one of the most successful barristers of the era. Although a Whig, he was offered and accepted the post of attorney-general in 1827 under Canning, with the consent of his party's leader. See G.F.R. Barker, 'Scarlett, James, first Baron Abinger (1769–1844)', rev. Elizabeth A. Cawthorn, *ODNB*, <http://www.oxforddnb.com/view/article/24783>, accessed 29 March 2005.

These consultations are generally of more use to create expense than for any other purpose. What this will be remains to be seen. M^r. Brougham had read his brief and had the leading features of it in his recollection. M^r. Evans who had gone heartily into the thing from the first was completely master of the Subject and M^r. Scarlet who had not read his brief knew next to nothing of the matter. At all the consultations I ever attended the councellors [*sic*] always were pettish – generally overbearing and insolent, this was not so here. No impatience was manifested but Scarlet stated so many doubts on unimportant points and talked in so much ignorance of the subject that, poor Fenn was all but crazy, this almost bewildered him and proceeded in an agony to give such explanations to Scarlet as he hoped might lead him to understand the main points of the case, and in endeavouring to do this shewed such a state of mental agony that Scarlet out of mere pity, suffered him to take his own course, in reading and speaking and endeavouring to make evidence of many things which by the rules of evidence could never be adduced in court. At length Evans fixed Scarlets attention to the three principal matters and after explaining them offered to make out from the brief a summary of all that the court would permit to be proved, and an elucidation of the three principal points of the case. Scarlet was well pleased with this. So Evans is to do it and then he and Scarlet are to talk of it. Went with Evans to his Chambers and here he told me that Scarlet had made the objections entirely from habit that half of them were absurd and really meant nothing, that he would make such an abstract of the <u>excellent</u> brief as he called it, and would converse with Scarlet until he made him thoroughly master of the subject, and then added I would rather have him for the leader than all the men at the bar together. You will see how well he will do it.

Called going home on M^r. Fenn who as I expected was sadly depressed told him what had passed at Evans's but could not make him easy.

Friday.   [December] 8.

Finished reading Godwin Vol. i.

M^r. Cousins on Miers Estate accounts gave him instructions.

M^r. Aimé respecting books and book sales.

Read and corrected 4 letter [*sic*] written by M^r. Geo White, on the report of the Emigration Committee – intended for insertion in the Morning Chronicle.

Read M^r. Colsons observations on the debate on Exportation of machinery.

Read and replied to a letter from Glasgow on petitioning against the Corn Laws.

Colonel Jones who had been to Sudbury, where it seems there is no chance of any one being returned to the Honourable House who will not bribe the independent electors to vote for him, he distributed some copies of his address which speaks too plainly and reproaches them too justly with their business to make any of them friendly towards him.

Read an excellent letter written in french by a Pole to M^r. Hume on Exportation of machinery.

Reading – Rapin – Hume – Reign of Jac. I – Commons Journals – d^o.

Saturday.   [December] 9.

M^r. Lang secretary to the trades newspaper. sundry matters relating to this newspaper, recommended to him for the committee to sell it while it was worth something to M^r. Northouse who is willing to purchase it at a fair price.

M^r. Fenn on his suit with the parish. The consultation has so discomposed him that he was utterly unable to attend to the matter until this morning.

Read and corrected the remainder of M^r. White's letters.

At M^r. Miers's – on their estate matters. Col^n Jones on sundries – Col^n Torrens d^o a dispute between Jones and I opposed to Torrens on his silly conduct in the house of Commons, he does not understand himself, is flattered by the attention of those who mean him no good, his vanity always great has become inordinate, and he will soon sink down to his level which will be very low. He is by far to [sic] ill read, too ill informed, and too poor a judge of men and things, to be able to have any standing now, but by a cautious and modest line of conduct which he is not wise enough to adopt.

M^r. Tijou — M^r. White.

Commons Journals – Jac. I. —

Godwin – Vol. II.

Miss Atkinson, case of a young lady badly treated, by her mother and apparently to them so by her Attorney. Will make enquiries and endeavour to assist her.

Sunday.   [December] 10.

Sticking papers – sundries —

Out from 12 to 3 – with M^r. Papworth to make arrangements to put out my son John to a builder.

208   1826

Writing from 4 to 6. my own memoirs.
Journals. – Rapin. Hume

Monday   [December] 11.

Long letter from M^r. Miers at Buenos Ayres. Colonel Jones
respecting Sudbury and also respecting, M^r. Northouse's project of
a Weekly Newspaper.
Out. 1 – to 3.
Closely occupied with the Journals and Hume. Rapin – and Petyt.

Tuesday.   [December] 12

Dr Thorpe – suggested to this poor gentleman that he never could
get any redress by continuing his complaints, led him on to his own
situation when I found as I had suspected that he was in great poverty.
His eldest daughter dying of a pulmonary consumption, his other two
daughters, attending her, and his son a clergyman without a living.
That he had not in fact a sixpence. Consoled him as well as I could,
and when he Asked him if he had ever applied officially and formally
for the usual pension, he said he had not, asked him if a pension could
be procured whether or not he would take whatever was offered and
be quiet, he said he would. So after he was gone, put his sad case on
paper with such suggestions as I thought likely to procure him a small
pension and sent the paper to M^r. Hume and Sir Francis Burdett.
Colⁿ Bradley – who for the twentieth time told me his case.
M^r. Hume, pressed the case of poor Dr Thorpe upon him, he said
he would see M^r. Wilmot Horton and read my paper to him. Thus I
hope I have put the poor mans case in train.
Conversation on the Kings message respecting Portugal, on the
atrocity of being thus lugged into a war from which none but evils can
result to this country, agreed what M^r. Hume should do or attempt to
do in the House.
Commons Journals – Jac. I —
To Covent Garden Playhouse to see The School for Scandal, and
the Marriage of Figaro. Both pieces were well played – but I do not
think I shall let my wife take me to the play again for some time.

Wednesday.   [December] 13

M^r. Tijou saw at 10 – went over with him – the deed of assignment
to secure payment of 500£ to each of his three daughters – d^o his will –
sent the deed to be executed and wrote out his will – sent that also to
him to be executed.

Journals – Rapin – Hume Rushworth Jac. I.

M^r. Blake and M^r. Barry —

Col^n Torrens, he is a shuffler and we do not agree, we shall soon cut.

~~Journals~~ – M^r. Miles's curious account of the Deveral Barrow in Dorsetshire.[376]

Thursday.   [December] 14

M^r. Burke the Attorney of M^r. Fenn desirous of another consultation with council [sic] – opposed this as not necessary.

Read M^r. Miles's account of the Kimmeridge Coal money.[377]

M^r. Fenn on parish matters, and the trial to come on Tomorrow.

Out from 1 to 3.

Journals – Rushworth. Hume, and the parliamentary history till midnight.

Friday.   [December] 15

In the Court of Kings Bench at 9 — a private consultation in court with the counsel – no doubt of a verdict. Special jury called – 5 only answered. Officers called in and sworn as to the service of notices – names of absent jurors taken down – Jurors called again, absent Jurors to be fined, our opponent refused to press a date [?], withdrew the record, and of course have to pay the costs of the day. These costs will not be less than 100£. home ½ 10–.

M^r. Fenn in sad low spirits, this matter will make him crazy – he has so far a victory, yet he is exceedingly discomposed.

M^r. Evans the Barrister – called and read to me the abstract of the case as it was completed and given to M^r. Scarlet. read references to support his view of the case, he is confident of our success.

Saw M^r. Purse [?] and ~~M^r.~~ Col^n Bradley and concerted a plan with them to raise money to keep M^r. Fenn from harm.

To see M^r. Scarlet and explains my view of the Jurisdiction of the Bishop of London in the antient Church of St Martin, to shew him that it could not be a parish.

Coln Torrens – and William Tijou. Reading Stat. 27 Eliz relating to the Government of Westminster.

M^r. Ellis and M^r. E^d Ellis – with a M. S – on Emigration &c

Journals Dom Com – till 11. p. m Reading as usual Cobbetts Register

---

[376] William Augustus Miles, *A Description of the Deveral Barrow, opened A.D. 1825. Also a minute account of the Kimmeridge Coal Money, a most mysterious and nondescript article* (Frome, 1826).
[377] *Ibid.*

M[r]. Hodgskin came at 7 and staid till near 9 – telling me of the arrangements made for bringing out the Peoples Library. He had been with M[r]. Longman. It will now succeed if not stopped by Broughams perversity.

Saturday.   [December] 16.

Read M[r]. Ellis's M. S – sent two sheets to him for emendation – a good essay – and may be made very useful.

Poor D[r] Thorpe told him what had passed between me and M[r]. Hume, of M[r]. Humes interview with S[r]. Francis Burdett, and of the measures M[r]. Hume proposed for procuring him a pension.

M[r]. Northouse. settled with him a plan for conducting the mechanical part of his intended newspaper.

Out from 12. to 3 – partly on Miers Estate matters.

Journals of Dom. Com. 18–19 Ja I. Reading Godwin.

Sunday.   [December] 17.

Reading in the Lords Report Dignity of a Peer – Constitution of the Legislature time of – Ed. I. II.

Out from ½ 11 to 3 – over Highgate and Hampstead hills – with my son John.

Looking at – the – Mirror. Mechanics Register – Literary Gazette. Hones Every Day Book – Carliles Republican.

Journals Dom. Com. 19 – Jac. I.

Godwin.

Monday.   [December] 18.

Looking at sundry matters relating to the parish for M[r]. Fenn. On saturday M[r]. Bailey of S[t] Martins Lane came and agreed to assist me to collect money to indemnify M[r]. Fenn – to meet him at M[r]. Purse's corner of S[t] Martins Lane at 10 – tomorrow morning.

M[r]. Fenn who had been reading Stat. 27 Eliz – Government of Westminster. Found it just as I had described it. Lent him Sayers, observation on the Govt at Westminster.[378]

Commons Journals – 19. Jac. I —

Rushworth —————— D°.

Godwins Commonwealth.

[378] Edward Sayer, *Observations on the Police or Civil Government of Westminster, with a proposal for a reform* (London, 1784).

Tuesday   [December] 19

Out early on M^r. Fenns business concerting with M^r. Bayley and
M^r. Purse the means of raising money to [illegible] M^r. Fenn harmless.
Writing to John Miers at Buenos Ayres
D^o. D. Leighton – Valparaiso.
With Messrs Cubbitts respecting my son John, they will take him
only for 7 years, and find him nothing whatsoever with a premium of
150 Guineas.
M^r. Blake — M^r. Evans
M^r. Barry — M^r. Lemaitre Junr
M^r. Tijou with his account between his father and himself, adjusted
it, made a copy, and opened accounts for him with his father and with
his sisters.
Journals —

Wednesday.   [December] 20.   Thursday.   [December] 21.
                                ~~Friday~~
Writing. Miers and Leighton.
Journals —
Composing and making fair copy, address to procure money for
M^r. Fenn.
M^r. Hume —
M^r. Hunt respecting the peoples library — Several other persons
— attended. M^r. Bailey and M^r. Purse arranged a plan to procure
money to indemnify M^r. Fenn.
Read – the comedy the way to keep him.[379]
At Covent Garden Play house to see the way to keep him came
home at the end of the play which in all well-represented.
Godwins Commonwealth.

Friday.   [December] 22.

Reading and noting three letters written by M^r. Bailey on Corn and
Currency, at his request.
Walked to Church St Stoke Newington to see my very old friend
Wm Frend who has been confined by severe illness for several months,
exceedingly glad to see me as I was to see him, rapidly recovering his
health, cheerful and happy with his family.

[379] Arthur Murphy, *The Way to Keep Him: a comedy in five acts* (London, 1760).

Writing letters to several persons. M^r. Thelwall wishes me to get
M^r. Hobhouse to speak to Murray the Bookseller respecting a poem
he wishes to have published without the author being known.

M^r. W^m. Prescot – a long conversation on currency – what really
constitutes the currency —

M^r. Smith on M^r. Whites affairs

M^r. Duttons clerk respecting M^r. Carlile's health – wrote to
M^r. Laurence to attend him forthwith

Journals – Hume – Rushworth. time of James. I.

This includes Saturday. 23.

Sunday.   [December] 24.

Writing several letters.

M^r. Worthington taking my portrait for Jos^h Parkes — 11 – to 2.

M^r. Wm Tijou — R^o Doane

Gossipping [*sic*] in the parlour 7 of my children being at home, that
is two more than usual.

Journals Dom Com. Godwin & Captn Rock.

Monday.   [December] 25.

Collecting from Prior examples of grossness – for manners and
morals of the people, Johnsons life of Prior.[380] Chalmers D^o [381] life
prefixed to his works Ed. 1754.

Own memoir, on the impropriety of drawing characters of ones
friends.

M^r. Mill, who is still very lame in his feet – a long conversation –
respecting – the conduct of Canning, Hume and Torrens, probable
result of the affairs in Portugal, absurdity of our treaties with that
barbarous nation. State of Ireland, &c &c.

[The following paragraph has been struck out in the original]

    Gossipping two hours after dinner with my children,
unfortunately for them my wife never enters into the spirit of any
thing subject which becomes matter of conversation, but thinking
as she does that all utility is combined and conducted in household
work, and the care of her family and being more [?] than indifferent
to the affairs of the world and averse [?] from all projects, and all

---

[380] Samuel Johnson, *The Works of the English Poets, with prefaces, biographical and critical, by
Samuel Johnson* (London, 1779–1781).

[381] Alexander Chalmers, *The Works of the English Poets, from Chaucer to Cowper including the
series edited, with prefaces, biographical and critical by Dr Samuel Johnson*, 21 vols (London, 1810).

conversation on projects, taking a ... [illegible] ... persons character, and putting it as a whole, denying that any one whose conduct or blemishes can be found, is anything but an unworthy person, she damps always and often extinguishes ... [illegible] ... conversations, and not unfrequently by applying words personally to herself she causes disputes. This has at length caused her elder children to pay less respect to her than they ought to do, and this again confirms her in her absurd notions, and causes her to impute motives to them, so that upon the whole the family is less social and less comfortable than but for her weakness in these respects it would be. In every other respect she is an acute [?] exemplary and in some respects an extraordinary woman. The Girls are diligence itself at various studies, seeking and obtaining knowledge in Art, Languages and Science continually. Not however to the exclusion of their other duties, except a little carelessness, as to disposing of things which are sometimes left about in rather a slovenly way.

In the evening. Commons Journals to the end of James I – Rushworth.

Out from ½ 1. to 3 – with my son John walked to the further end of Kensington Garden and back.

Tuesday.   [December] 26

Own memoir, put down certain matters to prevent them being lost.

Out from 11 – to 3. with M^r. John Evans respecting houses at Paddington.

Journals – Rapin – Rushworth – Pettit [sic].

Wednesday.   [December] 27.

Occupied all the morning and until 3. p. m. with various persons.

Journals &c &c —

Thursday.   [December] 28.

Arranging Parliamentary printed papers.

M^r. Worthington – painting at me, from 11 to ½ 2 – he may paint on for ever, but he will only make a very gross and vulgar portrait.

Reading quarterly review, N° 69 published to day.

Out 1 ¹/2 hour walking.

Several persons called.

Colonel Jones with a project for a Parliamentary Reform Club, an improvement on M^r. Marshalls plan with whom he has promised to cooperate.

Friday.   [December] 29

Reading Quarterly Review
Out to Paddington. 12 to 3
Looking over catalogues.
Writing to the Poor Weavers at Bolton answer to John Young – the secretarys' [*sic*] letter.
Hume. Reign of James I —
Parliamentary History – D°.

M^r. Northouse to read a letter he was going to send to M^r. Horton respecting the Emigration of poor weavers in the S. W– of Scotland. M^r. Horton having led him to expect the Government will defray the expense. He is very confident M^r. Horton will be able and willing to induce the Govt to send to Canada and settle there several thousand of these people. I expect he will do no such thing, and it is a horrible cruelty to do any thing which may lead these people to expect it and then to disappoint them. Before any such project could be accomplished, even if M^r. Horton were ever so intent upon the measure, there would be a couple of hundred thousand claimants, and it would be difficult to make a selection and impossible to take them all, and such would be the embarrassment that the project would come to nothing – the lowest estimate is 20£ a head. 20£ @ – 10.000 = 200.000£. and 50.000. @ 20. = 1.000.000£. but 50.000 from 15.000.000 the amount of the population of Great Britain would be on 1 in 300 and there is more than 1 in 300 ready to fill up the vacancy so that the population would not be reduced at all. But to take 50.000 supposing one person to a ton of shipping would require 50.000 tons, = 166 ships of 300 tons each, and supposing each ship to make two voyages it would require 83 ships, but in as much as the vessels which could be obtained would not upon an average exceed 200 tons it would require 250 or 125 ships. If 100.000 persons were taken or 1 every 150 the expense would be 2.000.000£, and no good would be done at home since 1 in 150 would be instantly supplied and the number of ships would be so increased that freight would rise and stores would increase in price and the people would be too many to be settled all at once in Canada. If they were sent to any other Colony the expense would be considerably increased. No doubt some 20.000 or 30.000 might be advantaged by being removed, but the poverty at home would not be mitigated. But when we add that if 100.000 could be removed from Great Britain at least as many more must be removed from Ireland the whole becomes absurd, they can neither be conveyed nor settled in such numbers, and if they could, the redundant population would not be in the least diminished.

M^r. Wm Tijou on the affairs of his family.
Reading and noting Hume – time of James. I.

Saturday.   [December] 30.

Reading Parliamentary Report on ~~Education~~ Emigration. I there
see by the evidence of practical men that not more than one grown
person or two children can be accomodated [*sic*] on board ship to a
greater extent, than two tons i.e. one grown person or two children
to every two tons register. Thus the number of ships and the amount
of the tonnage must be doubled. It is also shewn from the evidence
that it cannot cost less than 100£ to locate a man his wife and three
children or 20£ a head one with another.

M^r. Charles Blake for some papers respecting Pasco Peruvian
Mining which I gave him. He needs them to make himself master
of the subject previous to meeting on the business of Barings House,
the managing Director and some others who have the titles of mines
to sell, i.e. if they can find fools to be swindled. Their titles are not
worth a farthing, but if they were even so valid, the mines never can
be productive to those who may become purchasers.

At M^r. Carlile's he poor fellow is very ill and I apprehend in a bad
way.

At M^r. Sheriffs, with my son Frank and M^r. Tijou Sn^r to accept
as trustees a deed to secure payment of money from his son William,
to him and to his three daughters. He is a singular old man, yet an
example of how a very ignorant, stupid man may get on in the world.
He has however with a little persuasion done strict justice to both his
families.

M^r. De Vear on the business of Old M^r. Brooks's funeral.[382] When
M^r. Brooks, died some not very wise men thought that what they
called a public funeral would do honour to his memory and honour
also to Westminster. This is one of those common follies with which
men delude themselves. A number of persons therefore paid 15/ each
for the use of a cloak hatband &c – and ~~the~~ six others held the Pall,
namely, Burdett, Waithman, Kinnaird, Sturch,[383] Wood and Torrens
none of these paid any thing – The Undertakers charge was 58£ –
the sum collected 41£, but as no one took charge of the matter this
sum remained in the hands of two persons, who offered it to the

---

[382] Samuel Brooks, diamond-setter and glass cutter, member of the London Corresponding Society, and active in politics thereafter. See Hone, *For the Cause of Truth*, p. 25.

[383] William Sturch (1753?–1858), London radical, Unitarian, ironmonger, author of
Apeleutherus: or, an effort to attain intellectual freedom (London, 1799). See J. Ann Hone, *For
the Cause of Truth: radicalism in London, 1796–1821* (Oxford, 1982), pp. 24–25, 27, 117.

Undertakers if he would personally discharge them, this he refused to do and at length brought an action for the whole amount against M^r. Sturch. M^r. Sturch on his part defended the action without letting any one know that he had been sued until all the expenses short of going to trial had been incurred, he then waited on M^r. Adams told him how the matter stood and said he should let it go into court. Upon this M^r. Adams came to me for the absurd purpose of persuading me to let Burdett know the particulars, as he would he said no doubt pay the money. This I refused, observing to him that to obtain money from Burdett in the way he proposed was little better than swindling. Three days ago M^r. Adams came again, he had ascertained that the costs on both sides exceeded 30£ and he wanted me to subscribe some money to save the honour of Westminster and the honour of Brooks's family, but I could not see how I could be fairly called upon to subscribe money to what at the time I considered a foolery, and because also, that both James, and Henry Brooks whom Adams said could not afford to pay the money even for their own honour, spent each of them considerable sums of money every year, in luxuries which I in my circumstances did not think myself warranted to indulge, and that if I on the occasion gave money, I gave it to them to enable them to continue their luxurious mode of living at my cost, which I would not do. M^r. De Vear who is a good natured tolerably [?] liberal man, now came for the purpose of inducing me to give money myself and to assist him in obtaining money from others. I ~~defused~~ refused to do either, but rather than give him an alphabetical book of persons who on various occasions have given money for Westminster proceedings I consented to give him a list of names. He will I dare say raise the money, and thus the honour of Westminster and the Brooks's will be saved. There are in fact a large number of persons who rather than the action should come before the Court and the public would willingly give money, for notwithstanding there would be no disgrace in it to the people of Westminster who really had nothing to do with it, there are plenty of scribblers who would accuse them of meanness and fraud, a matter of but little importance certainly, but of great importance in the opinion of many who will give money to prevent it.

Reading Blackwoods Magazine for January, 1827.
Reading Godwins Commonwealth.

Sunday.   Decr. 31.

Intending to close this diary with the Year – shewed it to my son Frank who having read several columns in various parts, was of opinion, that as it cost but little time, I might as well continue it. I however feel a good deal of reluctance to going on with it.

Reading sundry small publications. Out from 12 to three, over Battersea fields and home by the Wandsworth Road.

M^r. Tijou Sn^r executed his will and signed a memorandum at the bottom that the two houses built by him in the Vauxhall Bridge Road were built with money belonging to his three daughters Mary Ann, Sarah and Caroline, and that they are their property solely. I witnessed his signature to this memorandum.

M^r. Gourlay sent me a note and a copy of his, "Appeal to the Common Sense, Mind, and Manhood of the British Nation."[384] Read the dedication to his daughter, and his address to the public, and looked at several parts of the book, he is as he long has been crazy, but he is a well meaning – and notwithstanding his outrageous conduct towards Brougham, he is a mild peaceable man.

Writing letters to the Sailors of Shields — Cutlers of Sheffield, and the Weavers of Bolton, in reply to letters received from them.

Reading and noting Parliamentary History. Reign of James. I.

Colouring a map to shew the antient boundary of St Margarets Parish – for Councellor [sic] Evans.

M^r. Blake, with some information respecting mining at Pasco. It seems that the holders of mines there which are not in the possession of the Pasco Company are desirous of selling and the Company of bu[y]ing these mines. They will therefore be bought with money of the Company. Pasco shares which once sold for 59£ now sell for 10/−. The directors of the Pasco Company will buy them up, make a display – raise the price sell again and pocket the difference.

With the year and as it happens at 12. at night finishes this diary. There is a minuteness about which I do not like, and which cannot I think be of any use whatever. There is more than enough to shew what are the habits of my life, if they are even worth being made known to any-body.

I shall not however at present cease from making notes of such circumstances as may seem to have any interest in them, and probably these after a while will be but seldom made and may perhaps cease to be made at all

No notes made till 19 – March. 1827.

---

[384] Robert Fleming Gourlay, *An Appeal to the Common Sense, Mind, and Manhood of the British Nation* (London, 1826).

1827

V. 5.

N⁰. 3 — Diary – for some portion of – 1827 ⎫ March. 19. Dec 31.
Journal – of another portion — 1827 ⎭

Monday.   [March] 19.

Sir Francis Burdett called this morning to talk of several matters, but principally respecting the Seamen of the Tyne and the Thames.

Soon after M^r. Canning made his rhodomontade speech in justification of his sending troops to Portugal when by the treaty we were not called upon to send ~~troops~~ any, the seamen became alarmed and their secretary at South Shields wrote to me for my opinion as to the probability of a naval war and the issuing of press warrants, this led to a desire among the sailors to petition parliament to abolish pressing, I ~~procured~~ caused a petition to be drawn up which they adopted and printed, 50 copies were sent to me two of those I sent to Sir Francis with a letter of information on the subject & a request to be informed if he was disposed to take up the matter. He replied by letter that he was and would do all he could. I now ~~explained to~~ informed him of the very extraordinary change which had taken place in the habits and intellectual acquirement of the sailors and shewed him that they could never again be treated in the brutish manner in which they had formerly been treated, and that unless the Government abolished pressing, they would not only lose the best of the seamen but the vessels they navigated the men being resolved in the event of a war and the expectation of being pressed to carry as many merchant ships as they could to North America and then desert them. That a plan was contemplated to hire several vessels and emigrate the sailors in large numbers to the same United States, which they affirm they can accomplish at a very small expense. Three vessels each of about 400 tons burthen were in the first instance to be hired and about 1000 men sent away.

Something must therefore be done or on the breaking out of a war we shall lose a large number of our prime seamen.

I have sent copies of the petition to the principal men on both sides of the house.

Much conversation with sir Francis on his absurd speech last week on the Corn Law project of M^r. Canning. His notions [several words crossed out] ~~so~~ are extremely absurd and so nonsensical that I cannot comprehend them. He has promised to put them on paper.

M^r. Hobhouse in the afternoon. He is one of a committee of the Honourable house on the mode of reducing the expense of County Elections and he came to me to request I would draw up a plan for taking the elections for the county of Middlesex in various places so as to save expense and to shorten the durations of Polls, he having promised the committee to produce such a plan on Friday next. Promised to give him a sketch of a plan, and this I shall do.

Tuesday.   [March] 19 [Place erred in recording the dates for the next ten days: Tuesday was the 20th, Wednesday the 21st, etc. His diary resumed the correct numerical date on Thursday, 29 March.]

M^r. Henry Drummond on sundry matters – ministers – Corn Laws – impressment, &c Gave him some copies for distribution of a Catechism on the Corn Laws – the author Major Thompson having sent me 100 copies.[385]

D^r. Hacley [?] wishing to be appointed one of the professors in the London University, he is I think a man remarkably well qualified, and I promised to assist him as much as I could.

Read a small pamphlet sent to me by M^r. John Wright called the Dolphin, a curious well written tract proving that the water served by the Grand Junction Water company is unfit for use, unwholesome &c &c.[386] This is a matter of ~~serious~~ great importance to the inhabitants of London, and I will assist M^r. Wright to the utmost of my power to obtain a remedy for so serious an evil.

M^r. Highley from D^r. James Johnson respecting the abuse of Dr Johnson in the Lancet.[387] Johnson wishes to bring an action against the ~~blackguard~~ the editor M^r. Wakley. Advised him not to do so. The circumstances are peculiar. D^r. Johnson would probably get little more than nominal damages, and this would be of no use to him, but of singular service to Wakley.

Wednesday   [March] 20

Reply to the Dolphin in the Times and threat of an action against M^r. Wright. the only remedy for the evil is an act of Parliament, forbidding after a certain time any water to be taken from the Thames by any Water company within seven or more miles of Blackfriars Bridge. M^r. Wright alarmed at the threat of an action.

[385] Thomas Perronet Thompson, *A Catechism on the Corn Laws: with a list of fallacies and the answers. By a member of the University of Cambridge* (London, 1827).

[386] John Wright, *The Dolphin: or, Grand Junction Nuisance, proving that seven thousand families in Westminster and its suburbs are supplied with water in a state offensive to the sight . . . and destructive to health* (London, 1827). It is unlikely that the author of this tract was the Grand Junction Water Works Company, which is how it appears in the catalogue of the British Library.

[387] The bad blood between Wakley and Johnson, surgeon to the Duke of Clarence (later William IV) and proprietor and editor of *The Medico-Chirurgical Review*, dated back to at least 1820. In the wake of the execution of the Cato Street conspirators, Wakley's home in Argyll Street was attacked and put to the torch for his alleged role in the decapitation of the conspirators. Johnson alleged that Wakely had burned down his own house for the insurance money. Wakely successfully prosecuted Johnson for libel and was awarded £100 in damages. See Peter Froggatt, 'John Snow, Thomas Wakley and *The Lancet*', *Anaesthesia*, vol. 57 (2002), pp. 669–670.

Wrote a plan for taking the votes of the Freeholders of Middlesex for M^r. Hobhouse and sent it to him, with a comment. This is not much better than a sheer loss of time for the committee will recommend nothing to the house which can be of any use to the nation, and if they were to recommend any thing useful the house would reject it. I see no reason why the purposes of a set of rich landowners should be spared, they have no desire to make elections free, they are the great corruptors [*sic*] of the people the wholesale suborners of perjury and so they will continue to be to the last possible moment. It is of little consequence how or where the poll is taken as long as open voting is practiced [*sic*]. Balloting would at once put an end to the abominable villainies practiced [*sic*] at Elections, and this they will never adopt if they can avoid doing it.

Thursday.   [March] 21

Early in the morning M^r. Wright who had been threatened with an action for what the Grand Junction company called a libel in his pamphlet.

M^r. Booth respecting his desire to be appointed professor of the English Language in the London University.

D^r. Thorpe on his own affairs

M^r. Adams with a petition respecting the Church at Hampsted [*sic*] for advice —

M^r. Lang and M^r. Adams from the committee on the Trades Newspaper to lay its affairs before me and to consult thereon.

All day occupied in the affairs of others without the possibility of preventing it.

Friday —   [March] 22.

Petitions received from Bolton respecting Minimum of wages – working to procure members of the house of Commons to present the petitions and move for a committee to hear the petitioners.

Sir Francis Burdett, M^r. Hobhouse M^r. John Smith, M^r. Hume, M^r. Warburton on this and the Water Companies.

Occupied with M^r. Wright on the subject of his publication.

Saturday.   [March] 23.

Occupied part of yesterday and to day in adjusting the accounts at Miers's.

Sunday.   Monday.   Tuesday.

As much as 20 hours occupied in the accounts of the Miers's. Nb. will never again undertake to administer, and never will administer any mans estate as I have done this, will be very careful how I undertake to be an executor, and if under peculiar circumstances I do consent I will take care to make all parties understand how much they are to expect from me and how much I shall expect from them. In this of Miers's, I have managed the complicated concern without the aid of lawyers, and instead of being assisted by any of the legatees have been embarrassed and delayed by their cupidity, every one of them . . . [words crossed out], refusing to assist in any way beyond the immediate interest of the individual. The brother, . . . [words crossed out] William, shuffling with the documents, and when detected treating the matter as one of the most perfect indifference, and as of no consequence whatever.

Taking much pains to induce members of the honourable house to procure a committee to hear the poor distressed cotton and silk weavers, in support of their petitions for a law to fix a minimum of wages. It is absurd for any one to expect that wages can be regulated by acts of parliament, as to the amount which shall be paid, no law can either fix the remuneration for the workman, neither can any arrangement even of the masters and men combined. Wages must and will be regulated by the supply and demand, of and for workmen, and when there are more hands on an average of two or three years than can be employed, the unemployed will undersell their fellow workmen until they bring down wages to the lowest possible amount and no law can prevent this. But if a law could be made so as to prevent this competition, it ought not to be made, and the reasons are so very obvious that it is unnecessary to state them. Spite of this however, not only are the cotton and silk weavers of opinion that a law can and ought to be made to fix a minimum of wages, but a large number of their employers are of the same opinion. This being so and it being of great importance that such absurd notions should be refuted and the best possible evidence given of their absurdity are the reasons which have induced me to move in the business. If a committee of the house of commons can be obtained, every man who comes before it may be made to shew the impracticability of the proposal and the absurdity of attempting it, a good yet a small book may be made of the most material parts of the evidence and the answer to all the loose objections now prevalent may be made familiar to multitudes of persons. This would be doing real service to the people, their prejudices do them very serious mischief and one at least if not the most important service that can be done for them is the removal of prejudice, yet I much doubt that a committee will be obtained. When the Combination laws were repealed it was contended that nothing but mischief would follow. I maintained that the hatreds, the ill will, the malice and the desire to do injury to one another which had existed would soon cease and that combinations of workmen instead of being general and perpetual would become particular and occasional, and this is now the case, masters and men meet in a way they never before met, there is little now to complain of, the men are satisfied that it was not the combination laws which kept down their wages, and the masters are convinced that it was not the law which kept wages from rising they are also convinced that the law was the perpetual occasion of many evils which have now ceased to exist. In fact a host of prejudices have died away and a committee of the house on the proposed minimum of wages would do away with another host of prejudices. The same may be said respecting the use of machinery. It is the duty of the legislature to see to these matters, and when an occasion offers to remove prejudices which lead to animosities, breeaches [*sic*] of the peace riots and plunderings, I know no more imperative duty than such easy means afford to prevent mischief.

Last night M^r. Hume moved as an amendment on the Corn Law project that instead of the proposed duty of 20/ a quarter on wheat when the average price should be 60/ that a duty of 15/ should be adopted and 1/ a year deducted therefrom until the duty shall be reduced to 10/[388] – yet in our Boroughmongering house of Commons only 16 were found to vote for M^r. Hume these were – R. Bernal[389] – Jo Birch[390] [–] Otway Cave[391] – Colⁿ Davies[392] – Ld. Folkstone[393] [–] D. W. Harvey[394] – Ld Howick[395] – Dr Lushington[396] [–] Jno Marshall. Jno Maberley.[397] W. L. Maberley[398] J. B. Monck[399] – Ld Nugent[400] – Ld Rancliffe[401] – C. P. Thompson[402]. Neither Sir Francis Burdett nor M^r. Hobhouse were present, both purposely staid away. And most assuredly I will stay away from the Hustings at the next

[388] *Hansard*, new series, 17, 27 March 1827, cols 95–106.
[389] Ralph Bernal (*c*.1785–1854), MP for Rochester.
[390] Joseph Birch (1755–1833), MP for Nottingham borough.
[391] Robert Otway-Cave (*c*.1796–1844), MP for Leicester borough.
[392] Thomas Henry Hastings Davies (1789–1846), MP for Worcester City.
[393] William Pleydell Bouverie (1779–1869), MP for Salisbury.
[394] Daniel Whittle Harvey (*c*.1786–1863), MP for Colchester.
[395] Henry George Grey (1802–1894), third Earl Grey, MP for Winchelsea.
[396] Stephen Lushington (1782–1873), MP for Ilchester.
[397] John Maberly (*c*.1780–1845), MP for Abingdon.
[398] William Leader Maberly (1798–1885), MP for Northampton borough.
[399] John Berkeley Monck (1769–1834), MP for Reading.
[400] George Nugent (1757–1849), MP for Buckingham borough.
[401] George Parkyns (1785–1850), MP for Nottingham borough.
[402] Charles Poulett Thompson (1799–1841), MP for Dover.

Westminster Election, so far at least as concerns them. Hobhouse last week made some objections to Hume's intended proposition, to my remonstrances he affected to attend and left me with a persuasion that he would vote for M^r. Humes propositions. This will be viewed with astonishment when the time shall come that men are wise enough to reflect with pity on the ignorance of those [who] can persuade themselves that so enormous a tax as 15/ on a quarter of wheat could be beneficial to the country, and with contempt on those who can consent as Burdett and Hobhouse have both done that a tax of 20/ a quarter shall be levied when wheat is at 60/ the quarter.

Neither Burdett nor Hobhouse opposed the grant of 9.000 a Year to the Duke of Clarence, in addition to his present income of 36.000£ a year.

This is the way the people are cheated, demoralized and degraded, men are selected as their friends, who like these two men mislead them, put them out of heart with all public men, lead them into a state of apathy from want of hope, and disqualify them from procuring or even from attempting to procure such reforms as can prevent multitudes of enormous evils. It is such conduct as these men are pursuing that retards the progress of all that is good and useful among mankind – luckily they can only retard, they can not prevent.

Wednesday.   [March] 27.

Yesterday I had a long conversation with M^r. John Smith, M. P – the Banker[403] respecting the Bolton petition for a minimum of wages and the several petitions against the use of machinery. M^r. Smith said he would speak to M^r. Hume, Sir Ronald Fergusson [*sic*].[404] M^r. Maxwell.[405] M^r. Abercrombie[406] and others and also to M^r. Peel who he thought might be prevailed upon to consent to the appointment of a committee, and that he would then present the petition. M^r. Smith called this evening, he had presented the petition, and had suggested the appointment of a committee. This was met by Peel who said that two committees had sat on the same subject some years ago, and that they in their reports had given reasons at length which were conclusive against any such law as that desired by the petitioners, and that to grant a committee would reflect on the proceedings of the former committees; this altho it was no reason at all was however enough to prevent a committee being appointed, but Peel did not

[403] John Smith (1767–1842), MP for Midhurst.
[404] Ronald Craufurd Ferguson (1773–1841), MP for Dysart burghs.
[405] John Maxwell (1791–1865), MP for Renfrewshire.
[406] James Abercromby (1776–1858), MP for Calne.

speak the truth, the report of the former committee was made on the
29 March 1809 Journals Vol 64. fol 196, and contains no reasons it
merely says — "the fixing a minimum for the price of ~~wages~~ Labour
is wholly inadmissible in principle, incapable of being reduced to
practice by any means which can possibly be devised, and if practicable
would be attended with the most fatal consequences." M^r. Smith on
receiving this information was offended at the conduct of M^r. Peel,
and will tell him so if he has another petition to present. He shall have
one — Sent the minutes of evidence of 1808 to M^r. Smith as a copy
cannot be procured at the house.

Thursday.   [March] 29

   M^r. John Fordham who says the Corn Bill will under certain
circumstances produce intolerable mischief to the farmer – e.g. if
a short crop which should raise the price to 90/– were to come the
actual price would not be more than from 60/ to 65 in consequence
of the foreign corn imported and taken out of bond, and this seems
probable. For as bad land is necessarily resorted to, it is plain that a
small deficiency of the crop would make a very high price necessary
to pay the farmer, but this he would not have, since the 500.000 qrs
in bond and the other 500.000 qrs, which would certainly be brought
in, would have a tendency to force down prices much lower than
the additional quantity would warrant, but as it would all be intended
~~from~~ for home consumption if the whole quantity of British and foreign
corn exceeded the supposed demand by only a very small quantity,
the price would be depressed, to a great extent, this would prevent
much misery among the working people but it would embarras [*sic*]
the farmers generally and ruin a great number. And this comes of
meddling.
   Assisting M^r. Wright to obtain a public meeting respecting the
state of the water companies, in the hope of procuring a plentiful
supply of wholesome water for the metropolis instead of the muddy
unwholesome water they now supply.
   Reading and remarking on a paper addressed by Dr Gilchrist to the
proprietors of East India stock. A difficult and disagreeable job which
I could not refuse to undertake.

Friday.   [March] 30.

   Reading and correcting Dr Thorpes petition, to the House of
Commons.

Interfering to procure a petition to be signed by the Lecturers Surgeons &c. &c to the house of Commons, which I drew some time ago respecting procuring subjects for dissection, as one step to breaking down the prejudices which make the obtaining [of] bodies difficult, expensive, and precarious, and also compelling the professions continually to countenance and promote a violation of the laws.[407]

Saturday —   [March] 31.

Finished reading and commenting on Dr Gilchrists papers. This good old man, mars all he touches, he is as good as an unsophisticated child, and like such a child he is defective ~~of~~ in respect to judgment, writes just what is agreeable to his own feelings quite unconscious of the effect, what he writes will have on others and then he is surprised that others do not fall in with his notions.

M^r. ~~Richard~~ Phillip Taylor of Norwich with the plans made three years ago for the project then on foot to bring water by a tunnel from Richmond to Hampstead to supply London. With M^r. Wright & M^r. Richard Taylor of Shoe Lane and concerted with him how to induce M^r. Burton and M^r. Deputy Routh [?] who were under M^r. Philip Taylor the original projectors of the plan, to take part again supposing, as seems probable that a number of Noblemen and Gentlemen should be willing to become members of a company.

[407] See Ruth Richardson, *Death, Dissection and the Destitute* (London, 1987).

Sunday.   [April] 1.

Long discussion with Dr Gilchrist on his papers, he agreed to expunge a considerable portion.

Monday.   [April] 2.

Up to this time reading and examining Journals Dom Com. Rapin. Hume Rushworth Nelson.[408] Whitelock[409] – Somers Collection of Tracts[410] – Burgh[411] – Prynne[412] – Ackerley[413] – Selden[414] – Marvel[415] – &c – for matters Relating to Parliament.

M^r. Marshall of Leeds, who is sick of publishing parliamentary Reports and Reviews, as well he may be since all he will procure is loss of money. Promised him to speak to M^r. Wright, respecting merging his Marshalls book in the Debates published by Hansard.

All the Westminster Electors, I speak to, are very much dissatisfied with the conduct of Burdett and Hobhouse, and I have no doubt, that it will be utterly impossible to procure volunteers at the next election, even, to form committees for them.

Tuesday.   [April] 3

Dr Gilcrhist with a pamphlet of 80 pages. Testimonials from James Sanders M. D. Of Edinburgh, wishing me to put them into the hands of some of the members of the Council of the London University

[408] Perhaps William Nelson, *The Office and Authority of a Justice of Peace* (London, 1710).

[409] Likely an edition of Bulstrode Whitelock's *Memorials of the English Affairs: or, an historical account of what passed from the beginning of the reign of King Charles the First, to King Charles the Second his happy restauration* (London, 1682).

[410] *A Collection of Scarce and Valuable Tracts, on the Most Interesting and Entertaining Subjects: but chiefly such as relate to the history and constitution of these kingdoms. Selected from an infinite number in print and manuscript, in the Royal, Cotton, Sion, and other publick, as well as private libraries; Particularly that of the late Lord Somers,* a new edition of which had been published between 1809 and 1815.

[411] Perhaps referring to Ulick Bourke, Earl of Clanricarde, *A Declaration of the Resolutions of His Majesties Forces, published by the Marquisse of Clanrickard against the Parliament of England also a declaration signed by the officers in Ulster. And a copy of a letter from Collonell Jones to the Lord Inchequeen* (London, 1648).

[412] Perhaps William Prynne, *The History of King John, King Henry III. and the most illustrious King Edward the I: wherein the ancient sovereign dominion of the kings of England, Scotland, France, and Ireland . . . is asserted and vindicated* (London, 1670).

[413] Roger Acherley, either *The Britannic Constitution: or, the fundamental form of government in Britain* (London, 1727) or *Free Parliaments: or, an argument on their constitution; proving some of their powers to be independent* (London, 1731).

[414] Perhaps John Selden's *A Brief Discourse concerning the Power of the Peers and Commons of Parliament in point of Judicature* (London, 1640).

[415] Perhaps Andrew Marvell's *An Account of the Growth of Popery and Arbitrary Government in England* (Amsterdam, 1677).

preparatory to his proposing himself for the Medical Chair. This I shall do.

M^r. Wright greatly agitated about the Water companies, great men make him promises but do nothing in the way of assisting him. Here is a man upwards of 50 years of age who has been living in the world all his life and has yet to learn that in a project such as his he must do his own business himself – and that to do it well he must do it promptly. Here is a man who has yet to learn that he can only be supported by Great men, when great men can make a public display, but that he must get every thing ready for them to make the display or it will not be made at all. Thus they do not give him money to pay expenses, and this frets him, yet he does not demand money, and unless he does demand money none will he have, and he will be left to pay the expenses himself. It is this want of knowledge want of tact and infirmity of purpose which mars many useful projects, while rogues whose object is plunder following up their object vigirously [*sic*] often succeed, and commit many extensive robberies.

Wednesday.   [April] 4

M^r. Hume to my surprise informed me that Sir Francis Burdett had on friday presented the petition of the seamen of Shields against impressment without saying a word on its contents.[416] On looking to the votes I see it was presented on monday. This is too bad by far. After promissing [*sic*] as he did, that he would, not only make a speech himself when he presented the petition but would speak to several other members to do the same. It is such conduct as this of Burdetts' [*sic*] that breaks the hearts of poor men who are led on with hopes, which are not only not realized, but no effort is even made to serve them,[417] [.] Nothing can now be done but to urge Burdett to make a specific motion after the Easter Holidays, and if he will not do that, the men can have no hearing not even of their petition, which was not read, beyond its title which was muttered over by the Clerk thus. [*sic*] "Sir Francis Burdett a petition from the seamen of Newcastle against impressment."

The way in which these matters are managed may be judged of by an occurrence in the house of Lords last week. A Noble lord, rose and said he begged their Lordships pardon for a mistake he made, in presenting to the house a petition which was addressed to the house of

---

[416] *JHC*, 82 (1826–1827), 2 April 1827, p. 381.
[417] Remainder of sentence crossed out.

commons, this he had done some days previously and he now wished the petition might be returned to him, which was ordered.[418]

A very long conversation with M^r. Hume respecting the law of debtor and creditor in Scotland and on the propriety of assimilating the law in England to the law in Scotland.[419] M^r. Hume is to frame a bill, which I am to see &c – M^r. Marshall was present during a considerable part of the discussion, after which we talked of a project which they supposed had been set on foot three or four years ago by Coln Torrens for a more correct mode [of] taking the parliamentary debates and of printing them, and I now learned that the proposition had failed in consequence of Torrens having represented the scheme as his and the dislike M^r. Hume M^r. Ricardo and others had to trusting him with the money necessary for the setting up and conducting the publication.

That plan was mine I wrote the prospectus, and offered if 5.000£ were raised to become the editor and manager, and to take no pay for the first session unless the publication produced profit. I laid down in writing the whole plan in all its details, but Torrens never once mentioned it as mine. "If he had," said M^r. Hume," [sic] "and we had known the project was yours and that you would have conducted the publication the money would have been raised without difficulty.["] M^r. Hume and M^r. Marshall both talked of reviving the project, but it will not now be agreeable to me to undertake the management. Promised to let M^r. Marshall have a copy of the plan.

Thursday   [April] 5   Friday.   [April] 6

Occupied a considerable portion of both days in examining the Journals of the house of Commons. Rapin Hume Rushworth, Nelson, May, Whitelock, Dugdale,[420] Prynne &[c] — as all the time I could bestow upon the subject has been occupied for several months past – and extracting matter. 1 for an article for the Westminster Review and 2 – as materials for a history of the origin construction and changes in parliament principally in respect to the House of Commons.

At, Mile End – Rotherhithe – Horslydown [sic] enquiring into the state of Mechanics Institutions at these places, at the request of Sir Francis Burdett to whom they have applied for pecuniary assistance.

Assisting M^r. Wright in preparing for a public meeting on the state of the water supplied by the water companies.

[418] I have not been able to find an account of this action in either *Hansard* or *JHC*.
[419] On 3 April, Hume introduced a motion to abolish imprisonment for debt. See *Hansard*, new series, 17, 3 April 1827, cols 223–234.
[420] Probably one of the numerous works of Sir William Dugdale (1605–1686).

Drew a petition to both houses and also resolutions to be proposed to the meeting next monday.

Dr Hales [?] with a proposition to dispose of his bookselling business to my son Fred in conjunction with a young german, this I declined being concerned in.

Saturday.   [April] 7

Narrative state of the Mechanics Institutions, in Spital Fields Bethnal Green &c — and at Horslydown [*sic*] – for Sir Francis Burdett —

Made up all the papers – viz – Resolutions, Petitions, and business sheet, for M^r. Wrights meeting at Willis's Rooms on Monday – Instructing him how to proceed. I should have taken a more active part in the matter, and should have attended at the meeting to have arranged the business and suggest to those who were to take part publically [?] the manner in which they should proceed so as to make a whole of it, as I have done on many other occasions, but M^r. Wright seeks not only payment for all the expenses he has incurred, which is very proper, and in obtaining which I would have assisted him, but he seeks what he calls a recompence [*sic*] for his time, and labour and anxiety. Now it so happens that when in public matters a man expects pecuniary profit, that he is looked upon as a mean fellow, who is more operated upon by the desire of gain than by any desire to do public service and he who condescends either to solicit or to permit even a public subscription for his personal use in such cases, is always shunned as one who would make money of the public improperly. I cannot therefore do any thing which would place me under a suspicion of a desire to participate with M^r. Wright and yet if I were to do any any [*sic*] thing personally at the meeting to promote his views I should incur the imputation. If there were a fund it might be proper to give M^r. Wright a small sum of money as payment for his time, but it will never do for me in any way to countenance an attempt to obtain a subscription of names to donations to an undefined amount that M^r. Wright may put the money into his pocket. I have told him thus much as reasons why I shall take no part in the management of the business at the public meeting.

Sunday —   [April] 8

M^r. Glazier, on the water companies. He is the gentleman who under the solicitors to Philip Taylor, Thames Water company got the consent of parties to set up matters and to make the proposed tunnel under their grounds — M^r. Richard Taylor says M^r. Philip will be in town to-morrow morning – and will attend the meeting – My notion now is that nothing should be said of M^r. Taylors project at the public meeting – A committee of the House of Commons will be appointed and M^r. Taylor and M^r. Glazier may be the first witnesses examined, they can expound the whole matter there, the drawings may be given in and the committee will print them. Names may be obtained for shares of Noblemen and Gentlemen, and a company formed as a company should be formed of respectable people, and not mere jobbers.

Monday.   [April] 9.

Meeting at Willis's Room on the Thames Water-supply – Many Noblemen and Gentlemen present, business conducted in a most disorderly manner, yet peaceably – Resolutions and petition both altered – Resolutions made three times too long, and petition not signed as [*sic*] in the room as it ought to have been a hundred signatures being as useful as five thousand, but this was a manuevore [*sic*] of Wrights, who caused a resolution for a committee to be appointed to whom he is to be secretary and thus he hopes to make money of the matter.

[At this point in the diaries, daily entries end.]

Sunday.   [April] 15

Variously employed all the week much as usual, in the concerns of others.

Tuesday.   [April] 17

M^r. Henry Drummond to consult with me on a project he had in embryo to portion out a considerable part of his estate at Aldbury [*sic*]^421 near Guildford in plots of 3 acres to build a cottage on each plot and let it to a labourer of good character. I advised him to do no such thing as the consequence would be the increase of human beings beyond the means of support, at a much greater rate than that which had already brought them to so much misery, and I instanced the plan which M^r. Gourlay^a had some 27 years ago ~~carried into effect for I~~

---

^a NB M^r. Gourlays statement taken from the Morning Chronicle Newspaper is pasted in the Guard Book – backed "Poor. Population. Emigration." dated Dec. 27. 1823. [Footnote.]

^421 Drummond's estate was at Albury Park, not 'Aldbury', Surrey.

~~think the Duke of Rutland~~ under the auspices of the Government, made enquiries into the state of the poor in Rutland and Lincolnshire and here where the cottage system was then carried to a considerable extent particularly by Lord Winchelsea, he in 1803 – ~~as he~~ says put up 21 cottages &c or just 23 years from the time he was aiding this cottage system, he now found the labourers were all paupers, and in every parish but one more people than there was work for. And M^r. Gourlay says this is the result of M^r. Arthur Young's Cow system. Lord Winchelsea he observe[d] had for some years abandoned the system lest he should be overwhelmed with paupers." [*sic*]

I represented to M^r. Drummond that this was an inevitable consequence of the cottage or Cow system, that as all his cottages would be occupied by married couples having children, their numbers would be tripled in less than 25 years and the whole mass ~~would~~ be reduced to as miserable a state as the Irish cottiers. He said the persons to whom he should let the land would at any rate be better off during his own lifetime and he should not for the future be annoyed by their poverty or misery as he now was, and he then, most inconsequently told me he had been with William Allen who had explained to him, minutely, the plan he Allen and M^r. John Smith had in hand in Hert – as M^r. Smith had a few days since explained it to me. The project was just such an one as M^r. Drummond now himself proposed, and yet, he said, I did not think William Allens project calculated to be of any permanent service, and I therefore refused to join him. Such are the reasonings and such the conduct of benevolent men who have much money and limited conceptions of the principle of utility.

M^r. Hume has made up his bill respecting debtor and creditor, and a M^r. Bell a barrister I believe from Edinburgh is to bring it to me and we are to examine all its provisions.

Thursday.   [April] 19.

There has been for some time past in consequence of the incapacity of Lord Liverpool, no Premier.[422] Many stories were propagated respecting his successor, but it at length appeared that M^r. Canning had succeeded with the King, and had received his commands to take upon himself that office and as in consequence of this command most of the ministers resigned their places. M^r. Canning was commanded to form a new administration, and this he has proceeded to do with apparent determination, to exclude all or nearly all who have either

---

[422] Lord Liverpool was incapacitated by a seizure on 17 February and Canning proceeded to form a coalition ministry with the Whigs. A detailed account of the negotiations is A. Aspinall, 'The coalition ministries of 1827', parts 1 and 2, *English Historical Review*, 42 (1927), pp. 201–226, 533–559.

resigned or rebelled against his authority. M^r. Canning it is said has obtained his present power through the influence of the Marchioness of Conyngham who is the specially [?] the Kings Mistress – Canning made her son his private and confidential secretary when he himself became foreign minister, and her wise and honest Lord is to be made a Duke. Many people, as well desponding Whigs, as malignant tories said that Cannings power ~~will~~ would be of short duration and that no ministry formed by him ~~can~~ will stand. It was no doubt the persuasion of the 7 ministers who resigned, that he would at once be embarrassed and subdued, but in this they were mistaken. Canning seems to have foreseen the kind of conduct he would have opposed to him and he took measures accordingly. He made the stupid Duke of Clarence the heir apparent of the Throne Lord high Admiral, the office being revived for him, and thus shut out the whole of the scotch connection of Lord Melville who had like an idiot resigned his office of first Lord of the Admiralty; and as he Canning will have to rearrange the business of that office, he can appoint efficient persons, without putting any business into the hands of the fool, the Duke of Clarence, who is scarcely fit to be left to himself in the most ordinary concerns of life. Thus however Canning fortifies [?] his own power and influence. Lord Eldon, the Lord Chancellor, may be said to have the good wishes of nobody as Chancellor, and the hatred of millions, his resignation gave Canning an opportunity of making M^r. Copley[423] (Sir S. Copley) – a man whom every body desired to see on the bench, Lord High Chancellor, and who since that obnoxious and pernicious court cannot be wholly abolished is perhaps the fittest man in the nation for the situation. Canning is it seems to advance, certain great Borough-mongering Lords a step or two in the peerage and will fill up the places vacated by ministers with men whom nobody in the present state of things will object to. Those who have resigned with the exception of M^r. Peel whom on account of the part he has taken in digesting the Laws every body wishes may consent to remain in office, are a set of men the least fit of any to govern such a nation as this in its present circumstances. They are all of the old stupid illiberal school, too ignorant of the state of mankind to be able to conduct themselves with even seeming propriety, and having therefore no hold on the wishes, or sympathies of the people. Chancellor Eldon, is in those respects just

---

[423] John Singleton Copley, later Lord Lyndhurst, who first came to prominence defending both Luddites and John Watson and Arthur Thistlewood, the latter of whom were indicted for treason after the failed uprising at Spa Fields in 1817. He was subsequently retained for the crown and, in that capacity, prosecuted the Cato Street conspirators, including Thistlewood. He was appointed Lord Chancellor in 1827. See Gareth H. Jones, 'Copley, John Singleton, Baron Lyndhurst (1772–1863)', *ODNB*, <http://www.oxforddnb.com/view/article/6272>, accessed 19 January 2006.

as wise as he was 50 years ago, society has progressed greatly, but he has been stationary. The enemy of all improvement, moral political, legal, & equitable, he sinks at once into utter insignificance.

Wellington, Duke of[424] – who had but just been appointed Commander in Chief in consequence of the Death of the Duke of York has in resigning acted an almost inconceivably silly part. Hated by the army, despised for his meanness, his ignorance his pride and his arrogance by everybody [words struck out] out of his profession[425] a man of ~~the~~ very mean intellectual endowments, everybody is pleased, at his being displaced, and as Canning will probably, place one of the Kings brothers in the Office of Commander in Chief, he will be as effectually shut out as Eldon is from the Chancellorship by the appointment of Copley to that office. Wellington is poor, notwithstanding he has received to the value of a million sterling from [the] Government and being out of office will be an object little short of contempt to ~~every one~~ a very great portion of the people. Lords Bathurst and Westmorland are two old women, conceited, insolent and capable of all manner of iniquity. As I have no doubt will yet be shewn both as to the, plots for which they and Castlereagh caused to be got up and for which Thistlewood and others were hanged, but also the Manchester Massacre. The nation can suffer neither loss nor inconvenience from the resignation of these men, and as no one will care a straw about them and as Canning will have the command of the loaves and fishes I see no reason why his power, barring unforseen [sic] circumstances, which cannot be calculated upon, should not stand.

At any rate the old, prejudiced, ignorant tories the remains as well as the worst of the Pitt school are now defunct and the notions which prevailed during his (Pitt's) reign of terror, may now be said to be obliterated and done with practically, and so far an advance towards a better government has been made, no thanks for this are however due to Canning, he would as willingly as the worst of them all keep the people in ignorance and the most degranding [sic] subjection but hated as he has all along been by the old-tories, and suspected and viewed with jealousy by the Whigs, he is compelled to support more liberal measures, and to conform more to the feelings and intelligence of the nation than he would otherwise be disposed to do. We may therefore expect, such liberal measures to be proposed as he has any hopes the aristocracy will any way permit, but he will take especial care not to propose or countenance any measure which has a direct

---

[424] This paragraph is twice overwritten with the words: 'Will not do in these times. 1874. FP' (that is, Francis Place, Jr).

[425] The phrase 'out of his profession' is inserted between lines in the original, and the precise point of insertion within this sentence is unclear.

tendency to make the people more free, or in any way to increase their political consequence. In other words, he will resolutely set himself to oppose every thing which has a tendency to lessen either his own power or patronage or that may in this way be calculated to operate upon the aristocracy.

Canning is not a man of long views, not a man having a profound judgment, nor even any considerable approximation to a profound judgment, and he will therefore as he has all along on occasions done, commit acts of folly, and when firmly seated in power, will probably do much mischief where he ~~has~~ will probably intend just the contrary.

The nation must gain by the present change. Any, every reform helps them, they sometimes clamour for reform and as soon as their object is accomplished ~~they~~ think but little of it and in a very short time ~~they~~ forget it, and go on for further reforms, and this feeling operates even on their opponents, excepting only on such of them as have been thoroughly bred and grown old in antiquated prejudices, of ~~which,~~ whom none will now remain in office, nor in the ~~face of the Earth many years~~ country very many years longer. Reform proceeds slowly but surely, intelligence amongst the people increases, and both will be accelerated in somewhat the proportion of the law of falling bodies.

This is no prophecy, for the march of intellect must necessarily produce its effects, and ultimately terminate in good, that is in a cheap republican government.

Monday.   [April] 23.

M^r. Bell W. S. Edinburgh and M^r. John Evans. Att^y at Law. Tooks Court London.

M^r. Bell a very gentlemanly person and well informed man brought with him, the draft of the bill of which M^r. Hume had given notice in the House of Commons, to put an end, to arrest on Mesne process and of imprisonment for debt.

M^r. Bell explained seriatim the scotch process for the recovery of debts. It seems that scarcely any english attorneys are conversant wether [*sic*] with the laws of Scotland in relation to debtor and creditor, and the Scotch writers are equally ignorant of the law and practice of England in the same matters. M^r. Evans explained the law and practice in England. We then made the necessary comparison, and agreed that the Scotch process was very far superior to the english process – Read M^r. Humes bill clause by clause, and as M^r. Bell now understood the practice followed here ~~and~~ the nature of our courts, and their modes of proceeding as well as of our legal officers, he was soon convinced that the bill was crude and inefficient. It appeared to me that as it was drawn it would not be even understood by the lawyers in the house or by any body out of the house, that its enactments would necessarily be viewed, in relation to, our courts and legal officers, and that it would at once be seen that it could not be carried into practice without several alterations being made in the legal machinery, and in this M^r. Bell and M^r. Evans both concurred. I suggested therefore that M^r. Hume should withdraw his motion, that M^r. Evans should consider the subject and write a comment both on the bill and the laws of arrest and imprisonment that other qualified persons should do the same, that then the bill, together with the remarks, &c should be left with me to be put into such a form, as should enable M^r. Hume to ~~understan~~ comprehend the whole subject. That then a bill should be drawn, containing the reasonings for every change proposed and every enactment and also an exposition of the principles on which the propositions were founded. The process to be had, step by step, and the alterations respecting courts and legal officers, expenses &c &c – all this to be printed as notes to the text of the bill. There appeared to me to be many reasons for pursuing the plan among others the absolute necessity in attempting so great a change, of shewing its advantages as well to debtors as to creditors, and also its moral effects upon the community. That it should be shewn to be easy in execution – that it should as far as possible be certain in its operation, that it should as far as possible be made to conform to present usages, and that upon the whole while the cavilling of those who would lose much of their practice was anticipated and set aside, it should be so plain to Merchants, Tradesmen and others whom it would materially concern that they might at once see that it was to their interest to support it. In all this M^r. Bell and M^r. Evans concurred. Finally it was agreed that it would do M^r. Hume no credit to introduce the bill in its present state, while it was very probable if he did, that he would impede rather than promote the end he aimed at. M^r. Evans took the bill with him.

Tuesday.   [April] 24.

Early this morning M^r. Bell came with the draft of a letter he had prepared, to be sent to M^r. Hume, in this he stated the matters in conference and advised M^r. Hume accordingly.

In the evening M^r. Florance an attorney who had been assisting M^r. Hume and had drawn the bill. He was disappointed at the result of the conference and was averse from ~~the~~ preparing the bill with reasons annexed. He wanted the bill to be laid before the house as it was, he said the enacting that no person should be arrested on mesne process would be understood easily enough, as would also the attaching of effects to answer process and this was as far as he went. I shewed him that this was doing next to nothing, and excepting in cases of Bonds,

Bills of Exchange and other specialties, not contested, neither time nor expense would be saved, and that one very large class of debts could never be recovered at all, namely all simple contract debts, as well as a large portion of debts due on bonds and bills, where the creditors could not at once lay their hands on the property of the debtor and ~~that~~ consequently in numerous instances the debtor would manage so to divest himself of property as to make it quite impossible for the creditor to attach it, and thus shut him out from all chance of either suing, or in any way obtaining payment, or of punishing the debtor for the fraud he had committed.

After nearly four hours discussion M^r. Florance confessed that enough was not done in the bill, that it was necessary to make it much more comprehensive, and to accompany it with a plan of procedure and reasons for the enactments, to print it, and cause it to be circulated all over the Country during the recess of parliament, in the next session to get a select committee to take evidence and finally to make the Bill as much as possible a code, for debtor and creditor and insolvency. I gave him ~~several~~ such information as I possessed on these matters, and a plan for simplifying the proceedings, in cases of insolvency – of discharging the unfortunate insolvent at once by consent of creditors, or of punishing him by the court, in case it appeared that he had acted with dishonesty, that thus while no man should be imprisoned for debt, none who were dishonest should escape punishment as criminals.

M^r. Florance promised to do what he could to promote my views, and said he would call on M^r. Evans. But M^r. Florance is a young man, exceedingly enamoured of his child, and will not I fear act as prudently as he ought. If M^r. Hume does not drop his motion, he will be laughed at for his folly. The great impediment to M^r. Hume in this and other matters is, his vanity, he will collect information privately from any one and will when it does not interfere with any display he wishes to make, take advice. But he will not permit any one to share with him in public the honour he covets of being seen and heard and looked upon as the originator and promoter of any measure, and this induces him, frequently to do things prematurely, of course to do them badly, ~~and~~ to miss his object and to prevent the concurrence of others whom had he consulted would have assisted him. I learned from M^r. Florance, that in the present matter M^r. Humes desire was to collect all the information he could as materials for a speech, and if he proceeds in this way as I fear he will he will sacrifice a most important subject for a silly display, which will not after all be so reported in the newspapers as either to please him, or be of much service to the public. If M^r. Humes vanity was not prompting him to this unwise course he would have been with me on the subject before this time.

Thursday.   [April] 26

M^r. Florance, a long discussion with him. He had seen M^r. Hume
and it appeared that both he and M^r. Hume were disheartened by
the proposition to recast the bill, to make it more comprehensive, for
the purpose of putting an end to imprisonment for debt altogether.
They were now willing simply to prevent arrest on mesne process – to
give the creditor means of attaching property and to leave the matter
there. They thought that neither the house nor the country were
likely to agree to go any further. I argued that this would never do,
that as it provided no remedy where property could not be attached
it would open a door to admit fraudulent debtors to a great extent
and would tend to make many men whose circumstances were getting
worse than they had previously been, become fraudulent debtors,
that as no means would remain but an action on a copy of a writ,
all the present vexations, delay and expense would remain as it is,
and the further evil of permitting a man to go on until the creditor
had obtained judgment would deter creditors from suing at all and
would consequently operate as a bar to their claims, and frauds would
be committed with impunity. That if a man did sue his debtor as
he must sue by a process not bailable the creditor could remove out
of the way at any time, as most likely he would do when he had
gained as much time as he could by the law's delay, and put his
creditor to as much expense as possible. That in fact by the proposed
law, the creditor would obtain no information as to the ability of the
debtor to pay until he had gone through the fire and brimstone of
the law, while by the present process he very frequently obtained that
information at once, and might therefore if he chose, either discharge
his debtor or permit him to go to prison. It appearing that nearly
half of those confined in debtors gaols, went to Gaol from inability
to justify bail. In this case the debtor goes to gaol at once and the
creditor generally knows before he does so that he has no property,
the number therefore who compromise the matter, and against whom
proceedings are dropped is very large compared with the number who
go to gaol. But if no bailable process could issue the creditor would
never discover the inability of the debtor until he had incurred all the
expense the law puts upon him in proceeding to obtain judgment and
issuing execution. It therefore seemed to me unreasonable to expect
that either the house or the public would go along with M^r. Hume
in so crude and inefficient a project. M^r. Florance was compelled to
assent to this.

I argued that much more must be done, and imprisonment for
debt be wholly set aside, as M^r. Hume had himself proposed, and
on which basis it was he proposed to legislate. That in cases where

property could not be attached, a debtor after certain notice and process entered should be declared insolvent and be brought before all his creditors by notice served on each by an officer of the Insolvent court. The debtor being compelled as he is now after imprisonment, ~~but~~ with this difference that instead of being sent to gaol he should be placed under the cognizance of the Insolvent Court and compelled to ~~sign a~~ make up a schedule of his debts, to enable the proper officer to summon his creditors who might if they pleased discharge him on any terms they chose, or they might send him before the court, the court having the power to sequester his effects present and prospective, to commit him to prison also if fraud was proved and to discharge him from personal annoyance if no fraud appeared. The court to have power to commit the debtor if he failed to appear or neglected to furnish a schedule, or gave a defective or false schedule. That this was absolutely necessary to ensure the least chance of success, and that I had no doubt at all, that if a bill as comprehensive as I pointed out, drawn up in the first instance as a code, with the reasonings[,] was printed and pretty widely distributed, its enactment would be petitioned for from all parts of the Kingdom. M^r. Florance admitted all this, but fairly hinted that it was more than he and M^r. Hume felt themselves competent to atchieve [*sic*] and he appeared to think the matter hopeless. I encouraged him to proceed, but I fear he and M^r. Hume will be deterred by the difficulties of composing such a code, and rather than do nothing will do mischief.

Consultation at M^r. Scarlets chambers, in M^r. Fenn's case, present M^r. Scarlet, M^r. Brougham, M^r. Evans – barristers. M^r. Burke Atty M^r. Fenn and self. The most pleasant, and also the most satisfactory consultation I ever attended. M^r. Scarlet elated, and in high good humour, on his being appointed Attorney General, he read to Brougham but in such a manner that we should all understand, two letters, one from M^r. Canning to M^r. Justice Abbott, and the other from M^r. Abbott in reply the one announcing M^r. Abbotts elevation to the peerage the other, of thanks in reply.[426] Discussed our case very freely, very fully and very candidly, every one of us is master of the whole case and of the whole law and success appears to be as certain as an undecided cause can be.

Friday.   [April] 27.

A long conversation with M^r. Bell on M^r. Hume's projected bill, in which I explained at length my notion of a proper adaptation of the Insolvent court, to the cases of Debtors, when their creditors could

---

[426] Charles Abbott was created first Baron Tenterden.

not find any property to attach. M^r. Bell admitted that, the mode I preferred would be as effectual as any mode could well be and that it would be an improvement on the law of Scotland and he concurred with me in thinking an attempt should be made wholly to prevent imprisonment for debt in any case.

Saturday.   [April] 28

M^r. Bell sent me a printed proof of maxims &c – respecting arrest on mesne process – and the remedy, for the evil, with a note requesting me to criticise the paper fully. Wrote him a letter containing some observations on his paper, and the substance of my proposition to prevent imprisonment for debt. (See the letter in the letter Book – this days date.)

Monday.   [April] 30.

M^r. Bell has adopted most of my suggestions, agrees with me, but cannot undertake to draw a bill from his ignorance of English Law.

Half inclined to set about it myself – thus to make a catalogue of heads, of subjects and to get as many persons as I can to put on paper, information, legal moral &c – objections &c – and then to make a sort of code in articles, which may be afterwards with or without the reasonings in the codified form be put in the form of enactments – this will occupy a large portion of time, yet I think, I shall if no one else will, go on with it.

Dr Thorpe has been communing with M^r. Hume on the subject of pressing Sailors, in consequence of my having conversed with him on the subject. The D^r says he can assist in giving useful information, and that he is authorized by M^r. Hume to say, that if I cannot induce Sir Francis Burdett to go on with the subject he will undertake it. If I can persuade Sir Francis, he will assist him all he can.

Letter through M^r. John Smith from Richard Thomason at Bolton, Secretary to the committee of Cotton weavers. There are 20 petitions to the house coming up, for a committee on a minimum of wages. Wrote to M^r. Smith on the subject, but with small expectations that he will stir the subject as he ought to do. He like every other member of the honourable house, Hume alone excepted, will not do as he ought to do, and as he wishes should be done lest it should occasion him more trouble than he is disposed to take, and thus none of them are of any use. And none will ever be of much use until the house shall be composed of men elected by the people, for short periods and by secret suffrage.

May

Tuesday.   1st

From 9 a. m. till ½ 6 p. m in the Court of Kings Bench on the Trial Goding. v. Fenn.

This is the action with the parish at the instance of M^r. Fenn. Verdict for the parish. It ought to have been for M^r. Fenn. By the process in the Ecclesiastical court, M^r. Fenn was compelled to become the defendant by which the council [*sic*] for the parish had to reply. The parish put in documents to shew that in the ~~reign~~ 13 Hen. 3 The Church and parish of St Martin were recognized by donations, of persons, of lands and tenements. We had a copy of the pope's nuncio in 1222 which shewed clearly that at that period there was no parish of St Martin, the whole being the parish of St Margaret, but as we could only produce the register book of the dean and Chapter, and consequently only a copy of the award [?] we could not make evidence of it and thus the parish was admitted to be a parish beyond time of memory. M^r. Scarlet for us, shewed great talent great zeal, ~~and~~ evinced great discrimination and sound judgment, he shewed most clearly that a select vestry could not be shewn to exist by custom, the customs having varied, and consequently was no custom in law, he shewed also that within the time in which the parish of St Martin was claimed to be a parish it was utterly unreasonable to suppose there could be select vestry, where there were so very few inhabitants, but if it were even granted that men had been selected by the parish, even in those times, it must have been by election of the parishioners, and afterwards when it was evident there was a select vestry, it was so elected by the people since they occasionally acted for themselves – and since also, the persons who composed the vestry continually varied[.] That in 1662 – a faculty was obtained constituting a select vestry of 49 persons, which if the custom had not been abrogated of a certain number destroyed the custom, and gave them power to elect one another as they have since done, except at intervals when the parishioners by force took their affairs into their own hands. ~~But~~ On this faculty the vestry has ever since acted. It was ordered to be read in the church as the power by which the Vestry existed. It was declared in a petition to the House of Commons in W. & M. To be the power under which the vestry acted, and by which it had been appointed to act, by which it had existence. But the faculty being of no validity, the Vestry was obliged to abandon it which they did. M^r. Scarlet conclusively argued that the Vestry could not use the faculty as a constitution for nearly 170 years & then lay it aside and say we are a vestry by custom, since the faculty

being taken as their constitution they had set aside the custom, if it
had previously existed.

M^r. Tindal replied ingeniously to M^r. Scarlet, avoiding all definition
of custom and scarcely using the word.

The Chief Justice Abbott who had shewn his teeth at us from the
first in his summing up, never once used the word custom, he was
bound in justice to have shewn what custom in law was, and had
he done this the verdict must have been for us. He told the Jury the
only question was, — was there a select vestry in antient times .i.e.
before the faculty was obtained and he said if all the parishioners did
not personally do the parish business there must have been a select
vestry to do it. Select he said was chosen, and he inferred that the
vestry chose one another. This he dwelt upon at much length and
this induced the Jury to find against us. But, according to the shewing
of the dishonest judge every vestry is a select vestry, and may safely
usurp power over the parish. Nothing was adduced to shew that the
vestry elected one another before the faculty was granted. Nothing
to shew that they ever levied taxes of their own authority and never
shewed their accounts, much was shewn to the contrary, but to these
matters the Judge never once alluded. He told the Jury that, a select
body had undoubtedly existed, that this was the only question for their
consideration and if they thought this was proved they would find for
the plaintiff, and under these directions they did find for the plaintiff.

I have no doubt at all that had the whole responsibility been laid
upon the judge, that if he had been obliged to decide, and to have
assigned the reasons for his judgment he would have decided in favour
of M^r. Fenn.

Brougham exceedingly animated with yesterdays proceedings at the
London University, agreed with him that it would be useful to print
an account of the proceedings.

A M^r. Badnall called upon me at 8. p. m. with a project, for mooring
ships, at anchor, and bringing them up in deep water, by means of an
iron parachute, near the anchor, or at the end of a cable without an
anchor. It is a simple & I think may be an an [sic] useful invention.

Wednesday.   [May] 2.

Dr Gilchrist and Major Turnbull with a paper of the heads of
a defence intended to be made by the Revd Robert Taylor, when
brought before the Court of Kings bench on a charge of having
uttered words charged as a blasphemous libel, from his pulpit, in his
chapel in Cannon Street. Went over the heads & from these it appears
that M^r. Taylor's intention is to make a display, that is to make a

fool of himself. Objected to several of his heads, and generally to the course he intends to pursue, and upon being seriously urged by the D^r and the Major, I consented to write a comment on the heads, and further to state seriatim the matters which I thought should compose the defence, this I have partly done, but M^r. Taylor will not I expect follow my advice, shut himself out of the matter personally and argue the case on broad [?] and public grounds, notwithstanding, in this consists his chance of acquittal, and at any rate the certainty of doing service to the cause of liberty of conscience.

Thursday.   [May] 3.

The proceedings in the House of Commons since it reassembled on Tuesday have been such as might make a dog sick. Burdett at the back of Canning, elegizing the avowed enemy of parliamentary reform, and for what? because, he appears friendly to Catholic Emancipation,[427] which is not by any means likely to be obtained whether he favour[s] it or not, and altho it is a thing which ought not to be witheld [sic] [it] is in fact of no great importance to the people of Ireland, what they want is government of their own, and one of their own making would be bad enough, but their evils would be made by themselves, so far as the Gov^t was concerned, and they would not then be as they are now in a constant state of irritation, from the knowledge that they are a conquered people held in subjection by the bayonets of their conquerors and oppressors.

Canning will do the people of Ireland no good, the people of England no good, in any fundamental matter, he loves power, and he sees by the help of M^r. Huskisson the absolute necessity of removing some of the restrictions which embarras [sic] trade, and he will therefore be disposed to go as far in these matters as the aristocracy will permit him, but their wishes will be his guide and whatever he finds them not likely to agree to, he will not propose and whatever he finds will please them and thus exalt himself he will propose. The people in every respect except so far as the Aristocracy may think the modification of some almost useless laws may be safely abridged or repealed will, be utterly disregarded by George Canning and his crew.

This entry has been provoked by a long conference with M^r. Hume, from whom I learned, that the soi-disant Whigs have not only consented to support the Canningites, but to hold every man for

---

[427] *Hansard*, new series, 17, 3 May 1827, cols 528–537, in which Burdett defended Canning against charges of 'overweening ambition' by insisting on his good character, honesty, and candor.

an enemy of his country who having been either in opposition merely
[?] or a parliamentary reformer who shall oppose the Canningites.
The shipping interest as it is called, have been bawling lustily against
the abrogation of the Navigation Laws, ~~and~~ in 181[?][428] and the
reciprocity act of 1822 – they have impudently asserted that these acts
are destroying, the British Merchant Shipping, and increasing that of
other nations, and this too in the face of returns which shew that,
the quantity of tonnage ~~in the~~ since the peace in 1814 has increased
greatly, ~~and~~ very considerably since the alteration of the Navigation
laws and also since the passing of the reciprocity acts.[429] The facts are
these since the peace capital has been accumulated faster than it could
be invested in profitable concerns, hence the low rate of interest for
money, and this has forced people to embark their capitals in trade
and commerce and has in several reduced profits as it necessarily must
do for some time, this is the case with the shipping interest. Ships are
held in shares, many in very small shares upwards of 100 in a ship,
and many persons have become ship owners ~~in~~ from the impossibility
of vesting their capital in other concerns with as they thought, and
perhaps correctly, as much chance of profit. The consequence is that
the number of ship owners has greatly increased, profits – i e freight
has fallen, and has to be divided among a larger number of persons
than formerly, hence as each gets less than he expected, and as many
large ship owners get much less than formerly they, say that the acts
have ruined them, or will ruin them, when in fact the acts have been
beneficial to them. But they like others are bad judges in their own
case, and in this instance do not look far enough. These men are to
have moved in the house to night that a select committee be appointed
to enquire into their case, they pledging themselves to prove the facts
they have alleged this they cannot do, but as they are a numerous a
rich and a noisy body, it would be wise to hear them, the more so as
they will not be put off but will annoy the house until they are heard.
Ministers have however ~~refused~~ resolved not to grant a committee and
the soi-disant whigs have agreed to concur with them. Hume took the
right view and ~~proposed professed~~ said he should vote for enquiry,
and has in consequence drawn down upon him the reprobation of the
drivellers, he has been called an enemy of M[r]. Canning, an opposer of
harmony, almost a breeder of animosity and a disturber of the public

---

[428] The final numeral of this date is omitted in the manuscript. This entry suggests a
reference to the 1819 agreement to allow US ships to carry British cargo to India and the
subsequent easing of the Navigation Acts in 1822. In general, see J.H. Clapham, 'The last
years of the Navigation Acts', *English Historical Review*, 25 (July 1910), pp. 481–484.

[429] On 7 May, General Gascoigne brought forward a motion to create a committee of
inquiry into the state of the shipping interest. See *Hansard*, new series, 17, 7 May 1827,
cols 592–665.

peace. Under these circumstances he came to me to consult, and I advised him as strenuously as I could not only to vote but to speak in favour of enquiry to say, the facts would out he was persuaded come not as the Ship-owners affirmed they would, but that – &c &c – it was advisable they should be heard, that the house had committed an absurdity in refusing to grant a committee on petition of the people, for a minimum of wages and on the tax on the use of machinery – since it was the short as well as the only way to set these questions at rest, and in refusing a committee to the ship-owners they would not only commit another absurdity, but would increase the persuasion but too generally entertained that the house was resolved not even to enquire respecting any alleged grievances. M^r. Hume went away resolved to do this, and to brave the obloquy of the late opposition and all others.

Sometime ago, Brougham promised he would attack the act passed in 1819 against small publications, he had done the same on other occasions, but he as usual did nothing because no eclat was likely to follow his attempt. Knowing that he would shirk the matter I talked with M^r. Hume about it, and to day we settled it that he should give notice of motion to repeal the acts. I gave him a copy of a letter I wrote three or four years ago for Bennet who with Brougham was to have made an effort, to procure the repeal of the acts, commonly called, Six Acts, of which that relating to small publications was one, but nothing was done. This will also bring down execration on M^r. Hume since Canning will oppose the repeal and the pretended friends of the people will support Canning. They will call Humes motion factious, ill timed mischievous &c. It relates only to the people and as they have nothing in common with the people, will for that reason reprobate Hume for his attempt to serve them.[430]

Thus we shall see that we have in the House of Commons, two parties as usual, or rather "two Battallions [sic] of the well paid regiment" as Burdett once called them, namely the old tories or Pittites, and the new tories or Canning-ites.

Wrote this morning to Sir Francis Burdett to request him to inform me in writing, if he intended to make a motion (as he had promised me he would do) respecting impressing of seamen if he did mean to move, then what he meant to move and when, as it was necessary for me to let the seamen know what they might rely upon as efforts to be made for their service.

[430] The motion was introduced on 31 May 1827: *Hansard*, new series, 17, 31 May 1827, cols 1062–1083.

Canning will not accede to the petitions of the seamen, and if Burdett moves in their favour he will have to go over to the other side of the house whence he ought not to have moved.

Deputation from the parish of St Paul Covent Garden on the affairs of that Parish as to a select vestry which they are about to bring before the court of Kings bench.

Saturday.   [May] 5

M^r. Florance on the subject of imprisonment for debt, he appeared to be satisfied that the best mode of proceeding would be to take in the whole subject. I said I would not hesitate to bestow three months on it, if I could arrange matters so as to have the time to myself – I said I would put down what I conceived were the principles, and illustrate them by arguments. That I would collect from him and other legal professional men, the modes of procedure in all its details, and illustrate the consequences by examples. That I would make a Code, all in short articles, with the reasons for each article, and when the whole was properly digested and arranged would submit it to him and others for their observations, that the articles might then be framed as a bill and M^r. Hume might take it as his. That I should not be desirous to appear in the transaction at all, and should not name it even to any excepting those whose assistance I thought requisite. But I feared I should not be able to apply my time to the subject. M^r. Florance said he would go on with the plan as I had sketched it and communicate with me. He does not however comprehend what is to be done and cannot therefore proceed to any considerable extent. If he does however proceed I will from his papers, make as complete a case as I can, for him.

Sunday   [May] 6.

Sir Francis Burdett. A long conversation on the recent change of ministers and on the conduct he had adopted. He justified himself by the opinion he entertained of the necessity of taking a decided part to exclude for ever the old stupid enemies of all improvements and he thought that until M^r. Canning was permanently seated, he should not be embarrassed by those who wished to keep the ex-ministers out. I thought M^r. Canning's Administration was safe enough, and that one of the best proofs in the house of commons was ~~that~~ the actual feebleness of the direct opposition, evinced by their permitting so incapable a person as Sir Thomas Lethbridge to become their leader. Sir F. Assented to this. ~~I said~~ I argued the propriety of granting

a committee to the Ship owners, notwithstanding M^r. Canning – &c –
had determined not to grant one, and I reasoned at some lenth [*sic*]
to shew him not only all the bearings of the case, but also, that, the
shipowners in a committee would be compelled to give evidence in
direct contradiction to the allegations of their petitions. That, if a
committee were refused they would call public meetings in London
and in all the principal ports and by the speeches and publications
~~would~~ persuade the people that the free trade laws were a national
evil, and ministers would lose considerably in consequence of their
uncontradicted misstatements. That as in respect to trade all they had
done, was good, and they were unwise to court opposition, when the
very grounds of complaint could so easily be shewn to be untenable,
and most likely after all be compelled to grant a committee. Sir Francis
assented to the propriety of ministers consenting to the appointment
of a committee.

Sir Francis promised that in a short time he would bring the subject
of impressment before the house.

Discussed the merits and defects of M^r. Peel's act for amending the
laws relative to Juries. Sir Francis agreed to attempt an amendment
of the bill so as to destroy its ambiguity, which is of some importance.
I promised to make extracts ~~from~~ of those parts of the Act which
needed amendment, to explain how the bill at present operated,
to relate some circumstances to shew its evils, and to write out the
amendments.

Monday.   [May] 7.

Performed my promise in respect to the Jury bill — Copies to be
made for Sir Francis Burdett – M^r. Hobhouse – M^r. Jno Smith –
M^r. Brougham – M^r. Denman. See Papers — Jury. &c

M^r. Florance with a prospectus of the Latitat.[431]

Tuesday. [May] 8 – to Tuesday. [May] 15.

Inte[n]sely occupied in the affairs of others, so as to fill up all my
time from 7 in the morning till 11 at night. scarcely able to obtain an
hour a day for exercise.

In writing out an abstract of the Act. "60. Geo III. cap. IX. to subject
certain publications to the duties of stamps upon newspapers and to
~~restrain~~ make other regulations for restraining the abuses arising from

---

[431] A latitat is a special writ issued out of the King's Bench, requiring appearance before
the court.

the publication of Blasphemous and seditious libels." 30 Dec. 1819"
[*sic*][432] Writing down the objections to this nefarious act, the reasons
on which these objections are founded and hints for the manner in
which they should be treated.

The same as to that other infamous "act, "for the more effectual prevention ~~of~~ and punishment of blasphemous and seditious libels – 60 G.
III. cap. VIII.["] 30 Dec. 1819"[433]

Sent these matters to M[r]. Hume for the purpose of assisting him in
his proposal to bring in two bills to repeal these two acts.

It will scarcely be credited hereafter

1. that two such acts should have been made in England in the year
1819.

2 – that from that time to the present no one should be found to
move the repeal of either.

3. That at the present moment, I cannot find a single man, a
member of the House of Commons on whom any dependence can
be placed that he will support M[r]. Hume as he ought to do, no one
indeed to whom I can even so much rely as would compensate me for
copying the papers sent to M[r]. Hume.

In the expectation that I was to be examined before the select
committee of the house of Commons on the manner of taking the
polls for members of par[l] in Cities and Boroughs, writing a short
account of the nature of elections in Westminster, how conducted in
former, how in recent times – an account of the changes – duration of
polls[,] treating bribery, intimidation, riots[,] paying expense, conduct
of parties &c &c — for M[r]. Hobhouse.[434]

Examined before the committee this day Tuesday 15. for two hours
and told the committee nearly all I wished to tell them.

Settling sundry matters relating to M[r]. Tijou and his son respecting
a law suit &c – brought by M[r]. Tijou against a customer of his into
which he had been induced to go by his son who, after all could not
verify the facts on which his father relied for the recovery of the money
due to him.

M[r]. Florance and his Latitat.

M[r]. Hobhouse respecting the meeting in Westminster held
yesterday. The leaders in which were — Pitt a vagabond, and the
two miscreants.

---

[432] One of the infamous Six Acts of 1819.

[433] The so-called Misdemeanours Act.

[434] Eventually published in the Sessional Papers as *PP*, 4 (1826–1827), *Report from the Select
Committee on the Mode of taking Polls at City and Borough Elections.*

Henry Hunt and
William Cobbett.[435]

Correspondence with the Woollen weavers in the west of England
and the Sailors in the North.

Mode of conducting elections in some of the U. S. Of N. America
as represented in some american publications.

M[r]. Fenn and his suit against the Vestry.

Miers's estate accounts &c. A laborious job in going over the heads
of the intended defence of the Rev[d] Robert Taylor and commenting
thereon. Writing out for him an essay on the law of libel as it is called
and an account, seriatim of the practice in libel cases – the mode of
defence most likely in my opinion to produce an acquittal, altho that is
unlikely but, such a defence as while it shocked the feelings of religious
men as little as possible should be when printed, such as men must
call respectable, and this too without giving up a particle of our claim
to free discussion on every subject.

Monday.   May. 20.

Wholly occupied in the affairs of others so as not to leave me any
time for reading. Among those who have occasionally come to me for
advice lately or assistance or both is a M[r]. William Augustus Miles.
I have known him about 20 years on and off. I knew his father full
30 years ago. This W[m] Augustus came to me the other day to consult
with me as to the mode he should pursue for the purpose of obtaining
~~some~~ employment in some Government office. He told me a story
which he has more than once before told me, namely, that the King
occasionally gave him 100£ upon his application to him for assistance,
and that on one occasion gave him an appointment in the West Indies,
to which as I at the time know, he went, and staid there until, if I mistake

---

[435] Henry Hunt (1773–1835) was 'the most famous and flamboyant figure in early
nineteenth-century radical politics', according to the historian John Belchem. Place,
however, called him 'an ignorant, turbulent, mischief-making fellow, a highly dangerous
one in turbulent times'. Place distrusted Hunt's strategy of mobilizing mass demonstrations
in favor of radical political reform and was particularly disturbed by Hunt's unwillingness to
do the difficult committee work that Place deemed necessary for the effective organization
of political pressure. To Place's consternation, this point marked the revival of relations
between Hunt and Cobbett, whose relationship had been strained by Hunt's prosecution
of Cobbett for libel in 1826. 'They buried their differences', Hunt's biographer has written,
'to unite against the old enemy, Burdett and the Westminster reformers' who supported
Canning and 'Liberal Toryism'. See John Belchem, *'Orator' Hunt: Henry Hunt and English
working-class radicalism* (Oxford, 1985), pp. 187–189; *idem*, 'Hunt, Henry [Orator Hunt] (1773–
1835)', *ODNB*, <http://www.oxforddnb.com/view/article/14193>, accessed 29 March 2007;
Wallas, *Life*, pp. 119–120.

not the business on which he went was completed. He said he was
tired of being a beggar, and receiving as he had now and then 100£
at the Treasury, from a gentleman who never spoke to him, and never
could by any thing he said, be induced to reply, not even yes or no. He
founds his claim to the countenance of the King on a circumstance
which he probably thinks is correct, namely that his father, is the son
of the late King by the Quaker woman whom it is said he married,
and he talks of papers in his fathers possession which would set the
nation in an uproar. The story told about this Wm Augustus was
born[,] credited at the time, and believed by many to the present
time, is that he is the son of the present King, and certainly as far as
the markings of breed in families goes he may claim to be a Guelph.
He is a tall, large man, with big limbs like the family he has the large
features, the goggle eye, the projecting pig ~~like~~ formed face, the low
and rapidly receding forehead which like the rest of them is bald to the
crown of the head, the small head a large carcass, altogether the want
of intellectual appearance and the strongly marked ~~character~~ animal
character. His father was one of the profligate friends of the Prince of
Wales, and like others of his friends then and now even, used to let the
Prince (King) have the use of his wife and thus it is said this M^r. W^m
Augustus was produced with the characteristics of Royalty strongly
marked upon him. (His father was a small man.) His father like most
of the Kings early friends was at lenth [*sic*] if not discarded treated
with coolness or contempt, as perhaps he deserved to be and then he
wrote a pamphlet against the Prince of Wales.[436] It had a prodigious
sale. ~~In so~~ Some time afterwards he wrote another pamphlet[437] and
this led to a compromise, M^r. Miles was pensioned for life and ever
afterwards held his tongue. I could of course give M^r. Wm Augustus
no advice that could be of any service to him, all I could do was to
tell him, what I believe, namely that he was better qualified for office
than many who were in office.

Thursday.   [May] 24.

Yesterday was celebrated the 20th Anniversary of the Triumph of
Westminster, in the election of Sir Francis Burdett by the Parliamentary Reformers against the opposition of the Whigs and Tories.
    The meeting (I was not present) was exceedingly tumultuous and
bordered on a riot, of a coarse description.

[436] William Augustus Miles, *A Letter to the Prince of Wales, in consequence of a second application
to parliament, for the payment of debts wantonly contracted since May 1787* (London, 1795).
    [437] Idem, *A Letter to his Royal Highness the Prince of Wales; with a sketch of the prospect before him,
appendix, and notes* (London, 1808).

I had been solicited by a very considerable number of Gentlemen to procure them seats at the top of the room and I recommended their names to the stewards. The applications were however so very numerous that not half the number that applied could be accommodated.

The cause of the riot was the conduct of Burdett and Hobhouse. Burdett not having of late years taken any prominent part for the people, and having therefore to some extent displeased them, his having gone over to Cannings side of the house, and the advantage these had given the miscreant Cobbett to stir up the ignorant & ill disposed to, assist him and Henry Hunt, in making a disturbance as they in an advertisement had promised they would do.

Another cause was the conduct of Hobhouse, who has on almost all occasions shewn himself a trifler.

The newspapers of to day contain an account of the proceedings yesterday, on which it is only necessary to remark that had the conduct of the two representatives been any thing like what it ought to have been, no confusion no interruption whatever could have taken place. M^r. Hobhouse was not even heard by the company, and this is conclusive proof of the feelings of the electors and others towards him. Had he acted as constituents expected he would have acted, and as he ought to have acted, no one would have dared to insult him in that or in any other place, as it was the electors who were present seemed scarcely to consider the conduct of Cobbett towards him as an insult. Sir Francis is not and never was a man of business, and is but ill qualified to represent the people of Westminster in the present times. M^r. Hobhouse is just such a man as one might have expected to meet 40 years ago, as a representative for Westminster, with nothing about him of General Principles, little actual knowledge of the people he represents, a trifling, disheartening conduct as a public man, and one who therefore must be thought less and less of by his constituents.

Much occupied in Mrs Harwoods affairs, I fear to no good purpose.

A deputation from a number of Benefit Societies associated by means of their delegates, on the apprehension that the committee of the House of Commons on friendly societies[438] mean them no good by their meddling. Gave them advice and put them in the way of obtaining the proceedings of the committee from time to time.

---

[438] The Committee's Report was published as *PP*, 3 (1826–1827), *Report on the Laws respecting Friendly Societies*.

Monday.   [May] 28.

On saturday M^r. Hobhouse called and after some conversation on the meeting on the 23rd at the Crown and Anchor Tavern, during which I told him the reasons for his being annoyed must be sought for in his own conduct, he urged me to write down some particulars I had mentioned ~~in rel~~ respecting the Solicitor Generals Bill, to limit ~~ass~~ arrests on mesne process to 20£, which I undertook to do.

M^r. Hobhouse then said, Hume has got himself into a pretty hobble, about his repeal bill, he promised Sir Robert Wilson to withdraw his notice and then in a day or two wrote him a note to say, he must persist in making his motion.^{a} I enquired how this could get him into a hobble. Hobhouse said, ~~He~~ he had given his word to Wilson and had broken it. I was indignant at hearing this from Hobhouse who as on other occasions was but too well disposed to take part against Hume, and I said very precisely, but not warmly – what I thought of Wilson. [Portion of sentence crossed out and indecipherable.] and thus I argued the matter at length, shewed M^r. Hobhouse that both he and Sir Francis Burdett had failed to do their duty in not moving the repeal of this bill in every session since it was passed, of the efforts I had at various times made to induce members to move the repeal of the 6 acts, and how I had failed, how they had broken their promises, how I had mentioned the matter to himself to no purpose and then I challenged him to give me a good reason why M^r. Hume should withdraw his motion, and he confessed he knew no one.

M^r. Hume this morning. He told me that on ~~entering~~ mentioning his intention to give notice of a Bill to repeal Act. 6 Geo 4. cap IX. M^r. Scarlet now Sir James Scarlet Attorney General called him aside and requested him not to make his motion, urging many topics, and amongst others the intention of ministers to cause the whole that remained of [the] 6 acts to be revised in the next session, that they were not prepared, and could not as yet be prepared to repeal an act which was made against ~~blasphemous~~ seditious libels, under their present circumstances. Upon this M^r. Hume observed that it was not "cap. 8 the act for preventing and punishing seditious libels but cap. 9, relating to small publications and Newspapers to which his notice applied.["] M^r. Scarlet said then he had made a mistake, and appeared to be reconciled to the repeal of that act, but the next day he made an objection, that the repeal would affect the Revenue by lessening the Stamp duties. This was a shuffle since no stamps have been used to small publications, the act being a complete prohibition. M^r. Hume

---

^{a} See copy of the correspondence. [Footnote.]

gave his notice, upon which Sir Robert Wilson came to him and urged all the arguments he possibly could, all the common place, vulgar topics of necessity of union, of the necessity of doing nothing to alarm or disturb [?] the newly formed administration or to give their opponents a handle against them, he observed as to what would be the conduct of Lord Redesdale and Lord Eldon, both of whom would appeal to the Lords against the bill as exhibiting the consequences of a so called liberal, or rather radical administration, and M^r. Hume at length consented to let his motion drop. (I was told these matters but somewhat incorrectly at the time, by M^r. Geo White and M^r. Florance and I therefore wrote an essay on the Refuge for the destitute and sent it to the Trades Newspaper, in this essay I explained the manner in which well meaning members are annoyed and operated upon by the vagabonds in others and either actually made or made to appear very infirm of purpose. In this essay I particularly mentioned an example of this in M^r. Hume – This had its effect on M^r. Hume).[439]

In a day or two the motion having been unavoidably delayed, M^r. Hume wrote to Sir R. Wilson that upon further consideration he felt he must persist in making his motion, and this caused Sir Robert to write an insolent letter to M^r. Hume, and has put an end to their acquaintance.

M^r. Hume observed that when Brougham several months ago seemed eager to have this act repealed, he encouraged Hume to move its repeal and promised to support him, and even so lately as three weeks ago repeated his promise but that now he had no person to support him but Alderman Wood who was incapable of making a Speech on the subject. To other entreaties he has replied that he shall certainly proceed. It has been suggested to him by Lord Duncannon, on the part of the Whigs, that his bill should relate only to so much of the act as regards small publications and periodical works leaving all that respects newspapers as it is. To this M^r. Hume has judiciously replied that provided he has a pledge of support from ministers and their whig friends for so much of the act he will limit it as requested, or if they will introduce the bill, he will withdraw his notice, to make way for them. They appear not to have calculated on this concession and are now at a loss how to proceed, had M^r. Hume refused compliance his refusal would have been made the ground of resistance. It is barely possible they may have consent to one or the other of his suggestions, but the probability is that a dead set will be made at him on his motion, for the purpose of putting him down, but he says if they do this he will then at once give notices of the repeal of other unpopular acts and make a speech to the country through the House on each of them, and

---

[439] 'The spoilers and the plunderers of the people', *TN*, 3 June 1827.

compel the whigs to expose themselves to the people as the supporters of all these bad and mischievous acts which they exclaimed against while out of office.

On thursday 31. M^r. Hume made his motion.[440]

[440] *Hansard*, new series, 17, 31 May 1827, cols 1062–1083.

Sunday   June 3

On M^r. Hume's motion none of the whigs attended, an especial circular from the Treasury was sent around in the following words, and scored as represented

Divisions.

Your attendance is most *earnestly & particularly* requested in the House of Commons to day, at the usual hour of commencing ~~business~~ Public Business on M^r. Humes motion to repeal the act imposing a stamp duty on certain publication.
Thursday 31 May.

Still it was not the intention of the now coalesced factions to make a house of all, but to let the motion fall from want of 40 members at 4 o clock. There were many committees public, select and private, sitting, and Sir Bobby Wilson, William alias Pat Homes, and others went into all the committee rooms and endeavoured to persuade every member they saw not to attend so that there might be no house. M^r. Hume was in one of these committees, and at half past 3 received a note from General Gascoigne telling him of these proceedings in other rooms, and saying that he himself among others had been requested not to attend the house. ~~As~~ The Whigs almost to a man staid away, and Holmes the Ministerial whipper in was busily employed in persuading members to withdraw from the house and many did so. This is not a new trick, the members who withdraw remain within call & come back if necessary, so it was in this case. The new opposition with M^r. Peel at its head, together with some three or four who had told M^r. Hume they would be present, made a house & Holmes sent for the Ministerial myrmidons, to make a large majority, when it was ascertained that a house must be formed. But the Whigs who had been sent back were not to be found, as usual they shuffled, and this so aggravated M^r. Herries that he threatened to resign his office,[441] since as he said, he would not continue a member of an administration made up of men who on such occasions as these refused to come to the house and do their duty.

M^r. Hume made his motion, and for remarks on the conduct of the house see the Trades Newspaper ~~and~~ of this day, and next sunday.[442]

Yesterday M^r. Hume came and told me all the circumstances of the case, & gave me the correspondence which had taken place.

[441] John Charles Herries, Chancellor of the Exchequer.
[442] 'The spoilers and plunderers of the people', *TN*, 3 June 1827.

As usual, employed in the affairs of others and that too to such an extent as to occupy my whole time. There is no remedy for this but absenting myself from London.

Dr Thorpe's case. Mrs Harwoods affairs The Rev^d M^r. Cruttwell, M^r. Florance M^r. Hume M^r. Hobhouse M^r. Ashby The Trades Newspaper, The Shipwrights Benefit Clubs, &c &c —

On Thursday, occupied several hours, making a case for M^r. Hobhouse against The bill to prevent arrests under 20£ unless an easy, speedy & cheap mode of recovering small debts was also adopted.

Made minutes under the head. Session 1827 – in the my Parliamentary memorandum book. Wrote an article on the Conduct of the Whigs and Tories for the Trades Newspaper.[443]

Monday.   [June] 4.

At Greenwich looking at the people quite changed from what they were some 35 or 40 years ago – see – some observations – in my memorandums respecting the improvement of the people.

M^r. Hume sent me two letters to read, addressed to M^r. Mill and a note to myself respecting Brougham['s] conduct on Thursday and Friday last.

M^r. Jno Evans. M^r. Barry. Col^n Jones M^r. Jno Fordham – Mrs Harwood. M^r. Grieve

To Saturday.   [June] 9.

Occupied as usual.

The conduct of the Whigs on M^r. Humes motion has produced much feeling among politicians, great and small, and has been the cause of many persons coming to me, all indignant and some outrageous. All are persuaded that Sir Francis Burdett is trifling with the people in the expectation of a peerage, I say I do not think he would accept one, and yet he makes me mistrust him. Hobhouse keeps away from me notwithstanding I am supplying him with facts and heads of arguments respecting the Bill to prevent arrests on Mesne Process about which his constituents are constantly annoying him, and notwithstanding he must be much in want of conversation with me on the subject. Electors go to him, and then come to me to express their dissatisfaction, which arises from his fidgettyness [sic] and want of knowledge on the subject, but as they suppose produced by his dislike to do them justice lest he should annoy the ministers.

[443] *Ibid.*

M^r. Florance several times respecting printing the debate on M^r. Humes motion at M^r. Humes expense.

Mill, Jones Col^n and others to talk of the course Hume must pursue.

M^r. Hume exceedingly desirous to make a motion on the state of the nation, which I suppose he will do, this I have told him it is not what he should do. He has erroneous notions on some part of his subject and now when trade and commerce and manufactures are all recovering from the recent state of depression, his motion would produce no effect. I indeed see nothing just now but matter of gratulations, and have no doubt at all that if the increase of population did not continually outrun the increase and application of capital, there would be very little poverty in the land.

A capital article as to matter in the Westminster Review. N° 14[444] – on education written in a strange stile, the progress of teaching as it regards the intellectual and moral improvement of the people is well marked.

Wrote an essay on the two infamous acts against the press. 60 Geo 3 – c.8. c 9.

Assisting Dr Thorpe, with some hope and I think some chance that the poor old man may at length obtain something from Government.

A M^r. Quin with a letter of introduction from M^r. Ensor, his case a very peculiar and a very hard one, read the papers he left with me and advised him, he cannot obtain redress in any way, misused by a magistrate and a Judge, and ruined as he is by their conduct he has no legal hold on them and parliament will not interfere. I have I think convinced him of this and he will I conclude endeavour to establish himself as a surgeon in America where he has friends and relations, he has been there, and knows something of the country.

M^r. Quin was accused of committing a rape was tried for it but acquitted before all the evidence was heard and he is silly enough to think that the notoriety of his case would procure him patients in London.

M^r. John Thelwall, with a cock and a bull story about a history of the political societies during the reign of George 3. He had he said proposed to Mess^r Hunt and Clark to write it for them, or rather that he would write it and they should have the copy right, he has seen M^r. Clarke and had told him it would probably make a moderate sized quarto volume, for which he should expect to receive a **Thousand Pounds** and M^r. Clark had made an objection. My opinion is that such a history would leave no nothing for the compiler after the

[444] John Bowring, 'Education of the people', *Westminster Review*, 7, no. 14, pp. 269–317.

Booksellers charges were paid. Thelwall would make a poor thing of it, he knows nothing of his subject, and were he to proceed would find he had ten times more to do than he supposes, he would make himself the hero of the tale, and would stuff it with his nonsensical poetry. He knows I have made some collections respecting these societies and he came to request my assistance, if he has any chance of getting his matter into print I will assist him, for since badly as he will do it, it will be better to have it badly done, than not done at all.

Thursday.   [June] 14.

Much to do with the people connected with the Trades, and the London Free Press Newspapers. M^r. Quin. The Tijous – Dr Thorpe Thomas Hardy and the subscription for his maintenance, took the accounts from M^r. Frend, and the balance in his hands, wrote letters to every subscriber, and to every other person whom I thought likely to assist.

M^r. Hume, annoyed by the negligent manner in which the debates in parl[iament] are reported has a strong inclination to advance money for the establishment of a paper to report the debates and to give an account of parliamentary proceedings, he has persuaded himself that others will also advance money and that a sufficiently large number of persons will be found to purchase the paper to pay its expenses. I have no such expectation, but since nothing but an attempt to ascertain the probability will satisfy him, and in as much as such a paper could it be established would be very useful, I have consented to revise the prospectus I formerly wrote, and adapt it to present circumstances.

Conversed on the subject with M^r. Mill and went through the principal advantages and disadvantages, the obstacles facilities, expense &c &c and our conclusion is that it will be quite impossible to make such a paper pay half of its expenses. It cannot be printed at all unless stamped as a newspaper unless two of 6 acts be repealed.

M^r. Dawson the member for Louth[445] having expressed his desire to become acquainted with me, I replied I was always at home till 11 a m, and seldom out ~~from~~ after 4. p. m. ~~But~~ M^r. Dawson having told this to M^r. Quin appears to have undertaken to bring us together and this gave rise to the following dialogue

M^r. Quin – M^r. Dawson Sir desires to make your acquaintance.

Place. So I have been given to understand.

Q. He is an early man Sir and I shall be with him tomorrow morning Sir.

P. On the business which has brought you to London.

445 Alexander Dawson.

Q. Yes Sir and to introduce you so Sir, we will go together at
10. o clock to M^r. Dawsons place.

P. That we shall not, for I never wait on any great man, except
on the urgent business of others, if M^r. Dawson wishes to see me he
knows where to find me, and if he thinks I can be of use to him in any
project for the good of the people I shall be glad to see him, but I shall
not go to him to claim his acquaintance. I am not, and never was and
never will be under the obligation to any such man, no political man
can say I owe him a turn or am in any way obliged to him for his
condescension, and I hope you have not led M^r. Dawson to expect I
am likely to court his acquaintance without having any public matter
as a basis. M^r. Quin was confounded and made no reply and I let the
matter drop.

Lord Rossmore who calls himself one of the 69 Irish Peers,[446] a long
conversation of on Irish affairs, he is a well informed [*sic*], and has
the manner and language of a man well disposed to promote the
prosperity of his country. His objects are. 1st Catholic Emancipation
2. Parliamentary Reform.

Endeavoured to impress upon Lord Rossmore and M^r. Quin both of
whom are well acquainted with the leaders of the Catholic Association,
the utility of abstaining from the silly conduct hitherto adopted by
these leaders. The Catholics want to be emancipated and this can
only be by making friends, and their whole conduct is and always
has been to make enemies. When in 1825. O Connel [*sic*] Bric,
Shiel, Lawless and others came to London as a deputation from the
Catholic Association for the purpose of obtaining emancipation of
which Burdett was the Champion, they instead of going to none but
respectable persons, went to Cobbett and he and they made common
case [*sic*], thus they at once affixed a mark of disrepute upon their
cause. At a meeting held at Sir Francis Burdetts house it was proposed
to call a public meeting of the Electors of Westminster to petition
for Catholic Emancipation, and Hobhouse came from the meeting
to consult with me about it. I put it to him thus does O Connel and
the rest of them propose to ground their demand on the broad basis
of the equal right of every man to the same privileges or does he
claim emancipation from any particular merit of their religion, are
they willing to put it on a broad ground and to hold their tongues at
the meetings not only on the peculiar merits of their religion, but also
on the accusations they are constantly making of former ill usage with

---

[446] Lord Rossmore, neither an Irish representative peer nor a UK peer, was a leading
proponent of reform of the system of representation of Irish peers. See A.P.W. Malcolmson,
'The Irish peerage and the Act of Union, 1800–1971', *Transactions of the Royal Historical Society*,
6th series, 10 (2000), pp. 289–327.

which the people have now nothing to do, and confine themselves to a simple claim because they are men. Hobhouse could not tell and I refused to have any thing to do with the matter until I was fully informed as to the wishes and intentions of the deputation. In a day or two I found the deputation so potatoe [*sic*] headed as to consider such a meeting of little consequence unless it gave them an opportunity of talking of their ill usage for centuries past and of the special claim their ridiculous and mischievous religion gave them. I therefore not only refused to promote a meeting but assured M^r. Hobhouse that I would do all I could to prevent a meeting, which would bring all the Irish from St Giles's into Covent Garden, and to make a riot to the disgrace of the electors of Westminster. He wished to introduce O Connel & me but I would not permit him — Bric called but I would not see him.

I mentioned these circumstances to Lord Rossmore as evidence of the folly of the Catholics. O Connel and the rest of them, exasperate the Catholics by their constant endeavours to revive and keep up their hatred to the protestants, and to make and keep the protestants enemies by constantly shewing their enmity, and the never failing desire they have to repossess themselves or rather to possess themselves of the estates which at some time or other belonged to catholics, thus alarming the very persons whose support is necessary to obtain for them, their civil rights. The only proper course for them to pursue is to cease talking of times gone by, to have no retrospect whatever. To shew what are the present privations & inconveniencies [*sic*] they suffer and to appeal to all men for assistance towards their removal. I have no doubt at all that were they to pursue this plan steadily they would soon have large bodies of English people to assist them, and that so long as they persisted in their present course they will effectually prevent such assistance. Lord Rossmore and M^r. Quin both assented to this and M^r. Quin said he was much obliged to me, since I had by convincing him prevented him committing an error, namely that in the event of his being examined at the bar of the house of commons he had intended to have taken that opportunity of stating the woes his country had endured for 5 or 6 centuries. But thus it is with all these potato headed people, they never can be rational for half an hour at a time.

Daniel Webb Webber Esqr[447] lately a ministerial member of Parliament an absurd Church and King and Pitt and Eldon and Castlereagh man, yet a man bearing a very good character in the neighbourhood of his own estate in County Sligo. He came as usual with a full apprehension that Catholic Emancipation would lead

[447] MP for Armagh borough, 1816–1818.

at once to the murder of all the protestants, and in the vain hope frequently disappointed of convincing me of my erroneous notions on the subject. He admitted that taking the Catholic Priests into Government pay and abolishing fees to almost nothing would break the influence the Priests at present had over the people. He admitted that the priests when thus paid would soon become careless of their duty. He admitted that a small sum paid as a gratuity would induce one half of them totally to neglect the people and he appeared to have no doubt at all that many of them would indirectly aid in converting the people to the Church of England, and he admitted that by various means which might then be successfully employed, a large proportion of the people might be converted. But he feared the consequence of the Catholics getting into parliament. He supposed that so many as 50 might be in the house of commons, but he admitted that they would not only disagree among themselves but would at first alarm, the people, and next disgust them. Yet notwithstanding he confessed all this, he was against their being emancipated. Such is prejudice. I told him I would not only emancipate them but I would withdraw all the troops unless money was raised in Ireland to the full amount of the expenses she occasioned, and thus reduce our own expenditure some 5.000.000£ a year which Ireland expends above its revenue.

Tuesday.   [June] 19.

From saturday evening to this morning at nine, no one for a wonder called upon me, excepting my my [*sic*] old very dear friend Jeremy Bentham,[a] who came with a volume of his book now in the press – a volume on evidence to request me to read the first 462 pages for the purpose of ascertaining whether.[448] 1. the matter was such as would interest the generality of readers who read on matters not quite frivolous. 2 – if as to stile it was such as would not deter them. 3 if yes on both these questions, how far it could be aided by notes and references to facts and practice, if no, on the second question, how it could be amended, the object being, to print so much of the work, in a separate volume.

This morning the very ingenious and very unsuccessful Mr. McCarthy with a request that I would do what I could to procure

---

[a] Visits from and to Mr. Benthams have not been hitherto mentioned as each of our houses were as freely entered by either as was his own. [Footnote.]

[448] Jeremy Bentham, *Rationale of Judicial Evidence, specially applied to English practice*, ed. J.S. Mill (London, 1827).

a son of his employment in the Greek Army – promised to go about the business this morning.

M^r. McCarthy then shewed me two drawings of a bridge to cross the Neva at St Petersbourgh [*sic*], the span 1000 feet, the bridge combines Popes plan of a lever bridge and the principle of a suspension bridge, is very ingenious simple strong and cheap. He also shewed me two drawings of a Cabriolet without shafts, a clever elegant thing. Suggested a mode of fixing the support which goes over the horses back, which he at once adopted.

During the last 10 or 12 days, some correspondence, which see [?] with that foolish old man M^r. Delegal [?] who has given me and M^r. Meabry notice of a bill in Chancery respecting Miers's Estate.

Assisting with notes &c – M^r. Mill for an article on the Liberty of the Press for the West^r Review.

Thursday.   [June] 21.

M^r. Hume to consult on the means of publishing the Parliamentary debates and other business of Parliament daily.

M^r. Quin. M^r. McCarthy.

Coln Jones respecting the London Free Press Newspaper, undertook to procure the names of the proprietors – did so – and find amongst them two men of substance. this will enable him to procure payment of the sum due to him and his partners.

Final plan to consolidate the Trades and London Free Press Newspapers – consented to read the deed when drawn, and to correct it if necessary.

At the Mile end and Bermondsey Mechanics Institutions – gave to each 10£ for Sir Francis Burdett.

Reading M^r. Benthams Book and Godwins – 3rd vol of the Commonwealth.

July.

Monday.   [July] 2.

Came from M^r. Mill's at Dorking at half past 10 and before I had time to speak with my family came M^r. Toplis, to tell me of some tricks Brougham had played him, respecting M. S he had prepared for the Library of useful Knowledge[449] and to ask my advice as to the course he should take.

Toplis was turned out by M^r. Fenn who came with M. S. He had composed on the proceedings of the select vestry in the Parish which he intended to send to the Rector together with a letter, and very earnestly entreated me to look over then correct and revise them by 4 o clock which I could not refuse to do.

Fenn was turned out by Lord Rossmore who has a project to unite all the dissenters in the North of Ireland in petitioning the parliament next session for a repeal of the Test and Corporation Acts, and this if he be really capable, of which I doubt of conducting the matter in a rational way, will be useful, he wants me to introduce some leading presbyterians, and some leading unitarians to him with whom he may correspond and thus if possible make common cause in both countries. Promised to endeavour to do as he requested.

Read a letter from M^r. Northouse containing the outline of a plan concocted by him and Lord Rossmore and submitted for my observations.

M^r. Carder respecting the Vestry of St Paul Covent Garden.

Mrs Kenney and her daughter Louisa just arrived from Paris[.] Mrs Kenneys tongue going as usual nineteen to the Dozen.

Harriette Dennett with the draft of brief for her council [sic] against the claim set up by a shake bag attorney to recover some 60£ on bills seven years old, went through the brief, examining her as I went on, and correcting and adding to the draft.

⁑ Read and corrected M^r. Fenns M. S but have not yet 9. P. M. had time to look at Lord Rossmores.

⁑ M^r. Mitchel of the house of Commons to tell me of certain matters, and to consult with me respecting the conduct of George White who had not kept his word in certain transactions. Enabled M^r. Mitchel to embargo some 50£ in the hands of a third person by which ~~means~~ he will probably obtain the money for himself.

[449] The phrase 'Library of useful Knowledge' was inserted in the manuscript.

Reading and ~~correctin~~ commenting on Lord Rossmores project, interrupted by M[r]. Charles Blake,[a] — bringing me some curious information respecting Mexico and the state of the mining companies, collected from some letters just received and from a German, a partner in one of the first houses in Mexico, and the only company who are making or at all are likely to make any profit by mining.

Finished a comment on Lord Rossmores project. His Lordship ~~has I see~~ evidently intends to compel the Government to raise him to the English Peerage or to seat him in the House of Lords as an Irish peer, and he most absurdly thinks, that by supporting the dissenters and telling all he knows respecting the tricks played at the Union he will be able to alarm ministers so as to induce them to comply with his wishes – I have advised him to go on with his plan of an association in which all men may join simply to repeal the corporation and test acts, lest the dissenters should be of opinion that he was only making use of them for another purpose, when they would certainly abandon him. That as far as the speeches and pamphlets he talks of as exposing and overawing ministers he will do well to say and print any thing he knows which may become matter for history, but that he will get nothing from them by any such speeches or publications. He will not take my advice, so that here as in but too many other cases my time will be wasted.

Finished at. $\frac{1}{2}$ past 11. p. m.

Tuesday.   [July] 3

Saw M[r]. Bowring[b] – and agreed with him that Lord Rossmore should call on him on thursday at 12 previous to the meeting of the sub-committee of Dissenters at. 1. o clock.

Tuesday.   [July] 30.

While with M[r]. Mill at Dorking, read some part of D[r] Arnotts Book[450] – a most excellent Book – proving decidedly the immense advance that has been made in right thinking and good teaching – It

---

[a] M[r]. Blake had resided some time in Chile and had been in Paris [Interlinear note, clearly intended for insertion in the text at this point.]

[b] Bowring is a leading Unitarian [Interlinear note, clearly intended for insertion in the text at this point.]

[450] Neil Arnott, *Elements of Physics or Natural Philosophy, General and Medical, explained independently of technical mathematics, and containing new disquisitions and practical suggestions* (London, 1827).

contains familiar explanation[s] in – Mechanics – Hydrostatics – Hydraulics [–] Pneumatics – Animal Life, and so well and so pleasantly is all this done, that it must give great pleasure to all who have the sense to read it, and must convey to all who do read it a large portion of information.

1827.   November

In the month of August I had a long conversation with M^r. W^m. Holmes – the late ministerial whipper in. On the changes of the administration, which as it was a conversation of the nature of most conversations, i.e. on matters and in manner, not to be repeated in its particulars I as usual shall not more particularly notice. We had also some conversation on the Law respecting Juries. M^r. Holmes had himself been sitting as a special Juror and saw that the law was defective but he did not know how it was to be corrected. I explained this to him, told him what I had done, and that M^r. Peele [*sic*] had objected to amend the act because he thought it would be invidious to designate, more particularly than was already done, those who should be liable to serve on special juries. I shewed M^r. Holmes that this objection was so far from deserving ~~any li~~ any weight as used by M^r. Peel that it ought to be used as the very reason for amending the law. Having fully explained the act and shewed how it was made to work iniquitously, he said he would consult M^r. Peel and was certain he could persuade him to amend the Act. I told him I would put down on paper the particulars I had mentioned ~~and~~ point out the mode of proceeding and give him the words necessary to correct the evil. I shall do this next month. I told M^r. Hume what had occurred, and about a fortnight ago M^r. Hume told me he had seen M^r. Peel [,] had read my remarks to him and had at his request left my letter with him, M^r. Peel having promised him to propose the amendments suggested. I shall notwithstanding this write to M^r. Holmes, and shew him how much better it will be to repeal the Act and reenact it with amendments so that there may be ~~but~~ one act only respecting Juries.

Consulted by a M^r. Barrows a gentleman who has been in the Gallery of the house of Commons, has cast in his terms and is about to be called to the Bar. He has a project to publish the debates in the Lords and Commons in weekly numbers and came to me for advice. He is a clever, quick and I dare say industrious fellow. He seems to be pretty well acquainted with the character of many of the members of honourable house, but like most young men too willing to confide in promises. Went over his plan, gave him the prospectus I wrote for a somewhat similar publication in 1823 — and subsequently upon his shewing that he had carefully compared his means of accomplishing his work and accurately calculated his expenses, I encouraged him to go on, provided he could procure as many subscribers at five guineas each as would cover all his expenses. On no account to touch it until he had thus secured himself and above all, not to take the word or even the hand writing of any member for the money, since if he did he would be sure to be cheated, but to have the money paid down.

He seems to be fully convinced that he must do so, and this as I told
him will I fear, put an end to his project.

Consulted – by M^r. Robson – and afterwards by him and M^r.
Lubbock a merchant in London, and a very clever man, respecting a
daily morning newspaper. Their plan is to raise 20.000£ in shares of
20£ each, and each share holder to take in the paper. On the plan of
this paper, there can be no doubt of success – provided the money can
be raised, of which they entertain no doubt. They say they have 400
subscribers already and that we have discussed the plan very minutely
and they understand it in all its details correctly, they say they shall be
able to put all their mercantile friends in motion in London and in all
the Ports and principal towns and shall soon have all the shares taken.
If it goes on the plan will be printed so I need not describe it here.

Monday.   Nov. 12. 1827

"Boswell. From the subject of death we passed to discourse of life,
whether it was upon the whole more happy or miserable. Johnson
was decidedly for the balance of misery, in confirmation of which I
maintained, that no man would choose to lead over again the life
which he had experienced. Johnson acceded to that opinion in the
strongest terms. This is an enquiry often made and its being a subject of
disquisition is a proof that much misery presses upon human feelings,
for those who are conscious of a felicity of existence will never hesitate
to accept of a repetition of it. I have met with very few who would."
~~Joh~~ Boswells Johnson

a.d — 1784.

The question put as it is may be answered as Boswell answered it
by almost every body. If I were asked will you consent to be born
again and live over your life again, I should say. **NO**. – no nor to
live over again the life of any one that ever did live, or such a life as
I can suppose any one ever will live. But if I were to be born over
again, chusing now what life I should lead, i.e. in what situation and
circumstances of life I should be placed in, I should at once say, My
own life over again, for I knew nothing of a balance of misery, and
should not like to be any other one instead of the one I am. Another
question has been asked – do you know any one into whom you should
like to be changed?, to this none but the very miserable would say yes.
If now I would say, my life over again, there never could have been a
time when I should not have said so, for there never was a time when
I was not quite satisfied I should succeed in doing those things which
in my situation and circumstances, it was essential should be done,

and now I am placed in the very worst circumstances – or rather have to endure the greatest of all afflictions a man in good health can endure, the loss of his wife. I knew ~~this would be so and~~ always said that the greatest loss that could happen to any man who had been long married and had a family was the ~~loss of~~ death of his wife, as it broke up or set aside the indulgence of his habits or compelled him to submit to new arrangements, to break in upon or break up a system which by time and the association of ideas, he could not change but with great reluctance, and which would require all the powers of his understanding to enable him to bear tranquilly – without moping or becoming obdurate.[a]

I was never like D[r] Johnson afraid to die, so far from it that the more I have contemplated dying the more I have thought it desirable to die, and these contemplations, ~~it was which~~ had a considerable share in inducing me to make a will as soon as I found I had any property, that thus having done my duty to my family to the utmost extent of my ability I might have nothing to regret on that account and as I could have no regret on any other account I might have nothing to make me afraid to die. My poor wife had no regret on account of any thing but her family, and she had no fear whatever of dying. Religious people cant on this subject, and like Johnson and Boswell talk nonsense about the terrors they must feel who think "death an eternal sleep," but I have no doubt at all that it is not the annihilation of existence as a sentient being that makes men fear death, but the contrary absurd and superstitious notion of being alive when they are dead, that produces terror.

[a] Dec. 31. The greatest present source of disquietude to me is that I have lost my companion, and am really notwithstanding [. . .]

See Post next page but one. ☞

[Footnote. Place's first wife, Elizabeth Chadd, died on 19 October 1827. The remainder of this entry does not appear to have survived.]

1828

1828

Every political man is agitated with the singular state of the Government. The Government cannot indeed be fairly considered as being guided by any body excepting the clerks in Office.

The King is sulky, gouty, occupied with his big bubbied woman, does not like to be disturbed by any body, will not be asked questions, has been snubbed by the late ministers, refused in his wishes by the present ministers. Annoyed by applications, from the Wellesleys, and other noble Peers their coadjutors, and will now attend to none of them. This might do well enough at all times in respect to a King of England, whose office not to be pernicious beyond the actual expense incurred, is but filled by a man who cares nothing about politics nothing about the country nothing about, any one excepting only they who immediately minister to his pleasures. A king in this country who has any will of his own and acts upon it in respect to government must be a mischievous animal no matter how good his intentions may be. At present the King does play the very devil with our wise men of the West. Ministers do not possess his confidence, they who were his ministers and are now out of office are also without his confidence, he leaves them to fight it out in their own way, which pleases no one, and a pretty mess they will make of it. There are now no whigs no tories, all are mixed up in one mess and the contention is who shall be in place. Happily the country takes no part in their squabbles. The newspapers talk nonsense but nobody moves, no body of people any where shews any indication of taking part either with the ins or the outs. Neither are now backed up by the people, the time has gone by when they could be deluded and led by the nose by such tricksters as, Fox, and Burke – and Sheridan, and Pitt, and Grenville. They now stand by, saying in fact by their conduct, we can wait and we will wait and see what it is you mean to do. This puts the rickety ministry in a most awkward situation, and I hope they will be kept in it [several words crossed out] (by far the greatest part) have been for years finding fault and justly so with the conduct of preceding ministers, but who now they are in office will hardly pursue those measures of their [word crossed out] opponents to the length even they would have gone, in favour of the people. Without the people to back them they are nothing, without fully committing themselves with the people they can be nothing, and as they will not do this they will be nothing. Swifts prayer need hardly be repeated now, for it is all but accomplished.

> "Thus I said whilst looking
> round them"
> May their God, the Devil
> Confound them.

As the time approaches when the parliament will meet, many are the reports of changes, and many the conjectures of as to the probable proceedings – and many are the persons who have called upon me to talk or the over these matters — Burdett, Hobhouse, Hume – Col^n Jones, Admiral Donelly. That most excellent man M^r. Bickersteth Mill Tooke, Campbell, some City men and others. I am not wise enough to conjecture what will be attempted, nor do I care one jot. I know that nothing will be attempted of any real importance to the Nation and am not at all solicitous on the subject.

Wrote a long letter very carefully to M^r. Holmes M. P. as I had promised him I would do, on the defects of Peele's [*sic*] Jury Act and pointing out remedies. He too is perplexed. See correspondence with Hobhouse – end of Dec. 1827 and, this day – 7. Jany 1828.

Only two days have passed and the ministry is at an end, all in confusion again — 9. Jan^y —

19 [January]

Ten days have elapsed and there is no administration. The King is led by Dr Knighton, the man-midwife, who has gained the ascendancy above Lady Cunningham, by M^r. Herries, and old Rothschild the rich Jew Broker, Speculator and Loan Jobber. So says report.[451] Joking with Brougham and Sir Ronald Ferguson the other day, it was agreed that this was as good a cabinet as was likely to be formed.

Soon after Cannings death, I was told by one not likely to be mistaken that it was in contemplation to turn, Copley out of his Lord Chancellor-ship and that Copley had discovered this, associated himself with Lord Wellington and was doing all he could to oust the ministry and this seems to have succeeded.

Wellington!!! has been commanded to form an administration, so great a disgrace as this, is more than even I had anticipated. He cannot form one which can remain long in office and ere three months have passed, there will be something like general disgust expressed at this

---

[451] This sentence was inserted.

man so remarkable for folly and ignorance having been appointed to select an administration.

Equally remarkable & admirable it is, that there is now no "man of the people." Not a single man amongst the whole aristocracy who to whom the people look up, from whom the people expect any thing. Some among the whigs talk of their wish to see the Duke of Bedford & Lord Althorpe in the cabinet, but their being put there would not produce the slightest sensation. The name. Bedford–Althorpe, have no charm in them, they are mere names, and were they to be called even personally by the King to take the lead and to form an administration and were they to come in at Hyde Park Corner in an open carriage and move from thence slowly to Whitehall to proceed to the business they would pass along with as little notice being taken of them as of any two unknown persons. There would be no spontaneous mob, no shouting [?] no huzzaing, no taking of horses from the carriage, as in former time, no fooling demonstrations of the ignorance of the people.

When in 1820 the Queen came from abroad, I set myself zealously to work, to procure addresses to her. I set on foot the first public meeting and wrote the address and resolution. I cared nothing for the queen as the queen, she had been ill used by her husband, had left the country to him and his mistresses,[a] and all that could be said against her was that she kept a man, a fine handsome fellow, this was no concern of any body's and if she liked to do so, it was a matter in which she ought to have been indulged without scandal, without reproach, while she could be no bad example at home.[452] She however received 40.000£ a year of the peoples money which she wasted and I could have no respect for a receiver of the plunder of the people but I saw very plainly, that if a public meeting was held, it would be followed by many others. (see the guard Books – "Queen") and that nearly the whole of the unprivileged unfrocked unpensioned unofficered part of the people would meet and address the Queen and go [to] the queen in thousands. I knew very well that the consequence would be a familiarity with Royalty highly injurious to its state, that the mystification of the throne would be greatly impaired, the "Divinity which doth hedge a King" – would to a great extent be set aside and that many thousands of people would lose their reverence of both for Royalty and Aristocracy, and this I assigned as the reason for my interference in favour of the Queen, as it was called. I doubted that whether or not so much stupidity existed amongst the Lords and especially in the Privy Council as would per induce them to push the

[a] What a very comfortable name. This is for a set of — . [Footnote.]

[452] This last phrase was inserted at a later date.

matter to extremities. But, when I saw them all commit themselves as they did I was exceeding pleased, and worked the harder on that account. I was now sure that the excitement would be general, and that the consequence would be, such a falling off of respect for Royalty and Aristocracy as had never before existed amongst the people in this country. I saw that to immense extent this falling off would be followed by contempt.

So it was, and now we see the consequence, no person who has any considerable portion of Understanding places any reliance on titles. Call a man what you will, it goes for very little indeed. The question is no longer **Who**, but **What**. What will he do for the people? is the question. No one will say what he will do, because every one knowes [*sic*] he can really do nothing which the people would think was worth praising to any considerable extent. Because they in whose hands the government is at all likely to be placed do not see the change which has taken place, and think to carry on the Government as it was carried on fifty years ago. Thus they are all at sea, and there they will remain for a long time. There has been no administration properly so called for twelve months past and there will be no permanent administration for twelve years to come unless some unforseen [*sic*] circumstance should produce unexpected changes.

A long conversation yesterday with Brougham, who if he had half the judgment, he has talent would do wonderful things. He has several good projects in hand, one a Parliamentary commission to inquire into the state of the law preparatory to a reform with a view to the formation of a Code, for which I am to furnish him some cases as proofs of the operation of the Law in trade. Brougham says his prime object is totally to abolish, common law and for this purpose he may command my time to any extent, and employ it in any way not dishonourable to me.

He has a capital project which will I dare say succeed. Making School Books, and story books and books of science for children and young persons, than which nothing can be of greater importance. I have promised my assistance. The "library of useful knowledge" sells he says 24.000 and will furnish ample means to pay the ablest persons for making school and other books – such as I have mentioned. This is a grand measure.

See Correspondence in Guard Book. "Parties" – respecting – the present and future government, between Hobhouse and Place.

30.   [January 1828].

Much occupied during the last two days, and to day with political people. No one of my quondam friends who are members of the

Den, knew what was to be done in honourable house yesterday, no one could decide what he himself would do. Several of the displaced whigs were eager to attack the new Tory administration, but then as they in consequence of taking office could not be in the house until re-elected, and it was said that it would be equally ungentlemanly and unmanly to attack them in their absence. This was one of the principle [*sic*] topics on which M^r. Brougham consulted me on the 18$^{th.}$ and we concurred in this that it would be improper to speak on any subject which personally concerned any of them when they ~~were~~ could not be there to reply, but I suggested, that he might make a speech which could not fail to be of use, and would become the text book for all the reformers in the Kingdom. It was simple to oppose the address on the ground that it had omitted to tell the people what were the real causes of their discontent so far as the government was actually concerned, and it also failed to point out any remedy. ~~That~~ The plan I suggested was to begin with the debt, and describe it, then complain that no plan for paying it had been even alluded to. Then the taxes – Then the Game Laws, and their criminal making effect. The Excise and Smuggling – The Army &c[453] – the state of the Laws – the Magistracy – and so on to the end of the chapter. Brougham said it would be excellent, upon which I observed that, I would willingly put the whole matter, into form, taking care to be perfectly correct, ~~and~~ referring for every statement to some parliamentary paper so that no one should be able to refute any particular part of the bill of Indictment. Brougham did not like this, it would have been a breach of decorum towards his party to do it without consulting them, and was quite sure to be rejected if laid before them. This I knew very well and did not therefore press him to do it. On monday I preached the whole or nearly the whole matter to M^r. Hobhouse, as he sat in my library, while I was walking up and down the room, it had a very considerable effect on him, animated him much, but altho I told him I would sit up all night ~~and~~ to arrange the matter of a speech for him, he had not the courage to undertake it.

In the evening I learned that Tierney[454] had threatened "to tell the whole story" of the Juggling respecting the recent changes, and this alarmed many honourable gentlemen, some I saw were so put out as not to know what to do, or what to say. At a consultation at Sir James Scarlets chambers at 10 o clock at night, present Sir James. M^r. Brougham, and M^r. Joshua Evans ~~besides~~ M^r. Fenn and M^r.

[453]This phrase was inserted.
[454]George Tierney, who had joined Canning's ministry in 1827, was dismissed by Wellington in January 1828. See D.R. Fisher, 'Tierney, George (1761–1830)', *ODNB*, <http://www.oxforddnb.com/view/article/27439>, accessed 19 January 2006.

Burke the attorney in the cause on which the consultation was held. Sir James who had resigned the seals of office only two days before, and was no longer Attorney General, was very dull, he was however attentive and did not hurry the business, but both he and Brougham displayed much restlessness. Yesterday when the cause was called in at 10 o clock, (it was a trial at bar) Golding v. Fenn) [sic] – it was supposed it would not occupy much time, but as our oponents [sic] had no law to stand upon, and as the Chief Justice was known to be opposed to us, the four counsel[s] on the other side ~~had to fin~~ whose duty it was to lead, had to find something like arguments, as excuses for the Judges to decide against us, and they did their duty to their clients to the utmost of their ability, no counsel ever took more pains, ~~shew~~ to make a bad case appear like a good one, never surely was more ingenuity displayed, but they were labouring in their vocation until nearly half past 2 o clock. Sir Ja^s Scarlet then spoke for us, and continued speaking till 3 o clock, when he concluded and the Judges adjourned the further hearing till thursday. What Scarlet said was good as far as it went, but he did not exhaust any one topic, neither did he notice several of considerable importance. It was not known with any thing like certainty, what would take place in the House of Commons and it had evidently been arranged ~~that~~ or was managed by some sort of understanding between the counsel and the bench that the ~~case~~ further hearing should be postponed that, Scarlet and Brougham might go to the House. Thus it is poor clients suffer. ~~B~~

Before I could reach home from the court I was attacked by an humble gentleman from the den to tell me all about the Kings – speech, and I was scarcely allowed time to swallow my dinner before other persons came and my whole evening was consumed.

On the Thursday the Trial at Bar proceeded, it was well argued by both Brougham and Evans – The Judges said they would take time to form their opinions.

February.   [1828]

Much occupied in assisting M^r. Hume respecting the Navy and the committee on Finance to be moved for by him.

Hunting out from various sources the state of our Navy in 1792 – that of France, and the other European Nations – and that of America, for the purpose of comparison. The object is to shew the enormous abuses which have been established, and are now in full practice, in every department, number of ships – of officers, &c &c – particularly those in half pay, over whose heads, as it were and frequently is, numbers are promoted who have seen no service. Vide Memoirs of Lord Collingwood as to these matters and his apprehension that upon the plan we are pursuing there can be very few good officers.[455]

M^r. Peels, intended Finance Committee is, in parliamentary language a special "humbug." It will consist of so many persons that responsibility even to meet to transact business will rest on no one. They may sit for years and yet do nothing and nothing will be done. Our plan is to have 5 committees of 7 members each whose attendance shall be compulsory. Each of these committees to take one department of the Receipt side of the accounts. A sixth committee to be formed of the chairman and one other member of the 5 committees, for the purpose of making a journal account. All 6 committees to report. Also 5 Committees on the Expenditure and also a 6th as before mentioned. A General committee to be formed of the two committees N°s 6. to report a general D^t a C^r account, under each head, and a general account or balance sheet of the whole.

All the committee so far as may be practicable to sit at the same time, to communicate with each other, & to meet each other, if necessary.

These committees to enquire into and to examine every matter and thing relating to money received and paid for national purposes, or in any way connected with the Government whether the accounts are delivered to the Exchequer or not, or annually reported or not.

With much labour digested the whole matter, I think clearly. M^r. Humes notions will not be adopted by the house, but they will be printed in all the newspapers, and will be ably commented on in the next volume of the Parliamentary Review, and thus many persons will be enabled to see what might be done with care in a matter which is mystified and made to appear so extremely ~~mysterious~~ abstruse and difficult, that no one seems to expect it can ever be carried into effect, nor any clear result be produced.

[455]Cuthbert Collingwood, *A Selection from the Public and Private Correspondence of Vice-Admiral Lord Collingwood: interspersed with memoirs of his life*, by G.L. Newnham Collingwood (London, 1828).

N.B. The Parliamentary Review for 1826–7 – published a few days ago is a most admirable book in every respect, but most especially as a teaching book for green Legislators.

On the 18 Jan^y – There was an article in the New Times relating to a Trial to recover some money from the proprietors of the London Free Press Newspaper. The Editor of the New Times imputes to Hume and me that we committed a fraud, and Hume has suffered himself to be irritated, and says he will commence a prosecution. I hope I shall be able to dissuade him from his purpose, for it is of no consequence either to him or to me what any one says on such subjects. There is not one word of truth in the account, and the Editor like many of the newspaper people is a great rascal, who lies to serve his own purposes, which I am sure he may with respect to M^r. Hume and me, do to any extent without damage to either of us.

M^r. Hume made nothing of the paper I gave him in the house, but he has made good use of it in the committee, and two or three sub-committees met ~~daily~~ on the three alternate days when the Finance committee does not sit ~~and~~ prepare matters, and collect information for the Committee.

Some disputing, with M^r. Hobhouse occasioned by his, neglect of the electors in the parish of St Paul Covent Garden which is likely to do him injury at the next election.

Much curious information from one of the clerks in the Army Pay Office. Digested it and gave it to M^r. Hume to be used at the Finance Committee.

[March 1828]

On the   M^r. Peel[456], made a speech in the house of Commons on the state of Crime in the Metropolis, he took however rather a discursive view but the gist of his argument was the great increase of the number of crimes committed in the Metropolis.[457] He concluded by moving for "a select committee, to enquire into the causes of the increase of the number of committments [*sic*] and convictions in London and Middlesex, and the state of the Police of the Metropolis, and the districts adjacent thereto, and to state their opinions thereon."

The committee consists of —

M^r. Peel.	M^r. Calvert.
— Estcourt.	— W. Peel.
— Byng.	Western.
Sir J. Brydges.	Pallmer.
M^r. Ferguson.	R. Gordon.
— Bankes.	G. Lamb
— Denison.	Ald. Wood.
Marquess Chandos.	Ld Lowther.
M^r. Spring Rice.	M^r. N. Calvert.
— Hobhouse.	Sir T. Freemantle.
Ald^m Thompson.	Mqs. Blandford.
Ld Jno Russell.	Major. Cust.

Urged by M^r. Hobhouse to supply him with materials, to enable him to push such an examination as would shew the former and present state of the Police of the Metropolis, the actual state of crime ~~then~~ during the last 50 years, and the comparative number of committments [*sic*]. This I was desirous enough to do, provided I had reasonable ground to conclude that after my time had been consumed in ~~coll~~ selecting and digesting the information, he would use it, so that my time on this as on other occasions might not be wasted, as however I could not be satisfied on this point I did nothing. At length M^r. Hobhouse after several conversations with me in which I shewed him pretty plainly that there was no increase of crime in the Metropolis, but probably a diminution, and after he had talked the matter over with several members of the committee and became convinced that my opinion was well founded ~~he~~ promised to use the matters I might furnish and push for such information in the committee as should elicit the truth. I now set to work, spent much time and furnished him with ample

[456]The date is left blank in the manuscript.
[457]*Hansard*, new series, 18, 28 February 1828, cols 784–816.

means to effect his purpose, but from ~~the~~ subsequent conversations I conclude that as usual he has been infirm of purpose, wearied with what he calls trouble, and that, what he has done will come out, as usual to nothing. M^r. Peel having most unwisely in his speech declared a great increase of crime, will no doubt do all he can to prove his case, and it is very probable that the Report will contain assertions of the increase of crime directly at variance with the facts, and that from not having had the proper witnesses before the committee, and from not putting the proper questions to those who were before it, the assertions in the Report may be born [sic] out, and thus a false shewing be made, which will be hereafter quoted by historians, as a proof of the demoralization of the population of London, when in fact no place on the earth has improved so much in morals.

The matter noticed in the next column[458] was finished in the morning of the 28$\underline{th}$ and by 2 o clock was concluded an arrangement which has set the disputes between Mrs Miller and her sons at rest, and now, for the first time since I can well remember, no, that is a mistake, but for the first time for many years past, I have no business of any sort, for any body on my hands.

With great care digested a plan to take the suffrages of the electors by ballot – put it into the form of enactments for M^r. Hume who is to move them as clauses in the bill to permit Birmingham to send two members to Parliament, and when they have been rejected as they will be on the plea that it would be improper to introduce the ballot partially, he will move their introduction, ~~into~~ the general Bill now before the House to regulate Polls.

NB. July. 23. M^r. Hume made no use of these papers. The matter stands over till the next session.

---

[458] The format of the manuscript has changed slightly at this point. The continuous, two-column, newspaper format previously employed now breaks horizontally across the page to distinguish the entries for the month of March from those for April. It is not entirely clear what material Place refers to as being 'in the next column', but the 'next' column in the manuscript appears in this transcription as the succeeding paragraph below.

April.

M^r. Hume was unable to use the matter relating to [the] Ballot in the way he intended and he therefore gave notice of a motion on the subject which has been unavoidably postponed, throughout the month.

M^r. Hobhouse has done next to nothing in the Committee on Committments [*sic*]. {July 23. M^r. Hobhouse shirked the business.[459]

Much occupied at times in the affairs of M^r. Fenn – but upon the whole less occupied in the affairs of others than usual, my situation being very different from what it was 6 months ago. I have gone out much more than I used to do, and people have not therefore been able to find me at all times as they used to do, and thus I have been prevented taking up the affairs of others to the extent I used to do.

Received a vast quantity of curious information from a M^r. Wallace or Wallis in the Army Pay Office relating to the shameful way in which it has been and is conducted. Digested it into form for M^r. Hume as a brief – M^r. Hume made good use of it in the Finance Committee and found it was quite correct, the committee was compelled to admit the abuses did exist, and to concur in [the] opinion that the office was useless and the whole expense upwards of 30.000£ per annum was wasted. Yet next to nothing will be done.

[459]This bracketed sentence was apparently added at a later date.

May. 1828.

A good deal occupied in the affairs of others, but not so much so as, formerly – My state or relative situation, being very different in consequence of the death of my wife, I have, since the middle of february last spent more time from home than I had ever before done – Seldom indeed did I ever dine from home; of late I have dined frequently from home, – and spent many evenings from home. One thing is somewhat remarkable. The time I now give to the affairs of others, leaves me in much the same state in respect to others as I was in when I gave up my whole time to them, and I can perceive that, if I were still willing to give up the whole of my time it would be as fully occupied as is the time which I do thus give up.

June.

Spent in much the same way as April.

July.

D°. — During this month and some portion of June, I have generally been occupied from about 7 in the morning till nearly 3 in the afternoon with the affairs of others, and so closely too, that I have written nothing, and have not read 100 pages of any book. After dinner, I generally go out, [remainder of sentence crossed out]. Walking, Reading, and about once in a fortnight on an average going to the Play.

August.

Same as July – no change – excepting, that my reading has been a little more extensive [remainder of sentence crossed out]. Once only to the Play – Much exercise taken during these two months.

September.

No change – occupied on the Report on the Police of the Metropolis. Attended the opening Lectures of the Medical and Surgical Professor of the University of London in the first and second weeks of October.

October.

Continued to attend the Opening Lectures at the London University, which is I now think, safe – it will I hope succeed rapidly as from its capabilities of being useful – it deserves to do so.

M^r. Lubbock and M^r. Robson with a revived project of their Daily Morning Paper. They have altered their plan in many respects – and have about 10.000£ —

November.

Much as usual, only rather more engaged, in the affairs of others —

December.

Less engaged in the affairs of others. Occupied most of my mornings – during this month, in extracting matter for my book of Manners &c. Principally relating to the Drama. [Section deleted.] Godwins Enquirer, This being composed of short [. . ..][460]

---

[460]The diary entries for 1828 end here.

1829

[4 May]   **1829**

Occupied much in the same way, noticed, in the memoranda dated December 1828.

M^r. Hobhouse had said in the House of Commons that early in the session of 1829 he should introduce a Bill to regulate the Parish Vestries in the Metropolis, as the meeting of the Parliament drew near, people came to me from many parishes, to learn if possible what the provisions of M^r. Hobhouse's bill were to be, and to suggest such matters as they thought should be introduced into it. M^r. H— had married and was in Italy,[461] and as I knew that he had declared his intentions to introduce a bill without having at all considered either the matter of which it should be composed or the extent of the trouble he was likely to bring upon himself, I could give no satisfactory information to the enquirers. I knew also that M^r. Hobhouse was but ill adapted, for such a measure, that he had neither the habits of business necessary for such an undertaking nor the patience to attend to the applications which would be made to him. He wrote to me from Italy saying he feared he could not not [sic] be in London at the opening of the parliament, and wished me to see M^r. Denison and request him to give notice of a motion for him. I saw M^r. Denison and in a long conversation in which M^r. Hobhouse was freely spoken of, it we concurred in opinion that the best way for him to proceed would be a motion for a select committee to take evidence. M^r. Hobhouse arrived before the houses met, and concurred in the view we had taken, and gave notice for a committee. The committee was appointed on the 29 April, and will sit for the first time tomorrow the 5 May.

M^r. Fenn's pertinacity in his proceedings against the self appointed Vestry of St Martin in the Fields during the last seven years had roused the attention of many other parishes, and had exposed many corruptions and abused [sic] and been led to many amendments. Many persons came to me from different parishes and in some cases it became requisite for me to take much pains to reconcile differences

---

[461] Hobhouse was married to Lady Julia Tomlinson Hay on 28 July 1828.

which had arisen amongst those whose object was reformation of
Parish Proceedings. These matters consumed much of my time. In
other respects I was not much occupied with public matters. The
proceedings in Parliament on the Catholic Relief Bill wholly occupied
the attention of political men and scarcely any other public matter
was attended to. The debates were long and frequent, numerous
were the meetings to procure petitions against the bill; flagrant and
infamous the attempts to excite the people to outrage and to overawe
the Parliament. But to the ~~great~~ credit of Ministers they neither
prosecuted, nor in any way molested the miscreants high or low, but
pushed on steadily to their object and carried it triumphantly. Men
will hereafter be astonished at the efforts made to prevent so useful a
measure from being accomplished, and more so at the monstrously
absurd predictions of the enemies of the measure, as well in as out
of Parliament. Already, has the dreadful measure passed away, and is
scarcely spoken of. Not a single column of debates in either house on
this subject did I read. I know well enough that no evil whatsoever
could be produced, and that within a very short time, no one scarcely
would think the concession even worth an acknowledgement. Its effects on Ireland, as a first step to important alterations is valuable and I
therefore rejoice that the Irish have been Emancipated — But the great
and important change, in mens opinions is the subject most worthy
of exultation. In 1780 Lord George Gordon, raised an immense mob
which threatened the destruction of the Metropolis, and now in 1829
– when it was proposed to proceed to lengths which no man at that
time dared to contemplate, when every means that ingenuity could
devise was resorted to, all over the country to excite dissatisfaction,
and produce riots, not a leg nor an arm could be set in motion in
that way. People have come to the knowledge that the pretences used
by the Church of England-men, the Parsons of every description, are
only meant to lead them astray to blind them to the corruptions of
their caste, to plunder them of their property, in proportion as they
stultify them, and are not now to be misled as they formerly were.
The Conduct of the Clergy in this affair has gone far to lessen their
consequence and happily to bring the necessity as has been pretended
of a state religion into more contempt than ever before existed.

The state of the Cotton manufacturers

The state of the Silk manufacturers

brought me a good deal of employment and will continue so to do
for some time. No permanent service can be done to either, but by
the people themselves who are not likely however to use the means
necessary to promote their own welfare.

The Catholic question having been settled, men now turned their
attention to matters which had been in abeyance and I was more

occupied with the business of others, than I had hitherto been since the commencement of last Autumn, and was in hopes I should not again be occupied so much in the affairs of others as I had formerly been the more so as I was rarely to be found at home after 3 o clock in the day and people became tired of coming to my house. But in this I was mistaken. Many projects were brought to me, numerous applications for many purposes, and excepting the time I could procure by rising early I have had very little of late which I could apply to any purpose of my own.

      Corn Laws. ————— Malt and Beer
      Silk Laws. ————— Trade Laws
      Police ————————— Parliamentary Reform

Petitions, Projects of various sorts all appeared to rise simultaneously and with one or another or more of my friends, and with strangers my time was and is likely to be for some time consumed. I cannot without offence and I fear without producing some evil refuse to interfere in the concerns of others and especially in those of the working people, and as it costs nothing to obtain such assistance as I can give numbers will always be seeking it.

Of late I have been very much occupied, one days diary will shew how this and stand as an example.

Monday 4 May. 1829.

At 7 – a.m. read several letters which were left for me yesterday, and made memorandums to reply to them.

Read in the Morning Chronicle.

Looked at the Parliamentary Papers delivered this morning.

Read a note from M^r. Hume requesting my attention and observations on the debate on the Silk Trade as reported in the Mirror of Parliament. Looked at it, and laid it aside 'till tomorrow.

Wrote a letter to Sir Francis Burdett respecting a petition to him for assistance from the man who made the Chairing Car in 1820.

Wrote another letter to him explaining the purpose of the inhabitants of St Paul Covent Garden, respecting an opposition they expected would be made to the second reading of their Vestry bill, this evening in the House of Lords.[462] Requesting his assistance with certain Lords.

Read a letter from Thomas Foster of Manchester, requesting me to draw a bill to amend the acts for the regulating of Cotton Mills and

---

[462]*Hansard* does not record any debate on this bill, the first reading of which had been on 28 April. See *Hansard*, new series, 21, 28 April 1829, cols 890–906.

Factories, so far as relates to the employment of poor children which
I had promised I would do.

While reading the Acts of Parliament came a deputation of Cotton
workers. 4 – from Manchester and Stockport, on the state of the Cotton
Trade, advised with them and promised to draw the bill immediately.
The draft bill to be shewn to M^r. Peel and several other members of
both houses tomorrow morning – copies to be made for that purpose.

Before I could proceed with the draft M^r. Fenn came in, he had
been endeavouring to frame a set of questions to be put to him before
the Select Committee on Vestries[463] but had not succeeded. Read his
notes, wrote out the ~~leading~~ heads of the matter he wished to have
investigated formed it into questions, so as to enable him to put in
several important documents and accounts, arranged the whole as a
brief of which he is to have three copies made, one for M^r. Hobhouse
the Chairman one for M^r. Hume and one for himself.

Deputation — M^r. Yockney, M^r. Phillips M^r. Pilt on ~~the~~ matters
relating to their /Covent Garden/ Parish Bill – read my letter to Sir
F Burdett and gave it to them to take to his house.

Letter from Colonel Jones requesting me to frame a set of questions,
to be put to him, before the Committee on Vestries.

Wrote an answer –
Wrote to M^r. Hume ⎫
——— to M^r. Hobhouse ⎬ same subject

M^r. Gray, M^r. Staton and another to beg money to build
the National Parish School, gave them 20/ reluctantly because these
schools are not as efficient as the Lancastrian Schools, and ~~because~~
what I give to the one must be witheld [*sic*] from the others.

M^r. Thomas Campbell Rector of the ~~University~~ College at Glasgow,
he gave me an account of certain proceedings there, calculated to
accelerate the instruction of the pupils. He had with him a young
man named Tennant who wished for employment as a reporter on
some London Morning Paper. Concerted the means of application,
and promised to do what I could to procure him employment.

Finished the draft of the Bill to amend the acts respecting the hours
of working, children in the Cotton Mills —

Arranged some papers relating to the Drama.

Dr Gillies, came with a message &c from M^r. Hume – gave him
some books.

---

[463]The Committee's reports were published in the Sessional Papers as *PP*, 4 (1830), *Two
Reports from the Select Committee on the Laws and Usages under which Select and other Vestries are
Constituted.*

Made memorandums – as above. M^r. Corder M^r. Dow from the Parish of St Paul Covent Garden.

M^r. Sullivan on his affairs – advised him.

Dined at 3 —

Walked off at 20 minutes to 4 to [several words crossed out] Sir Francis Burdett in the Park, talked with him of the matters before alluded to.

22 Sep. 1829

Towards the end of the Month of May Consulted by C. S. Cullen
the Barrister respecting a plan to promote a desire for Parliamentary
Reform, previous to a meeting to be held at Chichester. The meeting
was held on the 5th June at Chichester and certain resolutions were
passed. This was one amongst several indications that there would be
a large number of persons ~~who~~ willing to make exertions in the same
way.

Several others came to me on the same subject, but the most
determined by far was Colⁿ Leslie Grove Jones. I advised him to
see some of his friends and converse with them on the subject, he did
so and was in a hurry to proceed to business, but I checked him until
he could be sure of such cooperation as would warrant proceedings
— some days ago he saw the Earl of Radnor who said, he was a friend
to Universal Suffrage, Annual Parliaments and Voting by Ballott [sic],
and would become chairman of a Society to promote reform if Jones
could obtain a dozen respectable names to a list of gentlemen who
were willing to cooperate for that purpose. Colⁿ Jones now requested
me to draw up a plan for the formation of a society. This I did, and
yesterday I gave it to him. He was much pleased with it ~~and~~ said he
would shew it to Lord Radnor, have [. . .] lent their assistance.[464]

If this be carried into effect with vigour a society will be formed,
and correspondence opened with many places. Many associations will
be also be [sic] formed and there the effects of the society will end.
The declaration and regulations are so drawn as to induce others to
associate and correspond, and the names which may be procured will
be a guarantee against any delusion on the part of the London Society.
But this London Society will soon be alarmed at the proceedings and
resolutions of other societies and will abandon the position it has
taken.

[464]The manuscript appears to be missing a portion of the page at this point.

Nov. 15. 1830

The remainder of the year 1829 spent much in the same way, mornings at home afternoons and evenings at Brompton.

M^r. Hobhouse trifled in the Committee on Parish Vestries, he was overpowered and subdued by Sturges Bourne and did not push his examination of witnesses to the extent he ought to have done, when the report was to be made he received as I afterwards discovered a request from the Speaker that he would not move, "that the minutes be printed,["] so he went out of town and the minutes were simply laid on the Table of Honourable House by another member. It was some time before it was ascertained that they would not be printed and then M^r. Hobhouse was out of town and the parliament having been prorogued nothing could be done. This conduct of M^r. Hobhouse was highly reprehensible. A committee was recommended to him and adopted by him as the best means of making the subject familiar to all persons. It was not expected that any bill could be passed in the session, and it was therefore agreed on all sides that the best way to proceed would be to have a committee print the evidence that it ought to be circulated during the vacation and in the next session when the matter was well understood to propose a bill. M^r. Hobhouse's conduct gave great offence, and put his seat in jeopardy. It was certainly as weak as it was both treacherous, and injurious, when I saw him I spoke of it as I thought it deserved and in a letter to Col^n Jones, – dated. 5 Nov. 1829^a – I again said what I though[t] on the subject. ~~The~~ M^r. Hobhouse soon discovered that he had made many enemies and no friends and he therefore promised to have the report printed and the committee revived as soon as the Session commenced.

---

^{a} See it in the Political Letter Book. [Marginal note. See BL Add. MS 35148, fo. 36.]

V.5.

N° 6. From "the New Times" — London Newspaper[465]

"18 January. 1828"

"There was a newspaper called the Free Press established in February last, which lingered on until July, when it died of what ~~of what~~ the people in the north (whence its title was borrowed,) call a '"wasting."' It died, but its works did not ~~die with it~~ follow it, for there remained behind it a bill for 280£, for paper and stamps, due to Messr Battye and Co of Aldersgate Street. The paper was established by Col^n Jones and two respectable gentlemen, Joseph Hume, Esqr of Greek Bond memory; and the ingenious M^r. Place, the literary small clothes man, who writes bitter articles on politics and all that, in the Westminster Review. The Free Press was to be carried on in a bold and uncompromising manner; but in order that the literary charger might have a martingale as well as spurs for his guidance, if any libel were inserted in the bold and uncompromising journal, the editor was to forfeit half his salary. M^r. Hume is a clever man — he did not put his name to the bond – he had enough of trouble that way before – he acted under the disguise of a respectable gentleman. M^r. Place was equally provident, but the gallant Colonel, unluckily for himself, allowed his name to be announced, and hence the defeat which Messrs Battye and Co sustained in the Common Pleas yesterday, for it is so happened, that the Colonel was not only a partner with M^r. Hume and M^r. Place, the tailor and [illegible] on others in the property of the Free Press, but he was also a partner in the house of Battye and Co, citizens and stationers. We have no wish to remark on the manner in which the Colonel sought to slip the noose from himself, but it is not unamusing to observe the workings of the master passion in another of the Trio, who supported the bold and uncompromising Free Press for four whole months. This calculating gentleman is M^r. Hume, whose character wanted only a few finishing touches of this kind to perfect it."

Remarks on the matter

M^r. Hume demanded from the Editor a contradiction of the preceding paper, and threatened to commence an action against him if he did not insert the contradiction in his paper. M^r. Hume denied as he might truly do that he had, had any thing to do with the London

---

[465]This is a handwritten copy of an article that was transcribed into the Diary at this point.

Free Press and he invited the editor to call upon him to receive the proofs. I objected to this threat on the part of M^r. Hume, to which he replied that he cared not for what any man either said or printed respecting his public conduct but if any one accused him of fraud in his private transactions, he should feel the consequences. I still thought he had better have taken no notice of the matter. I said you know that I had no more to do with it than you had, yet I feel no disposition to take notice of it, and yet if the nonsense this editor talks could affect either of us injuriously it would be me, you have a public character the value of which is known and acknowledged and such things as these can have no effect against such a character. M^r. Hume however persisted an[d] caused his attorney to write to the editor on the subject. On Monday the 11th the following apology appeared in the New Times, and there the matter rests. "On the 18 of last month we made some remarks on the connection of M^r. Hume with a weekly paper called the Free Press. The fact of the connection was publicly talked of in Court during the trial, which gave occasion to the remarks in question. It was not until a very few days ago that we learned, that the report was an erroneous one. We are now authorized to state, that no connection existed at any time between the Free Press and M^r. Hume. Had we been earlier aware of the mistake into which we had been led, we should have made an earlier acknowledgment of it."

1830

V.5.

1830.

Nº. 7.

NB. This is a loose gossiping account – and must be greatly abridged as soon as I can find time to do it.[x]
    Feby. 17. 1831

                    NB. The time has not been found. Sep. 1838.
                                    nor yet — Sep 1845.

Since the above note was written some few memoranda have been made to June 1836. But no revision has been made, but the 3 papers – Numbered 7–8.9 – contain some indications of matters in which I was concerned, references to matters in my Letter Books, and to Matters more at length in M. S. S. In the Mahogany Chest. Jan[y]. 1850.

1830

$$\left.\begin{array}{c} \text{July} - 1830 \\ \text{to} \\ \text{Feby} - 1831 \end{array}\right\} \begin{array}{l} \text{Time when} \\ \text{written at} \\ \text{many intervals} \end{array}$$

At the close of 1829 I had detached myself very much from my political friends, and at the commencement of the present year, I had very few matters belonging to any body on my hands.[466]

I was to be married to Mrs Chatterly[467] as soon as my family arrangements by the marriage of my eldest son and some other family matters were accomplished. I would fain have remained at Brompton where [words struck out] to build a room for my books would have cost me less than putting my home at Charing Cross to rights was likely to occasion.

Mrs Chatterly's house N° 15 Brompton Square was neat in good condition and rather elegantly fitted up and furnished. The Square was occupied by genteel quiet people, and was nicely kept. The House was well situated the first on the Square, the back looking over a small garden had an uninterrupted view as far as Chiswick, and was so circumstanced in respect to situation that it was not at all likely it would be built in. It is in the neighbourhood of Hyde park and Kensington Gardens, and the walks in almost every direction are clear and pleasant, but here I could not remain without greatly deranging my family, so we agreed to remove to Charing Cross.

It was utterly impossible for me to detach myself from the business of others if I resided at Charing Cross. So I at once abandoned the schemes I would willingly have indulged, and more especially the attempt I had long since contemplated of writing a history of North America, and for which I have collected upwards of 600 volumes, and at once reconciled myself to my old way of consuming time.

M^r. Hume was pressing on some subjects, M^r. Hobhouse on others, they would however soon have ceased to expect much from me, if by remaining at Brompton I had made it inconvenient to them as well as others to come to me. M^r. Hume had promised to bring a motion before the house of Commons for a repeal of so much of the 60 Geo. 3– c.9 commonly called called [sic] one of 6 acts, as related to small publications. I therefore on the 7 Jany sent him an essay on the subject

[466] This entry is reproduced in Mary Thale (ed.), *The Autobiography of Francis Place, 1771–1854* (Cambridge, 1972), pp. 267–268.

[467] Place married Louisa Simeon Chatterley on 13 February 1830. Her surname has been struck out throughout the remainder of this entry. Their marriage eventually ended in separation in 1851. For an account, see Place, *The Autobiography*, pp. 258–260, 268–270.

which I wrote in 1827 for insertion in the Trades Newspaper but which owing to a change in the management of that paper was not inserted. I sent him a letter[a] also containing some information for him to proceed upon, and the case of a small weekly publication relating solely to the Drama, called the 'Harlequin' which had been extinguished by the Commissioners of Stamps by virtue of the act.

Several other members amongst whom were Sir Francis Burdett and M[r]. Hobhouse promised to assist M[r]. Hume but the session passed away without the subject ever once being mentioned in Parliament.

M[r]. Hume was also desirous to investigate the real utility of City and Borough Corporations and having promised to move for returns respecting them I drew up a motion to be made for that purpose,[b] this also came to nothing.

M[r]. Littleton[468] it was understood intended to move for a repeal of all the laws which related to the payment of wages in goods, or in any thing but money, and M[r]. Hume to enact a new law much more vigorously and effectually preventing the payment of wages in any thing but money. Thus putting an end to what had, obtained the name of "Tommy shops."

M[r]. Hume on the contrary was resolved to procure if possible the repeal of these laws and leave the matter there, so that the masters and men might make whatever bargains they pleased as to the mode of payment. At his request I wrote a short letter on this subject.[c]

M[r]. Littleton brought in his bill, M[r]. Hume opposed it, there were some short discussions, the bill was delayed and nothing was done, but an understanding prevailed that a committee to enquire respecting the practice of paying wages in goods, and the modes of conducting "Tommy shops," and other matters relating to the subject, should be moved for early in the next session.

Soon after the Session had commenced M[r]. Hobhouse moved that the evidence taking [sic] in the preceding session on Vestries should be printed, and he obtained the reappointment of the committee. As soon as the report of the last session was printed M[r]. Hobhouse sent me a copy, he was very desirous that I should read it and let him have such remarks on it as I might think useful to him. I read the whole of the minutes, made a marginal index, and wrote such comments as

[a] See Political Letter Book. 7 Jan[y] 1830. Six Acts. [Marginal note. See BL Add. MS 35148, fo. 37.]

[b] See. — l[etter]b[ook] — same date. Corporations. [Marginal note. See BL Add. MS 35148, fo. 41.]

[c] See l[etter]b[ook] — same date. Tommy Shops. [Marginal note. See BL Add. MS 35148, fo. 40.]

[468] Edward Littleton, MP for Staffordshire.

occurred to me, the time to do this, so as to make it useful, was short, and I worked hard [at] it.[a]

This done I commenced reading the minutes taken in the present session and on the 2 April sent M[r]. Hobhouse my observation thereon. My purpose was, to point out the most material parts of the evidence as data for M[r]. Hobhouse to frame his bill, and to furnish arguments for him to support it, with as little trouble as possible to himself. When the bill was prepared we went through it, together, and separately, and made it as perfect as we could. M[r]. Hobhouse had laboured hard at the bill and it did him great credit, we were however quite certain that Honourable house would not permit it to pass as it was drawn, but it was intended to put the onus of making it worse on those who made it so, after it had been presented as complete as it could be made. The bill went to a committee up stairs was altered delayed, and treated in the way obnoxious bills often are,[b] and the session terminated without any thing being done.

[a] See Political Letter Book. 22 March. 1830. [Marginal note. See BL Add. MS 35148, fos 42–47.]

[b] See l[etter]b[ook]. — 2 April — N.B. Several notes from M[r]. Hobhouse on the subject are also inserted. See also Parliamentary Papers. Select Vestries. [Marginal note. See BL Add. MS 35148, fos 49–56.]

March

Married the 13 Feb[y] at Kensington Church and resided at Brompton
'till the 15 April when we removed to Charing Cross.

Scarcely was I ~~again~~ settled at Charing Cross before ~~then~~ people
came again to me as usual, and my time was again occupied as usual.

On the 4 May a volume was delivered from the House of Commons
Intitled [*sic*] — Table of Stamp Duties, "proposed to be made payable
throughout the United Kingdoms." It proposed a stamp duty of [d]4
on every Newspaper and it defined the word thus

> "Newspaper. — containing public news – intelligence or
> occurence [*sic*], or any remarks or observations thereon in church
> or state, with or without advertisements, – that is to say – for any
> sheet half sheet or piece of paper whereof the same shall consist
> a stamp duty of four pence."
>
> "It exempted
>
> 1. Any paper printed and dispensed separately containing
> a single advertisement and not containing any other matter.
> 2. Daily accounts of Goods Imported and Exported.
> 3. The Weekly Bills of Mortality, provided such bills or accounts
> do not contain any other matters than hath been usually
> comprised therein."

The former objectionable act related only to papers sold, but here
the word dispensed is artfully introduced to prevent the giving away of
small publications, even ship bills which might contain more than one
advertisement would be chargeable with the duty, and so would every
Play Bill if printed as they now are. Every such bill contains several
advertisements and would therefore be liable to the stamp duty.

This was an attempt to obtain still more exorbitant power over
the press. I therefore wrote some remarks for the purpose of shewing
how this and the act 60 G. III.C.9. would operate together and sent
copies to several members.[a] Sir Francis Burdett M[r]. Hobhouse and
M[r]. Hume undertook to speak to as many members as they could,
and to make this the ground, not only of objection to the proposal
but also to 60 G 3 the repeal of which was to be strenuously urged.
Burdett more especially volunteered his services. Nothing was done,
or said in honourable house on the subject.

On the 21 May M[r]. Scarlet the Whig Attorney General who had
revived the Pitt mode of prosecuting the press, had also in deference
to the will of the house and the people, and to prevent its being done
by some member of opposition, brought in a bill to repeal so much

---

[a] See Political Letter book. 6 Acts Newspapers. [Illegible] [Marginal note. See BL Add.
MS 35148, fos 62–63.]

of the 60 Geo 3 c⁴⁶⁹   as related to the banishment of persons a second time convicted of libel, this he could not avoid, so he seized the opportunity to raise the amount of bail to be given by Newspaper proprietors from 300£ to 400£.

This was an atrocious proceeding, the Bonds are not as bonds usually are, to surrender the person or pay the money; but, to pay the money, if the person bailed should be convicted of libel. This coupled with the acts already in existence relating to small publications & the Stamp Duty proposal, was intended totally to prevent the publication of any tract Government might at any time for any reason dislike, whilst they would be at liberty to permit whatsoever they pleased and in any form they pleased to be published. The process being is this, The Commissioners of Stamps give notice to a publisher, if they wish to suppress his publication that if he continue his publication he must do so on a fourpenny stamp, and as such publications sells [*sic*] for perhaps one halfpenny, and thence up to three pence, demanding that they shall be stamped is demanding their discontinuance, and as it is optional with the commissioners to make the demand or not, so the power to prevent or to promote small publications is wholly transferred to Ministers.

This is perhaps the most effective way to extinguish such publications that has ever been devised. A most effectual mode of compelling the common people either to read such papers as the minister chuses they should read, or to refrain from reading altogether.

I therefore on the 25ᵗʰ May wrote another letterᵃ on the subject and sent copies to honourable members, and urged resistance to the bill, yet much as many of the members of the "Legion Club" had complained of these 6 acts, and much as many of them had promised to do towards procuring their repeal, scarcely any effort was made to prevent the bill passing and nothing was said on the subject of small publications.

These things sometimes vex me and almost make me resolve to cut my parliamentary acquaintances and this I certainly should do, were it not that the matters I have accomplished encourage me to hope I shall still be successful. It was only after 6 years of continued exertion in a great many ways that I at length induced Mʳ. Hume to procure a committee which led to the repeal of the laws against Combinations of Workmen, and the act which forbade Artizans leaving the country — it was only after long continued efforts that

ᵃ See Political Letter Book 25 May Libel Bill [Marginal note. See BL Add. MS 35148, fos 64–65.]

⁴⁶⁹ The chapter of 60 Geo 3 is left blank.

the exportation of Machinery was brought to the state it now is, it was in defiance to the opinion of the Speaker and the Attorney General that I procured the repeal of the Cutting and Flaying act, and it was only after efforts continued during 7 years that I at length was the means of a committee sitting on the conduct of the Commissioners of Hackney Coaches which will probably ~~be the means of putting~~ put an end to the abuses and to the absurd laws which incommode that business and inconvenience the public. If I did not console myself with these and similar results I should abandon all such efforts, shut out my political friends, and betake myself to more agreeable pursuits.

It is now the 19 November the Parliament has been sitting for business only three weeks and I have been requested to do as much in the way of research and statement as would occupy me for three months. I will do no one of these things unless I have very good reason to believe that my time will not be wasted, nor the matters on which I may employ myself be laid aside. With some I will insist that old matters be brought forward before I attend to any new ones, unless they shall be decidedly of as much urgency as importance.

M\ :sup. Lennard having given notice of a motion, to introduce a bill to abolish the office of Licensor of Plays I wrote[a] to him on the subject. His motion was however postponed from time to time, and I did not send the letter. His motion was not made until the session was too far advanced for any thing to be done, as however he promised to bring the business before the house again early in the next session, I am reading the debate in Hansards Debates, wrote in continuation of the letter[b] some matter which if he again gives notice of his motion I shall send to him.

Early in the month of May a committee of the house of commons was appointed to inquire in to the the [sic] duties, emoluments &c of the of the [sic] Commissioners of Hackney Coaches and the state of the public carriages in the Metropolis.[470] I had as I have mentioned taken much trouble in this business, and now hoped and was willing to expect that all the absurd regulations under the several acts of Parliament relating to Hackney Coaches and Short Stages might be repealed and a better system at once adopted. M\ :sup. Hume was a member of the

---

[a] See Political Letter Book, 25 May – 28 October   Drama [Marginal note. The letter does not appear to have survived, and there is no mention in *Hansard* of the bill having been introduced.]

[b] l[etter]b[ook] ——————— [Marginal note. The reference is unclear.]

[470] The Committee's report was eventually issued as *PP*, 10 (1830), *Report from the Select Committee on the Duties and Salaries of the Commissioners for Regulating Hackney-coaches, on the Present State of Public Carriages, and the Laws affecting the Same.*

committee, but was able to give very little attention to it, he was occupied in a committee up stairs on Scotch Affairs; he had mainly promoted the appointment of the Committee, but had not much attended to the subject, and therefore relied on me to give him information from time to time as the committee proceeded. My object on commenting on the printed evidence taken before the committee, which M^r. Hume sent to me as it came out, was to enable him with the least possible trouble to put the committee on the right path, from which it was not reasonable to conclude they would diverge. Not a man in the committee had the least suspicion that I had any thing to do with the business. Not even M^r. Warburton, until at the close I found it necessary to let him know that I had been conversant with the proceedings. The jealousy of these committees is childish in the extreme, and the apprehension of any one "out of doors" interfering would hardly in any case fail to do mischief.

M^r. Humes copy of the daily minutes were carefully read and marginal indexed and then a letter, in the manner of a comment was written and sent to him, and this enabled him to use the small quantity of time he could give the committee to be employed efficiently.

The business was well conducted by the committee. Whatever opinions or prejudices might have been entertained by any member of the committee at his appointments it is probable that no one left it unconvinced that the Hackney Coach Office, like many others, was a scandalous contrivance to plunder the public. That the regulations of Hackney Carriages were equally absurd in themselves and injurious, as well to the parties concerned, as to the public.

At the close of the examination it became a question in the committee whether they should make a formal report or agree to certain resolutions.

The first report made to the house of Commons in the form of resolutions was from the Committee on the Laws relating to Combinations of workmen in 1825. M^r. Hume who was chairman of that committee agreed in opinion with me that no report could be drawn which would not provoke a debate, and the session was drawing towards its close and, we feared, that unless a bill could be got through the house without delay, that it would not pass the Lords during the session, and that if it were postponed to the next session, it would not be passed at all; subsequent events proved the correctness of this notion.

Resolutions were accordingly drawn – some of them not much to my liking. M^r. Hume did not sufficiently comprehend the subject to enable him to prevent this and I was obliged to write out my objections at some length. At a meeting of the committee to consider the report held on the 4th of June some modifications and improvements were made,^{a} but M^r. Hume failed to procure the expulsion of what I thought a great blemish namely, regulation of the fares to be taken. I thought the reasons I had given conclusive on this point and am quite certain it is not in the power of the Legislature to fix the fares without doing injustice to the hackney man and disservice to the public.

Another objection which I could not get removed, was, registering the drivers, the short and simple and only efficient way, to secure good behaviour, is to make the master responsible as far as a pecuniary fine can make him so, for the conduct of his servant.

No bill passed the house, and as the matter is to come before the house again I shall then make an effort to procure these alterations in the bill.

A project for a New Daily morning Newspaper, formerly mentioned had been revived, ~~and~~ was countenanced by many clever men, and had been for some time pushed with vigour, the whole was admirably arranged, and several subjects of much importance to merchants, shipowners and traders were to be noticed in tables very cleverly constructed, whilst the literary [?] department was to be conducted by men very superior in every respect and all but infinitely more honest than the present conductors of the Daily papers are. I had been much and frequently pressed to write to Sir Francis Burdett on the subject and at length when there appeared some probability that the project would succeed I wrote to him.^{b} On a former occasion he had objected to assist a project for the establishment of a newspaper, because as he truly said, it was like the others, to follow and not to lead public opinion. All the arrangements of the intended paper were calculated to enable it to lead. This therefore being precisely such a paper as Sir Francis had said he would willingly support and his friend M^r. Davenport M. P.^{471} Having paid some attention to the subject and expressed a willingness to assist, as he was to meet Sir Francis in the country and had promised to communicate with Sir Francis my letter was given to him. They did not meet as they intended, and I have never heard that the letter was ever seen by Sir Francis.^{c}

---

^{a} See the rough draft and fair copy of these resolutions – Parl Papers – Hackney Coaches Vol.   . [Volume number left blank.];   See Political Letter book. 29 May. 1 July. Hackney Coaches. [Marginal note. See BL Add. MS 35148, fos 80–88.]

^{b} See l[etter] b[ook]. 24 July — Newspaper Project. [Marginal note. See BL Add. MS 35148, fos 71–72.]

^{c} See it in the Political Letter book. New Daily paper. [Marginal note.]

471 Davies Davenport, MP for Cheshire.

A project had been formed to colonize Australia. It originated with Edward Gibbon Wakefield who was confined in Newgate for the abduction of Miss Turner, here he set himself to work to understand the modes of life of the criminals[,] the causes of their criminality, and indeed as many points connected with them as he could. He also investigated the causes of poverty and the means of removing the general and the most mischievous, namely the abstraction of the redundant population, this he conceded could be effectually done by selling the land in the colonies, instead of giving it away – charging it also with a very small quit rent and supplying the money thus procured to pay the passage &c of as many young couples as would effectually relieve the working people here and promote the rapid progress of the Colonies. A society was formed of clever men, and as much display as possible was made. The project was however opposed by M^r. Wilmot Horton and Colonel Torrens, with both of whom I had conversations, and with M^r. Horton an extensive and somewhat elaborate correspondence.^{a} Some notes passed also with several other members of the Association and much conversation with a still larger number. The opposition of M^r. Horton combined with other circumstances dispersed the members of the association and the project fell to the ground. It has now – November, begun to revive again and one of its most active and intelligent members Charles Tennant having become a member of Parl^t and intending to press the subject on the attention of the House of Commons, I have again been drawn into a correspondence with him.^{b}

W$^{m.}$ IV

The King had been dangerously ill for some time and at length it was generally concluded he was near his end. Members of the House

---

^{a} See it in — d^o – d^o [.] [Marginal note.]

^{b} [The following has been added on the facing page, which is dedicated to marginal notes. Its proper placement in the text is unclear:]

A committee of the House of Commons was sitting on East India Affairs, they made several reports of evidence, and at length a long report, all of which I read and marginal indexed a large portion. This enabled me [to] cooperate with several persons of consequence respecting the propriety of permitting the Company's Charter to expire[.] I have no doubt at all that it should expire, the Debt charged on the Territory and not at all on the nation, and the debtors be compelled to take what the Territorial revenue after paying expenses would permit.

Arrangements might I think be made to promote the settlement of Europeans in India with a view to its being Independent at as early a period as possible, and that this would be advantageous to both Great Britain and India.

of Commons in the anticipation of a new parliament, to be called by W^{m}. 4. when he should come to the Crown, were endeavouring to secure their reelection.

Sir Francis Burdett and M^{r}. Hobhouse had both very much neglected their Parliamentary duties. Little beyond an occasional speech had ever been expected ~~for~~ from Sir Francis. He had stood up manfully for the people when no one else did, and he had on several occasions, done his ~~part manfully~~ duty remarkably well and he had suffered persecution on this account. Old associations were in his favour and notwithstanding the electors were generally disposed to require a more attractive representative they still respected him and would have returned him against any opposition.

M^{r}. Hobhouse had no such claims. He had very much offended the electors by his conduct on several occasions and especially by his behaviour in respect to the committee on Parish Vestries in the last session of Parliament, he had to be sure somewhat recovered his lost character by his conduct in the same matter in the present session,[a] still his return might be rendered precarious by the opposition of any man of character professing to be a sturdy Parliamentary Reformer. Advances had been made towards nominating M^{r}. Hume, and no doubt was entertained by any one who understood the matter that if the electors nominated M^{r}. Hume he would carry the election. M^{r}. Hobhouse understood this, and ~~he~~ applied himself to draw him off for Middlesex. M^{r}. Samuel Whitbread, had long since shewn his utter incapacity for the duties of a popular member of parliament, and his friends had often intimated their wish that he would not again become a candidate for that County, when therefore on the 16 June he resolved to withdraw, M^{r}. Hobhouse who was privy to the transaction, went immediately to Sir Francis Burdett and having settled some matters with him relating to M^{r}. Hume's being nominated for the County, came to me and related what had passed.

I concurred in the project. It was doubtful whether M^{r}. Hume would be again returned for the Scotch Burghs, and it was by no means certain he would be nominated for Westminster. It seemed to me quite certain that he might be returned for Middlesex, against any opposition, it was possible to make, and badly as M^{r}. Hobhouse performed his duty, it was pretty certain that if M^{r}. Hume were not returned for the County some man not even so useful as M^{r}. Hobhouse would be, and thus on every view of the case it was advisable that M^{r}. Hume should be nominated for the county.

[a] See the rough minutes as they were proposed, and the fair minutes as they were passed. [Marginal note.]

Cobbett had said he would become a candidate for Westminster and would at any rate give the old members fifteen days dressings [?]. That he would not spend any money of his own for the purpose, but that others had volunteered to pay his expenses, and he should therefore shew up the two "Shoy Hoys."[472] This was considered as mere boasting and so it proved. No independent man, unless supported, or rather unless invited by a considerable body of the people who by their exertions would save his purse was expected to put himself forward, – and the Whigs who when assisted by the Ministers had been beaten out of the field and were now in no repute with any body of men in Westminster were not at all desirous to go through another contested election add added to which was the conduct of Hobhouse, which had both publicly and privately been quite to their satisfaction.

M^r. Hume was therefore the only person likely to endanger the return of Hobhouse. Hobhouse knew that Hume would not put himself forward as a candidate but he was apprehensive that some of the electors might agree [,] carry on the election for him and if such a circumstance took place he clearly saw that he should be ousted. The opening for Middlesex was therefore most desirable and propitious. If Hume could be returned for the County he was for ever removed from Westminster, it was not to be supposed that he would abandon the County to come to Westminster, or that so useful a man as he would be would be abandoned by the freeholders. Some extraordinary combination of circumstances might to be sure induce him to consent to be returned for nothing for Westminster rather than pay a considerable portion of the expenses of a contested election for the County, but so remote was such a contingency that it might well be passed over.

Supposing too that he should not succeed in Middlesex – still as the election for the County and for Westminster would both be going on at the same time Hume would be cut off from the latter place and Hobhouse's purpose for the present answered accomplished.

The Whigs hate Hume even more than the ministers hate him. On every subject in which by a false pretense they hoped at any time to deceive the people into a belief of their desire to do them service, Hume by going further than they would ever profess to go took the ground from under them. The consequence was, every body saw that he was in earnest, and that they were not, it could not therefore be, but that they must hate him, and in this hatred both Hobhouse and Burdett concurred. It was not therefore from any respect to Hume

---

[472] Cobbett apparently often used this term as an epithet. According to the *OED*, a shoy-hoy is a person who scares birds away from a recently sown field. Two of the usages given are from Cobbett's *Weekly Political Register*.

that they now proposed him for Middlesex, nor from any desire they had to see him in parliament that they were willing to assist him. The sole object was to get him out of the way at Westminster.

The heads of the proceedings which followed may be seen in the Account of the Middlesex Election[a] in the months of June July and August 1830. These heads were taken from minutes made from day to day at the time they occurred.

This account contains as fair a picture of public men as need be drawn, all hollow hearted all utterly insincere even towards one another whilst acting together, all conscious of their own and of one anothers insincerity.

Sincerity is not practicable in civilized society, it is not practised however to any thing like the extent it might be, and ought to be, in any class of Society, but it is less practiced among public political men, than amongst any others excepting perhaps Lawyers and Priests.

People boast of their sincerity and ~~from~~ as a consequence of their vicious education, and the vicious people with whom they must associate, and by whom their manners are formed and their conduct regulated, habits of insincerity are ~~formed~~ acquired of which they are generally unconscious; and many, and indeed most really good meaning people seldom remark or take cognizance in any way of their own want of sincerity, excepting on particular occasions, when they happens [sic] to carry it to a considerable extent beyond their usual practice, and then they hardly ever fail to find a satisfactory excuse for their conduct.

Almost every person in every rank of life who desires to obtain or to pursue the ~~claim to be considered appellation of~~ appellation of respectable, has a limit to his insincerity beyond which on ordinary occasions he will not go, and in almost innumerable cases men predicate with something approximating to certainty on the result of other mens actions, who are well known to them, they know at least that they will neither do certain things nor encourage others to do them. Change the rank or materially alter the condition of the individual for the better let him associate with other persons than he has been accustomed to associate with, let his condition in life be such that to maintain it and keep up his own self-importance as it almost always is, ~~in the case supposed such cas~~, and he will become more and more insincere. Very few have the wisdom, and the courage to examine themselves, to any thing like the extent necessary to enable them to understand the more immediate motives (as they are called)

---

[a] This account is in the Guard book – Westminster Elections &c and in a M. S account in the mahogany chest. [Marginal note.]

which govern them, and still fewer have ever even thought or are capable of thinking of the more remote and general motives.

The general motive, that of desiring their own happiness they are familiar with, altho they do not understand it in the sense of a motive, they say indeed every one desires to be happy, but they have never attempted to analyse the ideas they seem to express. The morality of society is therefore very low, and religion so far from elevating it has all along prevented its rising to any desirable height. Sound Morality and Hypocricy [*sic*] are incompatible and cannot both exist to any great extent in the same person, yet religion grounds morality on hypocricy [*sic*], it teaches mankind to pretend to believe that which is impossible to believe and they who pretend ~~to~~ as well as they who think they do believe; shew by their conduct, that they do not believe, that they are either absurd or insincere; ~~are hypocrites~~ or both continually.

Sound morality can be based on the doctrine of motives and on nothing else, religon bases it on faith, which is precisely the reverse. "Do as you would be done by" – is not a Christian maxim, it is much older than Christianity, the Church has however appropriated it as its own, and constantly preaches it as sound doctrine. It is nevertheless absurd. No on can practice it in any society, much less in civilized society. He who is the best informed on the doctrine of motives, is ~~the~~ most likely to have the largest share of sincerity and consequently, to be more honest and more useful, than he who is not so well informed, other circumstances being equal or nearly equal. Yet strang[e] to say, whilst religion teaches every one to be a hypocrite, and refers for rules of conduct to a vague and false standard, there are no establishments, no settled rules in practice to teach the doctrine of motives and consequently none to teach morality, neither is there any where, any pretense set up to teach it, it is not expressly made a part of education at any public school or college.

Children should not do certain things, lest they should offend God – Men must conform to certain rules lest they risk eternal damnation. God Almighty and God the Devil are made bug-a-boos — to furnish one all comprehensive motive – fear – fear alone, and that too of an unintelligible, uncertain and distant punishment, with the comfortable assurance ~~of~~ that by discontinuing certain practices, and using certain set forms of words – praying devoutly, and as it is called in sincerity of heart, will enable the contrite criminal to escape punishment. The plain english of this is – by the faith that is in you, by the rules of hypocricy [*sic*] which you have been taught; so use your imagination that you may cheat your understanding, call this devoutness and sincerity of heart, and then persuade yourself that you have also cheated the God, whom you have been told is omniscient and omnipresent, and then you may take to yourself the comfortable

assurance that your sins are all forgiven and you may forget your
crimes, ~~or~~ and enjoy the property ~~with~~ you have fraudulently obtained
~~just~~ quite as much as you could do had you obtained it ever so justly.
Never mind the suffering of others whom you have wronged, you
having done so being pardoned has been forgiven, and their losses
and sufferings are their own concerns, only, they are no longer yours –
This is religious morality. The wonder is not that mankind are as
immoral as we see them, but that they are not all but infinitely more
so. Such is the practice, such the efficacy of the insincerity taught
as morality that scarcely any doubt, even while they are practicing
the greatest iniquity that they shall make the necessary compensation
~~required by their [illegible]~~ in good time; by faith with the consolatory
assurance of the priest of their own persuasion that when made they
shall be amongst those chosen for the Kingdom of Heaven. Thus they
reconcile themselves to themselves and continue to the hour of their
deaths in the practice of a detestable hypocricy [sic].

Much however of the insincerity now as commonly as disgracefully
practiced[sic] might be prevented by teaching the doctrine of motives
and enabling every one to understand the causes of their own actions
and their bearings on themselves and others to an extent which few
can have any thing like an accurate conception of. A man so taught,
could not even if he wished it, avoid referring to the causes which
had induced certain acts, and he would be much less likely than men
otherwise educated to mistake the causes, he would refer with certainty
to the causes of his thoughts, to the actions which had been the
consequences of his thoughts, he would trace back, the mental process
and discern the motives of his conduct, the practice when it had had
become familiar, would be rapid and performed with as much ease
as the excuses men make to themselves for not examining themselves
are now made and substituted for reasons. Men thus educated and
thus practiced [sic] would be all but infinitely more sincere and more
moral than men now are and society would be improved and mankind
benefitted [sic] to a great extent.

A man thus taught, thus placed in a position which would not
permit him to frame false and pitiful excuses for bad conduct and
to be satisfied with them, would be more moral than other men,
since immorality in him, would produce more pain than immoral
conduct had procured ~~of~~ his pleasure, pain too of longer continuance,
in most cases than the pleasure, and no man capable of reasoning
will ~~long~~ continue to inflict long continued pain upon himself, for
which he knows that he can receive no adequate compensation. Such
a man would be careful beyond all comparison with other men not to
commit injustice, nor to do injury to any one. He would to an almost
inconceivable extent avoid the acts of hypocricy [sic] and insincerity

now commonly practiced [*sic*] without reprehension, simply because he would not have the disagreeable reflections, which he could not otherwise avoid. and He would as carefully or more carefully avoid such acts of hypocricy [*sic*] and insincerity as usually lead to reprobation, for hence in addition to the disagreeable reflections, before mentioned would be added those which could not fail to be produced by his having outraged the popular sanction, and lost caste in the opinion of not only of those whose opinion in matters where he had committed no offence he would disregard, but as he had committed offence he would be compelled to respect, but also of better judging men for whose opinions he had been accustomed to respect. It can scarcely be doubted that the greatest possible good to society would result from having men thus instructed, and the time must come when, such men will be as common as they are now rare.

To expect that mankind will ever become sincere; which if examined in all its bearings will be found to include all the virtues, is to indulge an absurd imagination, but that they might may and that they will become more and more sincere as they become wiser, need not be doubted, and will not be doubted by any one who has ever thought seriously on the subject.

The numerous vices which insincerity engenders in even the most respectable men can be conceived appreciated only by a steady and accurate observer. My experience leads me to the conclusion, that the most insincere are they who other circumstances considered have the least reason to be insincere. I mean they who have any considerable fame which elevates them above others whose circumstances in other respects resemble theirs and they who have competent fortunes, or high situations, and move in polished society. I have never known a single instance to the contrary. I who whenever opportunities have occurred have pushed matters to extremities, or to an extent sufficient to elicit the fact, have found them as I have described them, pity it is to say, yet true it is, that as men were eminent in situation fame and fortune, they have been eminent liars and hypocrites. To this conclusion I expect every man must come, who carefully examines the matter, and declares not to deceive himself.

In June in consequence of the declining state of the Kings health and the expectation of a dissolution of parliament consequent thereon, and of other changes, many persons besides those who have been named, came to me, several of whom I had never before seen, and my time was wholly occupied in matters relating to Elections, about which however with the exception of Middlesex on the resignation of M^r. Whitbread I cared but little, still as some good could be done by exposing abuses and encouraging particular persons who were well disposed, I could not refuse the aid they requested.

The only remarkable circumstances connected with these transactions as they relate to myself were the arrangements made at my house by M^r. Hobhouse – M^r. Hume. Col^n Jones M^r. Lefevre, – and M^r. Wallis – for the purpose of preventing any whig candidate from standing for Middlesex – the contrivance as I doubt not of M^r. Hobhouse to induce his whig friends to object as they did to my being placed on the committee of middlesex freeholders, he supposing or rather taking for granted that I should have consented to have become a member in which he was however mistaken, as I had long since determined not to ~~become~~ be a member of any election committee. But the most curious circumstance was that the very same men who had done so passed a resolution, a fortnight before the election came on, putting the management of the committee into my hands and the uncontrould [*sic*] disposal of its funds at my discretion.

The account of the French Revolution of the 26 July was brought to M^r. Humes committee room when several members of parliament were present. M^r. Hobhouse was so animated by the news that he vociferated applause and was joined by every person present. This new revolution, produced a very extraordinary effect on the middle classes, and sent a vast number of persons to me with all sorts of projects and propositions; every one was glorified with the courage the humanity and the honesty of the Parisians, and the common people became eagerly desirous to prove that they too were brave and humane and honest, all soon seemed desirous to fight against the Government, if it should attempt to control ~~or [illegible]~~ the french government.

The Aristocracy and Gods own ministers, the beneficed Clergy were sorry the french King had not succeeded and would willingly have gone to war with the new Government, could they have indulged the least hope that the people could be again deluded as they had been in 1792, or could they even have had any chance of persuading them that it was their interest, as well as that of Priests and Nobles ~~that it was their interest~~ to go to war.

No such hope could be entertained and as the parliament was not to meet until ~~early in~~ late in the month of october, the time was occupied in making demonstrations not to be mistaken that war was looked forward to with the greatest apprehension of consequences, not to be encountered willingly, not at all if there were any means to prevent the Govern^t going to war.

All the well informed and reasonable men with whom I was acquainted deprecate war, our hopes were that, all the despotic states on the continent would remain quiet for some time, that the french people might have time to arrange their affairs, consolidate the new government, and by legislative means remove all obstacles to good government, they were sure that five years of peace in France would produce such beneficial arrangements, as would make ~~france~~ that country too formidable for any or all the powers on the continent ~~afraid~~ to ~~commence~~ make war upon her with any chance of successful issue.

We hoped that the humane yet determined conduct of the Parisians might be supported by the concurence [*sic*] of the people in all parts of France and that the New Government would act so wisely as to take from the despotic governments on the Continent all excuse for going to war with them, without bringing such obloquy on them as would deter our government from taking part with them. We had no doubt that declarations of war against France would lead to insurrections in all the Continental States, and probably terminate with advantage to the people, but we feared that the warlike disposition of the French eager to compensate for the disgraces of 1814 might end in a war mania, and this again to most undesirable consequences, we anxiously hoped that peace ~~should~~ would be preserved until the French people should have established a representative government, when all would go well with them, spite of all the Despots and would be despots in the world.

Matters were proceeding as well as could be wished when a revolution broke out at Brussels. This at the moment was considered a revolt against certain measure [*sic*] taken by the King of Holland, but it was soon found to be a revolt of the whole of Belgium, against the King of Holland as their King and a determination to be an independent people. Almost all the newspapers had praised the French Revolution, so incessant were their eulogies, so well adapted to circumstances were their reasonings, that it was almost impossible to suppose, that at the opening of Parliament ministers would venture to shew any hostile disposition towards the French, but the tumult at Brussels we feared would be used as a pretext by ministers to commit the Government, so as to lead in time, to active exertions with Russia – Prussia and Austria ~~to in~~ and bring on a general war.

We expected that arrangements would be made privately for Prussia to assist Holland to recover the Netherlands, that France would then interfere and there would be a general war. The Kings speech was therefore expected with anxiety, when the time for the parliament to meet came the people in the Metropolis ~~became~~ were unusually agitated, Parliament assembled on the 26 october, and the hopes of the people were dashed to the ground by the passage it contained respecting Belgium, war seemed inevitable, and many were the suggestions to place impediments in its way. Amongst others a refusal of the housekeepers to pay taxes, and to form themselves into a National Guard. These two projects obtained pretty extensive attention. Vast numbers of persons became apprehensive of consequences, the pauperized, discontented, miserable peasantry were burning stacks & barns, and such was the terror that almost every body anticipated a revolution.

I did not expect that any hostile expressions would be put into the Kings Speech, and I had therefore no expectation of any extraordinary proceedings nor of any change of ministers.[a]

I dined with M[r]. Bentham in the evening, and when the Kings speech was brought to us, we were greatly disconcerted and vexed. Our forebodings were dismal enough. But when next morning I read in the newspaper, the out of the way absurd declaration of the Duke of Wellington against Reform of Parliament, I was at once relieved from all apprehension, I saw at once, that the Duke and his friends could not remain in office, and Earl Grey who had in the debate declared that Reform must be had, — as he deprecated all interference with Belgium, my fears and those of my friends were all at an end.[b]

Ministers did not however at once resign, though they saw that, they were universally condemned, attacked on all sides in every way, and in every place, whilst large mobs assembled in the street and fought with the Police. These mobs were composed of sad vagabonds, but they would not have assembled, but for the general feeling, and greatly excited state of the people.

On the 1 November I wrote a letter to M[r]. Hume,[c] on the subject and on the silly conduct of the King deprecating his going to the Lord Mayors feast on the 9 Nov[r], as the procession was sure to be attended with violence, robbery and a slaughter of the people. This letter I read to M[r]. Hobhouse who urged me to give him a copy and I did so —

See Political Letter Book.[d]

Great preparations had been made to receive the King, and there would have been a monstrous parade.[e] I was in communication with M[r]. Thomas the Police Inspector and through him got my opinion of the consequences of the Kings going to the Mansion House made known to many.[f] The Duke of Wellington was so unpopular that he would have been the excuse for all sorts of outrages.[g]

---

[a] October [Marginal note.]
[b] Oct. Meeting of the New Parliament. [Marginal note.]
[c] November. [Marginal note.]
[d] Nov. 6. Letter to M[r]. Hume
                    Copy to M[r]. Hobhouse
  see. Political Letter Book. [Marginal note.]
[e] Wellingtons folly [Marginal note.]
[f] Lord Mayors feast [Marginal note.]
[g] Mobs. [Marginal note.]

This unpopularity was the alleged reason of ministers for advising the King not to go to the Lord Mayors.[a] It was expected that Ministers would have resigned but they did not. They were attacked on all sides and in every way as well within the house as out of the house. The laws against the press were disregarded, and many small publications were printed and sold at from one halfpenny to four pence each. Attorney General Scarlet whose enmity to the press was not only well known from his acts but by his declarations, did not now think it was worth while to file ex officio informations and every one published whatever ~~they~~ he pleased.[b]

Large mobs were constantly in the Streets, their cry was down with the Police, and as the new police was obnoxious to many persons in better circumstances than the rabble who made all the riots, they appeared at least to have the countenance of their betters, they therefore attacked the police men beat them off – and were as they supposed all but masters of them; This was owing to the dislike of the Police commissioners to give an appearance of too much power or an officious use of power to the police men, who were not authorized to disperse these mobs as promptly as they ought to have been.

I advised M[r]. Thomas yet again to wait until his men were attacked and then when they had been maltreated and bruised to take a few vagabonds into custody, but when he saw a mob prepared to make an attack to lead his men on, and thrash those who composed the mob with their staves, as long as any of them remained together, but to take none into custody – and that if this were done once or twice there would be no more such mobs — On the 9th November, a large mob, gathered in the City and sallied through Temple bar, and with pieces of wood from a fence in Chancery Lane, for the purpose of beating the Police, my advice was followed[;] the Police ~~to the number of 60~~ retreated up Wyld Street and collected to about 60 men in Catherine Street from whence they sallied and beat the mob before them to Temple Bar – This at once put an end to all rioting no one was killed no limb was broken but many were bruised and many heads were broken but there were no more mobs.

Ministers being beaten on a question concerning the Civil List resigned on the 16 – and a new Ministry with Earl Grey at the Head was appointed —

Parliament was adjourned on the 24 to 3 Feby 1831.[c]

---

[a] Nov. 8 Letter to M[r]. Hobhouse
     Atwoods proposal not to pay taxes
     Conduct of the Gentry. [Marginal note.]
[b] Every one published whatever he pleased [Marginal note.]
[c] Parl. prorogued 24 November [Marginal note.]

The new ministers having declared ~~in~~ themselves friendly to Parliamentary Reform, people thought it wise to meet and petition for Reform in aid as they intended of ministers and many came to me to concert meetings and construct Petitions and resolutions. I assisted freely – not because I thought it would aid ministers but because it was right in itself ~~and because~~ for I had a strong persuasion that Ministers would not propose any reform which would in any way destroy the corruption of parliament and give the people the influence they ought to posses [*sic*] in the Commons House.[a]

Every ~~body~~ one I saw was greatly alarmed at the conduct of the Husbandry Labourers, in burning Stacks and Barns and the rapidity with which those atrocities spread from county to county, many were the conjectures ~~as to~~ respecting the cause and consequences, many the projects, but no one saw any actual remedy.[b]

Towards the end of November I had several serious conversations with M[r]. Mill on these matters and on ~~expla~~ my detailing my opinion of the way in which the husbandry labourers would affect the community he urged me to put the matter on paper. I had also a long and serious conversation with M[r]. Warburton and M[r]. Hume, and they also desired me to put the matter on paper.[c]

Amongst others who came to me was Colonel Torrens; he and I have been friends many years and he is in some respects a particularly well informed man. He was even more at a loss than any one else to discover a remedy, and this was occasioned by his taking a larger view of the case than most others. He was in communication with some friends of Lord Wellingtons and he came to me almost daily. He said he was continually talked to of schemes to put a stop to the mischief, but he could not see a remedy in any of them. To him I communicated my view of the case and he also urged me to put my opinions in writing. I therefore made a rough draft – which was read for the purpose of remark and correction by Col[n] Torrens Col[n] Stanhope – Col[n] Jones M[r] John Mill. M[r] E. G. Wakefield M[r] Hume M[r] Hobhouse M[r] Roebuck M[r] Graham D[r] Bowring – Col[n] Thompson M[r] Bentham — and several other persons at their leisure, all of whom wished me to print it.

NB. It was circulated in MS. 'till the middle of February 1831.[d]

Early in December The Right Honourable George Lamb, the brother of Lord Melbourne the Secretary of State for the Home

[a] Nov. 22. Political Letter Book to M[r]. Hume Middlesex Meeting. [Marginal note.]

[b] Husbandry Labourers – Outrages. Fires. [Marginal note.]

[c] My opinions — [Marginal note.]

[d] The matter relating to Husbandry Labourers was printed at the end of Feb[y] 1831. with the title of "An Essay on the State of the Country In respect to the condition and conduct of the Husbandry Labourers and the Consequences likely to result therefrom.["] Not for Sale [Marginal note.]

Department came to me, for the purpose of requesting me to write an address to the husbandry labourers, on the conduct they were pursuing and to persuade them to desist from the enormities they were committing.[a]

I had thought a good deal on the subject and had come to the conclusion that it would do [more] harm than good to address them at this time. M[r] Lamb said we are of opinions you can write to them so as to produce more effect than any one else, and he went on to explain how his friends thought they should be spoken to. I told him my opinion, and gave the reasons with which he was satisfied. I then took the opportunity to speak to him on ~~the subject of~~ Reform of Parliament. I detailed to him my view of the probable consequences of the conduct of the husbandry labourers, and then said, that the right course for his friends to pursue was straight and clear. That I however feared they would prefer a crooked way and if they did they would do mischief to the country and totally destroy their own reputation. That Lord Grey had on the preceding sunday, told a friend of mine, that whatever proposition for reform was made it must be such a one as the house of Commons would entertain. That if this course were followed nothing but mischieff [sic] could result from it.

That if we were thus handed over to the Borough mongering house there would be [the] greatest outcry against ministers that ever had been heard, that their popularity being thus destroyed, their small majority in the house would at once become a minority and they would be thrust out with ignominy.

That if on the contrary they proposed a plan of reform which should destroy the corruptions by which the members were returned, so that the body of the people having property should recover their influence they would be lauded beyond any men who had ever before existed.

That it was almost certain if they did so ~~that~~ they would be outvoted and compelled to resign, but if they would fall back upon the people, and be supported by them.

That no set of men the King could chuse could remain in office six months, probably not six weeks, and he would be forced to take them again when backed as they would be by the whole nation they might carry any measures they pleased.

M[r] Lamb assented to this but took care as he was bound to do not to give a distinct opinion on any ~~one~~ point, but one and that was his fear that his friends would not propose a sufficient reform.

---

[a] [The following marginal notes were appended in parallel columns on the recto:]

see Political Letter Book – Letter   Visit of George Lamb.
to M[r]. Hobhouse 1 December
conduct of the Gentry. &c &c.

1831

V. 5.

N°. 8.   1831.

1. The New Whig Administration.
2. Swing —— Trial of R. Carlile.
3. Letter to a Minister of State.
4. Essay on the State of the Country.
5. Duty on Printed Cottons.
6. Reform Bill Introduced by Lord John Russell 1st March.
7. Parliament Candidates Society.

Nº. 8.   V. 5.

1831

January.[473]

Occupied as usual and very busy. Scarcely had the new administration been formed and Mr Denman appointed Attorney
General than he presented, or rather caused to be presented a bill
to the London Grand Jury a bill against Richard Carlile for a libel.
This was an exceedingly absurd proceeding – as it could forward no
one purpose of the government, deter no one from writing, and cause
a very large circulation of the obnoxious matter of which a very small
quantity had been sold. I saw Carlile on the 6 Jany his trial had then
been fixed for the 11 at the Old Bailey, and he was in a state of high
exultation. On the 7 I wrote a letter to Coln Jones – (see it in Political
letter book[474]) – respecting this prosecution in the hope that it might
be abandoned. Coln Jones took the letter to the Right Honbl Edward
Ellis and read it to him. Ellis seemed to think the prosecution was
injudicious, and recommended Jones to go to George Lamb, he did
so and Lamb promised to lay it before his brother Lord Melbourne
the minister of the home department.

Carlile was tried on the 11 and after a very extraordinary course of
proceeding of the Jury was found guilty and sentenced to[475]

This is the heaviest sentence ever inflicted on a libeller within ones
memory. Brougham had written that Pitts administration was upon
the whole a mild administration and this seems something like a proof
that they ministers will prove it so, when compared with theirs.

About the 16 Coln Jones wrote to Sir Thomas Denman to request
he would dine at his house on the 30 Jany – at his calves head dinner
and in his letter he made some remarks on the prosecution of Carlile.
In his reply after excusing himself on account of a prior engagement
for the 30th he went on to excuse himself for having prosecuted Carlile
by several fallacies of which he ought to have been ashamed. He

[473] The marginal headings and references in the following section appear on separate
pages from the manuscript's text and do not always correspond exactly to what appear to
be the relevant passages. I have made every effort to link in the footnotes the marginalia to
the appropriate text, but this is admittedly nothing more than a 'best guess'.

[474] See BL Add. MS 35149, fos 12–17.

[475] Remainder of sentence is left blank in the manuscript. Carlile was convicted on four
counts of seditious libel and was fined and sentenced to two years' imprisonment. See
Joel H. Wiener, *Radicalism and Freethought in Nineteenth-Century Britain: the life of Richard Carlile*
(Westport, CT, 1983), pp. 174–177.

disclaimed all intention, to prosecute generally, and almost said that Carlile was alone to be prosecuted.[476]

Brougham had written, that, "for they who would be satisfied with a whig administration there would be favour, but, that for their opponents, there was" the "Strong Arm of the Law." And notwithstanding what M[r] Denman wrote in his letter to Col[n] Jones, I am persuaded that prosecution for libel will not stop here.

On the 12 Col[n] Thompson shewed me some queries sent to him by M[r] Hume, respecting taxes on knowledge in which he said ministers could not reduce the amount of the taxes produced." I therefore on the 12 (see letter[a]) wrote to him on his folly being convinced not only that he had taken a false view but was likely to do himself great injury and thus impair his usefulness.

February

On the 6 I wrote a letter to the Right Honourable Charles Poulett Thompson, M. P.[b] – under secretary of state for the Colonies, respecting the Stamp duty on Newspapers – M[r] Thompson had taken a decidedly prominent part with those who were exerting themselves to procure a repeal of the Taxes on Knowledge and had given notice of a motion on the subject, before he was in office. I therefore chose him as the proper person to be addressed and the more particularly so just now as ministers had avowed their intention to reduce the duty on stamps and advertisement and as the Budget was to be brought in shortly. The letter will shew that by a particular arrangement the Post Office would produce a much greater amount of revenue than the stamp duty did. D[r] Bowring read a considerable portion of the Letter in M. S. to M[r] Thompson who promised to read the remainder and consider the proposition it contained.

A copy of the letter was handed to several persons all of whom and more especially M[r] Hume M[r] Hobhouse and M[r] Warburton concurred in the view I had taken – and wished to have it put into the hands of some of their political friends.

On the 10th M[r] Hume who had the M. S returned it to me with a note in which he said that "the minister had done as much in his budget as he thought he could carry and that next year my proposition

---

[a] See Political Letter Book 12 Jan[y] [.] [Marginal note. See BL Add. MS 35149, fos 22–24.]

[b] I was acquainted with M[r] Thompson and thought I understood him well and this it was which induced me to address the tract to him under the title of a Minister of State. [Marginal note.]

[476] See BL Add. MS 35149, Place to Jones, 17 January 1831.

must be considered." On the 13 I wrote a letter to Mr Hume (see it^a)
– in which I resented the conduct of him and others and shewed him
the folly of confiding in Ministers — This produced another note in
which he says he has sent the printer to me to obtain an estimate for
printing it. I gave the printer orders to print it,^b and on friday 18 –
sent 25 copies to the committee of the society for procuring the repeal
of the taxes on knowledge; the committee at once adopted the letter
and ordered the printer to be paid from their funds.

Writing petitions and resolutions for reform of parliament, and
consulting with persons on this subject.

Deputation of four principal Manufacturers and Calico printers
from Lancashire, to procure a repeal of the duty on printed calicos –
met them at Mr Hobhouses, and became acquainted with two of
them, intelligent and well disposed men, cooperated with them,
as I understood the subject thoroughly in consequence of my
correspondence &c on the same matter in 1829.^c

This partial and unjust tax is to be repealed.

See the papers. Calico Printing.^d

On the 27. Printed. "An Essay on the State of the Country["] – &c^477
– which as well as the, Letter to Poulett Thompson is appended.^478

The Society for promoting the repeal of Taxes on Knowledge
having had some communication with Lord Althorpe, it was settled
that ~~they~~ some of their members headed by Mr Hume were to have
an interview with his Lordship, and Mr Roebuck came to me, to tell
me this and to settle the words of a petition to the House of Commons
praying for the repeal of the Stamp duty on Newspapers

the Duty on Advertisements —

the Duty on Paper.^e

---

^a Political Letter Book 13 Feb^y. [Marginal note. See BL Add. MS 35149, fos 27–30. The letter was first drafted on the 13th, but the final version was only dispatched on 16 February, after some hesitation.]

^b Letter to a Minister of State printed 13 Feb^y [.] [Marginal note. See Francis Place, *A Letter to a Minister of State, respecting Taxes on Knowledge* (London, 1831).]

^c Duty on Printed Calicoes. [Marginal note. Notes and swatches were included as appendices to this volume. See BL Add. MS 35146, fos 148–160.]

^d See the papers on Calico Printing. Appendix to N°. 2 ante. [Marginal note.]

^e See the Petition in the Political Letter Book. [Marginal note. See BL Add. MS 35149, fo. 33.]

---

^477 Francis Place, *An Essay on the State of the Country, in respect to the condition and conduct of the husbandry labourers, and to the consequences likely to result therefrom* (London, 1831).

^478 Neither the pamphlet nor the letter remain appended to this volume.

Mr Chadwick[479] had some time before mentioned, the placing a penny stamp on a publication, with approbation, and notwithstanding the objection I had made Mr Roebuck again mentioned the matter, and I learned from him that others entertained the same notion, and as a meeting of the committee of the society was to be held on the 23 feb^y – I on the 22 sent a letter – dated 22 feb with a request that it might be read to the meeting.[a]

The conference has not been held, the question of reform having superseded any other consideration for the present.

March. 1. Lord John Russell made the ministerial statement respecting Reform in Parliament. It surprised all parties – the reformers, the enemies of reform and the Boroughmongers, were all equally surprised – and all for the same reason, namely that the plan of reform – has had been made so extensive. None believed none expected any such proposition. But as they were plain and easily understood as there was no leaning to party, as the fear of a revolution if they were not passed, and the sneaking – servility, of the ridiculously loyal who will go with the King – made the propositions acceptable to a much more decided majority of the whole people than any other measure proposed to Parliament had ever before within the memory of any man living.

Any general description of the state of feeling would but feebly depict the excitement caused by the proposed reform. [Words struck out and illegible.] But much may be learned from the leading Newspapers, and the accounts they contain of the many meetings had all over the Country.

It was impossible for me to be an idle spectator, many persons came to me and urged an immediate meeting of the people of Westminster without waiting till a regular requisition could be sent to the High Bailiff and the meeting be called by him. I therefore agreed to call a meeting – and one was accordingly held at the Crown and Anchor Tavern in the Strand on the 4 —[b]

On the 6 Mr Erskine Perry[480] came to me, to say that several of his friends wished to form a society for the purpose of providing

---

[a]   See it in Political Letter Book[.] [Marginal note. See BL Add. MS 35149, fos 31–32.]
[b]   See the Spectator in the Guard Book Lettered. [Marginal note.]

[479] Edwin Chadwick (1800–1890), well-known for his later contributions to public health reform, was also active in the free press and postal reform movement. See Joel H. Wiener, *The War of the Unstamped: the movement to repeal the British newspaper tax, 1830–1836* (Ithaca, NY, 1969), pp. 43–46.
[480] Thomas Erskine Perry, recently returned from Munich, joined the reform campaign and eventually founded the Parliamentary Candidate Society. See G.F.R. Barker, 'Perry, Sir Thomas Erskine (1806–1882)', rev. Katherine Prior, *ODNB*, <http://www.oxforddnb.com/view/article/22000>, accessed 19 January 2006.

candidates at the next election for such places as might require them. As I did not mean to join any society I gave my opinions cautiously but encouragingly —

On the next day M̶r̶ W̶ Sunday Mʳ Wakefield came to me with a copy of the Spectator Newspaper read the Leading Article, and said it was intended to publish a list of persons who for various reasons ought to be returned to parliament, and that, a suggestion would be made for the formation of a society similar to the "aid toi" society which had been of great use in France in procuring the return of proper persons to the chamber of deputies.[a]

On tuesday the 9 Mʳ Perry came again saying that his friends had resolved to commence such a society as he had before indicated. I therefore advised him to lose no time in procuring its establishment. A meeting was to be held he said at his chambers on Wednesday at 4 o clock and I promised to write an address for him and let him have it in time for the meeting. I was however so broken in upon that I was unable to write the address till late in the evening. I sent it to him early in the morning and early the next morning the 11– read a note from him,[b] which satisfied me nothing would be done by his friends notwithstanding they, "had exceedingly applauded my address" – so I wrote to Mʳ Hume a letter telling him my opinion and the determination some persons had taken to form such a society at once and I gave him till the sunday morning to decide on the course he would take. I sent him Mʳ Perry's note a copy of the address, and I requested him to become the Chairman of the society. In his answer he concurred in every thing proposed and consented to be the chairman.[c]

Mʳ Perry had been with me and urged me to take up the matter myself saying nothing would be done if I did not take it up; at least a dozen other persons had done the same, and as the matter was of importance, as a means of intimidating many opponents of the reform bills, I consented. I was of opinion that the address should be published before the second reading of the bill on monday week, and I saw that unless I exerted myself t̶h̶e̶n̶ nothing would be done.

Mʳ Perry agreed to summons his friends about 8 or 10 and I promised to summons about as many more to meet at the British Coffee House on the 14ᵗʰ — and on the evening of that day about

[a] See Proceedings in Westʳ Book. [Marginal note.]
[b] See Political Letter Book. [Marginal note. See BL Add. MS 35149, fo. 38.]
[c] See his note in Political Letter Book. [Marginal note. BL Add. MS 35149, fos 34r and 37v.]

20 gentlemen attended, and voted the resolutions and address I had
prepared, appointed a committee, that committee a sub[-]committee
for a week, and referred the address to the sub-committee with power
to alter it as they might think proper and then print it.[a]

On the 15. I sent a copy the minutes of the proceedings to M[r]
Bentham a another copy of the resolutions to Sir Francis Burdett and
a third also to M[r] Hobhouse, requesting each to become a member.

M[r] Bentham wrote —

"I have the instant of reception heard read the book you sent me
in relation to the '"Parliamentary Candidate Society"' approve of it
highly and intirely [sic] and am ready to attach my signature to any
document you may send me for that purpose."

Sir Francis Burdett wrote —

"I have only to say, make what use you please of me. The plan seems
very like Jeremy Benthams no small recommendation to me."

M[r] Hobhouse sent a shuffling excuse to M[r] De Vear.

The sub[-]committee met in the evening, and a good deal of
cavilling took place. I now learned for the first time, that the society
projected by M[r] Perry's friends, was an absurd and impracticable
project, a general reform, nothing at all society.

One disliked the name, we had taken another disliked the plan one
disliked the dis address another was for [word struck out and illegible]
for softening it down so as to make it contemptible as usual the thing
was to be frittered away to suit the views of men who had no real
comprehension of the matter, or had some personal object to obtain,
at length however it was agreed to give the address to M[r] Perry and
M[r] Roebuck to make alterations for the consideration of the sub-
committee at 10 o clock the next morning when the objections to all
and every part of the proceedings by Col[n] Thompson the consequence
of his fears we were occupied for three hours when he went away and
left us to settle the address which we did as follows.[481]

I had sent a copy of the Address and resolutions to M[r] Hume with
a request that he would shew them to M[r] Warburton and ask him to
become a member of the general committee. On my return from the
committee I found a note from him full of doubt and apprehension
and absurd suggestion – I replied that he need not be a chairman
but might merge in the committee or withdraw his name – so he
consented to be on the committee.

A Room was taken at the Crown and Anchor Tavern and the
address was printed and other steps taken. No sooner however did

---

[a] The meeting appointed me Treasurer. [Marginal note.]

[481] A copy of the handbill is inserted in the manuscript here.

the advertisement of the society (as follows[482]) appear than a howl was set up by the torys and by some of the Whigs too against it, and when the address was distributed, all sorts of imputations were put upon us, and by some the society was declared to be illegal. This alarmed ~~some~~ several of the committee and I have been assailed all day long for two days past with thier [*sic*] doubts and fears and absurd suggestions, but the thing is on its course and cant [?] now be set aside. Copies of the address have been sent to many persons at many places and some have been requested to reprint it, and this I have no doubt has been done at Birmingham, Manchester and Stamford and probably at some other places.

These are all the notices in the way of a Journal taken in 1831 – excepting some few memorandums in the Political Letter Book relating to the Parliamentary Candidates Society.

---

[482] A copy of the notice is inserted in the manuscript at the end of this paragraph, followed by this comment: 'The members of the General Committee; at least they who assembled none agreed on no one measure[.]'

1835

N°. 9.   1835   April

Much occupied in conjunction with Dr Robert Black of Kentucky[483] who has undertaken to superintend a number of young men, who are pledged to act together to promote petitions, from all parts of the Kingdom for the repeal of the stamp duty on Newspapers – wrote some 50 letters of introduction for them to members of parliament and to others. To procure money for current expenses, and names of persons with whom to open a correspondence &c &c — arranging &c &c

17 Mr Ashton Yates with an address he had drawn up and another, which had been drawn by Dr Bowring for the Middlesex club.[484] Yates's was prozy [*sic*] Bowrings was poetry, requested to draw one – did so sent it on the 19th to Mr Yates.

Pestering every public man and every club of reformers as far as able to procure the repeal of so much of the 27th clause of the reform Bill as relates to the ~~stamp on news papers 27 clause~~ so far as it disfranchises electors for non payment of rates by a day certain. This in consequence of a bill brought in by Lord John Russell for the registration of votes – The payment clause has enabled overseers in many places to make fraudulent lists – and to reduce the number of electors very considerably. The non payment of rates and the tricks of overseers have caused the disfranchisement of more than 4000 electors in Westminster and in some places as many as ^{2}/$_3$rd of all the 10£ house holders – Lord Johns Bill will still further reduce the number. The purpose of my letter is to procure the repeal of the words which relates [*sic*] to the payment of rates and regulate the conduct of overseers.

June 20 – yesterday in committee on the Registration Bill – Lord John Russell argued in favour of retaining the rate paying disfranchising clause – and when put to the vote 9 including Lord

---

[483] Dr James Robert Black was president of the Association for the Abolition of the Stamp Duty on Newspapers, a group organized under Place's influence. See Wiener, *War of the Unstamped*, pp. 98–99.

[484] That is, the Middlesex Registration Society, in which both Yates and Bowring were active.

John and the sneaking Wm Tooke the pretended reformer, M. P. for
Truro voted for the clause – Mr Hume and M^r H Elphinstone being
the only two who voted against it. Lord John is at heart a great rogue.

Occupied since the commencement of the month in the Municipal
Corporation Reform matter – for which see – Papers relating thereto.

Not less than 70.000 copies of the prospectus of the Municipal
Reformer have been printed and distributed. A goodly mass of
republican notions these.

Examined before the Committee Dom Com on Education.

July

8 to 11. Advising with a Mr Holt to bring out a daily unstamped paper. I expect that the stir the announcement has made among the unprincipled stamped newspaper people will provoke prosecution to any extent which will so injure the sale of this unstamped twopenny, and that the prosecutions of the printers publishers and venders will be so severe that it will be extinguished in a short time but even then another step will be gained towards the abolition of the Stamp duty on newspapers. Pamphlet for Roebuck {Taxes on Knowledge.[485]

The daily unstamped paper ceased at the end of a week —

Augst. 2. Requested to attend a meeting at the House of M^r parkes – the Lords are expected to throw out the Corporation Bill. Attended – discussion – Wrote letter to Mr Parkes dated Augst 3. Copied by Mr Parkes – original sent to Lord Melbourne —

Bill in jeopardy. Lord Melbourne spoke out distinctly – took a much more determined line of conduct than the whig cabinet had ever before done.

13. Wrote a pamphlet for Mr Roebuck in anticipation of the bill being rejected.[486]

---

[485] This bracketed phrase was apparently added at a later date.
[486] Perhaps J.A. Roebuck, *On the Qualification Clause of the Corporation Bill* (London, 1835).

December

See Letter book correspondence with Mr Hume and Mr Parkes – Augst to Decr. respecting corporation bill and conduct of Administration.

See papers – Municipal Corporations.

Occupied in reading and commenting on Municipal Corporation commissioners enquiry respecting London, with a view to obtaining further particulars and framing a bill for the City of London.

The printed papers I have are the matters set up as proofs of which there are only three copies.[a]

20. Finished a paper on taxes on knowledge for Roebuck. Published by him.[487]

School – see my evidence before the House of Commons Committee on Education – Printed by order 3 Augst fols 67 – to 90. {It was cut down and sadly mangled after it had been corrected by me.[488]

Wrote – a set of abstract[s] of political proceedings respecting Reform of parliament – in

1830 and 1831 – Bristol Riots &c

---

[a] Sent all the Printed papers on this subject – The Corporation of London (a very large number) to Mr Joseph Fletcher for his use. [Marginal note. Joseph Fletcher served on several royal commissions, including the commission on handloom weavers, children's employment, and the health of towns. See Timothy L. Alborn, 'Fletcher, Joseph (1813–1852)', *ODNB*, <http://www.oxforddnb.com/view/article/9736>, accessed 19 January 2006.]

[487] Included in J.A. Roebuck (ed.), *Pamphlets for the People* (London, 1835).

[488] This bracketed phrase was apparently added at a later date.

1836

Jan^y – continue reading enquiring and writing in conjunction with Joseph Fletcher – on London Corporation – and the report of the commissioners – / the proofs only.

Persecution of the unstamped very fierce – Government determined to put them down this cannot be done.

Proceedings of the last year revised by us.

Feb^y —

Proceedings to procure repeal of the Stamp on Newspapers – are
becoming very extensive —
    Meeting at Hoopers Pall Mall
    D° — Lord Melbournes —
    Persecution virulent —
    Opposition increases —
    Public meetings increasing.

Proceedings to procure a meeting in the Guildhall London —
Extraordinary & successful exertions of Dr Black [?]
See Paper on this subject
Meeting at the Guildhall on monday 7 – [489]
Much occupied in this matter.

---

[489] On this large and successful meeting, see Wiener, *War of the Unstamped*, pp. 109–110.

1836

June

Lugged [?] into a newspaper project and my time greatly occupied therewith very foolishly — Appointed with Mr Harrison to examine certain statements respecting arrangements – Consumed much time took much trouble, and made a report to the committee – on the 8 July. The whole scheme was made as perfect as possible – None took the pains necessary to understand the matter, and John Crawford who with Ashton Yates[490] were deputed to find a wonderful man for an editor found one whom they represented as better qualified to take the command in the concern than "any other man in Great Britain," and yet neither of them understood what his office would require of him. They found this man in a small scotchman a protegé of Crawford, the editor of the Spectator which never paid its expenses and is heavily in debt. These men want no system for to secure regularity and efficiency, they say Make Mr Rintoul – the Editor and leave all the rest to him. The others – John Travers, Thomas Gibson – Wm Pritchard. Wm Wansey [?] Edwin Field, Ben Wood.

These are are [sic] desirous that the paper should be established, and I have no doubt that it would succeed, the London daily papers are one and all despicable tools of either the paltry whig administration or their opponents the Tory faction. The people are now forward enough to support a well conducted newspaper which would be the mean and dirty tool of neither faction, but there will be no such nor any paper at all, set up by these men[.]

Rintoul is a dabbler whose latents [sic, perhaps 'talents'?] are mediocre, and is a shuffling tricky scotsman, men whom as shufflers when they become shufflers beat all the world in that capacity.

[490] Both members of the Association for the Abolition of the Stamp Duty on Newspapers.

INDEX

Abbott, Chief Justice 242, 245
Abercromby, James (MP) 227
Abernethy, John 105
Ackerman, Mr 179
Adams, Mr 67, 216, 224
Adams, William (father) 56, 96, 98, 99, 102, 105, 110, 116, 188
Adams, William (son) 99, 100, 101, 108, 127, 130, 134–135, 146, 147, 162, 163, 176, 188
Adcock, Henry and James 181
Aimé, Mr 79, 93, 104, 118, 133, 162, 205
Allen, William 235
Althorpe, Lord 277, 336
Anderson, John (editor, *The Trades Newspaper*) 65, 76, 84, 86, 90, 91, 101, 108, 119, 125, 127, 133, 149, 152, 192
Andrews, Capt 135
Argelick, Mr 163
Army Pay Office (*see also* Wallace (Wallis), Mr (Army Pay Office)) 282, 285
Arnott, Neil 42–43, 267–268
Ashby, Mr 70, 259
Atkinson, Miss 207
Atlas Weekly 83, 95
Auban, Mr (of the *Westminster Review*) 133
Auckland, George Eden, Earl of 115
Aust, Mr 124, 125, 126, 128, 129, 195
Austin, Charles (barrister) 181
Austin, John 132
Austin, Mrs 176, 177
Austria 326

Badnall, Mr 245
Bailey, Mr 210
Baines, Edward, Jr, (editor, *Leeds Mercury*) 87, 115, 167, 169
Baldwin's (London printers) 46, 59, 70, 188
Bankes, Mr 283
Banvise, Mr 85, 115
Barber, Alderman 93
Baring, Mssrs (banking house) 159, 160, 215
Barrow, Mr 269–270
Barry, Mr 55, 58, 59, 60, 62, 63, 65, 79, 83, 85, 86, 87, 88, 92, 94, 97, 100, 101, 102, 110, 117, 118, 121, 125, 128, 133, 134, 142, 143, 144, 147, 148, 149, 150, 156, 157, 160, 163, 166, 167, 172, 176, 197, 205, 209, 211, 259; and Irish emigration scheme 152, 153
Bathurst, Henry, third Earl Bathurst 154, 204, 237
Battye & Co (publishers) 304–305
Bayley, Mr 211
Beaumont, Barber 103
Bedford, John Russell, sixth Duke of 277
Belgian Revolt (1830) 326–327
Bell, W.S. (barrister) 235, 238–239, 242–243
Bennet, Henry Grey 41, 64, 95, 161, 170
Bentham, Jeremy 7, 14, 61, 62, 63, 117, 128, 178, 183, 204, 264, 265, 327, 329, 339
Bernal, Ralph (MP) 226
Best, Mr 162
Beveridge, John (seaman) 86
Bickersteth, Henry 276
Bingham, Peregrine 60, 62, 63, 86, 169
Birch, Joseph (MP) 226
Birkbeck, George 45, 108, 139, 181
Birmingham 202, 284
Black, John (editor, *The Morning Chronicle*) 117, 176
Black, Dr Robert 136, 171, 174, 343, 351
Blackwood's Magazine 72, 125, 126, 151, 169, 189, 216
Blake, Charles 52, 54, 55, 58, 59, 60, 61, 62, 63, 75, 79, 83, 84, 87, 89, 91, 92, 94, 96, 97, 99, 100, 101, 103, 105, 107, 108, 110, 111, 114, 119, 121, 125, 127, 130, 133, 135, 141, 150, 152, 157, 158, 159, 160, 162, 163, 176, 178, 187, 191, 205, 209, 211, 215, 267
Blandford, George Spencer-Churchill, Marquess of (later sixth Duke of Marlborough) 283
Bolton Chronicle 54, 74, 120, 123, 136, 163, 185
Booth, Mr 224
Boswell, James 270–271
Bowring, Sir John 124, 125, 128, 133, 141, 156, 167, 174, 176, 178, 183, 184, 267
Bozzelli, Chevalier 90, 114
Bradford, Mr (secretary to London seamen) 72

Bradley, Lt-Col Thomas 54, 60, 91, 199, 200, 201, 204, 208, 209
Bramah, Timothy 44
Bric, Mr 262
Bristol Riots 346
British Iron Company 177
British Museum 164
Brooks, Henry 53, 111, 216
Brooks, James 178, 216
Brooks, J.W. 111
Brooks, Samuel 215–216
Brougham, Henry 43, 112, 145, 174–175, 187, 191–192, 196, 198, 203, 204, 205–206, 242, 245, 248, 250, 256, 259, 266, 276, 278, 279–280, 334–335
Brown, Mr (attorney) 97, 178
Bruce, Mr 167
Brunel, Isambard Kingdom 63, 78
Brydges, Sir E. 116, 117, 283
Buckingham, Mr 80, 85
Buenos Aires 62, 63, 114, 165
Bull-Dog, The 135, 137, 141
Burdett, Sir Francis 6, 7–8, 22, 53, 55, 56–57, 58, 63, 64, 65, 85, 95, 97, 98, 99, 100, 111, 138, 166, 167, 177, 179, 180, 181, 184, 186, 187, 195, 204, 208, 210, 215, 216, 222, 224, 226, 227, 230, 231, 232, 233, 243, 248–250, 253–254, 259, 262, 276, 299, 301, 310, 313, 317, 319–320, 339
Burgess, Henry 198, 200
Burke, Edmund 275
Burke, Mr 205, 209, 279–280
Burnet, Richard 142
Burton, Mr 229
Byng, G. (MP) 283

Calcutta 164
Calder, Mr 161, 165
calico: duties on printed 51, 153, 336; newspaper printing 195–196, 198, 204
Calvert, Mr (MP) 283
Calvert, N. (MP) 283
Campbell, Mr 276
Campbell, Thomas (see also University of London) 43, 90, 110, 112, 115, 122, 124, 125, 192, 300
Canada, emigration to 214
Canning, George 73, 79, 94, 186–187, 188, 193, 194, 212, 242, 246–249, 276; and Portugal 222; premiership 235–238
Carder, Mr 266

Carlile, Richard 55, 59, 63, 69, 76, 79, 81, 82, 83, 84, 87, 89, 91, 93, 96, 100, 101, 102, 104, 105, 106, 108, 122, 128, 133, 134, 142, 148, 149, 153, 158, 163, 178, 197, 212, 215; Every Woman's Book 59, 76; prosecution for libel 333–334; The Republican 62, 72, 79, 89, 126, 148, 151, 152, 156, 210
Caroline, Queen, wife of George IV 121, 122, 277–278
Cartwright, Major John 155
Catholic Association 262–263
Catholic Emancipation 246, 262–264, 298
Cato Street Conspiracy 237
Chadd, Elizabeth (see Place, Elizabeth)
Chadwick, Edwin 337
Chairing Car 299
Chandos, Richard Plantagenet Temple-Nugent-Brydges-Chandos-Grenville, Marquess of (later second duke of Buckingham and Chandos) 283
Chapman, Mr 178
Charing Cross Improvement Bill 26, 54, 65–66
Charles I, King of England, Scotland, and Ireland 162, 182–183
Chatterley, Louisa (later Louisa Place) 69, 71, 80, 81, 97, 99, 161, 164, 183
Chichester 302
child labor in cotton factories 299–300
Chile 46, 52, 54, 63, 66, 75, 97, 134, 150, 166
Chile and Peruvian Mining Company 60, 83, 88
Chile Loan Scheme 59, 148, 149
Clarence, Duke of (see William IV, King of the United Kingdom of Great Britain and Ireland)
Clark, Mr 94, 97
Coates, Mr (see also University of London) 115, 118, 130
Cobbett, William 58, 59, 63, 68, 69–70, 74, 80, 89, 116, 128, 185, 189, 254, 262, 320; Cobbett's Register, 59, 63, 67, 72, 79, 89, 93, 116, 148, 150, 185, 209
Cochrane, Lady 180
Cochrane, Lord Thomas (later tenth Earl of Dundonald) 78, 82, 117, 137–139, 165, 177, 179, 180, 184
Collingwood, Lord Cuthbert 281
Colls, John 88
Colson, Mr 174, 226
Combination Acts 6–7, 21–24, 40–42, 61, 226; repeal of 314–315, 316

Commission for Inquiring into the Collec-
    tion and Management of Revenue 136
Commissioner of Stamps 314
Committee on Commitments 285
Committee on Scotch Affairs 316
Connellan, Thaddeus 100, 101, 104, 106
Conyngham, Elizabeth, Marchioness Con-
    yngham 276
Coombes, Mr 119, 133
Cooper, Sir Astley 141
Copley, John Singleton 236, 276
Corder, Mr 301
Corn Laws 73–74, 79, 83, 113, 148, 149, 152,
    153, 154–155, 156, 160, 162, 165, 166,
    167, 169, 171, 172, 175, 181, 182, 185,
    186, 187, 188, 192–193, 201, 207, 222,
    223, 226, 227, 228, 299
cottage system 234–235
cotton: manufacturers 298; taxes on 150;
    workers 76, 225–226, 243, 300
Courts of Request 66, 68
Cousins, Mr 206
Covent Garden Playhouse 208, 211
Crawford, John 352
Cruden, Robert Pierce 82
Cruttwell, Revd Mr 259
Cullen, C.S. (barrister) 165, 302
Cunningham, Sir George 65
Cunningham, Lady (see Conyngham,
    Elizabeth, Marchioness Conyngham)
Cust, Major P. 283
Cutting and Flaying Act, repeal of 41, 315

Daily Morning Paper 270, 291
Darnley, Lord 65
Davenport, Davies (MP) 317
Davies, Thomas H.H. (MP) 226
Dawson, Alexander (MP) 156, 187
Dean, Thomas 64
debtor and creditor, law of 232, 235, 238–
    243, 249, 255, 259
Denison, W. (MP) 283, 297
Denman, Thomas 104, 174, 250, 334–335
Dennett, Harriet 266
DeVere (DeVear), Mr 94, 96, 97, 98, 99, 101,
    102, 339
Dibdin's Theatre 179
Diggins, Colonel 94
Doane (Doanne), Richard 80, 204
Doherty, John 185
Dolphin, The 223
Donelly, Admiral 276
Donkin, Bryan 44

Dow, Mr (machinist) 301
Drew, Mr 63
Drummond, Henry 56, 77, 82, 90, 96, 103,
    104, 105, 134, 149, 150, 152, 165, 166,
    174, 223, 234–235
Dryden, John 191
Duncannon, John William Ponsonby, Lord
    (later fourth Earl of Bessborough) 87,
    118, 256
Dutton, Mr 212

Eden, Frederick Morton 53
Edinburgh Review 56, 69, 71, 154, 169, 171, 172,
    199
Egypt, Pacha of 80
Eldon, John Scott, first Earl of 236–237, 256
electoral reform 222, 224, 251, 285
Ellice (Ellis), Edward 114, 165, 166, 174, 175,
    177, 179, 180, 181, 184, 209, 334
Elliot, Mr 191, 204
Ellis, Mr 209, 210
Elphinstone, H. 344
emigration 206, 209, 214, 215
English Opera House 142
Ensor, George 75, 76, 77, 81, 89, 91, 92, 94,
    260
Estcourt, T.G. (MP) 283
Evans, James 92
Evans, John (attorney) 52, 133, 134, 169, 213,
    238–240, 242, 259
Evans, Joshua (barrister) 58, 94, 95, 101, 111,
    125, 143, 165, 203, 205–206, 209, 211,
    242, 279–280
Evans, Mr 217
Evans, Mr (bookseller) 165
Excise and Smuggling Laws 279
exportation of machinery 63, 66, 78, 206,
    207, 314–315

Farrar, Mr (of Bradford) 162
Fearon, Henry Bradshaw 76
Fenn, William (see also St Martin-in-the-
    Fields parish vestry) 26, 54, 58, 65–66,
    91, 97, 99, 100, 102, 106, 108, 110, 113,
    123, 133, 134, 135, 137, 142, 143, 146,
    148, 149, 150, 159, 160, 162, 163, 164,
    171, 174, 182, 200, 203, 205–206, 207,
    209, 210, 211, 242, 244–245, 252, 266,
    279–280, 285, 297–298, 300
Ferguson, Mr 283
Ferguson, Sir Ronald 80, 227, 276
Field, Edwin 352

Finance Committee 281, 282, 285
Fisher, Clara (actress) 142–143
Fletcher, Joseph 349
Flight, Mr (organ-builder) 175
Florance, Mr (attorney) 239–242, 249, 250, 251, 256, 259, 260
Folkestone, William Pleydell-Bouverie, Viscount (later third Earl of Radnor) 226, 302
Fordham, John 93, 141, 155, 228, 259
Forster, Dr 59, 160
Foster, Mr 88
Foster, Thomas 299
Fox, Charles James 275
Freemantle, Sir T. 283
Frend, William 133, 211, 261

Galloway, Alexander 44, 66, 77, 80, 82, 84, 118, 137–139, 140, 165, 177, 179, 184
Galloway, John 141
Game Laws 279
Garcia del Rio, Juan (see also Peruvian Loan Scheme) 125
Gast, John 8
George IV, King of the United Kingdom of Great Britain and Ireland 185–186, 253, 275–277, 280, 318–319, 324
Gibson, Thomas 45, 352
Gilbee, Mr (attorney) 75, 77, 80, 82, 85, 100, 178
Gilchrist, Dr John Borthwick 85, 90–91, 99, 102, 106, 108, 118, 121, 193, 204, 228, 229, 230, 245–246
Gillies, Mr 300
Glazier, Mr 233–234
Goding v. Fenn (see also Fenn, William; St Martin-in-the-Fields parish vestry) 244–245, 280
Godwin, William 171, 174, 175, 176, 177, 178, 179, 180, 182, 191
Goldschmidt, T.L. 119
Gordon, Lord George 298
Gordon, R. (MP) 283
Gourlay, R.F. 217, 234–235
Graham, George 156
Graham, James 116, 132, 135
Graham, Mr 329
Graham, Mrs 103, 106
Grand Junction Water Works Company (see also Thames Water Company; Thames water supply) 223, 224
Grant, Charles 81
Grant, Horace 133

Gray, Mr 300
Greek Loan Scandal 26, 167–168, 171, 172, 173–174, 176, 177, 179, 180, 181, 184, 195
Greek War Committee 80, 82, 83, 137–139, 166, 167
Greek War of Independence (see also Cochrane, Lord Thomas) 82, 165
Green, Mr 101
Gregory, Mr 112
Grenville, William Wyndham, Baron Grenville 275
Grey, Charles, second Earl Grey 327, 330; premiership 328
Grieve, Mr 259
Grote, George 115, 118, 121, 174
Grote, Harriet 156
Gurney, Mr 104

Hackett, Mr (carpenter) 98, 130
Hackney Coaches, Commissioners of 315–316
Hacley, Dr 223
Hale, Mr (bookseller) 233
Hale, William 84
Halhed, Nathaniel Brassey (MP) 205
Hammerton, Miss 87, 88, 103, 111, 114, 115, 116, 182
Hanniford v Hume 86
Hansard 78, 230
Hansard, Mr 78, 315
Hardy, Thomas 43, 82, 96, 98, 99, 103, 104, 147, 197, 199, 200, 204, 261
Harlequin, The, suppression of 310–311
Harrison, Mr (printer) 175
Harrison, Mrs 89
Harvey, D.W. (MP) 226
Harwood, Mrs 75, 77, 79, 80, 84, 85, 91, 95, 96, 97, 99, 100, 101, 102, 104, 122, 143, 178, 254, 259
Hassell, Richard 96, 123
Haymarket Theatre 143, 157
Hayne, Mr (engineer) 181
Henson, Gravenor 104
Herries, John Charles 258, 276
Highley, Mr 223
Hobhouse, Sir Benjamin 101
Hobhouse, J.C. 6, 39–40, 53, 54, 58, 65–66, 70–71, 82, 85, 90, 96, 98, 99, 100, 104, 163, 184, 186, 187, 194, 199, 200, 201, 202, 204, 212, 222, 224, 227, 230, 251, 254, 255, 259, 263, 276, 278, 279, 282, 283, 297, 300, 303, 310–312, 313, 319–321, 325, 327, 329, 335, 336, 339; Greek

War Committee 138, 165, 167, 177, 179, 180, 181, 195

Hobley, Mr 201

Hodgskin, Elizabeth (née Hagerwich) 67, 76, 105, 135, 195

Hodgskin, Thomas 57, 76, 145, 161, 199, 210

Holland, King of (*see* William I, King of the Netherlands)

Holland, Mr (wine merchant) 163, 164

Holmes, William 41, 258, 269, 276

Holt, Mr 345

Hone, William 52, 55, 70, 77, 78, 79, 84; *Hone's Every Day Book* 67, 72, 210

Hook, Miss 103

Hope, Thomas 132

Howick, Lord 226

Hulletts & Bros 205

Hulme, Mr (pawnbroker) 201, 204–205

Hume, David 171

Hume, Joseph (*see also* Corn Laws; debtor and creditor, law of; Greek Loan Scandal; Greek War Committee) 7–8, 23, 26–27, 40, 44, 53, 54, 58, 78, 82, 83, 84, 100, 113, 118, 119, 121, 124, 125, 127, 148, 149, 153, 157, 163, 164, 166, 167–168, 172, 173, 174, 176, 180, 184, 186, 187, 189–190, 192–194, 195, 196–197, 199, 204–205, 207, 208, 210, 211, 212, 224, 226, 227, 232, 235, 238–243, 246–249, 251, 255–260, 261, 265, 269, 276, 281, 282, 284, 299; address on the King's Speech 153, 155, 163, 176, 180, 182, 184–185, 186, 187, 208, 300, 304–305, 310–312, 313, 315–321, 325, 327, 329, 335–336, 338, 339, 344, 346

Hunt, Henry 251–252, 254

Hunt, Henry Leigh 77, 79, 86, 90, 114, 195, 204, 211

Huskisson, William 42–44, 94, 202, 205, 246

impressment of seamen 231, 243, 248–249

imprisonment for debt (*see* debtor and creditor, law of)

Ireland, Mr 166

Irisarri, Antonio (*see also* Chile Loan Scheme) 59, 63, 148

Jackson, Mr (publican) 46, 94, 95, 96, 97, 98, 99, 102, 178

Jacob, Mr 74, 97

Jeffrey, Francis 56

John Bull 121, 182

Johnson, Dr James 223

Johnson, Samuel 270–271

joint-stock companies 39–40

Jones, John Gale 95, 108, 161, 162, 178, 181

Jones, Col Leslie Grove 64, 96, 194, 195, 300, 302, 303, 304, 325, 329, 334–335

Jones, William 204

July Revolution (1830), effects of 325–326, 338

Juries Bill and Act (*see also* Peel, Sir Robert) 149, 156, 165, 250, 269, 276

Keating, Mr 191, 204

Kendall, Mr 98

Kennedy, Mr 92

Kenney, Miss Louisa 266

Kenney, Mrs 133, 141, 143, 161, 266

Kenrick, Judge 64

Kinder, Thomas, Jr, 125–126

King, Mr 86, 191

Kinnaird, Douglass 56, 85, 94, 95, 97, 170, 215

Knight, John 108

Knighton, Sir William 276

Lacey, Henry 108

Lamb, George 283, 329–330, 334

Lancashire 81

Lancet, The 141, 223

Lang, Jonathan (London Hatters Union and secretary to *The Trades' Newspaper*) 65, 101, 148, 207, 224

La Plata 63

Laurence, Mr 212

Lawless, John 262

Lawrence, William 59

Lee, William 82, 83

Legion Club 314

Leighton, Dr 134, 135, 184, 188, 191, 204, 211

Lemaitre, Paul 92, 98, 211

Lennard, T.B. 315

Lethbridge, Sir Thomas 249

Library for the People 199, 204, 210, 211

Library of Useful Knowledge 266, 278

Licensor of Plays, abolition of 315

Literary Gazette, The 52, 67, 72, 79, 93, 149, 152, 165

Littleton, Edward (MP) 311

Liverpool, Robert Banks Jenkinson, second Earl of 152, 204, 235

Lomax, Benjamin (Thames shipwright) 71, 85, 91, 92, 96

London: docks, construction of 127, 128, 129; plan for morning paper 300, 317; University of (*see* University of London)

London Corresponding Society 4, 6, 93, 97

London Free Press 154, 157, 159, 167, 261, 265, 282, 304–305

London Mechanics' Institution (*see also* Mechanics' Institutions) 45, 46, 70, 98, 108–109, 145, 175–176

London Mechanics' Register 67, 210

London Spy 171, 172

Longman (publisher) 56, 191–192, 199, 210

Longson, William 88, 118, 167

Lowther, William Lowther, Viscount (later second Earl of Lonsdale) 283

Lubbock, Mr (London merchant) 270, 291

Luriottis, Andreas (*see also* Greek Loan Scandal) 173, 174, 180

Lushington, Dr Stephen 174, 226

Lyceum Playhouse 114

Maberley, John (MP) 226

Maberley, William (MP) 226

Macaulay, Z. 119, 122

Mackintosh, James 170

Maclaren, John 124

MacLean, Dr 55, 82, 85, 91, 92

Madrid 151

malt and beer taxes 299

Manchester 300

Manchester Massacre (Peterloo) 125, 237

Marbot, Colonel 140

Marriot, Mr (editor, *Taunton Mercury*) 195–196, 198, 204

Marshall, James (editor, *Parliamentary History and Review*) 60, 230

Marshall, John (MP) 171, 184–185, 186, 200, 226

Marshall, Mr 201, 202, 213

Marshall, William (MP) 200

Martineau, John (*see also* Taylor and Martineau) 42–43, 44, 97, 177

Maudslay, Henry 44

Maxwell, John (MP) 227

Maynard, Mr 165

Mayse, Mr (potter) 53

McCarthy, Mr (inventor) 81, 91, 264–265

McCreevey, Mr 165

McCulloch, J.R. 53, 55, 59, 62, 63, 65, 76, 77, 79, 80, 81, 85, 87, 89–90, 169, 189

McDougall, Mr (Glasgow cotton spinner) 169

McWilliam, Mr 145

Meabry, Mr (co-executor with FP of Miers's estate) 116, 119, 149, 188, 265

Mechanics' Institutions (*see also* London Mechanics' Institution) 62, 65, 69, 193, 202, 232, 233, 265

Mechanics' Magazine 57, 108

Mechanics' Register (*see London Mechanics' Register*)

Melbourne, William Lamb, second Viscount 345, 350

Melville, Robert Saunders Dundas, second Viscount 235–236

Memoir of Robert Blincoe, A, manuscript of 118, 120, 122

Merle, Mr 157, 159

Mesne process (*see* debtor and creditor, law of)

Mexico 43

Middlesex 222, 224, 320, 324, 325

Middlesex Registration Society 343

Miers, John (FP's son-in-law) 28, 46, 62, 103, 116, 118, 132, 142, 165, 179, 181, 184, 211; *Travels in Chile and La Plata*, FP's editing of and revisions to 46, 53, 55, 59, 61, 62, 63, 65, 66, 68, 70, 71, 73, 75, 79, 81, 84, 86, 87, 89, 90, 91, 92, 97

Miers, John (father) 164

Miers, Mr 196

Miers, William 149, 169, 183, 184, 225

Miles, William Augustus 252–253

Mill, James 7, 14, 88, 89–90, 117, 118, 119, 122, 128, 130, 137, 142, 146, 151, 153, 155, 156, 159, 167–168, 172, 173, 174, 175, 181, 182, 188, 191, 195, 212, 259, 260, 261, 266, 267, 276, 329

Mill, John Stuart 103, 132, 133, 151, 165, 176, 329

Miller, Mr (Joseph Hume's secretary) 90, 176

Miller, Samuel 92

Mirror, The 52, 67, 79, 93, 149

Mirror of Parliament, The 299

Mitchell, Mr 171, 266

Monck, J.B. (MP) 226

Moncrief, Mr 192

Money, Mr (carpenter) 129, 133

Morland, George 192

Morning Chronicle, The 39, 54, 56, 74, 79, 105, 120, 150, 190, 194, 195, 203, 206, 299

Morning Herald 54, 59, 74, 75, 89, 92, 105, 113, 114, 195

Morrison, Mr 92, 96

Municipal Corporation Reform 344, 345–346, 349

Murray, Mr (bookseller) 212
Mutual Insurance Benefit Society 64

Navigation Acts 247–248
Neal, Mr 176
Netherlands, The 326
Nettlefield, Mr 119
Nettleford, Mr 181
New Monthly Magazine and Literary Journal, The 199
newspapers: printing on calico (*see also* calico, duties on printed) 195–196, 204
New Times 35, 282, 304–305
Northouse, Mr (editor, *The Glasgow Free Press*) 150, 151–152, 153, 154, 157, 159, 167, 169, 195, 203, 204, 207, 208, 214, 266
Northumberland, Henry Percy, third Duke of 106
Nugent, Mr (British consul at Valparaiso) 60

O'Connell, Daniel 262–263
O'Higgins, Bernardo 59
Old Price Riots 108
Oliver, Mr (attorney) 156, 161, 165
Oriental Herald, The 108
Orlando, Jean (*see also* Chile Loan Scheme) 136, 180
Otway-Cave, Robert (MP) 226

Paget, Lord Henry 65
Pallmer, C.N. 283
Papworth, Mr (surveyor) 179, 297–298, 299
Parish Vestry Bill (*see also* Fenn, William; St Martin-in-the-Fields parish vestry) 97, 99, 101, 297–298, 299
Parisian Greek Committee 184
Parkes, Joseph 81, 175, 183, 202, 212, 345–346
Parkinson, Mr (trade unionist) 160
parliament: opening 326–327; reform 329, 330, 338, 343–344, 346; reporting on proceedings 230, 232, 261, 265, 269–270
Parliamentary Abstracts 60–61
Parliamentary Candidate Society 337–340
Parliamentary History and Review (*see also* Marshall, James) 60, 155, 281–282
Parliamentary Review and Debates 68
Paroissien, James 125, 134
Pasco Peruvian Mining Co 215
Paskin, Charles 188
Paull, James 58, 105

Peel, Sir Robert (*see also* Finance Committee; Juries Bill and Act; police in the metropolis) 64, 83, 142, 146, 205, 227–228, 236, 250, 269, 276, 300
Peel, W. 283
Pepys, Sir Lucas 89
Perry, Thomas Erskine 337–339
Peru 60, 72
Peruvian Loan Scheme 125–126
Peterloo (*see* Manchester Massacre)
Phillips, Mr 300
Phillips, Sir Richard 76, 105, 122
Pilt, Mr 300
Pitt, Mr (London radical) 251
Pitt, William (the Younger) 237, 275, 313, 334
Place, Anne 54, 62
Place, Caroline 59, 61, 63, 75, 86, 89, 99, 101, 102, 104, 106, 108, 110, 134, 147
Place, Elizabeth, née Chadd (FP's first wife): death of 271; Jane's wedding proposal 130; personality 212–213; the theatre 142, 143–144, 147, 157, 161, 208; walks with FP 4, 25, 28–29, 47, 54, 58, 59, 61, 86, 87, 89, 93, 96, 97, 98, 99, 100, 102, 103, 104, 105, 106, 108, 110, 111, 112, 113, 114, 117, 121, 122, 123, 126, 127, 132, 133, 134, 135, 136, 137, 139, 140, 142, 143, 146, 147, 149, 150, 151, 157, 161, 169, 171, 179, 181
Place, Francis (*see also* Burdett, Sir Francis; Corn Laws; debtor and creditor, law of; Hobhouse, J.C.; Hume, Joseph; St Martin-in-the-Fields parish vestry; Westminster elections): administration of John Miers's estate 116, 184, 196, 207, 210, 224, 225, 252; annuity 161; on aristocracy 5–6, 277–278; bankruptcy laws 201–202; birth and childhood 1–3; burials in London 147, 149, 157, 164; Combination Acts 6–7, 21–24, 40; conduct of electors in Westminster 251–252; Corn Laws 26, 64, 65, 73–74, 84; Cutting and Flaying Act 41, 315; death of first wife 271, 286; diary 12, 19, 74, 110, 198, 216, 217; diet 120; dispute with London *New Times* 304–305; on dissection 229; on drama 300; exportation of machinery 202–203, 205, 207; Finance Committee 281; *Free Press* 304–305; free trade 250; French and Belgian Revolutions of 1830 325–327; friendly societies 254; historians' view of 6, 8–12; *History of America*

39, 135, 310; history of parliamentary reform, research on 117, 127–128, 148, 153, 162, 163, 164, 171, 177, 178, 179, 180, 181, 182–183, 188, 190, 191, 194, 197, 199, 200, 203, 204, 205, 208, 209, 210, 211, 212, 214, 215, 217, 230, 232; husbandry labourers 329–330; London Mechanics' Institution 45, 108, 113, 127, 130; London 'mob' 327–328; Luddites 145, 146; manners and morals of the working class 91, 92, 93, 119, 125, 127, 130, 141, 148, 158, 161, 167, 171, 172, 174, 212, 259, 293; marriage to Elizabeth Chadd and early career 3–5; marriage to Louisa Chatterley 310, 313; moral sincerity 321–324; Navy Committee 281; parliamentary reform movement 279, 299, 302, 330, 336, 337–338, 346; personality 28–29, 46–47, 158, 261–262; play-going (see also Place, Elizabeth) 289; political economy 7–8, 22–23, 118–119, 123; political history of Westminster (see also Westminster elections) 61, 62, 63, 67, 72, 119; public opinion 298; rate-payers' franchise clause, repeal of 343–344; renovation to shop 129; republicanism 17–18, 20–21, 23; review of Felix Mengin, Histoire de l'Egypte 137, 139, 140, 154; Scottish judges 170; Six Acts 198, 248, 250–251, 255–260; state lotteries 159; Swing Riots 329–330, 336; Trades' Newspaper 52, 64, 87, 88, 90, 91, 92, 99, 205, 259
Place, Frank 86, 93, 118, 130, 158, 161, 202, 216
Place, Fred 86, 233
Place, Jane 99, 112, 114, 121, 130, 161
Place, John 89, 121, 203, 207, 210, 211, 213
Place, Louisa (see Chatterley, Louisa)
Place, Mary 130, 155, 195
Place, Revd Matthew 105
Place, Tom 184
police in the metropolis 283–284, 290, 299
Political Economy Club 81
Ponsonby, Lord (see Duncannon, John William Ponsonby, Viscount)
Poor Laws 123
Portales, José (see also Chile Loan Scheme) 59, 63
Potosí, Bolivia 134–135
Prescot, William 212
Pringle, Capt 131, 132
Pritchard, William 352

Prowse, Mr (accountant) 163
Prussia 326
Prussia, Friedrich II, King of 158

Quarterly Review, The 104, 140, 144, 150, 213, 214
Quin, Mr 260, 261–263, 265

Radnor, Earl of (see Folkestone, William Pleydell-Bouverie, Viscount)
Rancliffe, George Augustus Henry Anne Parkyns, second Baron 226
Rankin, Mrs and Miss 117
Redesdale, John Freeman-Mitford, first Baron 256
Reece, Mr (bookseller) 141
Registration Bill 343–344
Rey, Mr 60
Reynolds, Sir Joshua 179
Ricardo, David 42
Ricardo, Moses 42, 177, 184, 195
Ricardo, Mr 232
Richter, Henry 106
Richter, John 106
Rintoul, Robert Stephen 83, 95, 352
Rio de la Plata Mining Company 142
Rivadavia, Bernardo 205
Robertson, J.C. 57, 108, 145
Robertson, John Parish 205
Robinson, Frederick John, first Viscount Goderich (later first Earl of Ripon) 150
Robinson, William 63, 100, 108, 134, 157
Robson, Mr 270
Roebuck, J.A. 134, 329, 337, 339, 345–346
Romeo, Capt 64, 75, 80, 91
Rossmore, Warner William Westenra, second Baron 262–263, 266–267
Rothschild, Nathan 276
Routh, Mr Deputy 229
Russell, Lord John (later first Earl Russell) 283, 337, 343–344
Russell, Mr (engraver) 55, 135
Russia 326

Saint Margaret's, Westminster (see St Margaret's Parish, Westminster)
Saint Martin-in-the-Fields (see St Martin-in-the-Fields)
Samida, Abraham 85, 87, 99, 167, 199, 204
Sanders, James (MP) 230–231
Savery, Mr 161
Say, Jean-Baptiste 184

Scarlett, Sir James 104, 174, 203, 205–206, 209, 242, 244–245, 250, 255, 279–280, 313–314, 328, 334–345
schooling, methods of 129, 300
Select Committee on Artizans and Machinery 26, 44
Select Committee on Education 344, 346
Select Committee on Emigration 134, 135, 136, 137
Service, Mr 133, 142
Sheffield 202
Shelton, Mr 97, 115
Sheridan, Richard Brinsley 275
Sheriff, Capt 78, 138
Sheriff, Mr (attorney) 86, 87, 88, 160, 215
Shiel, R.L. 262
Shipwrights' Benefit Club 259
Sidney, George 57, 139, 179, 181, 191–192
Sidney (publisher) 199
Silk Laws 299
silk manufacturers 298, 299
silk weavers 225–226
Six Acts (see also newspapers, printing on calico; Stamp Act) 41, 198, 248, 250–251, 255–260, 310–311
Smith, John (Bolton, Lancs) 84, 94, 98, 99, 106, 121, 133, 202, 203, 243
Smith, John (MP), 56, 115, 119, 121, 189, 224, 227–228, 235, 250
Smith, Mr 212
Smith, Mr (laceman) 89, 108
Smith, Robert (vice-consul) 64
Smith, William (MP) 196
Society for Promoting the Repeal of Taxes on Knowledge 336
Society for the Diffusion of Useful Knowledge 174–175
Southern, Mr 142
Spencer, Miss 103, 111, 115, 116
Spring Rice, Thomas (later first Baron Monteagle of Brandon) 283
Stamp Act (see also Six Acts) 255–260, 310, 313–314, 335, 337, 343, 345, 349, 350, 351
St Margaret's Parish, Westminster 217, 144
St Martin-in-the-Fields parish vestry (see also Fenn, William; Goding v Fenn; Parish Vestry Bill) 26, 119, 123, 124, 126, 131, 135, 142, 149, 159, 162, 171, 174, 244–245, 266, 297–298, 300
Stokes, Miss 106
Strachan, Mr 110
Sturch, William 215–216

Sturges Bourne's Act 26
Swift, Jonathan 276
Swinburne, Sir John 146, 147
Sydney, Mr 133, 166, 175
Sykes, Mr (Solicitor to the Commissioner of Stamps) 204

Talbot, Jonathan 155
Tanner, J.J. 204–205
taxes on knowledge 335–336, 345, 346
Taylor and Martineau (engineers) 177
Taylor, Edward 176, 177
Taylor, John 176
Taylor, Mr 134
Taylor, Phillip (solicitor) 176, 177, 229, 233–234
Taylor, Richard 177, 229, 233
Taylor, Rev Robert (deist) 196–197, 245–246, 252
Temple, Sir William 134
Tennant, Mr (attorney) 201–202
Test and Corporation Acts 27–28, 266
Tester, John 57, 136
Thames Tunnel 63, 65
Thames Water Company 233–234
Thames water supply 223, 224, 228, 229, 231, 232, 234
Thelwall, John 76, 77, 81, 83, 89, 91, 100, 102, 118–119, 182, 212, 260–261
Thistlewood, Arthur 237
Thomas, Mr (London police inspector) 327–328
Thomason, Richard (secretary, Bolton cotton weavers) 243
Thompson, Alderman 283
Thompson, Charles Poulett 226
Thompson, Thomas Perronet 223
Thorpe, Dr Robert 53, 58, 63, 64, 75, 76, 91, 150, 199, 208, 210, 224, 228, 243, 259, 260, 261
Thwaites, Henry (proprietor, Morning Herald) 105, 111, 113
Tierney, George 279
Tijou, Mary Ann, Sarah, and Caroline (daughters of William Tijou, Sr) 217
Tijou, William, Jr, 211, 215, 251, 261
Tijou, William, Sr, 46, 54, 75, 77–78, 81, 86, 87, 88, 91, 94, 97, 105, 136, 148, 156, 158, 160, 176, 178, 179, 188, 191, 202, 207, 208, 209, 215, 217, 251, 262
Times, The 189–190, 194
Tindal (Tindall), Mr (barrister) 80, 100, 245
Tommy shops 311

Tooke, B. 91

Tooke, E. Eyton 160

Tooke, John Horn 147

Tooke, Mr 176

Tooke, Thomas 79

Tooke, William Eyton 101, 111, 112, 113, 119, 134, 160

Toplis, Mr 85, 98, 175, 204, 266

Torrens, Robert (*see also* Corn Laws) 43, 81, 104, 113, 119, 155, 156, 157, 166, 171, 182, 183, 184–185, 187, 188, 192, 196, 201, 202–203, 205, 207, 209, 212, 215, 232

Trades' Newspaper, The (*see also* Anderson, John; Lang, Jonathan) 76, 78, 81, 86, 152, 205, 207, 224, 258, 259, 261, 265

Trade Unions: Bolton Cotton Weavers 214, 217, 243; Durham Sailors 46; Linen Drapers' Shopmen 45; London Coopers 191; London Engineers 44; London Gold Lacemen 108; London Tanners 41; Loyal Standard Association of Seamen 160; North of England Seamen 252; Sailors of Tyne and Wear 160; Seamen of South Shields 175, 217, 222, 231; Sheffield Cutlers 217; Sheffield Mechanics 46; Spitalfields Weavers 45, 108; West of England Woollen Weavers 252; Woollen Manufacturers' Journeymen, Frome 204

Truck Act (*see* Tommy shops)

Turnbull, Major 102, 245–246

Twiss, Horace (MP) 205

University of London 26, 43, 110, 112, 113, 115, 117, 119, 121, 122, 123, 124, 125, 127, 130, 142, 223, 224, 245, 290–291

Urquhart, Mr 117

Valparaiso 135

Vestris, Eliza (actress) 144

wages, minimum 224, 225–226, 227–228, 243

Waithman, Alderman Robert 76, 215

Wakefield, Edward Gibbon 91, 92

Wakefield, Felix 117

Wakley, Thomas 223

Wallace (Wallis), Mr (Army Pay Office) 285

Wallace (Wallis), Mr (Spitalfields weaver) 102, 149

Warburton, Henry 115, 121, 125, 201, 202, 224

Waterfield, Miss 114

Watkins, Mr 158

Webb, Joseph 117

Webber, Daniel Webb 263–264

Wellington, Arthur Wellesley, first Duke of 237; ministry 276–277, 279

Western, C.C. 283

Western Literary Institution 85, 97, 179

Westminster 110, 111, 209, 210

Westminster elections 185, 226–227, 230, 251; of 1790 103, 104; of 1796–1797 93; of 1806 56, 100, 101, 102, 103, 105; of 1807 58, 96, 102, 105, 107; of 1809 108; of 1817 253–254; of 1818–1819 96, 102; of 1820 53, 96, 102; of 1826 85, 90, 93, 94, 95, 97, 98, 99, 109–110, 184; of 1830 319–321, 324; of 1831 337–340

Westminster Review 60, 61, 136, 137, 139, 142, 154, 155, 156, 163, 165, 199, 232, 260

Westmorland, John Fane, tenth Earl of 237

Whitbread, Samuel 319, 324

White, George 54, 58, 73, 81, 84, 85, 90, 97, 104, 119, 122, 124, 128, 133, 139, 156, 163, 166, 171, 174, 175, 176, 177, 179, 181, 182, 187–188, 191, 201, 207, 256, 266

Whitmore, Mr 166

Wilkes, Revd Mark 88

Wilkinson, Thomas 78, 89

William I, King of the Netherlands 326

William IV, King of the United Kingdom of Great Britain and Ireland 318–319, 327, 328, 330, 337; as Duke of Clarence 227, 236

Wilmot-Horton, Robert John 151–152, 153, 154

Wilson, Sir Robert 255–258

Wood, Alderman Matthew 94, 215, 256, 283

Wool Laws 40, 58

Wooler, T.J. (editor, *Black Dwarf*) 203

Worthington, Mr (painter) 63, 212, 213

Wright, John 58, 74, 84, 87, 95, 97, 99, 104, 105, 106, 110, 121, 122, 124, 223, 224, 228, 230, 231, 232, 233, 234

York, Frederick, Duke of 204, 237

Young, Arthur 235

Young, John (secretary, Bolton Weavers' Union) 214